Woman's Proper Place

WOMAN'S PROPER PLACE

A History of Changing
Ideals and Practices,
1870 to the Present

SHEILA M. ROTHMAN

Basic Books, Inc., Publishers

NEW YORK

Library of Congress Cataloging in Publication Data

Rothman, Sheila M
  Woman's proper place.

  Includes bibliographical references and index.
      1. Women—United States—History.   2. Women—
United States—Social conditions.   3. United States—
Social policy.   I. Title.
HQ1420.R67   301.41'2'0973   78–55000
ISBN: 0–465–09203–9 (cloth)
ISBN: 0–465–09204–7 (paper)

For David

With Love

What is certain is that hitherto woman's possibilities have been suppressed and lost to humanity, and that it is high time she be permitted to take her chances in her own interest and in the interest of all.

Simone de Beauvoir
The Second Sex (1953)

Contents

Illustrations

Following page 146

Listed in the order in which they appear

Acknowledgments

It is pleasant to note the important assistance that I received from various people as I worked on this manuscript. Irving Kristol encouraged me to investigate the assumptions of social policy toward women, children, and the family for the Rockefeller Commission on Critical Choices; Erwin Glikes was in large part responsible for persuading me to make that essay the starting point for this book. I have been fortunate to have access to the libraries of Columbia University. The extensive collections at Teacher's College and at the School of Social Work provided a wealth of sources on women's roles in education, charity, and health; Florence Wilkinson and her staff at Teacher's College and Harriet Hoptner and her assistants in the Social Work Library were never too busy to locate buried material. The staffs at the New York State Library at Albany, the New York Academy of Medicine, the Sophia Smith Collection of the Smith College Library, the Schlesinger Library of Radcliffe College, the Library of Congress, the National Archives, and the Rockefeller Foundation Fund were also especially helpful.

In various stages of writing and research I benefited from interviews and discussions with Annette Baxter, Jay Cutler, Richard Hausknecht, Frederick Jaffe, Charles Halpern, Barbara Harris, Stacey Jacobs, Flora Kimmich, Eve Merriam, Jeannie Rosoff, Leslie Scalett, Margaret Stern, and Andrew von Hirsch. Amitai Etzioni and Herbert Gans, my colleagues at the Center for Policy Research, were not only encouraging of my work but always willing to answer particular questions. Oscar and Lillian Handlin and Pauline and Charles Maier reviewed the entire manuscript; their comments were especially helpful. I owe a special debt to Fritz Stern who has gone well beyond the duties of friendship in his careful reading of all of my work. I also profited from the opportunity to present preliminary findings to fellow members of the Columbia University Seminar on Women and Society and to the Organization of American Historians at its 1976 meeting. Evelyn Ledyard typed the manuscript with particular care and patience.

Over the years that I researched and wrote this book, Ellen Coaxum, Sherry Edmunds, and Diane Ellison Grabos assisted me with many household and childcare duties. My parents, Rose and Harry Miller, once again did all that they could to facilitate my work. More times than I can remember they belied the popular notion that supportive kin networks have become a thing of the past. So, too, my children, Matthew and Micol have learned the delights and difficulties of growing up in a family in which both parents are devoted to long-term and time-consuming projects. Matthew not only performed babysitting chores but, when I completed the manuscript, surprised me with a collection of stamps on American women. Micol took great pleasure in writing her own books as she sat patiently beside her mother on many a rainy or snowy day. Lastly, I profited greatly from the assistance of my husband, David Rothman. His knowledge of the discipline of history allowed us to spend many hours relating the experience of women to the changes that have occurred in society at large. He also did manuscript research with me in various libraries and edited, in his meticulous style, the entire manuscript. I will always treasure his ability to combine all this with encouragement and affection.

S. M. R.
Barnard, Vermont
New York City
March, 1978

INTRODUCTION

THIS book grew out of my attempt to understand the principles and consequences of American social policy toward women. I began with a modest effort—an essay on the present—and went on to a book about the past and present, because the subject turned out to be unexplored, fascinating, and marvelously intricate.

As soon as I opened this investigation, I confronted the intense and deep conflicts that now mark the design and implementation of social policy toward women. Competing claims and clashes of interest appeared everywhere. Programs that supporters believed would promote the welfare of women, opponents thought would undermine the needs of children or the integrity of the family or the cohesion of the society. At the same time, when I attempted to identify the premises that underlay social policies and to account for the sharp disagreements, I repeatedly came up against diverse judgments of what constituted woman's proper place. Invariably, controversies over programs represented a conflict over the models and ideals that should shape women's lives. The debates on day care, abortion, and the Equal Rights Amendment ultimately reflected this more fundamental dispute.

The clashes that affected social policy in the 1960s and 1970s appeared all the more glaring to me because they stood in striking and significant contrast to the harmony that characterized attitudes and practices in earlier periods. During the nineteenth century and for most of the twentieth, it seemed logical and sensible to link the welfare of women directly to the welfare of their children, their family, and their society, and to assume that the best interests of women were at one with all these other interests. Our predecessors found interdependence just where we perceive competition and conflict. And hence my effort to understand the novel character of contemporary policy took me back to the 1870s, to the Progressive period, and to the 1920s. What principles had created a sense of cohesion in their world? Why had accord given way to conflict? By what route did we reach our present state of affairs?

The historical record revealed many more changes in notions of woman's proper place than traditional surveys suggest. Definitions of proper womanhood have shifted remarkably from the 1870s to the present. Before the 1960s traditional assumptions about woman's place did consistently involve some form or another of domestic obligations. But even within this framework, important variations occurred over time. Expectations of what constituted the ideal type of mother or wife differed from one period to another. In the 1880s, child-rearing manuals gave primacy to notions of maternal instincts and the innate and all-beneficial effects of motherly affection. By the 1920s, the literature emphasized the need for parental insights and reflected an acute suspicion of motherly love. So, too, in the earlier years, sexuality seemed to threaten the marriage bond; later, it was expected to sustain it. And each of these shifts affected women's everyday life experiences in profound ways.

To a surprising degree, women's conceptions of their domestic responsibilities have often led them out of the household and into the community. American women have not been so caught up in a familial world as to ignore public responsibilities. Ours is not the first generation of women to undertake social action. Rather, in the 1880s and in the Progressive era, as well as in the 1970s, women played a vigorous and significant role in the politics of American reform, particularly in shaping social policy toward women, children, and the family. Once again, the premises that took women into the political arena and the causes that they attempted to promote differed from one era to another. The focus on feminine purity and sensibility in the 1880s gave way to a new concern for child health and welfare in the 1900s. In the first decades after the Civil War, women organized themselves into private and philanthropic societies to fulfill their aims. After 1900, they turned more and more frequently to the state.

It is the purpose of this book to describe these changes and to analyze their origins and implications. Put briefly, every generation has advanced its special definition of woman's proper place, and every generation has devised public and private programs to promote and enhance that definition. Thus, my goals here are threefold: to describe the varying principles establishing woman's proper place, to understand their links to social programs, and finally, to explore the effects of these programs and their consequences, both intended and unintended.

The text traces four major shifts in policy from the post-Civil War era to the present. In the closing decades of the nineteenth century, precepts of "virtuous womanhood" guided middle-class women as they confronted a new and unusually open urban environment. Novel opportunities for leisure, education, and employment coexisted with an inherited code of behavior that demanded that women embody and propagate an inherently feminine kind of morality, chastity, and sensibility in their families and throughout the society. The results were at once activating and confining. Women's clubs and reform associations assumed an unprecedented vitality and importance; at the same time, they attempted to implant these highly restrictive precepts not only in the middle but also in the lower classes. A network of philanthropic societies, from the Charity Organization Society to the Woman's Christian Temperance Union to the Young Women's Christian Association, set out to rescue women at risk, be they poor or new arrivals in the city, and to make all women over in the image of virtuous womanhood.

Beginning in the twentieth century, with the coming of Progressivism, a new definition of proper womanhood emerged, a model of "educated motherhood." Focusing with a new intensity on the needs of the child, the ideal looked to *train* women to the tasks of motherhood. Women's insights into child development were now to take precedence over their virtuous and maternal instincts. Again, these notions helped to shape social policy. Public, state-supported preventive programs replaced private, charitable rescue efforts. Legislation aimed to guard the health and welfare of children and their mothers. A series of institutions, from child and maternal health clinics to kindergartens, new types of public schools, and protective codes, looked to remove children from the workplace and to improve conditions for the women who remained there. These institutions dominated the reform enterprise. Indeed, women's mission provided the essential rationale for the suffrage movement and contributed to its victory.

The 1920s witnessed a third turn: the rise of the concept of woman as "wife-companion." It was a romantic and sexual definition, moving women from the nursery to the bedroom even as it kept them at home. The implications of this shift for public policy are nowhere more apparent than in the career of Margaret Sanger and the course of the birth control movement.

The norms established for women in the 1920s were revived in the 1950s (after the interruptions of the Great Depression and World War II), and they provided the setting for the emergence of the women's liberation movement. In contrast to the concepts of educated motherhood and wife-companion, the new ideal defined "woman as person." She was to find fulfillment not in the role of mother or wife but in her own accomplishments. To this end, agitation for equal rights, for day care, for reproductive freedom, and—by reaction—for children's rights has dominated social policy concerns. The agenda is in many ways novel, emphasizing rights over needs, but it cannot be understood apart from its historical antecedents.

Changes in conceptions, it should be clear, were never complete from one era to another. The model of virtuous womanhood, for example, had its origins in the pre-Civil War decades, and it was then recast in the 1870s and 1880s. Commitments to the notion of educated motherhood that began in the Progressive era continued among some women into the 1920s, indeed into the 1960s. And the 1920s notion of wife-companion has certainly not disappeared today. The models, in other words, are not unique to any one chronological period—there are links before and survivals afterward. Nevertheless, one can identify in each period one central ideal that had a critical role in shaping women's behavior, one that took center stage without monopolizing it. Even more important perhaps, one can identify in each period an ideal of proper womanhood that underlay reform programs, that set the directions for social policy. Hence, the analysis here focuses in turn on each dominant model and the institutions that embodied its principles. It explores, for example, the activities of the settlement house in the 1900s rather than the efforts of an older organization like the YWCA to adapt to the Progressive style. In this way, the dimensions as well as the process of change may be best understood.

To turn to causes, the institution that has exerted a primary, but certainly not exclusive, influence in shaping and popularizing different concepts of proper womanhood has been the college and university. The rise of women's colleges in the 1870s, the introduction of a social science curriculum into colleges and universities in the

1890s and 1900s, and the popularity of sororities in the coeducational state colleges and universities in the 1920s at once represent and begin to explain shifts in ideals. To understand why women's allegiances went initially to women's clubs, then to settlement houses, and later to country clubs, one properly looks first to the colleges.

As would also be expected, technology has exerted a powerful influence on women's lives, as it has on men's. The effects, however, have not been similar. In urban life, the advent of electricity had very special implications for women, which will later take us into kitchens and apartment houses; in the job market, the invention of the typewriter was no less significant for them, a fact that will take us into business offices. And technology too is intimately connected to the rise in the late nineteenth century of department stores, which will take us both in front of the counters, to the customers, and behind them, to the salesgirls.

Finally, the professions, most notably the medical profession, have shaped attitudes toward womanhood and exerted a profound influence on women's sense of self. In every generation women have confronted their doctors—in the 1870s and 1880s in a dispute over the propriety of collegiate education, in the 1920s over who should dispense birth control, offer sexual counseling, and give preventive health care, and again in the 1960s over what should define disease and its prevention and treatment. The outcomes have not been consistent: at some times, women have reached a compromise with physicians; at others, abdicated to their expertise. The dialogue, however, has had a persistent centrality in women's lives.

Because so much of our understanding of woman's place has come to us filtered through the world of men, I have chosen quite self-consciously to try and right the balance, to examine institutions, practices, and ideas primarily as they influenced and were influenced by women. I am not unaware of the fact that some of the critical elements affecting women also had an impact upon men; the stress on physical education in the women's colleges can also be detected in the men's schools, and both men and women were involved in settlement houses. But the extensive programs of physical education had a special meaning in female colleges because the need for women to balance mental activity with exercise appeared to be so pressing. So, too, the emphasis in the post-Civil War period on the precarious state of female health not only shaped the college experience of one generation of women, but also the reforms that another generation enacted on behalf of the immigrant child. Hence, to lump the contributions of women settlement house workers with those of men has meant that historians have slighted the peculiar cast that women gave to settlement house activities and the particular kinds of programs that they promoted. Moreover, a sufficient amount of information is already available on the men's world for readers to be able to make their own comparisons and supplement what I have had to relegate to footnotes. When Vassar opened in the 1860s, it pledged to admit women through the front not the side door. This is my effort to bring to history and social policy this same kind of commitment.

To move to consequences, the efforts of women to structure social policy have invariably come up against one central problem, and that problem will appear again and again in these pages: the bonds of sex have not been able to overcome the differences between classes. In retrospect, this failure is clear and will be illustrated in many contexts. Yet, women reformers have all too typically not recognized the issue, let alone responded to it. Each generation seems to believe that social policies devised and implemented by middle-class women will be in the best interests of lower-class women. The programs formulated by what we may label "Protestant nuns" in the 1880s, and by settlement house workers in the 1910s and birth controllers in the 1920s, invariably promised to improve the lot of all women, even to create a new and better social order. The results, however, have been quite different. The enterprise of reform has invigorated middle-class women, giving them a keen sense of solidarity and purpose, and it may also have brought them some tangible benefits. But insofar as lower-class women were concerned, the results have been at best uneven, and more than occasionally mischievous and counterproductive. However strong the sense of solidarity that brings women into social policy, it has not been able to bridge the gap between the social classes.

For the women's movement today to ignore this legacy would be foolhardy and self-defeating. Like other reformers, feminists have a distinct sense of their own novelty, and they are understandably reluctant to look back to a record that is replete with failures and mistakes, perhaps fearing that it might immobilize them. But the aim of this account, and perhaps the purpose of history, is not to inhibit action but to inform it.

The contemporary definition of woman as person has energized its proponents, both in their personal lives and public commitments. The movement has bred its own sense of solidarity and generated

an optimism about the prospects of social reforms to promote freedom of action. But again, when these views are translated into programs, the outcomes, however unintentionally so, are often unsatis-
fying. In no simple sense has this latest reform endeavor been able to
benefit all women in all social classes; it certainly has not promoted
a more harmonious or cohesive social order. To the contrary: there
is ample reason to believe that the politics of women's liberation,
with its vigorous expression of its members' rights, has—like so many
other contemporary expressions of a group's interest—sparked conflict.
Yet an awareness of this conflict, a clear recognition of diversity of
interests, the limits of a sexual identification, and the differences between classes may well represent in the world of social policy the
beginnings of wisdom.

CHAPTER

I

Woman's Special Sphere

THE CLOSING DECADES of the nineteenth century present two contradictory and yet authentic images. In the first instance, the period appears to be remarkably open and fluid, filled with marvelous innovations and technological advances. Over these thirty years, America did become modern. Industrial production transformed the economic life of the nation: large-scale corporations distributed mass-produced goods to national markets over an elaborate network of railroads. Americans in unprecedented numbers began to move to the cities. A restless energy drove them from the countryside and the small towns to the new urban centers. At the same time, great numbers of Europeans, particularly Eastern Europeans, migrated to take their chances in a New World. A sense of ambition and adventure seemed to pervade every place and enterprise. But these same decades were no less marked by constraints and restrictions. The gap between the rich and the poor widened, the distance between mansion and tenement becoming so great that only a very lucky few could ever bridge it. The discipline of work took on a new relentlessness: the factory machine and the office routine imposed their own kind of tyranny. Thus one vacillates, properly, between a sense of opportunity and creativity and a sense of fixity and rigidity.[1]

Although many of these images come from the world of men, the same tension predominated in the world of women. In a variety of ways, technological innovations transformed women's lives and particularly the lives of middle-class, urban women. Technology liberated them from much of the drudgery of household tasks. The appliances that electricity powered freed women from traditional and incredibly onerous household chores. Further, new types of institutions for women, particularly the women's colleges, came into existence during these years, providing an altogether novel kind of experience. Still further, new occupations opened up to women, especially in offices and department stores, while the number of teaching positions in the public schools increased. Finally, this era witnessed the vigorous and energetic activities of women's clubs; benevolent-minded women set out to reform the almshouses and eliminate the saloon. As the Woman's Christian Temperance Union (WCTU) motto proclaimed: "Woman will bless and brighten every place she enters, and will enter every place."

Yet again, in each of these instances, liberation seems to be only part of the story. A very special ideology defined women's proper social roles in narrow and restricted ways. Ideas that we may label "virtuous womanhood" dominated their lives, closing off opportunities, fostering a sex-stereotyping of jobs, and ruling out options. Both in the private and public arena—in the home, in the club, and in the workplace—women's actions had to be consistent with moral sensibility, purity, and maternal affection, and no other code of behavior was acceptable. Hence, to understand the experience of women in the post-Civil War decades, particularly as it helped to shape social policy by women and on behalf of women, requires a full appreciation of the interaction between opportunity and obligation, between social reality and ideology.

Technology and the White Woman's Burden

Almost every technological innovation in the period 1870–1900 significantly altered the daily routine of middle-class women. During these years, city after city, responding to the demands of engineers and real estate promoters, constructed and extended water and sewerage lines. It was not unusual for as much as one-third of a municipal budget to go to improving sanitation.[2] By 1890, even moderate-priced homes in many cities were equipped with hot and cold water, water closets, and bathrooms. These conveniences are so much a part of our lives that we may easily forget their significance to the first generation of women who enjoyed them: they reduced—almost eliminated—an extraordinary amount of menial tasks. Hot and cold running water within a private dwelling simplified the most demanding domestic task that a woman faced, the weekly wash. Laundering probably took as much as one-third of her working hours. To Marion Harland, one of the most prolific writers of household advice books, laundry was "the white woman's burden . . . the bane of American housemother's professional life." [3] The new water supply eliminated not only the endless parade of bucket-carrying from the outdoor well to the kitchen, but also the enervating task of pumping water from a hand pump, then lifting and lowering heavy washtubs of hot water from the stove. More, the piping of water prepared the way for the arrival of the great household appliance, the washing machine.[4] The hand pump, the copper washtub, and the wooden scrubbing board were on their way to becoming antiques, relics of a primitive past.

So, too, the municipal power companies began to harness electricity to light city streets and stores, and before very long they were providing electric light for private dwellings.[5] Electricity expanded the hours of the day in a literal sense, and it was soon reducing the drudgery of housework. Electricity, reported one architect by 1903, "is used in operating telephones, call bells . . . for driving laundry, kitchen ventilating and pumping apparatus, and in some cases for refrigerating machinery." [6] And each of these appliances saved women time and energy.

The technological improvements in water supply, sewerage, and electricity all contributed directly to the creation of a novel form of residential living, and one that would prove exceptionally convenient for women—the apartment house. Part of the stimulus for the erection of apartment houses came from real estate developers. As the cost of land climbed in every major urban area and as real estate values doubled and tripled in short periods of time, the use of commercial residential space was fundamentally altered. When land values soared, so did buildings—and hence the new office skyscrapers. At the same time, the possibility of owning a private home within the city became more and more the prerogative of the very rich, the mansion dwellers along New York's Fifth Avenue. For the middle classes there was the suburb, and they did flock to the perimeters of the city along the new urban transportation networks.[7] But many middle-class families were eager to remain close to the urban core, and for them the apartment dwelling was eminently attractive.[8]

Developers quickly understood the need to build not only offices but also apartment houses as high as possible. But before they could carry out the plan, they had to be able to deliver critical kinds of services. In the case of the office building, electricity made the essential service of an elevator easily available. But home residences required more complex facilities, particularly in the kitchen. Some apartment houses had been constructed before the advent of electricity, but invariably they served a very limited clientele, generally the rich, precisely because they could not provide kitchens. The first apartment buildings were appropriately known as "apartment hotels," buildings that substituted a communal dining room for a private kitchen. The family took its meals on the hotel's main floor with other residents. The lack of privacy under this arrangement did prompt some buildings to offer an additional service—the private servants of the family could prepare meals in the downstairs kitchen and then use dumbwaiters to lift the food upstairs. In either case, apartment hotels were suitable only for a very wealthy minority.[9]

By the late 1880s, technological developments transformed apartment hotels into apartment houses. Builders installed a central refrigeration plant that cooled each apartment refrigerator. They piped gas into kitchen stoves and, of course, provided elevators to move the tenant and her groceries upstairs.[10] Thus, in 1901 the apartment, to quote one architect, became "a substitute for the home," able to supply "what the house gives."[11]

The innovation was quick to spread. Developers found that economies of scale paid well, and so they built apartment houses taller and wider. The first structures occupied one city lot; the newer ones covered two or three. The high initial cost of wiring and providing elevators could be offset by increasing the number of units in each building.[12] Thus, middle-class families who did not wish to move to the suburbs could live comfortably and even cheaply within the city. Apartments were less costly to maintain than homes and were more efficient besides. The new kitchens were especially attractive: the floors were typically covered with rubber tile, and the lower half of the walls had white tile that was easy to clean. A gas stove, a hot water heater, a sink with hot and cold running water, and a refrigerator with "glass or tile linings and compartments for every conceivable use" were all in place, simplifying almost every household task. Further, the entire arrangement obviated the need for servants just at a time when domestic help was becoming less available. In 1870, one of every eight families had a servant; by 1900 the number had dropped to one in fifteen.[13] Clearly, an apartment kitchen made full-time help much less necessary.

Technological innovations and apartment units became more available to still larger numbers of American families in the opening decades of the twentieth century. More electrical power was harnessed to light homes, to drive washing machines, and to heat ovens. More apartment dwellings were built as land costs rose in small as well as large municipalities. Indeed, to a local chamber of commerce, apartment houses represented municipal prosperity, a sign that land in the town was too valuable for constructing private homes. To the tenants, the units symbolized the quintessence of modern living. "Apartment dwelling is both simplified and intensive living," one observer reported. "The smoothly run private house, with one or two good servants doing practically all the work, is for those of moderate means largely a recollection of the happy past. . . . We may contrast with this the life of the well-managed apartment house. At once is the heating problem disposed of, with its laborious care of the furnace and its coal and dirt. . . . Packages, mail, and messages are received, receipted for, and delivered by attendants. Rubbish and garbage are taken away daily, and papers, milk, bread, and ice are brought to the apartment doors. . . . If plumbing or electrical trouble develops, the engineer is at hand; if a trunk or piece of furniture needs shifting, there is the elevator man." So, too, the "servantless electric kitchen" became popular. Builders substituted refrigerators, electric ranges, and even dishwashers for roomy kitchens, pantries, and maids' rooms. One favorite cartoon of the 1920s portrayed the servantless housewife asleep while her electric machines did all the chores.[14]

In the newly expanded city, women found a host of labor-saving services. In 1870, for example, most urban women were still canning and preserving fruits and vegetables; over the course of the next two decades, the technology of commercial canning advanced so that women could vary the family diet in little time and at little expense. The Campbell soup jingle now boasted that "it only takes a ten-cent can to make enough for six," and the Heinz Company had developed not only their famous ketchup but also fifty-seven varieties of pickles and relishes. (To advertise their products, Heinz in 1897 erected a fifty-foot electric sign in mid-Manhattan, whose green bulbs made up an enormous pickle.) At the same time, the combination of national railway lines and refrigerated railway cars brought fresh meat from Midwestern slaughterhouses to butchers and to housewives in

well-wrapped and precisely cut packages. The presence of commercial local bakeries in the cities and the distribution of national
food company products like Uneeda Biscuits meant that women no
longer had to reserve one day of the week to bake the family bread
and cakes. (Uneeda Biscuits promised that its inner wrap seal would
deliver a product "as fresh as mother's.") By 1900, 90 percent of
urban homes used bakers' bread only, and two-thirds of urban families
sent some laundry out of the home to be finished. All these developments represented a fundamental change in the consumption patterns.
More middle-class families were spending a larger proportion of their
funds on durable goods and services and less on purchasing homes
and the services of domestic servants.[15]

Only a few nostalgic critics lamented these changes. " 'The Home-
made Loaf,' " Marion Harland declared, "stands with so many of us
as a symbol of the wholesome good cheer beloved in our childhood's
days that we are disposed to class the phrase with the traditional
open fireplaces, doughnuts 'such as mother used to make,' and other
reminiscences of 'the days that are no more.' " [16] But others, like
Thomas Edison, spread a very different message. Praising the wonders
of electricity, he predicted that woman "will give less attention to
the home, because the home will need less; she will be rather a
domestic engineer than a domestic laborer, with the greatest of all
handmaidens, electricity, at her service. This and other mechanical
forces will so revolutionize the woman's world that a large portion
of the aggregate of woman's energy will be conserved for use in
broader, more constructive fields." [17] Technology had the potential
to make women's lives much less isolated and home-bound.

No change better exemplified the way in which technology increased women's efficiency and encouraged their movement outside
the home than the department store. Just as Americans quickly incorporated the variety of new, mass-produced products in their
homes, so, too, women with equal ease moved to take advantage of
the bargains and delights of shopping in the new department stores.
These stores, another innovation of the post-Civil War decades,
revolutionized the patterns of retail trade and the shopping habits
of middle-class women. Wanamaker's in Philadelphia, Marshall Field's
in Chicago, and Macy's in New York wanted to make it more
economical for women to shop at their stores. They defended a
cash-only system of business by claiming that it allowed them to
offer lower prices than the local shops. "For every cent expended
in our store," Macy's told their customers, "we return full value,

because we give no credit and, therefore, incur no losses. . . . Every article in our store is a BARGAIN." [18] The stores' size also enabled them to eliminate many middleman costs; they could buy directly from the manufacturer or even produce the goods themselves. By 1885, Macy's manufactured "ladies' and children's underwear, men's shirts, linen collars and cuffs for both men and women, women's dresses, bustles . . . velvet wraps and linen handkerchiefs," selling the goods under their private label.[19] They were further able to reduce prices by placing orders in bulk. John Wanamaker proudly noted that a purchase of pins for his store took an entire freight car to transport and that he could then sell pins to his customers at a lower cost.

The department store also offered women a dazzling variety of products. Macy's boasted that it had the "most extensive assortment of china [and] glassware . . . ever displayed in America." [20] And the opening of a new Wanamaker's store gave President William Howard Taft the occasion to declare that Americans could now purchase "under one roof . . . at the lowest reasonable, constant, and fixed price, everything that is usually needed upon the person or in the household for the sustaining of life, for recreation, and for intellectual enjoyment." [21]

The department store added other efficiencies to attract women. It delivered packages to apartments in the city, to the suburbs, or to nearby summer communities. It repaired jewelry and watches and framed pictures. It even stored furs during the hot summer months, a particular convenience to customers living in small apartments.[22]

The department store's popularity also testified to its ability to capture the imagination and interest of the middle-class woman. It resorted to so many promotional devices that a trip to the department store had the quality of an adventure. *The New York World* was right to call Macy's "a bazaar, a museum, a hotel and a great fancy store all combined." [23]

The architecture of the new stores was monumental in design. The "cast-iron palaces" were almost cathedral-like in character. Wanamaker, for example, instructed his architect: "What you must do for me is to strive to say in stone what this business has said to the world in deed. You must make a building that is solid and true. It shall be granite and steel throughout . . . simple, unpretentious, noble, classic—a work of art, and, humanly speaking, a monument for all time." The result was a building that contained a huge auditorium with almost 2,000 seats, a pipe organ of nearly 3,000 pipes, a Grand

Court with towering marble columns, and a Greek Hall with 600 more seats.[24] Shoppers entering New York's Siegel & Cooper Company faced an enormous fountain of a Greek goddess over twenty feet high. Plush and ornate trimmings ran through every corner of the stores. The ladies' waiting room at Macy's was described as "the most luxurious and beautiful department devoted to the comforts of ladies to be found in a mercantile establishment in the city. The style of decoration is Louis XV, and no expense has been spared in the adornment and furnishing of this room." [25] Adjoining the waiting room was an art gallery with an extensive exhibit of oil paintings.

The department store provided customers with still more comforts and conveniences. As early as 1878, Macy's set aside space where women could sit and write letters or read its collection of the latest editions of the daily newspapers. The newspapers, of course, always contained the store's advertisement, usually placed directly across the page from an article of special interest to women. The Wanamaker advertisement was seemingly so popular a feature of the Philadelphia press that the store claimed: "Women of the city and suburbs refused to take a daily paper that did not contain the Wanamaker advertisement." [26] In 1890, when a biking craze swept New York City, women could not only purchase their bicycles at Macy's but also learn to ride them there. In all, these stores had an irresistible appeal. As Macy's told its customers: "Ride our bicycles, read our books, cook in our saucepans, dine off our china, wear our silks, get under our blankets, smoke our cigars, drink our wines—Shop at Macy's—and life will Cost You Less and Yield You More Than You Dreamed Possible." [27]

Department store customers were among the first to experience technological innovations. New York City streets were not lit by electricity until 1882, but in 1879 Macy's display windows were "brilliantly illuminated with electric lights until 10 o'clock." In 1878 the first telephone was installed in the White House, and within two years Macy's had the device. One of the earliest steam-powered elevators in the country ran in Strawbridge and Clothier of Philadelphia. The Otis hydraulic model in the Eiffel Tower took tourists to the top in seven minutes in 1889. The electric elevators installed by Macy's and Wanamaker's in 1888 went faster.[28]

Urban living meant that many middle-class women did not have to be at home to prepare a noonday meal. Men's workplaces were typically too distant from their residences to allow the family to lunch together. So daytime visiting between women, once confined to the parlor, more frequently took place in centrally located public restaurants. The department stores, as well as the commercial tea parlors, offered a Ladies' Luncheon. The first ladies' lunchroom opened at Macy's in 1878, the same year the Sixth Avenue Elevated brought rapid transit to Fourteenth Street. The lunchroom was so successful that, when opening its new Herald Square store in 1902, Macy's installed a public restaurant for 2,500 people.[29] The Womans Exchange, a charitable and social organization commonly found in cities, also ran dining rooms. The Boston Exchange, with its several thousand women members, was reputedly "the one place we can surely find good food at moderate prices." [30] By 1910, as Marion Talbot, Dean of Women at the University of Chicago, aptly concluded, "the sewing circle, the husking bee, the afternoon visit are things of the past." [31] Now women would meet in the grand reception hall of the department store, see the newest sights, shop with friends, and then lunch together. A stop before returning home allowed them to purchase a "home-baked" bread or cake to place on the table.

The Concept of Virtuous Womanhood

As the activities of the department store indicate, middle-class women used the new leisure gained from technological innovation and urban living in very particular ways. They became consumers, not producers, of the new technology. They did not translate free time into employment opportunities or careers. They did not compete in the world of men—employment was legitimate only for a brief period before marriage. Technology freed them from the menial labor that had dominated the lives of their mothers and offered them opportunities to go outside the home, but it did not free them from the commitment and obligation to the home that had structured their mothers' aspirations and choices. They, too, although in new and perhaps more insidious ways, were dominated by an outlook that ultimately confined and narrowed their sense of possibilities.

The definition of virtuous womanhood that prevailed in post-Civil War America has become almost so trite that we may forget its impact and significance. Ministers, moralists, writers of advice books for young girls and mothers, public lecturers, indeed, almost every commentator on social roles consigned men and women to separate and distinct tasks.[32] "The sum total of general belief of the most enlightened of both sexes," one orator told the 1876 graduating class of Mount Holyoke College, "appears to be that there is a difference of kind in their natural endowments and that there is for each an appropriate field of development and action." The appropriate field for women was caretaking and nurturing inside and outside the home. Catharine Beecher, perhaps the most influential writer of advice books through the 1860s and 1870s, urged women to obtain "appropriate *scientific and practical training* for her distinctive *profession* as housekeeper, nurse of infants and the sick, educator of childhood, trainer of servants and minister of charities." In this way women would "develop the intellectual, social and moral powers in the most perfect manner," becoming better mothers, wives, and social reformers.[33]

Although the definition of virtuous womanhood was reminiscent of ideas that prevailed in the pre-Civil War decades, continuing a tradition of describing women as the repository of special sensibility and refinement, the 1870s and 1880s nevertheless brought novel interpretations to these general views. For one, a new ideal took hold in childrearing. The primary task of the mother in the Jacksonian period had been to instill obedience in her offspring, a trait that the father might have inculcated as easily or even more easily. In the post-Civil War period, women were to raise children as only a mother could, with love and affection. "We still unhappily hear of 'breaking a child's will,' " noted one typical child-rearing tract. "But I hope the expression is only used by very narrow or ignorant persons. For it is to the will . . . that we must look for all that is strong and valuable." [34] Newton Riddell, author of the best-seller *Our Little Ones*, recommended that "a parent who does not know how to govern a child without whipping it ought to surrender the care of that child to some wiser person." And suffrage reformers like Frances Power Cobbe, in her widely read *The Duties of Women*, advised mothers "to drop, as completely as possible, the tone of command, and assume that of the loving, sympathetic, ever-disinterested guide and friend." [35]

This view of feminine traits also gave wives an enlarged and awesome responsibility within the marital relationship. Post-Civil War women had a new and urgent charge to civilize their husbands by curbing their "animal" instincts. "Few women understand at the outset," insisted one female writer in 1886, "that in marrying, they have

simply captured a wild animal . . . the taming of which is to be the
life work of the woman who has taken him in charge. . . . The duty
is imposed upon her by high heaven, to reduce all these grand, un-
tamed life-forces to order . . . to make them subservient to the behests
of her nature, and to those vast undying interests which, to these
two and to their posterity, center in the home." [36]

Finally, women in these decades, far more keenly than their pre-
Civil War sisters, had the mandate to "tame" society. One no longer
spoke merely of aiding a neighbor or improving the welfare of a particular community but of transforming, even feminizing, an entire
culture. "We owe to women," one educator declared, "the charm
and the beauty of life; for purity of thought and heart, for patient
courage, for recklessly unselfish devotion, for the love that rests,
strengthens and inspires, we look to women. These are the best things
in women; these are the best things in life; in them men cannot compete with women." Or, as Cobby's tract, distributed by the American Woman Suffrage Association argued, women were to "use their
power to purify and amend society. If a woman be herself pure and
noble-hearted, she will come into every circle as a person does into
a heated room who carries with him the freshness of the woods." [37]

To a significant degree, medical authorities reinforced the idea of a
separate women's sphere, that "the home is woman's kingdom" and
her only kingdom. Physicians insisted that biological characteristics
permitted women to pursue only certain special activities. Their very
refinement and moral sensibility was the root cause of the prevalent
female maladies—and these maladies made active participation in the
world outside the home impossible. Students of gynecology learned
about the anatomy of female patients in order both to treat their
physical illnesses and to understand their moral makeup. "You shall
have to explore," Dr. Charles Meigs explained to his class, "the history of those functions and destinies which her sexual nature enables
her to fulfill, and the strange and secret influences which her organs by their nervous constitution . . . are capable of exerting, not on
the body alone, but on the heart, the mind, and the very soul of
women. The medical practitioner has, then, much to study as to
the female, that is not purely medical—but psychological and
moral." [38] And Meigs was not unique in assuming that a woman's
anatomy shaped her destiny. As another physician bluntly concluded,
it was "as if the Almighty, in creating the female sex, had taken the
uterus and built up a woman around it." [39]

According to practically every physician and manual on female health, women had to fit their daily routine to their peculiar bodily structure. "Woman has a sum total of nervous force equivalent to a man's," contended one doctor, but this force was "distributed over a greater multiplicity of organs. . . . The nervous force is therefore weakened in each organ . . . it is more sensitive, more liable to derangement." [40] The onset of menstruation introduced and exemplified the debilitating process; the burden of a "uterus heavy and engorged with blood," had to be carefully reckoned with.[41] Thus, through puberty in general, but particularly at the time of their monthly periods, girls were to curtail both their physical and their intellectual activities. "Long walks are to be avoided," counseled one physician, "also long wheel rides . . . in fact, all severe physical exertion. . . . Intense mental excitement as a fit of anger or grief or even intense joy may be injurious." [42] And women took this advice seriously. A rare critic of this school of thought, Dr. Mary Putnam Jacobi, noted that all too many women "expect to go to bed every menstrual period, expect to collapse if by chance they find themselves on their feet for a few hours during such a crisis." [43]

The rules that a woman was to follow during menstruation applied throughout her pregnancy. The growing fetus drained physical strength and consumed mental energy. All forms of exercise—and all expressions of emotionality—had to be avoided; again, the safest place seemed to be in bed. The penalties for disregarding these rules were heavy. "Many a young wife has died in childbirth," a physician warned, "because of the uterine ailments contracted in girlhood through improper dress or injudicious conduct." [44] And clearly, the pregnant woman who did not follow the right regimen risked not only miscarriage but her own death as well. Put another way, the woman who would be active, who would enter the man's world and compete with him, was pursuing nothing less than a suicidal course.

By associating the normal bodily functions of women with disease and ill health, this ideology perpetuated the notion that women were not only inherently frail but also predisposed to insanity. Women were far more prone than men to nervous exhaustion—neurasthenia, as it was called. The precise etiology of the disease was unclear, but it was linked somehow or other to femininity itself. The neurasthenic was delicate and high strung, subject to fits of anxiety or even hysteria that could erupt at any time. Women who appeared particularly delicate had to exercise great caution, but by virtue of their anatomy, all women were susceptible and therefore had to avoid anxiety-producing and enervating situations.[45]

A host of popular magazines and newspapers spread these notions, especially through their advertising columns. No group more consistently preached the doctrine of woman at risk than the patent medicine industry. Medicine manufacturers defined menstruation as an illness, and a serious one, that required (of course) a daily dose of their compound. Although they advertised their nostrums as vegetable derivatives, such tonics as Lydia Pinkham were actually composed of opium, and others were laced with alcohol. Their advertisements not only disseminated the ideology of feminine frailty but promoted addiction as well. To persuade women to buy its medicine, Lydia Pinkham described the symptoms of menstrual illness as a "taste for solitude," eyes with "strange lustre," "headaches, sluggishness of thought, dizziness and disposition to sleep," and "pains . . . in the back and lower limbs." The young girl who first exhibited these characteristics, who was about to enter puberty, was "stepping into a NEW LIFE." [46] But it was obviously a cursed one—and even allowing for readers' ability to discount advertising hyperbole, many women were bound to see themselves in a most precarious state of health.

Physicians and advice books cautioned women who might think of themselves as exceptional, with special talents or robust health, that they too were prone to the perils of femininity. Every woman, for example, experienced "*the temporary insanity of her menstruation.*" During their monthly periods, as one physician explained, women were "more prone than men to commit any unusual or outrageous act," [47] and that fact alone ought to keep them at home. Isaac Ray, probably the leading psychiatrist of the time, was certain that "with women it is but a step from extreme nervous susceptibility to downright hysteria and from that to overt insanity. In the sexual evolution, in pregnancy, in the parturient period, in lactation, strange thoughts, extraordinary feelings, unreasonable appetites, criminal impulses may haunt a mind at other times innocent and pure." [48] While doctors conceded that women in a few "exceptional cases may have all the courage, tact, ability, pecuniary means, education and patience necessary to fit persons for the cares and responsibilities of professional life, they still are and must be subject to the periodical *infirmity* of their sex; which for the time and in every case, *however unattended by physical suffering*, unfits them for any responsible effort of mind, and in many cases of body also." [49] So it did not matter whether a woman actually experienced discomfort during menstruation or was out of sorts during pregnancy or nursing; even those who believed themselves healthy were highly susceptible to attacks of insanity. Hence, women from puberty onward had to organize their lives to compensate for the special and onerous demands of their bodies. It was in society's interest, and in their own best interest, too, to follow domestic pursuits.

That women were at once the more civilized, the more moral, and the more virtuous of the two sexes and at the same time the victims of precarious health made for an odd duality of traits. Women were frequently sickly, temporarily insane, and always susceptible to mental and physical derangement—and at the same time they possessed extraordinary moral strength, saintly devotion, and exemplary virtue. The ideology rendered them at once incompetent and competent, broken and whole, to be pitied and to be emulated. But whatever the contradictions in this perspective, they disappeared in one grand edict: Women had better stay very much in their own sphere. They did not belong in the world of men.

All effort to expand options for women had to take into account both the social assumptions about woman's appropriate sphere of influence and, even more important, the medical judgments about her predisposition to frailty and derangement. Any new program would have to reckon with her inherent weaknesses and to compensate for them. The task was not an easy one, and it placed a heavy burden upon any would-be innovator.

The Vassar Model for Health

The female colleges established in the post-Civil War decades represented both an acknowledgment of societal assumptions about the peculiarities of the female sex and a novel response to them. The founders of these colleges, such as Matthew Vassar, could insist that "woman having received from her Creator the same intellectual constitution as man, has the same right as man to intellectual culture and development." [50] The college that bore his name, however, had to provide women not only with an opportunity for education but also with ways of overcoming their seeming predisposition to illness. No sooner did Vassar, the first of the women's colleges, open its doors in 1865, than it confronted a barrage of medical warnings about women's infirmities.[51] The college was not unprepared. Vassar, and later its sister schools, devised a regimen to counter the objections, which they continued to refine over the next several decades. The colleges designed programs that promised to provide an education equal to a man's and at the same time to preserve, in college and throughout life, the students' mental and physical health.

Vassar was not to be just another female seminary, devoted exclusively to instilling in well-bred girls the correct female graces. Nor was it to be a normal school, offering a two-year course to qualify women for teaching positions. It had a far grander vision. At a liberal arts college of their own, the girls were to be admitted not "by a side door [as] into a man's college," to be seated "at the lower end of the bench as mere tolerated intruders." [52] At Vassar they were at the core, the focus of all educational efforts.*

From the start, the trustees confronted conflicting pressures. On the one hand, they were bombarded by the judgments of male doctors warning that "the physical organization and function of woman naturally disqualify her for severe study, and that an education es-

---

* Vassar's determination to make female education *equal* to a man's turned it, and not the midwestern coeducational colleges or female seminaries, into the battleground between women and physicians. Vassar was not the first institution to provide women with the opportunity for a collegiate training; it was, however, the first to insist that women were entitled to take all courses deemed appropriate for a man, that women would not come to this college through the side door. Although women had been attending Oberlin since 1834, they lacked the rights and privileges of the male students. "The founders," recalled President James Fairchild about the first days of Oberlin, "certainly held no new or special views on the rights or the sphere of women." Even after admission a woman had to demonstrate her individual ability to enroll in courses that were routinely open to a man. Women were admitted only to the Ladies Course; after completing one term, they could request permission to take courses in other branches. So, too, until 1874, female graduates were not allowed to read their essays at Commencement Day as the men did.

Although midwestern state schools also admitted women before Vassar opened, their policy reflected an ad hoc response to the determination of a small group of women to get some form or other of college training. Thus, at Michigan, one woman applied and was admitted to the college; within a year thirty-four others joined her. But this band of females differed from the men students in many ways. They were generally older; many of them had been teachers or in some other way self-supporting. More, the administration made no attempt to integrate them into the school. "The women were welcomed by a small minority," noted one observer, "and by most of the students were usually treated with an indifferent courtesy." Medical instruction, for example, was kept separate: any professor willing to teach women medical science was paid an additional $500. At Wisconsin, women were initially admitted into the normal school and then only slowly integrated into the university. At Ohio State, too, the women although not excluded were not welcomed either. Thus, when Vassar declared itself determined to let women in the front door, to give all women an education identical to men, they were, in a genuine way, breaking new ground. The doctors' special response to Vassar, their fears and concerns, reflected its novel premises.

sentially popular and largely ornamental is alone suited to her sphere." [53] Yet a group of women did insist upon a more rigorous education, if for no other reason than that its "mental and moral discipline" would improve the quality of home life. "In intellectual cultivation," wrote one supporter, "who is more called on for cleverness of thought and vigor of expression than the mother? . . . In moral culture, who has more need of it than woman in every part of her life, especially if she be yoked with a drunkard or has a harsh, overbearing, and tyrannical husband [the male animal come to life]?" [54]

Vassar's response was to try to satisfy all claims. It offered a wide variety of courses in the sciences as well as in the humanities. It did not neglect the female graces, providing instruction in the "arts of design and music." "Whatever might be added to the former ideals of womanly culture on the score of breadth and thoroughness," insisted Vassar's first president, "there must be no lowering of the standard of womanly refinement and grace." [55] Vassar also presented courses for future teachers and gave instruction in domestic economy, "to maintain a just appreciation of the dignity of woman's home sphere . . . to teach a correct *theory*, at least, of the household and its management." [56] Even more important, the formal instruction was to be supplemented by a regimen that made certain that students did not succumb to nervous exhaustion or ill health. "The social and sanitary care," the health of the students, was of critical concern to the administration.

Although the educational curriculum bore some similarity to the male colleges, the daily routine of the students seemed closer to the ways that medical superintendents of the Jacksonian asylum administered institutions to cure the insane. Vassar's trustees assumed that they were dealing not only with a class of young women who needed maternal supervision and moral guidance but who were prone to insanity as well. By organizing the lives of their students around the precepts of a well-ordered household, the trustees, like the medical superintendents, were trying to provide "moral treatment" and so guard their students from attacks. [57]

A highly structured schedule was at the heart of the design. The college (adopting a plan that would be followed later by most other Eastern women's colleges) constructed one large dormitory in which every student was to live and to study. [58] A female principal was at the head of the dormitory to "exercise a maternal supervision over the deportment, health, social connections, personal habits and wants of the students." [59] The college supplied three "abundant" meals a day and insisted on a regimen of early rising and lights out not later than ten o'clock.

The trustees, again following the asylum superintendents, encouraged outdoor activities among the students. They provided open-air instruction, physical activity, and after-class excursions. "For amusements," recounted one student, "there were baseball clubs, croquet clubs and a chess club. A bowling alley was in the basement of the museum; there was horseback riding . . . light calisthenics . . . trips to the Catskills and Lake Mohonk . . . and in the Easter vacations extensive geological excursions were taken to various places of interest." [60] Vassar also taught the value of personal hygiene. "How many years of torture," declared the college's trustees, "how often a whole life of suffering would be avoided; what numbers of the loveliest of the sex would be rescued from an early grave, if all our young girls were properly informed respecting those natural laws, the violation of which never goes unpunished." [61]

Most notably, physical education assumed a novel prominence at Vassar. So worried were the trustees about the effects of strenuous mental labor on a group prone to mental derangement that they placed this department first in the "General Scheme of Education." Physical education, the original *Prospectus* noted, is *"Fundamental* to all the rest, and in order to indicate the purpose of the Managers of this Institution to give it . . . its true place in their plan." [62]

Despite all these precautions, college education for women in the 1860s and 1870s was still considered a hazardous business. As one alumna of Vassar recalled: "It was impressed upon the whole family that the higher education of women was an experiment, and that the world was looking on, watching its success or defeat. The good of the college was the watchword, and not mere gratification of individual preferences."

Each Vassar applicant was carefully screened not only for intellectual competence but physical fitness as well. Matthew Vassar had first intended the school to be a charity institution, educating talented but poor young women. But by the time Vassar opened, that goal had disappeared. The trustees looked to secure the "patronage of intelligent and discriminating parents," to make the college "so attractive to gifted and aspiring young ladies that our most affluent and aristocratic families will contend for the honor of placing their daughters in Vassar." [63] Behind this shift was not just a loss of reform ardor but a determination to turn what was clearly a risky experiment into a success. Given the stakes, Vassar wanted to admit only the brightest and the most vigorous students and, with a clear class bias, it assumed that that meant the well-born. Thus Maria Mitchell, Vassar's most prominent professor, advised potential benefactors not to provide scholarships for girls from very poor families. "Do not attempt," she cautioned, "to put the daughters of the *very* poor through a college course. It is barely possible that a rare genius may be found even among the unworthy poor, but the chance is so small that we shall waste time in looking for it." So, too, Mitchell made it clear that Vassar preferred the healthiest candidates. "Do not aid the sickly girl to enter college," she continued. "Harm has already been done in this way. . . . I should dissuade the delicate girl from the attempt to take a regular college course." [64] The college knew well that its success rested on the intellectual and physical fitness of every student.

Soon after opening, Vassar did gain support from diverse sources that helped to legitimate its enterprise and to broaden the appeal of female education. First, Vassar benefited from some physicians' efforts to demonstrate that the concept of women's illness was highly exaggerated. These doctors were usually themselves women—and although they did not discount altogether the validity of the idea, they were eager to establish that the health of *all* women was not so precarious as the manuals insisted. Dr. Mary Putnam Jacobi formulated the most important response of the period—*The Question of Rest For Women During Menstruation* (1877). Jacobi argued that pain in menstruation was abnormal, a symptom of "an imperfection of the uterus." Menstrual pain originated in an anatomical defect of some women, not in the physical structure of all women. Those whose "nutrition was adequate" and who exercised frequently did not have difficulty during their monthly periods. "*There is nothing in the nature of menstruation,*" Jacobi forcefully concluded, "*to imply the necessity, or even the desirability, of rest, for women whose nutrition is really normal.*" [65]

On the basis of this finding, Jacobi insisted that higher education in and of itself did not threaten female health. The routine and precepts of the college were more than adequate protections. "When nervous exhaustion is observed after prolonged mental effort," Jacobi argued, "one of two other conditions, or both, has nearly always coexisted, namely *deficiency of physical exercise or presence of active emotion, as ardent ambitions, or harrassing anxieties.*" [66] A number of other women physicians shared this perspective, no less certain that physical exercise was an effective antidote to women's maladies. "Nature teaches us from the cradle to maturity" insisted Dr. Mary Taylor Bissell, "that some definite, voluntary, physical *exertion* is indispensable to healthful growth. . . . When we give children systematic physical exercise we are not only increasing the strength of their external muscles, but are also promoting the even development of heart and lungs, bone and brain and blood vessel." [67] More, physical education benefited mental health. Muscular control promoted mental control. "Systematic physical training," declared Bissell, "will improve the functional working of the nervous system, will increase its control over the body, will re-enforce its power of determining voluntary, accurate and definite movements." [68] So Vassar was on the right track, and the women doctors lauded the "well-ordered gymnasium." "It is precisely such training that young girls and all young persons need," Bissell maintained, "and so far as we know, it is a form of training which is only to be gained in the discipline and opportunity of a well-ordered gymnasium, under the conditions which are included in the term 'physical culture.' " [69]

These conclusions justified both the routine that Vassar offered its students and also its determination to keep education for women as a separate venture, apart from men and apart from purposes of professional advancement. While doctors like Jacobi and Bissell provided a powerful medical rationale for the college, they certainly did not minimize, even indirectly, the need for a separate woman's sphere. Female health might not be as precarious as most doctors insisted, but a woman had to take extra precautions. She could never altogether escape from her special biology.

As standard as these recommendations were, they did not placate an apprehensive medical profession, nor did the growing number of women who appeared to be flourishing, physically and mentally, under a college life routine. The doctors continued to define the woman's college as an affront to their wisdom and, in fact, agitated for a statistical report of the actual health of college students and graduates. Only such a survey, they insisted, could inform the public "if the future mothers of our country are being ruined physically by our methods of education." [70] The Association of Collegiate Alumnae accepted the challenge and sent questionnaires to all female college students and alumnae, requesting detailed information on social backgrounds, health, conjugal status, and even on the health of their children. [71] So important was the venture that the Association employed Carroll D. Wright, the leading statistician of the period, to analyze the results. Wright's conclusion was unequivocal: college women were healthy and so were their children. Intellectual endeavor did not endanger the mother's well-being or her offspring's.

The very fact that the medical profession demanded the data and the Association so quickly and so carefully responded reveals just how intense was the controversy surrounding female higher education. And more, it showed how vital the special routine was to the enterprise. "The stringent rules," reported Annie G. Howe, head of the Association's Committee, "drawn in accordance with hygienic principles that govern the daily conduct of most of our women's colleges made it impossible for any large number of women to transgress against the ordinary regulations of a systematic life." [72] But at the least, despite all their qualifications and special routines, colleges did demonstrate that physical health and intellectual capacity could be combined in a highly disciplined, middle-class woman.

The Vassar system became the model for other Eastern women's colleges in the post-Civil War period. They, too, put physical education and an orderly routine at the core of their curriculum. They, too, set out to educate women in very special ways. All of them remained locked in a dialogue with the physicians, assuming that women were at risk and in need of a compensating program. Thus, when Bryn Mawr opened in 1885, its trustees at once followed Vassar, confident of success. As its first president observed, "Four years of college study is a tax upon the bodily strength," but Bryn Mawr had a scheme to protect its women. "Students at college should have better health than elsewhere," the president asserted, "just as they have better mental training." So Bryn Mawr was "carefully limiting the hours spent in the classroom, by instruction in hygiene, by the supervision of an accomplished physician, by outdoor sports, by the best sanitary conditions, by cheerfulness and joyousness, and, finally, by the use of our excellent gymnasium." [73]

Smith College also followed the Vassar model, placing physical education very prominently in its curriculum. "The number and arrangement of studies and the mode of life," noted one of its circulars, "are carefully adapted to the demands of an enlightened physiology." [74] (Perhaps no phrase better expresses the precepts that guided all these institutions than "an enlightened physiology.") The danger of ill health in college students ran deep and was not to be disregarded. "When the question of offering a liberal education to women was first agitated," Dr. Mary Taylor Bissell recounted to the

Association of Collegiate Alumnae, "one of the objections immediately urged against it was the physical inability of the sex to sustain long-continued, severe application to work. This objection has never ceased to be urged by a certain portion of the community—an honorable portion, be it remembered—and it is not likely that it will ever cease to be urged until girls and women, in their own persons, have demonstrated it invalid." [75] And this process would take time.

No sooner was the Smith Alumnae Association formed in 1881 than it began to raise funds "for purchasing Sargent apparatus for the gymnasium." The college was so overwhelmed, one of the first alumna recalled, "by the criticism that girls could not stand the strain of college life, [that] it is not surprising that the first work of the Association should have been in the line of increasing the equipment of the Physical Department at the college." [76] Appropriately, the popular magazines reported on the success of the institution and linked it to the fitness of its students. Just two years after Smith opened, *Scribner's Monthly* observed: "Those who are watching with some anxiety to see what will be the effect of this higher education for women upon the health of the students, will be glad to know that the experience of Smith College has been most encouraging in this respect; and that the majority of the students have improved in their physical condition during their connection with the college." [77] Indeed, Smith's successes were so impressive that by 1889 the Alumnae Association could begin to use its funds for other than physical education purposes. "When the needs of the college were discussed," an alumna recalled, "the physical side still appealed to most of them, though the old criticism was heard much less frequently." [78]

As might be expected, the women's colleges during the 1880s began to rely on the services of women physicians. Perhaps the Jacobi essay led them to see the woman doctor as a valuable ally in qualifying male medical opinions. Or perhaps the presence of a woman physician as a healthy figure who had survived a rigorous professional education was a useful model for the girls. In all events, the female physician found a place on practically every women's campus. "The health of the students," noted the Smith circular, "is cared for by a resident physician who gives familiar lectures upon Hygiene and instruction in Physiology and Anatomy. She may be consulted without charge in her office at regular hours during the day." If the girls wished to visit a doctor in the community, the college had no objection. But no one could miss the doctor's lectures. The rules she taught the students, soon to be labeled "preventive gynecology," were another protection against ill health.[79]

These women physicians frequently lectured to public audiences, again stressing the value of physical training. Physical exercise for women assumed "scientific" respectability. "When it is objected that girls do not need great *muscular* strength," Dr. Mary Taylor Bissell declared, "and therefore systematic physical training is unnecessary for them, we answer that judicious physical training has larger aims than the development of external muscles only." Bissell was certain that physical exercise provided women, as well as men, with "endurance, activity, and energy, presence of mind, and dexterity, . . . and the girl or woman who has gained these by systematic physical training is of more use, more comfort and more value to herself and to her country than without them she ever would have been." The woman who followed these precepts would avoid the ominous predictions of the doctor. "The value of physical exercise," Bissell concluded, "cannot be overestimated as a sedative to emotional disturbances, and a relief from that nervous irritability and hypochondria too often engendered by a sedentary or an idle life." Physical exercise became, in effect, the favorite prescription of the women doctors.[80]

The model of vigorous femininity that the colleges offered was so compelling that even some among their male medical opponents conceded, if only reluctantly and indirectly, the success and value of their methods. The changing prescriptions of S. Weir Mitchell, a prominent alienist and neurologist and, incidentally, now the bane of women historians for his rest cures, points to the concessions that physicians made as a result of the college experience. In 1878 Mitchell published *Fat and Blood*, in which he recommended an extensive period of rest as the cure for delicate and debilitated women. The treatment consisted of one to two months' confinement in bed, overfeeding, extensive applications of electricity, and frequent bodily massages, all under continuous medical supervision.[81] To Mitchell, women's diseases represented, at their core, a moral failure. Long-established and hard-to-break habits of self-indulgence caused illness; and while his own treatment might first appear as still more pampering, Mitchell intended to carry the self-indulgences of his patients to such an extreme that they would learn their lesson. "Enforced rest [had] a moral use." He would, in effect, remove the pleasant associations of days in bed (which, when combined with sewing and reading, tended to be "both interesting and excite sympathy"), and make them repugnant. Mitchell's bed rest would constitute "moral medication" precisely because it would train the patients to exercise "order and control." "When they are bidden to stay in bed a month, and neither to read, write nor sew, and to have one nurse—who is not a relative—then rest becomes for some women a rather bitter medicine." [82] These women would soon enough leave the sickroom once and for all. To illustrate the effectiveness of his cure, Mitchell presented the case of Miss L., a 26-year-old who suffered first from an "irritable spine," then "anorexia," and finally "an overuse of drugs"—and all the while, of course, her selfish demands tyrannized the household. After completing his treatment, Miss L. not only gave up drugs but also gained 21 pounds. The change in her physical appearance "was so remarkable that the process of repair might well have been called a renewal of life." A spiritual renewal occurred as well. "She went home changed," Mitchell proudly concluded, "no less morally than physically, and resumed her place in the family circle and in social life, a healthy and well-cured woman." [83]

Over the course of the next decade, Mitchell came to prefer a very different method of treatment, one that emulated the routine of the female college. Rather than confining women to bed, he became convinced that despite its "moral force," the rest cure should only be a last resort when "*every other plan has failed*." [84] Instead, he emphasized the value of frequent physical exercise. "When I see young girls sweating from a good row or the tennis field," he wrote in *Doctor and Patient* (1887), "I know that it is preventive medicine." Such exertions promoted self-control. "Physical strength and an outdoor life, will make this lesson [of health] easy and natural. Be certain that weakness of body fosters and excuses emotional nonrestraint." As he told mothers, "Crave then, for your girls strength and bodily power of endurance." [85]

Mitchell remained apprehensive about the effects of collegiate education. "That it does not work satisfactorily I am sure, from the many cases I have seen of women who have told me their histories of defeat and broken health. The reason is clear. The general feeling (shall I say prejudices?) of such groups of women is bitterly opposed to conceding the belief held by physicians, that there are in woman's physiological life disqualifications for such continuous labor of mind as is easy and natural to man. The public sentiment of these great schools is against any such creed, and every girl feels called upon to sustain the general view, so that this acts as a constant goad for such as are at times unfit to use their fullest possibility of energy." And he certainly continued to insist on separate spheres of influence for men and women. "The woman's desire to be on a level of competition with man and to assume his duties is, I am sure, making mischief, for it is my belief that no length of generations of change in her education and modes of activity will ever really alter her characteristics. She is physiologically other than the man." [86]

But Mitchell's distrust of the colleges did not prevent him from conceding their good effects on some women, even if he gave his compliments grudgingly. "Let me once and for all admit," he conceded, "that many girls improve in health at these colleges, and that in some of them the machinery of organization for care of the mental and physical health of their students seems to be all that is desirable." [87] More, he was prepared to offer a cure for women patients that had them follow a type of life he had once believed only "desirable for men." "I wish now," he declared, "to correct my error of omission." The new illustrative case was a woman cured by a long and rigorous camping trip when she lived essentially as a man. The patient went into an isolated wilderness area for a six-month period (accompanied only by a woman companion and two guides). The group pitched their camp "by the lonely waters of a Western lake in May," sleeping in two "good wall tents," without letters from relatives or newspapers, just a good supply of books and a camera. The patient not only became interested in botany, but took up rowing, fishing, swimming, and even shooting. "Before August came she could walk for miles with a light gun, and stand for hours in wait for a deer." Thus, Mitchell concluded, "she led a man's life until the snow fell and in the fall she came back to report, a thoroughly well woman." [88]

In light of this shift in medical opinion and the college women's own sense of success, it is not surprising that the administrators of the women's schools believed that they had won an important battle. They had demonstrated the efficacy of a vigorous femininity. "The old notion that low vitality is a matter of course with women," wrote Alice Freeman Palmer, the president of Wellesley in 1897, "that to be delicate is a mark of superior refinement . . . that sickness is a dispensation of Providence—all these notions meet with no acceptance in college." [89] Ill health in a woman was not a biological truth, nor did its cure demand enforced rest. The colleges had demonstrated that a sickly girl was nothing other than an individual who was unable to abide by a well-ordered and active regimen. "I have often noticed among college girls," continued President Palmer, "an air of humiliation and shame when obliged to confess to a lack of physical vigor, as if they were convicted of managing life with bad judgment, or of some moral delinquency." [90] Indeed, Palmer's very use of the phrase "moral delinquency" amply testified to the colleges' sense of victory. Right was on their side.

So armed, the colleges were ready to admit the sickly girl, certain that they could transform her into a healthy woman. "The young student," declared President Palmer, "cannot afford quivering nerves or small lungs or an aching head any more than bad taste, rough manners or a weak will. Handicapped by inheritance or bad training, she finds the plan of college itself her supporter and friend." [91] Through the strictly enforced routine of early rising and regular eating habits, with hours of work alternating with vigorous exercise and outdoor activity, college life was the "salvation" of the sickly. As Palmer boasted: " 'I can never afford a sick headache again; life is so interesting and there is so much to do,' a delicate girl said to me at the end of her first college year. And while her mother was in a far-off invalid retreat, she undertook the battle against fate with the same intelligence and courage which she put into her calculus problems and her translations of Sophocles." Accordingly, Palmer concluded, "colleges for girls are pledged by their very constitution to make a persistent war on the water cure, the nervine retreat, the insane asylum, the hospital—those bitter fruits of the emotional lives of thousands of women." [92] Other administrators shared Palmer's sense of triumph. M. Carey Thomas, the president of Bryn Mawr, looked back in 1908 to the early battles and confessed that "we did not *know* whether colleges might not produce a corps of . . . invalids. Doctors insisted that they would. . . . Now we have tried it, and tried it for more than a generation, and we know that college women are not only not invalids, but that they are better physically than other women in their own class of life." [93] Within thirty years, the college graduate had become the model woman.

Despite this success, colleges did not provide women with an intellectual education equal to that of men. In their determination to produce healthy women, the trustees at Vassar and at other women's colleges devised a system of liberal education that was so responsive to the so-called feminine traits of women as to relegate intellectual accomplishments to second place. To be sure, women appeared no less capable of learning than men, but in setting out to devise a system of education that would compensate for female frailties, the colleges implemented a program that was both separate and unequal. They answered the doctors well but did not challenge the notion of woman's traditional sphere.

The ambivalent attitudes underlying the organization of the new women's colleges emerge vividly in an essay that Vassar president, John Raymond, wrote soon after the institution opened. Raymond, like so many of his colleagues, was caught between a determination to encourage the individual talents of his students and a commitment to uphold prevailing social norms about woman's proper roles. On the one hand, Raymond looked to a liberal education to free women from the bondage of marriage. "If one holds," he declared, "that the chief end of women is *to be married*—that every individual woman was created to be the adjunct and complement of some individual man, missing whom she misses her destiny . . . to one, I say . . . the argument for her higher culture, though not entirely destroyed, must certainly lose much of its weight. . . . 'Marriage is honorable in all'—in man and woman both—but it is absolutely necessary for neither." Raymond went on to note: "Thousands of the girls now under training in our schools and seminaries are destined to live and die unmarried. God pity such, if the great business of women is to wait for 'the coming man.' The suggestion is an insult alike to woman and to God." Accordingly, Raymond insisted that Vassar .ought to train women to become teachers and doctors.[94]

But then, the point made, Raymond suddenly retreated, as if shocked by his own arguments. Marriage must come first. "God forbid, that I should breathe a syllable that could lessen in any mind the sense of its exalted sanctity." And Vassar did not intend to train women to enter the bar or politics. "I am more than doubtful, whether, as these are at present organized, woman has a vocation to either." Raymond was not about to do battle for equal opportunity and choice; rather, the female colleges would perpetuate the definition of virtuous womanhood. "No one need fear," he continued, "that she will be made any the less *woman* by [the Vassar] process— though woman, we will hope (just as we hope for man), may be made a nobler thing and more potent for the universal good. *She will not need to handle the ballot, or mount the hustings, or mingle in the debates of Congress, in order to make her influence felt in moulding and purifying politics and ennobling the national character and life*." To the contrary, Vassar would encourage her to use her

moral refinements to civilize society. "Without invading any law of
social propriety or doing violence to one of the sacred instincts of
her nature," concluded Raymond, "she will find a thousand womanly
ways to serve." [95]

To ensure that feminine sensibilities were not violated, the
college atmosphere had to be protective, duplicating the life style of
a well-ordered family. At Vassar the administration, the faculty,
and the students were all to live together as "members of the college family." In an essentially domestic circle, the students and staff
were "bound together by a community of interests, aims and pursuits,
every member communicating and receiving kindly and ennobling
impulses and each contributing to the harmony and happiness of the
whole." [96] And the model of the family circle set the tone for the
entire curriculum. "Let every opportunity be given," contended
Wellesley's President Palmer, "for developing accomplished, yes, even
learned women, but let the process of acquiring knowledge take
place under careful guardianship, among the refinement of home life
with graceful women their instructors and companions." [97]

Notions of female virtue and morality intruded in still more significant ways on the intellectual life of the colleges. The institutions
rarely employed teachers of scholarly stature. Their hiring practices
did not aim to promote intellectual achievement. Rather, the faculty
was to be a model of female grace and virtue. Alice Freeman Palmer
outlined the requirements succinctly: a woman faculty member had
to be "a lady of unobjectionable manners and influential character;
she should have amiability and a discreet temper for she is to be a
guiding force in a complex community . . . an officer of administration and government no less than of instruction." As President
Palmer concluded: "Neither Wellesley nor any other woman's college could find a place on its faculty for a woman Sophocles or
Sylvester. Learning alone is not enough for women." [98] *

The colleges were so deeply involved in a dialogue with the physicians that health also had to take precedence over learning. The
gymnasium was more important than the classroom. Indeed, it is

---

* That men's colleges had very few Sophocles in their ranks is true, but it does
not weaken the point. First, it is doubtful that a male college president in the 1890s
would have felt compelled to state so baldly that "learning alone is not enough for
men." More, if the innovative women's program still subscribed to the doctrine of
female graces, then even the most adventuresome woman who dared to enroll in
college would graduate with a clear sense of the need to remain in her own special
and vital, but still separate, sphere.

hard for us to capture the intensity of the colleges' determination to counter the standard medical position. Observers who evaluated the new women's institutions reported first about their effect on health. Thus, when one writer in *The Journal of Social Science* in 1888 posed the rhetorical question, "What has been the effect of a college education upon women?", he noted immediately: "The work of the full college course is favorable to health. The regularity of life . . . tends in that direction. There is high medical authority for saying that for 'nervous' young women even, 'the higher education is a conservative, rather than a destructive force.' " [99] And college administrators' pronouncements often followed this pattern. Bryn Mawr's President, James Rhoads, included prominently among the accomplishments of the graduating class of 1889 "that all of them left the college in their best state of health, with the exception of some temporary fatigue that soon passed away." [100]

Despite the early rhetoric proclaiming the equality of women's "intellectual constitutions" with men's, it is not surprising that the administrators of the women's colleges were eminently comfortable in perpetuating a view of separate female spheres of influence. They were, after all, the direct beneficiaries of a system of special education for women—and they linked their own ventures to the broader theme of women's special social roles. "Women, not men," insisted M. Carey Thomas, "should solve the problems of women's education. And women can do this only, I think, in colleges for women in which they are practically in control." What was good for the administrators was good for their students. "It is very depressing," Thomas declared, "for large bodies of young women to study where no women hold positions of influence or honor on boards of trustees, or in college faculties." There was "the incalculable loss to women students of the influence of women scholars and teachers. . . . Whereas in a women's college everything exists for women students and is theirs by right and not by favor." [101] Moreover, as Dean Briggs explained to the alumnae of Smith, women's colleges "exist not for the competition of women with men, but for the ennobling of women as women. They do not, or they should not exist primarily for higher learning." Dean Briggs warned of the dire consequences to both the colleges and their students if this precept were ignored. "If women's colleges . . . teach women to compete with men, they will fall—or, what is worse, they will make women ignoble." [102]

As a result, the colleges won the battle with the physicians, but not the war. They did demonstrate that middle-class and even delicate middle-class women could attain a liberal education without risking their health. But they accomplished this purpose without ever challenging the underlying assumptions on which these views rested. The colleges would not provide women with the type of education that would encourage many of them to enter men's professions or businesses—and thus they had the ultimate effect of further legitimating the traditional social definitions of male and female roles. The colleges may have widened a woman's angle of vision and offered her the opportunity to leave home, but they perpetuated and strengthened the idea that her activities had to be limited to a sphere suitable to her sex.*

Still, it would be inappropriate to conclude on so dark a note. Given the prevailing views on feminine frailty, the establishment of colleges for women was a major achievement. To fault them for not liberating women would be ahistorical and unfair. Further, the colleges provided participants with an awareness of their own physical and mental health, and as more and more young women shared this experience, the vigor and confidence that the colleges instilled affected not only their lives but also the lives of women in general. The emphasis on living together and sharing experiences promoted friendships during college life, and afterwards as well. In fact, the ties that women formed in college were of lasting importance to them. "I have forgotten my chemistry and my classical philology cannot bear examination," Alice Freeman Palmer declared, "but all around the world there are men and women at work, my intimates of college days who have made the wide earth a friendly place for me." [103] These friendships also helped the graduates to go out into their communities and spread to others their new and sturdy sense of self. In this way, the colleges altered the private and the public lives of

---

* Male colleges, it should be clear, did not neglect the physical well-being of their students; they also provided for regular exercise in well-equipped gymnasiums. The psychiatric notion that mental stimulation had to be balanced with physical exercise held for males as well as females. But the administrators of the men's colleges did not attach nearly so much importance to physical exercise; nor did they assume as much responsibility for students' health. The men's colleges would not close if a few students suffered mental breakdowns—in men, ill health was an individual, not a collective, problem. Hence, the administrators of men's colleges did not find it necessary to report at graduation on the physical state of their students; the alumni did not have to provide information on the state of their health to angry physicians. Finally, male students, unlike female students, paid little heed to rules of right conduct, certainly insofar as dormitory living was concerned. "A man dwelling there," reported one Yale student in the 1880s, "can come or go whenever he will at any hour of the day or night and no one need be the wiser. . . . His room is his castle." It is doubtful if any Vassar girl would have considered her room to be her castle.

women, promoting the importance of female friendship and organized female activities.

Defining Woman's Work: Typewriters, Salesgirls, and Teachers

The contrast between opportunity and rigidity, innovation and fixity that marked the world of urban women and college girls also characterized the world of working women. To many observers, women were enjoying an unparalleled freedom to enter traditional professions and to hold newly created positions in an expanding economy. And yet, their actual distribution in the labor force and their chances for promotion do not bear out such optimistic pronouncements. In fact, the late nineteenth century began a sex-stereotyping of occupations that would persist through most of the twentieth century. This was the moment when typists, stenographers, department store clerks, and school teachers all became prototypically female.

The definition of what constituted a woman's occupation owed much to purely market forces. Employers hired women when men, because of their social class or education, were either unwilling or unable to fill the positions—or, put another way, when women made up the cheapest available and suitable labor pool. Yet the prevailing concepts of virtuous womanhood that we have been exploring had an impact, too; they helped to buttress and support this process of selection and labeling. Notions of when women could properly work and what they could properly do contributed in critical ways to legitimating distinctions that were frankly discriminatory.

It was those women most active in public life—heading up newly established clubs or agitating for suffrage—who were most convinced of novel opportunities in the work force. Taking as their point of comparison Harriet Martineau's observation in the 1830s that only seven occupations were open to women in the United States, these women insisted that nothing less than a revolution had occurred: in 1900, women could be found in 295 of the 303 occupations listed in the United States Census. "When I was a girl," recalled suffrage leader Lucy Stone, "I seemed to be shut out of everything I wanted to do. I might teach school . . . I might go out dress-making or tailoring, or trim bonnets, or I might work in a factory or go out to domestic service; there the mights ended and the might nots began."

For her children, however, conditions seemed altogether different. "A few years ago when my daughter left Boston University with her degree of B.A., she might do what she chose; all the professions were open to her; she could enter any line of business." Frances Willard, another suffragist, agreed. "Nowadays, a girl may be anything, from a college president down to a seamstress or a cash girl. It depends only upon the girl what rank she shall take in her chosen calling." Opportunities appeared to be limitless, bounded only by individual choice. "Set the goal of your ambitions," Willard advised young women, "and then climb to it by steady, earnest steps." So too, Marion Harland told her many readers: "Choose Something to Do *and do it!* Thirty years back this injunction would have meant to a young woman, reputably-born and in moderate circumstances, 'Prepare yourself to become a governess or the principal of a school.' Now—what may it not signify and include? If we would know how times have changed, and we with them . . . survey . . . the fallen and disintegrating boundary-walls." [104]

This insistence that unmarried women could and should "do something" reflected a belief that the chance to work would relieve the tedium that often afflicted their lives. Specifically, new job opportunities seemed not only to explain but to justify the fact that so many country girls were flocking to the city. "Young girls," declared Arnold Wolfe, a remarkably perceptive student of urban lodging and boardinghouses, "come from rocky farms and hill towns to escape the irksome drudgery and monotony of petty household duties; girls who have grown tired . . . of helping their mothers wash the dishes and pare the potatoes . . . have set their eyes to the city as a sort of Mecca for all in search of opportunity." [105] Nor were they likely to be disappointed: "If a girl has the right sort of business ability behind her ambition," noted one advice-book writer, "the city holds wonderful possibilities for her. There is always room for the girl with an idea; for the girl who does one thing well; for the girl who is willing, nay anxious to learn to work." To be sure, in this Mecca a woman would have to be careful to preserve her virtue: "No mother should permit her daughter to go to a strange city unless she can provide the girl with funds to pay for board and room for a month. . . . The mother who recklessly allows her unskilled daughter to enter a strange city armed with only a week's board and high hopes is guilty of criminal neglect as the guardian of her child's future." But as long as the girl had good moral training or skill and something of a financial stake, she would realize the promise of the city.[106]

Even more important, employment possibilities would rescue not only country girls from the farm, but all girls from the perils of a hasty and unwise marriage. To this end, the concepts of virtuous womanhood actually encouraged work for single and middle-class girls. To a suffragist like Mary Livermore, women's entrance into the labor force was another way to bring feminine, as opposed to masculine, qualities into the society. Pleased that "the doors of colleges, professional schools, and universities, closed against them [women] for ages, are opening to them," and that "trades, business, remunerative vocations and learned professions seek them," Livermore contended that such changes demonstrated that "the leadership of the world is being taken from the hands of the brutal and low, and the race is groping its way to a higher ideal than once it knew. It is the evolution of this tendency that is lifting women out of their subject condition, that is emancipating them from the seclusion of the past." But Livermore herself, and others as well, placed these general observations into a more specific context: the woman who could earn her own living would not be a captive of the male beast. "This fact," declared Laura Clay, the daughter of Henry Clay and a noted feminist, "would avail more to prevent unworthy and loveless marriages, entered into for the sake of support, than all the exhortations of moralists." [107]

Marion Harland, a far more traditional-minded writer, was no less certain that a young girl should abandon altogether the precept, "Do nothing, but be as happy as the day is long," precisely because "in the endeavor to follow the prescription, she falls in love." And that kind of fall could be disastrous: "Many a woman, after wasting years of time and wealth of devotion upon an undeserving object, has died of a broken heart, who would never have loved a worthless man and suffered unto death if she had had regular employment for her thoughts and hands. Occupation, congenial and continuous, is the best panacea for ill-directed fancies." [108]

Livermore elaborated this message in her 1883 volume, *What Shall We Do With Our Daughters?* "The substance of this book," she explained, "has been before the public for more than a decade, in the form of lyceum lectures, delivered hundreds of times to audiences in all sections of the country from Maine to California." The core of the advice that she spread so energetically was that parents should train daughters to support themselves, to enable them "to maintain themselves by their own labor." Livermore insisted that "it is not safe, neither is it wise or kind, to rear our daughters as if marriage were their only legitimate business." First, some of them would not find husbands, because men were killing themselves off through addiction to corruption and vice: "If it were possible to obtain statistics on drunkenness," noted Livermore, "we should see that its draughts on the male population exceed that made by war." Remember, too, "the inevitable fatalities attending the pursuits of men in pleasure and business, by overwork and excessive haste to be rich." More, the men who did survive were not always "good or competent husbands. Some become permanent invalids; others are dissolute and unambitious [Livermore damned men either way], and not a few desert entirely both wives and children." Thus, women had to choose their mates wisely and even then be prepared for all sorts of contingencies. Only a "practical knowledge of a trade, a paying business, or a profession" would allow for that.

Such training, Livermore argued, had another advantage: "Girls would then escape one of the most serious dangers to which inefficient women are liable—the danger of regarding marriage as a means of a livelihood." The self-sufficient woman who married would not view the future with "the vague terror with which aimless untrained women regard it." Clearly, a moral imperative informed all these dicta, drawn directly from the precepts of virtuous womanhood. "No woman," Livermore declared, "has the moral right to become the mother of children whose father is drunken and immoral. For this perpetuates the brutishness of the race and extends evils that should be eliminated from humanity." In sum, concluded Livermore, when women "are trained and self-poised, they will not be in bondage to ignorance; nor will they be as liable to become dupes or the prey of others. A wife and mother should be mistress of herself and of her department and never a slave of another—not even when that other is her husband, and the slavery is founded on her undying love." [109]

In fact, mothers learned that working was less dangerous to their daughter's health than attending college, provided, that is, that the work was not too intellectual. Physicians believed that even physically demanding occupations were not as harmful as concentrated study. "There are two reasons," maintained Dr. Edward Clarke, "why female operatives of all sorts are likely to suffer less, and actually do suffer less, from such persistent work than female students; why Jane in the factory can work more steadily with the loom than Jane in college with the dictionary." The average female worker, Clarke argued, had already passed puberty, the time when reproductive organs placed their heaviest demands on the body; the female student, on the other hand, has "these tasks before her." (Clarke's chronology, incidentally, was inaccurate—the majority of women in the work force were actually between 14 and 18, just the ages that doctors found so worrisome.) Clarke also insisted, in the tradition of Jacksonian medical superintendents, that factory girls were healthier because they "work their brains less." Finally, he and his colleagues were acutely concerned about the ill effects of idleness, convinced that moral degeneration and corrupt habits had their source in a life of leisure. Hence, just as medical superintendents instituted a routine of steady work to cure the mentally ill, so these doctors advocated it to protect the young woman.[110]

College presidents used a variant of Livermore's arguments as another justification for female higher education. A college experience, like training for a job, would enable graduates to marry better than others. A liberal education, contended Vassar President John Raymond, made a young woman into "a fit companion for a wiser and nobler man, than she otherwise would have been. If he be a professional man, she will feel an enlightened sympathy in his intellectual pursuits, and may often find it in her power to render him valuable counsel and effective aid." And many others agreed. "Educated women," reported one journalist, "subject their impulses to the test of their reason in study; this gives them an advantage in choice of husbands." Insisted still another: "The college woman is not only more exacting in her standards of marriage, but under less pressure to accept what falls below her standard than the average woman. . . . Unhappy marriages are almost unknown among college women." [111]

These comments, to be sure, were intended to offset the popular assumption that college unfitted girls to marry—a notion that did have a base in reality. The 1885 survey of the Association of Collegiate Alumnae (which reported so favorably upon the health of college women) noted that only 28 percent of women graduates were married. Vassar, surveying its first twenty-four graduating classes in 1894, discovered that of the 815 living graduates, only 315 (39 percent) had married, and most of them did so many years after graduation. But proponents of women's education had a ready answer. Maria Mitchell coined the slogan that would be heard well into the twentieth century: "Vassar girls marry late, but they marry well." [112]

All of these claims exaggerated and distorted both the number of opportunities that women enjoyed in the labor force and, no less important, the amount of freedom of choice that the role of virtuous womanhood allowed them outside the home. The occupational distribution of women was nowhere near as balanced as the rhetoric of Lucy Stone implied. The principles that were to guide women in selecting a job and remaining at work were far more confining than the language of Mary Livermore suggested.

Frances Willard once described the reality of the situation accurately when noting, "The American woman . . . has taken a *dip* into every occupation." Although one could find a woman here or there in many job categories, most women were grouped into a select few. College graduates ended up as school teachers (of those 815 Vassar graduates, 805 worked at some time as teachers). Women with less education entered offices; those with still less, retail stores. (In 1870 the number of women in offices and stores was 10,798 or under 1.0 percent of the women employed in nonagricultural jobs; by 1900 the number had risen to 394,747 or 9.1 percent of the total.[113]) And no matter what the job, women remained at the lower end of the ladder. In the public schools they were the classroom teachers, not the principals or superintendents; in offices, they made up the ranks of typists and stenographers, not the executives; in the retail stores, they were the clerks and cashiers, not the floorwalkers or managers. In other words, the job that a woman first assumed was generally the one that she kept as long as she worked. Men had careers, rising from clerks to become managers, from teachers to become principals; women remained locked in the same position. Once a typist, always a typist; once a clerk, always a clerk. Indeed, the job discrimination that they suffered was so obvious, the situation that they confronted so bleak, that the point that needs explaining is why some jobs opened up for women at all.

By the same token, even the staunchest proponents of women's work wanted them—and everyone else—to think of labor essentially as a temporary state (something to do until the right man came along), as a form of insurance (something to do if an emergency arose), or, in a still more restricted way, as a last resort (something to do if the sex ratio remained grossly imbalanced). A woman's job skills were to improve her marital choices, to allow her and her husband to sleep more securely, and to demonstrate her moral worth through self-support under the most trying circumstances. But a woman was not to work in order to advance a career. In fact, these postulates assumed a self-fulfilling quality. Encouraged to think of themselves in some sense or other as part-time workers, women did not generally expect or press for promotion and equal pay. So, too, employers defined women as temporary workers and were accordingly reluctant to advance them or to raise their salaries. The graduate and professional schools also took refuge in this argument (more or less honestly). Why invest in so expensive a training program for a woman if she would only practice law or medicine temporarily? Again, what now seems most puzzling is that *any* job actually became a woman's job.

The dynamic that operated in the post-Civil War decades to create new and exclusive positions for women emerges with special clarity in white-collar occupations. An expanding and modernizing economy did increase the number of clerical and office jobs, particularly for typists and stenographers—and it was women who filled them. In the 1870s, men typically worked as stenographers and scriveners; women composed less than 5 percent of this group. By 1900, the women held fully three-quarters of these jobs.[114]

The change began with the typewriter. It altered both the style of office work and the composition of the office staff. Although the Remington Company developed the first writing machines in 1874, typewriters were not sold in significant numbers until the 1880s. They remained a novelty, mostly because few people had the necessary skills to use them. Remington soon understood that to market its product it would have to train operators; only when typists, like spare parts, were available on demand would businesses invest in the machines. The company therefore opened typewriting schools in the large cities and established an employment bureau as an adjunct to each of them. The strategy worked well. By 1890, Remington could barely keep up with orders for machines and demands for operators. Between 1897 and 1902 it supplied New York City alone with 25,262 typists, and Chicago with 23,368.[115]

Nearly all of Remington's students were women. One of the designers of the machine even boasted that its most important achievement "was to allow women an easier way to earn a living." But why did Remington's schools recruit—and recruit successfully—among women? Because the company recognized that a typist had to "be a good speller, a good grammarian and have the correct knowledge of the use of capitals and the rules of punctuation." [116] Where might it find a ready source of labor with such educational qualifications? Lower-class men did not have the literacy skills necessary for the job; skilled male workers were well paid in other positions. Middle-class men with high school educations had still more opportunities for responsible and upwardly mobile employment elsewhere. Recognizing that men were either ineligible or uninterested, the company then turned to women, to the large pool of female high school graduates.

The high school system had only recently come to hold a significant place in urban educational systems, and its new popularity was linked in part to its filling up a young girl's time. "Boys drop out of high school," as one superintendent explained, "some [to] go to college; others because they get tired of school; others to engage in business; and still others because they had formed bad associations; but the girls remain and graduate if not obliged to quit." [117] Put another way, boys had options (to go to college or into business); girls did not, so they stayed on to graduate. But what were they to do when commencement finally came? For many of them, as we shall see, a teaching position was the answer. But over the 1870s and 1880s, competition so increased that a sizable number of girls could no longer find open posts. There was always the factory, but that was a last resort. Clearly, work at the typewriter in an office was a far more attractive option. The girls could remain in a middle-class, respectable setting, one that was clean, well lit, quiet, and safe. The typewriter was an easy machine to run, and the wages paid were no lower than those of skilled female machine operators. How much better, then, to be a typewriter (as these girls were called) than a factory worker. This fact of life gave Remington and other companies like Royal their labor supply.

Given the desirability of this sort of office work, the manufacturers, the commercial schools, and soon the high schools themselves, rushed to train girls at typewriting. In the early 1880s, one commercial school, Prospectus, still had to concede that "it was an uncommon thing to find a girl living in a respectable home and moving in good society who would not consider herself somewhat degraded by going into a business office and earning a living. And more than that, her father and brother—if she had them—would feel it would be greatly to their discredit to permit such a thing." [118] But by the 1890s, views had changed. The mayor of New York could now tell the graduating class at the Packard Commercial School, "You will lift the tone of those offices . . . and win the lasting respect of your associates. The men around you will grow nobler and better." He assured them that the women working in his office had not only made it a finer place, but "they have made me better, and there is not a person about the office who has not been improved by the presence of the ladies." [119]

From the employers' perspective, women were perfectly suited to be "typewriters." The temporary nature of their work commitment posed no problem; if one operator left to be married, a call to the Remington Company quickly produced another. And since each typing assignment was discrete, the continuity of service of any particular operator was unimportant. Another typist could just as well copy the next letter or bill. Further, wages could be kept low —office managers recognized that their working conditions were superior to those in the factory. Finally, the women's presence did not threaten the ambitions of the men in the office. They could be added to the staff with a minimum of trouble.

In much the same way, women took over stenographic positions, mastering the skills of shorthand and learning to take dictation and then to type the letters. These were well-paying jobs, and women eagerly filled them; a typist earned $6 to $10 a week, a stenographer between $12 and $16. An income of $700 a year put a stenographer well up on the scale of earnings at a time when unskilled labor received about $200 annually, and semi-skilled workers about $400 to $500.

Why did these remunerative positions go to women? Why did a job that in the pre-1860 period was held almost exclusively by men now become defined as female work? Obviously, lower-class men lacked the educational qualifications (or in the case of immigrants, the necessary language skills) to compete for these positions; nor were they about to enroll in a 6- to 9-month course in stenography. As for middle-class men, they did remain the first choice for some employers. (In 1902, when women filled over three-quarters of the positions, the Remington Bureau noted that 40 percent of perspective employers still first requested male stenographers.[120]) But in most cases, office work had become so much more specialized that neither employers nor middle-class men continued to define stenography as a desirable position, that is, one with a potential for promotion. As offices grew larger and the routine within them more specialized, stenography became one of several bureaucratic chores; the time when the male clerk worked alongside the proprietor and might well anticipate advancement had passed. And then it became appropriate to make stenography, and so many other office positions, women's work. Women had the requisite skills, and again, the tasks were so discrete that turnover did not matter.

From one perspective, it is clear that specialization in office work did create new job opportunities for women. The number of all types of female clerks climbed dramatically over the period. In 1880, women composed only 6 percent of the half million clerical workers. By 1910, they were 35 percent of a group that numbered over one and a half million.[121] Yet, at the same time, office work offered few occasions for promotion. It really could not have been different—had the positions allowed for upward mobility, men would have held them. Only because they were dead-end jobs did these positions go to women. One poll taken in the 1920s reported that two-thirds of typists and stenographers never expected advancement. And the companies themselves frankly admitted the correctness of these negative expectations. "It is a commonly accepted fact," noted Grace Coyle, a student of office work, "that such promotion as does exist is much more common for men than for women." Part of the explanation that employers offered was frankly sexist: "It is not assumed that they [women] have the calibre for executive positions." They suggested, too, that the temporary character of women's work ruled out promotion. "The fact that they are likely to marry and leave the business also tends to keep them out of positions which are regarded as training for the higher levels." Whatever the reason, Coyle concluded—accurately—that such assumptions were likely to persist, so that the number of women working in offices would increase but the number who would be promoted would not. "The nature of the work seems to be well adapted to women; they afford a less expensive labor supply than men and their more or less temporary relation to the job enables them to adjust themselves to the lack of opportunity for advancement which is characteristic of many office positions. There seems to be every reason to expect that succeeding census figures will show a growing proportion of women in the major clerical fields."[122]

In the exceptional instance when stenography retained its traditional place as a starting point for a career, it was men, and not women, who filled the posts. Thus one trade journal reported that some employers "are actually seeking the boy who understands shorthand." Why? For "no other purpose than to train him with a view of placing him ultimately in some responsible position." When the goal was promotion, the right employee was a male. So, too, the Chicago and Northwestern Railroad announced in 1898 that it was no longer hiring women stenographers. "The move is not because women proved inefficient," they reported, "but it is simply carrying out the company's policy in the matter of promotion of employees. The Northwestern will advance its employees from low positions to officers of trust. Can you imagine a woman as general superintendent or general manager of the affairs of its great railroad system? I think not. But just as long as we have women in clerical positions, the source from which to draw valuable officials in the future is narrowed to small limits." [123] A policy to promote up through the ranks was therefore a policy that prohibited bringing women into the ranks at any level.

The department stores, which revolutionized the buying habits of one class of women, also provided novel employment opportunities for another. As they proliferated, so did the number of women employed as cash girls, saleswomen, and cashiers. Because middle-class men (and in this case, middle-class women, too) did not want these low-paying and tedious jobs, and because store owners considered lower-class men unsuitable, it was lower-class women who filled them.

In the pre-Civil War decades, men had typically worked as clerks in small retail stores, doing the bargaining and selling, and even purchasing the merchandise. To be a clerk in a dry goods shop was a position of some responsibility. The post-Civil War department store, however, with its "one price" formula and specialized buying staff, made the sales clerk's job into a menial position. Department stores actually prided themselves on the passive and routine quality of the help. One general manager boasted that his "salespersons do not urge the customer to buy, and dilate upon the beauties of his wares. They simply ask the customer what he or she wants, and make a record of the sale." [124] The stores generally did not pay their clerks a commission on sales, reducing in still another way the possible returns from the position. Under these circumstances, middle-class men preferred to look elsewhere for jobs that valued their initiative or allowed more responsibility and better prospects for advancement.

But young women whose only other choice was factory work or domestic service found the department store a very attractive option. Since it was designed to attract middle-class women as customers, the store was far cleaner and more pleasant than a factory. The work was also less tiring. However demanding the customer might be, the machine was much more ruthless. A department store clerk was much less isolated than a domestic. (Indeed, more than one reformer worried that salesgirls met *too many* people.) And even the most dictatorial company rules and autocratic managers were mild in comparison to the regimen that middle-class housewives imposed on their maids.

Department store employment created its own hierarchy. The youngest workers, those around fourteen years old, took their first jobs as cash girls and moved up to become wrappers and stock girls. Each promotion carried a slight increase in pay—a stock girl earned between $2 and $3 a week, less than an unskilled factory worker. The cash girls raced between salesclerks and cashiers, delivering payments and bringing back change. (In the twentieth century the pneumatic tube and then the computerized cash register would take over this job.) The wrapper "artfully" packaged the merchandise, and the stock girl "neatly" replenished the shelves. At age 16, usually after two years of service, a girl might become a salesclerk (receiving $6 to $7 weekly, better than an unskilled factory worker and about the same as a typist). Clerks who proved both "intelligent and responsible" went on to become cashiers (earning $8 to $10 a week).[125]

Owners preferred to hire women for all these positions, so that three-quarters of department store employees were female. They believed that women were more honest than men. In an establishment with two or three thousand workers, owners and managers—unlike their counterparts in a retail shop—could not expect to oversee every detail. "Honesty on the part of employees," one observer reported, "must of necessity be taken for granted." Therefore, as one manager told Helen Campbell, an investigator of conditions of women's work, "We don't want men; we wouldn't have them even if they came at the same price. No, give me a woman every time. I've been a manager thirteen years, and we never had but four dishonest girls, and we've had to discharge over forty boys in the same time." [126]

Women also seemed easier to discipline and manage. "Boys smoke and lose at cards," Helen Campbell learned, "and do a hundred things that women don't and they get worse instead of better." The girls, drilled in obedience and politeness in an almost military manner, proved tractable. "We want it said of our employees that they are a credit to the house," the Siegel and Cooper Company told its workers. "Be civil and polite to your superiors. Should those in

authority not be civil to you, OBEY." The store's manual went on
to establish the following rules:

THINGS NOT TO DO

Do not stand in groups.
Do not chew gum, read books, or sew.
Do not giggle, flirt, or idle away your time.
Do not walk together through the store.
Do not be out of your place.
Do not be late at any time.
Do not take over fifteen minutes on a pass.
Do not make a noise when going up in elevators.
Do not push when going into elevators, but always stand in line.
Do not talk across aisles, or in a loud voice.
Do not gossip; mind your own affairs and you will have enough to do.
Do not sit in front of the counter.

TRY TO BE

Polite, neat; dress in black.
Serious in your work.
Punctual, obliging, painstaking.
Keep your stock in good order, and follow the rules of the house.[127]

To enforce these regulations, the stores hired floorwalkers, a post
that always went to men. Better paid than the female help (receiving
up to $40 a week), the floorwalker was the sergeant in charge of the
army of clerks. It was his duty "to keep his salespeople up to the
standard in dress, deportment and activities." He was to be the
"arbiter on conduct and store etiquette." In addition, the companies relied not only on the threat of dismissal but also on a system of fines to implement their codes. They docked the girls' pay for
lateness, for gum chewing, and for standing in front of (instead of
behind) the sales counter. Some stores were even prepared to police
the moral habits of their employees after work hours. As Siegel and
Cooper informed the girls: "You would be very much surprised if
you knew the trouble and expense we go to find out character and
habits. Detectives you don't know often are detailed to report on
all your doings for a week. Don't flirt. . . . Don't lie. . . . Don't live
beyond your income, or go into debt. . . . DON'T BORROW OR
LEND. . . . Entertaining, even while selling goods in a long, drawn-
out way, will not be allowed. Floor managers are particularly instructed to enforce this rule and are to remember that they are to
guard the young ladies from annoying visitors." [128]
Most important of all, the department stores hired women for

their manners, or, more precisely, for their suitability in dealing with middle-class women customers. The owners did not hire lower-class males to do the job, on the assumption that the ladies simply would not buy household goods and clothing from rough-and-ready immigrant men. Indeed, the owners did not want to hire just any type of female worker. "A girl who obtains employment at even the lowest work in any department store I know of," one salesgirl reported, "must be neat, bright, smart, in good health and have some education." Or, as another journalist noted: "For every woman who means to enter the retail trade, manners should be considered by her and her employer as necessary as neat dress or stools to sit on, or ability to add and subtract, or English speech. They should be learned and cultivated, like typewriting and stenography, as among the qualifications for a particular kind of business." [129]

Given the attractions the job had for women, the managers could be particular about whom they hired. And given the styles of their customers, they kept the social habits of their employees very much in mind. Just as middle-class women preferred to employ servants of English stock or second- and third-generation Irish, so did the department stores. During these decades, almost every Macy's employee was English or second- or third-generation immigrant. Not until 1900 did German or Eastern European girls begin to appear in the sales ranks. As late as 1909, native-born girls made up the majority of employees in Baltimore's retail stores. "Two stores employ only American girls," one researcher noted. "This preponderance is due to the fact that many customers prefer to be served by Americans, and in part to the fact that native-born girls of Anglo-Saxon stock prefer, when possible, to choose an occupation socially superior to factory work." [130] The department stores also preferred to hire only young women who lived at home, reducing the possibility of a scandal, and—in terms of the girls' appearance—getting more for their money. "Two-thirds of the girls here are public school girls and live at home," one manager boasted to Helen Campbell. "You see that makes things pretty easy, for the family pool their earnings and they dress well and live well." [131]

In the department store, as in the office, the women's jobs were the dead-end jobs. Girls did not rise from clerical positions to become floorwalkers; they did not earn promotions to become buyers or assistants to the managers. They could move from cash girl to cashier, but never beyond that. Had the position held out more promise, it might well have become the preserve of middle-class men. So once again, opportunity for women in the post-Civil War decades came in a very particular way: through novel job openings that were preferable to factory work but that led nowhere.

For all the availability of novel types of employment, teaching remained women's primary role in the work force. Large numbers of women had entered the profession in the pre-Civil War decades, and the dynamic that first made teaching a woman's job continued to operate through the post-Civil War period. In schools, as in offices and factories, women did what men would not or could not do.

No sooner were public schools founded in the 1820s than a seemingly endless number of complaints began to circulate about the unsatisfactory nature of the teaching staffs. School reformers had assumed that educated, sober, and even refined middle-class men would make a career of teaching the young. Instead, the male teachers either were poorly educated or were using the post as a stepping-stone to another career; many would-be lawyers, for example, supported themselves by classroom teaching. In 1837, George Emerson, one of Massachusetts' most distinguished educators, drew a discouraging portrait of the average teacher for the state legislature. Public school teachers, he contended, were either "young men in the course of their studies, teaching from necessity, and often with a strong dislike for the pursuit," or they were "mechanics and others wanting present employment," or "persons who, having failed in other callings, take to teaching as a last resort with no qualifications for it, and no desire of continuing in it longer than they are obliged by absolute necessity." Emerson believed that local boards were "baffled by the want of good teachers; that they have been sought for in vain; the highest salaries have been offered, to no purpose; that they *are not to be found* in sufficient numbers to supply the demand." As a remedy, he proposed a system of state normal schools. Emerson's ideal teacher was "to know *how* to teach," to "have a thorough knowledge of whatever he undertakes to teach," and to have such an "understanding of *the ordering and discipline* of a school, as to be able at once to introduce system, and to keep it constantly in force." [132] He insisted that the state normal school would inculcate just such traits in its students. Graduates would be able to fulfill the seemingly masculine task of ordering and disciplining a classroom.

But it was women, and not men, who flocked to the normal schools. The men found better opportunities elsewhere. "When we consider the claims of the learned professions," explained Catharine

Beecher, "the excitement and profits of commerce, manufactures, agriculture, and the arts; when we consider the aversion of most men to the sedentary, confining, and toilsome duties of teaching and governing young children; when we consider the scanty pittance that is allowed to the majority of teachers; and that few men will enter a business that will not support a family, when there are multitudes of other employments that will afford competence, and lead to wealth; it is chimerical to hope that the supply of such immense deficiencies in our national education is to come from that sex." Yet, the very reasons that made teaching so unattractive to men made it more suitable and appealing for women. "It is woman," Beecher continued, "fitted by disposition, and habits, and circumstances for such duties, who, to a very wide extent, must aid in educating the childhood and youth of this nation; and therefore it is, that females must be trained and educated for this employment." In following a teaching career, a woman helped herself as well as improved society. "Most happily," concluded Beecher, "the education necessary to fit a woman to be a teacher, is exactly the one that best fits her for that domestic relation she is primarily designed to fill." [133]

The fit between women and teaching seemed no less ideal to local school boards. Women not only were willing to work for low salaries but, in the absence of competing opportunities, composed a very pliable staff. Thus, one Ohio school superintendent confidently told his fellow educators: "As the business of teaching is made more respectable, more females engage in it, and the wages are reduced. Females do not . . . expect to accumulate much property by this occupation; if it affords them a respectable support and a situation where they can be useful, it is as much as they demand. I, therefore, most earnestly commend this subject to the attention of those counties which are in the habit of paying men for instructing little children, when females would do it for less than half the sum, and generally much better than men can." [134]

These judgments on the suitability and convenience of employing women teachers persisted through the post-Civil War decades. As school systems expanded, so did the percentage of women on their staffs. In 1870, women constituted 60 percent of the nation's teachers; by 1900 they made up 70 percent, and by 1910, 80 percent. [135] That boards continued to find them so satisfactory is not surprising —middle-class men still looked for opportunities elsewhere and the newly arrived immigrant men were obviously unsuitable for the positions. But why did women continue to seek out teaching? Indeed, why did college graduates as well as normal school graduates persist in moving into the classroom?

In the first instance, college girls learned that teaching was a significant task and one that they could perform exceptionally well. From the moment that Vassar opened, its president lectured on the graduates' duty to improve the quality of public schools. "I do not hesitate to avow the belief," John Raymond declared, "that the education of the nation is today emasculate and weak, compared with what it might easily be made by simply raising the qualifications of its female instructors. . . . Elevating the character of women instructors alone might raise the standard of the national intelligence a hundred percent in a generation," [136] and Vassar was going to help do just that. In fact, as the colleges grew confident of their ability to train vigorous young women, they became even more certain that their students belonged in teaching. "The college woman is also proving herself the most efficient of all women," contended M. Carey Thomas in 1901. "She makes so successful a teacher that she is swiftly driving untrained women teachers out of the private and public secondary schools and will soon begin to drive them from the elementary schools; she is also driving men from the schools."

Women heeded the message. Perhaps they did so in a spirit of resignation, recognizing that business and the professions were closed to them. Or perhaps, in keeping with the precepts of virtuous womanhood, they were most comfortable in the role of moral counselor and teacher to the young. "There are more reasons," insisted Marion Harland, "for the press of women who are obliged to earn a livelihood, into the profession of teaching than the one usually assigned and accepted, namely, that it is an eminently respectable occupation and involves little physical drudgery. It is the nature of being of the mother-sex to gather together into her care and brood over and instruct creatures younger and feebler than herself." [137] Or perhaps women calculated that teaching wages were the best available for the least onerous work. The salaries were higher than factory girls earned and identical with those of stenographers. In all events, women crowded into teaching jobs.

Despite their numerical dominance in the teaching ranks and seemingly natural suitability for the jobs, female teachers suffered the same kind of discrimination in school systems that their counterparts did in offices and department stores. School boards paid men more than women for carrying out the same assignments ($35 a week compared to $14). As the Massachusetts Board of Education reported in 1893, women's wages, when contrasted with men's, "are so low as to make it humiliating to report the two in connection. Moreover, the advance in the wages of male teachers in ten years has been at the rate of 36.2 percent, while that for female teachers has been at the rate of 14.8 percent." [138] Even more important, the men held practically all the influential and well-paying administrative positions. (Probably the boards hired men as school teachers so as to be able to promote them up the ranks to run the system.) If men composed only a small minority of classroom teachers, they made up a heavy majority of the principals and superintendents. "There is some slight relief from . . . the steady falling off of male teachers," declared the Massachusetts Board of Education, "in the fact that it is more than compensated for in the number of male teachers transferred to the ranks of school superintendents." Put another way, women with similar credentials remained elementary and secondary school teachers. "While 67 percent of all the teachers in the country are women," one investigator reported to the Association for the Advancement of Women in 1888, "less than 4 percent of those who direct what shall be taught and teaching what shall be done are women." Women were permitted to teach children in every state of the union, but in only 13 states were they even eligible to hold all school offices. In 1900, only two women held the position of state superintendent of schools and only twelve were superintendents of city school systems. [139]

School boards explained the situation in terms of rapid turnover and immaturity, as though female teachers were typically young girls of sixteen or seventeen with two years of high school education. But such a claim was inaccurate. The average city school teacher was in her early twenties when first appointed and had completed at least a normal school course. She also tended to hold her teaching position for almost a decade. The tenure of the teaching staff in Columbus, Ohio was one case in point. As the Columbus school system grew, so did the length of service of its female teachers. In 1875, Columbus employed 97 teachers, 91 of whom were women who remained on the job for an average of 5.3 years. In 1891, the city employed 256 teachers, 251 of whom were women who typically served 9 years. In 1875, only 5 percent of the women had been employed for over 19 years; by 1888, the figure climbed to 34 percent. So, too, in neighboring Indianapolis the average length of tenure for women teachers in 1888 was 8 years; 29 percent of the female staff had taught more than a decade. Indeed, the keen competition for the positions made such an outcome logical and predictable.

Cities or states that had created normal schools in the 1850s and 1860s to ensure a ready supply of teachers found themselves in the 1880s and 1890s with a surplus of highly qualified applicants. Waiting lists for jobs were commonplace, and the larger the city, the longer the list. In 1898, Columbus, Ohio could no longer place the graduates of its normal school into the system. "If the order of the present reserve list is followed," declared the principal of the normal school, "it will be some time before many of the class are assigned to duty in our schools." [140] Thus, despite their degrees, women could not translate their qualifications into better positions. A diploma became an entry card into a profession already overcrowded with women—and one that would not allow for mobility.

In the world of work as elsewhere, new opportunities were counterbalanced, if not quite canceled out, by restrictions and qualifications. The post-Civil War decades created many types of novel settings for women, and yet within each of them women had to know their very special place.

CHAPTER

2

The Protestant Nun

IN THE PUBLIC ARENA, in the formulation and implementation of programs that were to promote the best interests of women, the concepts of virtuous womanhood assumed a critical importance. The ideas were remarkably energizing to the post-Civil War generation. Women organized themselves in novel ways so as to be able to popularize the precepts and to realize them. Far more vigorously and systematically than their predecessors (with the exception of the handful of determined female abolitionists), women set forth to implement a broad variety of goals on a national scale. So, too, virtuous womanhood set clear guidelines for action by benevolent-minded women. The agenda now reflected (as it had not before) a determination to transform institutions and organizations in the spirit of feminine virtues, and to protect and preserve the purity and respectability of all women, but particularly of country girls, working girls, and street girls. If women in the 1820s were eager to bring their virtues into the homes of needy neighbors, women in the 1880s, to paraphrase the WCTU slogan, were resolved to bring their virtues out into the world.

At the same time, the ideal of virtuous womanhood gave a distinctly narrow and class-bound quality to social programs. It ultimately defined problems in moral terms and, therefore, focused ameliorative efforts more on the person than on the system. This orientation also carried a distinctly negative thrust. Virtue was something that had to be protected, guarded, and surrounded, and so programs looked to the elimination of corruption. An institution like the saloon was to be done away with; a practice such as contraception was to be banned. Finally, the ideal of virtuous womanhood bred an outlook that was more comfortable with voluntary than with state action. Since social problems were finally moral ones, solutions demanded the sensitive intervention of the philanthropic individual, not the heavy-handed involvement of the state. As one of the favorite images of the period had it, social policy was the proper domain for a Protestant Nun.

Female Fellowship: The Club World

The post-Civil War organizations that best exemplified the effort to popularize and fulfill the principles of virtuous womanhood were the women's clubs. Through these associations, female fellowship would work to elevate the moral character of society. Charlotte Perkins Gilman, one of the leading feminists of the period, did not exaggerate when describing the club movement as "one of the most important sociological phenomena of the century—indeed, of all centuries, marking as it does the first timid steps towards social organization of these so long unsocialized members of our race." Although this was not the first time that women participated in club life, the new organizations were very different from their antebellum predecessors. "Societies have always existed," one member told her associates in 1889, but the earlier societies were "generally desultory gatherings, without organization or parliamentary method, while for a very large class of intelligent women, no means of association existed, such as were common to men." [1] The clubs now were formal in organization and nationwide in scope. The General Federation of Women's Clubs, organized in 1892, had 495 affiliates and 100,000 members. More, the clubs defined their purposes broadly; they were not narrow or sectarian associations. "The growth of clubs," declared Jennie Croly, one chronicler of the movement, "has been accompanied by an equally common determination to avoid those religious and political differences which separate and antagonize common interests." The organizations aim to "cultivate on broad grounds the spirit of unity and good fellowship." Gilman, then, was right to exclaim: "The whole country is budding into women's clubs. The clubs are uniting and federating by towns, states, nations." [2]

One initial impetus to the founding of women's clubs was the desire to provide a forum for literary discussion. These associations would offer a kind of classroom experience for women who had not attended college and, at the same time, provide graduates with a way of maintaining intellectual activities. Jennie Croly was persuaded that the clubs reflected the "desire among women engaged mainly in domestic duties for the exercise of mental faculty, and the cultivation of a more intimate knowledge of vital questions and issues." The clubs, in other words, were "the 'school' of the middle-aged women," "the 'university extension' of the home." Mary I. Woods, another chronicler of the movement, defined the club as a school in which women might "*teach and be taught, a mutual improvement society, which should educate them and lead them out into better hopes, nobler aspirations and larger life.*" And if the lectures that the members delivered were not erudite, still the meetings "gave to women, unaccustomed to the sound of their own voices, courage to speak before an audience; they gave women an ability to express their thoughts in logical sequence . . . they gave an interchange of ideas whereby other thoughts, fresh and creative, had birth."

The clubs were also reminiscent of the colleges in promoting female fellowship—women joined with others of similar interests and tastes to create an intellectual and social atmosphere that might not be available in a family circle or a neighborhood church. "What college life is to the young woman," Ella D. Clymer told the National Council of Women in 1891, "club life is to the woman of riper years, who amidst the responsibilities and cares of home life still wishes to keep abreast of the time, still longs for the companionship of those who, like herself, do not wish to cease to be students because they have left school." [3] Club life, in fact, fit well with city life. It did not demand a full-time commitment from women with families, and its obligations were sporadic. Yet, it did promise to structure leisure in an interesting and pleasant way.

The first and most noteworthy of these school-like clubs, founded in 1868, was Sorosis. "We have proposed," announced its first circular, "to enter our protest against an idle gossip, against all demoralizing waste of time, against the follies and tyrannies of fashion, in short, against everything that opposes the full development and use of the faculties conferred upon us by our Creator." But Sorosis was not designed exclusively for intellectual discourse. The meetings were marvelous opportunities for forming and maintaining female friendships, for encouraging a "great awakening" of an "isolated and unsocialized sex." Attending the sessions was an invigorating experience for its members. "It is the spirit of the meetings," declared Croly, "even more than the word or written speech, which gives them a peculiarly uplifting quality. There is a sense of freedom, of social exhilaration which is hard to define. To the surprise of their posessors, latent talents have been unfolded into joyous, useful activities."

Still more important to the clubs was the judgment that such intellectual and social activity would enhance women's ability to effect social betterment. Sorosis proposed to help its members "to think for themselves not so much because it is their right, but their duty." And duty had a very special meaning—to encourage women to assume their proper responsibilities, to enlarge women's sphere of interest both for self and for communal improvement.[4]

Sorosis, its bylaws declared, would inspire "the discussion and dissemination of principles and facts which promise to exert a salutary influence on women and on society, and the establishment of an order which shall render the female sex helpful to each other, and actively benevolent in the world." The Association for the Advancement of Women, founded in 1873, followed on the design of Sorosis. By "securing for women higher intellectual, moral and physical conditions," it would "improve all domestic and social relations." And Croly at least was confident that club life had "changed the whole tone of the communities and raised it to a higher intellectual and social level. It has taught women how to think, how to speak, how to act, for the best good of the community in which they lived."[5]

None of this activity, of course, was to make women any less feminine. It was not to challenge but to fulfill their special attributes. "The attractiveness of woman, instead of being diminished," one Sorosis leader insisted, "will be increased in direct ratio to her broader culture and more varied responsibilities." In spite of the opposition of doctors and conservative men, "the terrible spelling-book got into her hands and there was the beginning of the end. . . . Every advance involved another, and with each she has grown more womanly; more a social power, and centre of influence; more a creator of beauty and good."[6] In effect, clubs, like colleges, not only preserved women's virtues but also brought them into the community.

Of all the women's clubs, none were more determined to respond to this mandate to bring women's influence into the larger society than the Woman's Christian Temperance Union (WCTU). Founded in 1873, the WCTU rapidly gained popularity; by 1890 its 160,000 members came from all political persuasions and Protestant denominations. Its purpose was clear: to organize virtuous womanhood so as to transform the masculine world, to have feminine traits counterbalance men's brutal and animal qualities. As its motto boldly proclaimed: "Woman will bless and brighten every place she enters, and will enter every place"—not to compete with men but to reform them.[7]

In this spirit, the WCTU looked to recast social institutions. "Its manner," declared WCTU's president, Frances Willard, "is not that of the street, the court, the mart, or the office; it is the manner of the home. Men take one line and travel onward to success. . . . But women in the home must be mistresses as well as maids of all work." The most prominent goal of the organization was temperance reform, but its purposes were really much grander. "The best workers," declared one of its members, "soon found out that whatever makes for Christianity counts also for temperance; whatever improves the social atmosphere of the home or town, whatever helps men and women laboring to support a competent home, that also counts for temperance." In this spirit Willard described her organization as "the home going forth into the world." [8]

By preventing the sale and consumption of alcohol throughout the nation, the WCTU hoped to eliminate an incredible number of social evils; it would eradicate drunkenness, prostitution, disease (venereal, at least), and political corruption. Moreover, it would promote a new ethic—to close the saloon was to do war with male (read "beast") values. So every time a group of women banded together to shut a tavern, they learned about the efficacy and import of cooperative efforts. WCTU membership was a transforming experience, at one with attending a college.

Willard liked to recall how the act of closing down a saloon affected women. In their initial effort, the ladies usually made up "a gentle, well-dressed and altogether peaceable mob." But, much to her delight, repeated ventures turned them into an "army drilled and disciplined." And it was an army composed of "beloved homemakers and housekeepers [who] give us scraps and fragments of their time, finding in our Union a nobler form of social interchange than in the ceremonious calls and visits of the older time." Members of the WCTU were nothing other than "our Protestant Nuns." [9]

The WCTU "nuns," appropriately enough, worked for the glory

of the home under a pledge of abstinence, wearing a white ribbon to symbolize their moral purity. Even their wifely obligations shrank in importance. In the new Union, they were mothers rather than wives, fighting for the goals of "organized motherhood." "Save the children today and you have saved the nation to-morrow." Thus, with missionary zeal, the Union established free kindergartens for the children of the poor in an effort (which we will explore in more detail later) to provide an environment free of vice and moral contamination. The WCTU organized Sunday schools and even attempted to reform the public schools. The schools were to convey in "their architecture and adornment a means of education to the little ones, so that they shall from the first have placed before them images of the highest beauty and grace." They should also teach "the scientific truth concerning the effects of alcohol, tobacco and other narcotics" and provide courses in physical fitness. So firm was the WCTU's faith in the beneficial effects of vigorous exercise that Willard called the bicycle "our new temperance reformer." [10]

The WCTU also intended to reform the prison, the jail, and the juvenile asylum—all of whose inmates were victims of the saloon. Since the male criminals were probably beyond redemption, the Union focused its energies on the institutions' women and children. It set out to rescue the "fallen woman," through the personal encounters of female wardens and police matrons with female prostitutes and drunkards. "The arrested woman is at all times in the custody of a man," women reformers complained. "She may be in such a state of intoxication that no man should see her. These women . . . are often so intoxicated as to be wholly irresponsible, and may at any time disrobe themselves and stand at their cell doors." Better that a virtuous woman jailor, rather than a lustful male warden, should hold the key to her cell. "Every honest woman *must* demand that her unhappy sisters shall be protected at all times by a woman official." So, too, the WCTU demanded that women serve on boards of trustees of institutions caring for dependent or delinquent children. The responsibility was appropriate to "organized motherhood." [11]

Finally, the WCTU was staunchly committed to securing the vote for women: the ballot would further its campaign to recast social institutions. "In popular government," declared the WCTU, "the ballot is the most potent means of all moral and social reform." In fact, Willard believed that the very act of working for the goals of the WCTU raised women's awareness about the need for suffrage.

"When women come to consciousness," she argued, "they must inevitably ask questions like these: Why should we have no voice in making the laws under which we may be imprisoned or executed? Why should women have no hand in pleading woman's cause or determining her penalties? Why should men, and men alone, have the power of life and death over women, in all cases of indecorous or outrageous conduct toward us? . . . Who has so great a stake in the Government as the Nation's motherhood? Yet every law and penalty on every statute book of this and every other land was placed there by men, and men only." [12] Suffrage would further collective feminine (not feminist) goals; it was a woman's duty to agitate for the ballot, not because she deserved it as a citizen but because she required it as a Protestant Nun.

The WCTU mission attracted an enthusiastic following in rural areas and small Midwestern towns and in Northeastern urban communities as well. The late nineteenth-century city was an ideal breeding ground for female clubs: a generation of women who at once enjoyed a new degree of leisure and agreed on their obligation to uplift and purify the world inside and outside of the home, confronted a series of more-or-less obvious social problems. Virtuous womanhood came up against a distinctly virtueless society. Indeed, to an occasional critic, the city was too hospitable an environment for women's clubs; these associations were beginning to rival the family as so many women gave over so much of their time to them. "A woman who lives in an apartment hotel," began a typical attack, "has nothing to do. She resigns in favor of the manager. Her personal preferences and standards are completely swallowed up in the general public standards of the institution. She cannot have food cooked as she likes. . . . She cannot create that atmosphere of manner and things around her own personality, which is the chief source of her effectiveness and power. If she makes anything out of life at all, she is obliged to do it through outside activities—through her club membership and charitable works." But the women had a ready answer. City living did reduce "materially the amount of work demanded of women in the home," observed Marion Talbot. "The result is not to free her from responsibility; on the contrary, there arises here a new duty for women, that of intelligently and effectively cooperating with the other members of the community. . . . The home does not stop at the street door; it is as wide as the world into which the individual steps forth. The determination of the character of that world and the preservation of those interests which she has safeguarded in the home, constitute the real duty resting upon woman." [13]

This message had a critical meaning for middle-class urban women. Clubs would satisfy their individual desires for companionship and allow them to realize their particular mission. In a sense, the women's clubs were the late nineteenth-century successor to the earlier women's church societies. The shift represented a change in the locus of benevolent activity and in its content as well. These women were determined to address the entire range of the city's problems in novel fashion.

As women reformers well understood, urban life did pose unusual problems. It was no longer possible to be charitable in the way of one's parents or grandparents. As Josephine Shaw Lowell, one of the moving spirits in the new philanthropic organizations, explained: "It seems most easy and natural and right in one's own neighborhood, where one knows everyone, to step into the house of a poor friend and give him the help he requires in his unexpected distress." But such conditions no longer prevailed. "Gradually there come strangers, both rich and poor, to live in the village; suddenly the knowing of everyone is discovered to have become a thing of the past." [14] The scale and anonymity of the city required an altered style of benevolence.

The leaders of the new charitable societies were not dismayed by the challenge. They had a model at hand to implement, one that they had acquired during their Civil War service in the United States Sanitary Commission. In the Commission, women had joined with men to provide humane and efficient care for wounded, sick, and dying soldiers. The men directed the Commission's financial and political affairs; the women nursed, maintained sanitary conditions, and coordinated the delivery of provisions. Each sex, it seemed, had used its special attributes to meet the exigencies of war, to do good under very trying and unusual circumstances. [15]

Those who participated in the Commission's massive effort underwent a transforming experience, and it guided their philanthropic activities after the war. These women had learned that seemingly "feminine" virtues (such as patience and sympathy) and skills (such as knowledge of household organization and sickroom care) had a vital part to play in humanizing the brutalities of war. More, they, like the girls who would attend Vassar, undertook demanding and fatiguing work without ruining their health or losing their virtue. The Sanitary Commission experience gave workers a sense of vigor and confidence that would soon inspire them to reform urban charitable institutions.

With predictable ease, the Commission's graduates shifted attention from field hospitals to municipal hospitals and almshouses, the institutions that provided a last home for the helplessly ill and disabled poor. The organization and activities of the New York State Charities Aid Association (CAS) were one case in point. The moving force in the new association was Louisa Lee Schuyler, who had served as the Corresponding Secretary of the Women's Central Association for Relief during the Civil War. Before the war, Schuyler had been a volunteer sewing instructor in an industrial school for immigrant children. During the war, she worked to supply the Union's hospitals with the nurses and equipment necessary for caring for the wounded. After the war and her Sanitary Commission experience, Schuyler gave herself over to another group of victims in another series of buildings, the poor confined in public charitable institutions.[16] The CAS would upgrade the facilities so as to accomplish, in the words of its constitution, "the physical, mental and moral improvement of their pauper inmates." It would reform "the present pauper system . . . in accordance with the most enlightened views of Christianity, Science and Philanthropy." These goals, Schuyler was certain, were the logical outgrowth of the Sanitary Commission experience. "Many of the members of the State Charities Aid Association have worked together before," she noted. "When our country was bleeding, in the great war of the rebellion, for four years they stood shoulder to shoulder in the ranks of the Sanitary Commission." They "know the earnestness, the fidelity to principle, the self-sacrificing spirit which lie hidden in the homes throughout our State." It was now time for "our old fellow workers" to join in a "new and difficult work," and Schuyler correctly anticipated an enthusiastic response. "We believe they are ready to stand by us in memory of those old war-days when we worked together for our soldiers and our country." [17]

One of the first targets of CAS activity, appropriately enough, was Bellevue Hospital. "To those of us whose favored connection with the U.S. Sanitary Commission during the rebellion had brought some knowledge of the first principles at least of modern hospital construction," Schuyler explained, "our first visit to Bellevue Hospital was a painful surprise. We could not believe that this was the celebrated Bellevue Hospital of American and European fame." The wards spilled one into the other, the ventilation was totally inadequate, and the kitchen and laundry were "simply disgraceful." Bellevue, in other words, violated "all scientific principles of hospital construction." The CAS turned next to conditions in almshouses and jails. As with Bellevue, visiting committees of women investigated the institutions and were shocked and dismayed at what they found. At Blackwell's Island they reported "stifling odors" and clothes coming back from the wash "still alive with vermin"; at other places, the roofs were in such disrepair that tubs were scattered around the floors to catch the dripping water; the women learned, too, "how washing of the foulest description can be carried on without air and without light." [18] In all, municipal institutions were in desperate need of reform.

The very fact that Schuyler and her friends even visited such dismal places on a regular basis is striking testimony to the way the legacy of the Sanitary Commission combined with the ideology of virtuous womanhood to lead women to enter every place so as to try to brighten it. Dorothea Dix had attempted to do something of this sort in the Jacksonian period. However, she went alone and was considered something of a saint, the wonder of her times. Now, such work was almost commonplace, the task of all good-hearted charitable ladies. Moreover, the concepts of virtuous womanhood shaped the nature of the women's response. Schuyler was convinced that change could be accomplished through publicity. Once visiting commissions informed the public of the evils that they found, improvement would be immediately forthcoming. "Our people are essentially humane," declared Schuyler. "It is because they are ignorant of its existence that they allow human suffering to go unchecked or unrelieved." [19] In other words, vice flourished only because of secrecy. To bring in the light was to effect the cure.

The CAS assumed that the very presence of women on the wards would promote reform. Their personal involvement—in a very real sense, their virtue—would transform the character of the institution. The handbook that the Association prepared, *Visitors to the Poorhouse*, testified to the significance with which middle-class women endowed these tours. "Every visit, therefore, which gives the impression that a sincere and lasting interest is taken in the welfare of its inmates, will tend to reform all its evils. . . . What is chiefly to be desired . . . is a disposition to be thoroughly and in the best sense charitable."

Finally, Schuyler and her associates were determined to bring women's skills to the service of the institution in another and more permanent way. They founded the Bellevue School of Nursing to train women in the sanitary care of the sick. Its graduates, replacing the workhouse inmates, would improve the hospital's internal management. The nurses, as women in white, would minister to the sick —a model of unselfish and virtuous femininity—and help to manage the institution efficiently—a model of careful and frugal housekeeping.[20]

The impact of the concepts of virtuous womanhood on the new style of philanthropy was nowhere more evident than in the founding of the Charity Organization Society (COS). Although men did play a major role in the program (they were particularly eager to establish a complete roster of charity recipients so as to prevent fraud and to make philanthropy "efficient and businesslike"), much of the COS agenda reflected the special views and goals of female reformers. It is no accident that Josephine Shaw Lowell, one of the moving spirits of the COS, had been deeply involved in the activities of the Sanitary Commission. And Lowell's design for the COS gave primary importance to virtue, character, and morality.

To Lowell, the greatest danger in any relief effort was its potential to corrupt the recipient. "It has been proved," she declared, "and surely it scarcely needed proving, that no amount of money scattered among people who are without character and virtue will insure even physical comfort. It is for this reason that nothing should be done under the guise of charity, which tends to break down character." For philanthropy to destroy the integrity of a poor man, insisted Lowell, would constitute "the greatest wrong that could be done to him." The needy had to be relieved without incurring such a cost, without charitable impulses "increasing the evils they seek to cure."[21]

Lowell's solution depended particularly upon the discriminating and diligent efforts of women. "Charity must tend to raise the character and elevate the moral nature . . . by care in whom it is given and how it is given." Philanthropy dared not reward a lack of virtue. If a rogue abandoned his wife and children, or if a drunk squandered household money on alcohol, the good-hearted philanthropist must not intervene to feed and clothe the family. "It ought to be understood in every community," argued Lowell in no uncertain terms, "that where a man deserts his wife and children and neglects his most pressing duties to them and to the public, that they will be left to suffer the fate he has prepared for them. . . . It is a *wrong* and a great wrong, to give help to the family of a drunkard or an immoral man who will not support them."[22]

To this end, it was women's duty to organize groups of friendly visitors whose first charge was to investigate the moral character of the poor. Towns and cities were to be divided into districts, with visitors assigned to "a special territory," enabling them to "become thoroughly acquainted with all who live within its limits." Then the COS representative, as one member explained, "visited each [of the needy] in her own home, listened to her pitiful story, and gave practical suggestions concerning personal and domestic cleanliness and order which effected a marked improvement and created in sluggish minds a real ambition to make a home." The visitor was to teach the poor "how to run a better house" and to instruct "a widow how to best handle a boy inclined to be a rover." In this way, the COS could "create a neighborly good feeling, to help forward all good objects and put down all bad ones. . . . Such a Society, acquainted with the town and all its people, would in great measure prevent the growth of pauperism." [23] Lowell and the supporters of the COS, like Schuyler and the supporters of the CAS, were certain that face-to-face contacts and one-to-one relationships would promote reform. "The main instrument to be depended upon, to raise the standard of decency, cleanliness, providence and morality among them," concluded Lowell, "must be personal influence, which means that a constant and continued intercourse must be kept up between those who have a high standard and those who have it not, and that the educated and happy and good are to give some of their time regularly and as a duty, year in and year out, to the ignorant, miserable and the vicious." [24] Here was the way for virtuous women to recreate traditional ties in an urban setting and to teach morality to the alien poor.

Protecting the Country Girl

The facts of city life prompted still other women to establish charitable and educational programs to protect the virtue of the newly arrived country girls, a particularly innocent and vulnerable class. The most outstanding organization was the Young Women's Christian Association. First founded in Boston in 1866, the YWCA was soon running chapters in practically every American city. Patterned on that of the Young Men's Christian Association, its motto was: "The temporal, moral and religious welfare of self-supporting women." But its leaders adapted these broad aims to fit the roster of virtuous womanhood.

The New York YWCA, established in 1870, provided a great variety of services. It aimed "to extend Christian kindness to the multitudes of young women who come from quiet country homes to this city in search of employment or educational advantages. . . . To the average young woman engaged in self-support in large cities, the word 'home' means a cheerless room in some crowded tenement, or scarcely less solitary boarding house; and it often means associations and acquaintances that are full of danger to young and inexperienced women, whose very loneliness opens their hearts to the approach of anything that offers itself in the guise of friendship." [25] So acute was the YWCAs' fear of the city's temptations and corruptions that its workers scoured the railroad depots in order to meet the country girl the moment she arrived. In this way, her first contact would be with virtuous women.

The YWCA agents often found boarding places for the girls with respectable families. Because making these arrangements could be difficult (identifying the right family and suiting it to the girl and the girl to it), most YWCAs soon established their own dormitory facilities. And with the rooms came a program of moral uplift. The weekly religious service included a sermon on the need for purity in the face of adversity, and evening lectures preached the value of female chastity. The library books were selected for their "moral worth"; before borrowing, the girls were required to pass the inspection of the female librarian, who not only gave them privileges but also gave them "earnest Christian sympathy and counsel." The YWCAs typically established a Provident Savings Bank to encourage thrift among the girls. So, too, the reception rooms of the New York YWCA were open from 8 A.M. to 9 P.M. every Sunday, and members were expected to be on hand "to welcome those who called." To combat the anonymity of the city, "this intercourse will result in each member becoming personally interested in the welfare of some young girl, and extending to her a sister's kindness." [26] Through these encounters, the YWCA would protect the female virtues that were so clearly at risk when girls were away from their families.

The organization also founded employment bureaus to aid the girls in finding respectable jobs—that is, to encourage them to take up some form of domestic service. "No young woman can be too well-qualified, either by education or culture," insisted the New York YWCA, "to find fitting employment in the care of infancy, nor are such talents lost in the performance of these domestic duties which are essential in every household." [27] But the YWCA, after all, was serving ambitious country girls ready to run the risks of migrating to the city. Those content to be domestics would have remained at home; clearly, those who had moved did not wish to end up in a kitchen. The YWCAs, therefore, modified their programs to offer more varied employment choices, to devise variations on the "domestic" theme. They provided training in child care and then obtained positions for the girls as nursemaids and governesses. They offered instruction in the care of the sick, enabling the girls to become nurses in private families. They taught courses in "fancy sewing," providing the girls with jobs as seamstresses in good homes.

But such solutions were not altogether satisfactory. Those who came to the YWCA employment bureau had usually taught school for a year or more in a rural community and were expecting to teach in the city. "A very large number of the applicants have been teachers unable to do anything but teach," lamented Mary McCready, head of the New York YWCA employment committee. "The number of teachers throughout the country being immense, but few (say one in ten) have found employment at anything like remunerative prices." Fearful that these girls might turn in their disappointment to factory or shop work, the YWCA adopted a novel alternative: it began to offer training in skilled office work. In the 1880s at the New York YWCA, a girl could take courses in shorthand, typewriting, and bookkeeping.[28] In this way, the YWCA helped to place many former teachers in office work and to legitimate this employment for respectable women.

So convinced were reformers that women belonged in virtuous homes that they tried to persuade factory girls (just as they tried to influence YWCA girls) to take up household service. Philanthropic society representatives visited them at work to lecture on the advantages of domestic positions and to warn them of the perils in their present situation. "Factory employment," one charity worker declared, "has proved to be dangerous and demoralizing to young women, who without proper early education and discipline, are obliged to aid in the support of the family to maintain themselves. The farther the woman drifts from the family and the home, the more she is in danger from the shoals and quicksands of society."

The reports of the first female factory inspectors appointed by state boards of labor in the 1880s (of whom we will hear more later) repeated these conclusions. The factories not only bred poor health but failed to provide moral oversight. "Continuous factory toil has a tendency also to physically unfit women for the duties of motherhood," reported inspector Mary Halley from Massachusetts. Further, "it deprives them of training in social and domestic duties and in many cases brings a premature decline." And, since all laborers were, by definition, lower class, the setting was still more hazardous. "In a large number, particularly of those who go to work young," continued Halley, "much of the modesty which so becomes a woman is lost, and this is due mainly to the coarse, immodest language which is so common in some rooms." The open familiarity between men and women, the fact that "young people of both sexes work together, particularly where discipline is in a measure lax," had to be corrupting. "In such conditions the delicacy and modesty of thought, deportment and speech which are so precious and lovely in the character of young women are in danger." [29] Thus it became a middle-class mission to convince the girls to work in a refined and uplifting middle-class home.

Women philanthropists also attempted to supervise the leisure of working girls. They established clubs, modeled on their own, to inculcate the precepts of virtuous womanhood. The associations were to be centers "where enjoyment, friendship, and opportunity for improvement can be found." But it was "opportunity for improvement" that most concerned the women. "Wherever there are girls with whom the material side of life is emphasized," insisted one proponent, "there is a need for club life, with all it brings of mental activity and social relaxation, with the stimulus it gives to all spiritual life." Accordingly, working girls' clubs were devoted to moral uplift; friendship between members was not as critical as the relationship between leaders and members. The organizations provided the occasion for middle-class women "to come into *direct* personal contact" with working girls and "to exert a *personal* rather than general influence upon their lives." [30] In other words, the clubs, reminiscent of the COS, were committed to elevating the virtues of their members, not to improving working conditions or raising wages. The sponsors looked to self-improvement, not to social improvement.

It was Grace Dodge, the heiress to the Dodge copper fortune, who organized the first working girls' club. In 1881, with the help of a worker who was a member of her Sunday school class, Dodge arranged for a group of factory girls of about her own age (twenty-five) to meet for discussions. Within 3 years, the discussion group had become a formal club, with its own meeting place. The Dodge venture seemed so appropriate and successful that many women rushed to emulate the example; before long, they could consult a detailed list of "how-to" instructions. "A good plan," one organizer suggested, "is to gain admission to the factories during lunch hour and to speak to the girls yourself, distributing among them afterwards cards of invitation to opening night." [31] Through this activity, a philanthropic-minded woman could demonstrate "that she is especially called on to do something for other girls and women, as well as herself."

Philanthropists carefully designed every aspect of the working girls' clubs. "It is well to have two or three good speeches," counseled one leader, "in which the objects and aims of the Society are clearly explained. A little music will serve for entertainment, and ice cream and cake if announced on the invitation cards, will provide a great attraction." The girls could join the club for a nominal fee and in return have access to the clubhouse (usually one floor of a brownstone). In it they could read books, talk together ("they should feel as though the rooms were part of their homes and be social and friendly to all they meet there"), and sing along with that indispensable instrument of middle-class respectability—the piano.[32] Clubs also provided cooking, sewing, millinery, and even dressmaking classes. And often a few clubs joined together to rent a house in the country, so that members could spend a week or two during the summer with "sufficient exercise." The girls were also encouraged to "take walks to the lake, to the brooks," and, of course, "to the town and public library." [33]

The clubs did provide a comfortable meeting place for the hours after work, but the heavy hand of middle-class morality hovered over all activities. Dodge did not merely want to provide a pleasant occasion but to do good, to encourage "the development of higher types of daughters, sisters, wives, mothers, companions, friends." The clubs took such names as Endeavor Club, Goodwill Club, and Steadfast Club, with such mottoes as, "The Three P's—Purity, Perseverance and Pleasantness." Dodge used the weekly meetings to discuss "household matters, the grandeur of womanhood, her powers and possibilities, or the influences she possesses over men and boys, health, dress and so on." The clubs were also attentive to the girls' physical health. A female physician provided medical assistance and gave advice on personal hygiene and rules for right living. Dodge also discussed the "traits of womanhood," with illustrations from "the lives of famous women" (such as Joan of Arc) and extensive quotations from WCTU tracts. "We must," she told the girls, "respect ourselves and learn to control the different parts of our being, the physical or bodily side with its appetites and desires, the intellectual side with its brain ready for educational help, and the spiritual nature with its wonderful possibilities." [34]

The club founders were determined to promote sexual purity in the girls. Dodge's lectures were filled with warnings about men's animal passions, and she went so far as to draw up a list of twenty-one *don'ts* to guide female behavior, including:

Don't allow young men to be too familiar in words or action.
Don't let a young man know that you think too much of him.
Don't allow a young man to stay too late at your home.
Don't accept a present from a young man if you are not engaged to him.
Don't visit a young man at his place of business.
Don't forget to deserve respect and then demand it.
Don't have anything to do with a young man who sneers at religion.
Don't expect to reform a young man by marrying him.
Don't marry a man who drinks.[35]

In sum, the clubs were to give the girls the training they probably had not received in their own homes and certainly would not receive in the factory. They were, in brief, the middle-class antidote to lower-class evils.

In still another determined effort to bring the principles of sexual purity directly to the lower classes—indeed, to those who had flouted them—women reformers organized a network of rescue societies. These associations would prevent the once-fallen, the unmarried mother, from descending deeper into vice; they would also work to uplift the most pitiable of all women, the prostitute. To these twin purposes, benevolent-minded women established a variety of "homes" for destitute mothers and young girls—and among the most widespread of them was the Florence Crittenton Mission. The society opened its first home in New York City in 1883, and by 1897 it had 53 branches operating in cities all over the country. The clients were typically alcoholic women, one-time prostitutes, and unmarried mothers with infants. As the Mission slogan advertised, Florence Crittenton looked to assist any girl "Wishing to Leave a Crooked Life." At the Mission she would find: "Friends, Food, Shelter, and a HELPING HAND by Coming Just as She Is." [36]

To the Mission founders, the girls were not so much irredeemable sinners as they were the victims of passion, particularly as manipulated by unscrupulous men. "Most of our girls in the first place fell through love," declared Mrs. Kate Barrett, the general superintendent of the Mission, "and they will be redeemed through love; not the blind love that coddles and pampers but the wise love that guides and controls." So the Mission workers went out to deliver the message of redemption, not waiting for the girls to come to them. They visited train depots, police stations, jails, reformatories, massage parlors (not inventions of the 1970s), poorhouses, and houses of prostitution. They distributed pamphlets that warned about the wiles of men and encouraged reformation. They even enlisted the aid of policemen (to them a symbol of male lust) in the hope that, despite the officers' "loyalty to these girls" (a polite way of referring to bribes), they might send them to the Mission.[37]

A long period of residence at the Mission was to transform a woman from "idleness, filth, drunkenness and sin . . . into a neat, industrious, sober, godly woman." The change could not be quickly accomplished. "It is to be remembered," cautioned Josephine Shaw Lowell, who was as interested in rescue as in poor relief operations, "that every one of these young women needs training, physical, mental, industrial and moral education, and that education takes time. They are probably in a perverted state of body and mind and therefore . . . [the] institution should retain its inmates long enough to really cure them and develop them, and form habits of good living, that is, for at least two years, and probably five or more." And the missions followed a policy of isolation. "It is a great help having them break all outside ties completely," contended Mrs. Barrett, "and to teach them to have resources within themselves. They soon become interested in the simple home pleasures that we give them and are entirely weaned from the reckless life of excitement which they have lived in the past."[38]

Life in the Florence Crittenton institutions followed a well-ordered routine that emphasized moral elevation and training for domestic service. Mrs. Barrett's rhetoric notwithstanding, there was far more control than love. The schedule was that of a servant residing in a moral Christian home. The girls rose at six and recited a prayer before breakfast. The matron gave them their work assignments for the day, usually chosen from a variety of household chores including laundry work. The girls washed their own clothing, their infants', the matron's, and, in an effort to meet expenses and keep them busy,

laundry taken in from families in the community. They also attended
Bible classes and psalm singing two hours a day.[39]

To the managers, this program constituted moral rehabilitation.
They insisted that the drudgery of laundry work offered the inmates
a "means of grace" and would curb "the animal spirit of our charges"
and cure their restlessness. "We are trying to equip these human
beings for self-sustainment and honorable lives," explained one of the
Missions. "They come to us idle, ignorant. . . . By the end of their
stay . . . they learn to be good cooks, laundresses, nurses and seamstresses." [40] At the same time, tedious domestic labor in the Mission
gave the girls a good sense of what lay in store for them when they
left.

The managers of the institutions, ever sensitive to the moral vulnerability of the inmates, tried to formulate plans that would lessen
the likelihood of another fall. For one, they insisted that the girls
keep their infants with them, believing that the children would stim-
ulate maternal spirit, thereby deterring misconduct. For another,
they found positions for the girls as domestics in rural settings, isolated from the corruptions of urban life. Josephine Shaw Lowell
urged the managers to "place the women upon their release, in situations where they will be protected, where they will not be exposed
to temptation, nor where they can tempt others. For instance, I
should think that the ideal training would be such as would fit a young
woman to go into the country, and help an old couple in the care
of their home, or their horse, cow, chickens, garden, etc." And the
Florence Crittenton Missions pursued such practices. "The baby fur-
nishes all the amusement the mother desires," declared Mrs. Barrett,
"and we find that our girls are contented and happy in country
homes for the good of their child, when in ordinary circumstances
they could not be persuaded to leave the excitements of the city." [41]

The Discipline of Abstinence

The identification of virtuous womanhood with sexually pure and
abstinent womanhood was also evident in the passage of anticontra-
ception and antiabortion legislation in the post-Civil War decades.
Although it is often assumed that such statutes have a long history,

that Americans have always banned the distribution of contraception and made abortion a heinous crime, in fact such actions became major offenses only beginning in the 1870s. It was women reformers and women physicians of the period, particularly Frances Willard and Elizabeth Blackwell, who led a purity crusade that made the suppression of birth control information a major plank in the moral reform agenda. They, along with male doctors, ministers, and an occasional layman, supported legislation defining contraceptive information and devices as "obscene material." A federal statute of 1873 (known for its most flamboyant proponent, Anthony Comstock, but backed by women reformers as well) made it a felony (not even a misdemeanor) "to sell, or lend, or give away or in any manner exhibit . . . or have in [one's possession] for any purpose or purposes, any obscene book, pamphlet, paper . . . or any drug or medicine, any article whatever, for the prevention of conception, or for causing unlawful abortion." [42] State after state quickly enacted similar legislation. Through the 1920s, the distribution of contraception was illegal in practically every jurisdiction.

The social purity legislation presupposed, just as the concepts of virtuous womanhood taught, that the male was a savage beast who would subvert and corrupt women in order to satisfy his animal impulses. Contraceptive practices were so reprehensible precisely because they separated sexual activity from procreation, thus enabling the male to indulge all his lusts while free of the responsibility of rearing children. Contraception would turn woman into a "slave to her husband's desires." With birth control devices allowing her to avoid an "unwanted and unregulated maternity," her time and energy would be devoted to satisfying his needs. There was no way, it seemed, that a woman could be both a wife and a mother. Since the practice of contraception elevated the role of wife at the expense of the role of mother, it had to be banned.

The virtuous woman was first and foremost—even exclusively— a mother, not only to her children but also to her husband. "It is the motherly element which is the hope, and is to be the salvation of the world," declared one woman reformer in 1876. "The real woman regards all men, be they older or younger than herself, not as possible lovers, but as a sort of stepsons towards whom her heart goes out in motherly tenderness." To virtuous women, "their husbands are . . . only children of larger growth, to be loved and cared for very much in the same way as their real children." [43]

In this type of relationship, the only permissible way to limit family size was through abstinence. As Frances Willard contended, under the discipline of abstinence "the sanctities of fatherhood shall be seen to exceed all others . . . and the malarious dream of wicked self-indulgence shall slowly but surely give place to sacred self-restraint." Abstinence was the only morally healthy practice that a couple could follow. Any woman who disregarded such precepts was nothing but a prostitute—hence, the final logic of linking contraceptive devices to obscene material. (This was, by the way, a self-fulfilling logic, for contraceptives became part of the stock of pornography shops during these years.) "When two people are determined to live together as husband and wife," concluded one minister, "and evade the consequences and responsibilities of marriage, they are simply engaging in prostitution without the infamy which attaches to that vice and crime." Another physician concurred, in language almost indistinguishable from that of his clerical colleague. The use of contraceptives "certainly must produce a feeling of shame and disgust utterly destructive of the true delight of pure hearts and refined sensibilities. They are suggestive of licentiousness and the brothel, and their employment degrades to bestiality the true feelings of manhood and the holy state of matrimony." [44] Marriage allowed women one role and one role only: that of mother.

These same decades also witnessed the passage of strict criminal abortion statutes. Before 1860, performing an abortion before "quickening," when the fetus first moved, seems not to have been a crime at all, at least under the common law; an abortion after quickening was not more than a minor offense, and one that may well have been frequently ignored. Beginning in the 1860s, however, state after state criminalized the procedure. Although the campaign was led by doctors and not by women reformers (who seem to have been content to allow medical men to condemn so horrendous a medical procedure), the language of the movement faithfully repeated the principles of virtuous womanhood. Physicians did note what they took to be the injurious effects of an abortion upon women's health: "We cannot recall to mind," insisted one doctor, "an individual who has been guilty of this crime (for it must be called a crime under every aspect), who has not suffered for many years afterward in consequence. And when health is finally restored, the freshness of life had gone, the vigor of mind and energy of body have forever departed." [45] Yet physicians also went on to argue that abortion was a gross violation of proper and moral womanhood: "It is a swift witness against their purity and nobleness and shows an utter recklessness in the pursuit of sensual pleasure." Like contraception, abortion indicated that a woman had succumbed to "the *increasing* sensualism of men and their determination to gratify it without regard to consequences for their wives and mothers." A wife who underwent an abortion had "mistaken notions of conjugal duty"; that is, she placed her "fear of losing a husband's love and confidence" above her maternal duties.[46]

Thus, women reformers and physicians were at one in condemning contraception and abortion—as they had not been in judging the propriety of women's collegiate education. The difference between the two cases is not difficult to account for; both camps were consistent and faithful to their own principles. The women and the doctors both agreed that proper womanhood did not allow for sexual expression. The doctors emphasized the deleterious physical effects of frequent or regular sex. "With some," went one medical argument, "once a week may do them no harm and neither cause disease or increase the liability to suffer from other causes. It is quite certain that no one can gratify this passion much more frequently than this without doing himself future or present harm and injuring his offspring." Other physicians found this advice too liberal. Doctor Wood-Allen recommended sex once a month—and then only under the most ideal of circumstances. "Sexual union," she cautioned, "should never be indulged in when either or both are fatigued in mind or body, as at the close of a day of hard work . . . never when either is actually ill or even ailing; never when under strong emotions, such as anger, grief, or even excessive joy; never during pregnancy or lactation; never when conception would be unwelcome." [47] The women reformers, for their part, thought of sexual expression as incompatible with the feminine mission. It represented an elevation of the role of wifehood over motherhood, of private interest over public concern.

From the medical perspective, the need for economy of energy and moderation not only ruled in sexual matters but also dictated that women avoid the strains of a collegiate education. The precepts of moderation could be violated as easily in the library as in the bedroom; an excess of study, like an excess of sexual activity, would ruin a woman's health. But here the female reformers separated themselves from the doctors. The whole point of virtuous womanhood was to invigorate and energize women so that they could take their principles from the home into the world. Vassar was so significant an experiment and refutation of traditional medical advice because it demonstrated that a proper regimen permitted women to be active—at first in the library, if you will, and then later in Sorosis, the WCTU, the CAS, the COS, and the YWCA. Sexual relations, then, were not so much debilitating as they were distracting and corrupting—and for that reason, their expression had to be severely restricted, practically to the point of abstinence.

Moneymaking for Ladies

Of the reform efforts carried out in the name of virtuous womanhood it might well be said that it was far better to give than to receive such help. Clearly, the model of a Protestant Nun did spur women's efforts on, making them all the more ready to bring the home out into the world and to promote the moral welfare of the poor, the country girl, and the fallen woman. But in instance after instance, the programs were inadequate to the problems that they addressed, obfuscating the issues, not clarifying them, and substituting rhetoric and morality for care and assistance.

The limits of a social policy based on these principles are evident first in the case of married women who fell on hard times, the respectable ladies who were victims of misfortune. There was no shortage of such persons. Middle-class families did suffer disasters when husbands succumbed to business failure or to illness, when women were left widowed and without resources. Life insurance in the post-Civil War decades was still a rare commodity and to a degree even suspect (a kind of gamble with the devil). Pensions were unusual and savings did not last long enough. For all the popularity of the notion that training a young girl to a trade or occupation would serve as protection against just such a desperate moment, reality was far more grim. Married women who had once worked as teachers could not typically re-enter the profession; school boards did not wish to hire them and, with a long list of applicants from colleges and normal schools, were under no pressure to do so. So, too, offices and department stores would not often employ an older married woman. No less important, the married woman herself was very reluctant to accept such positions. To work openly had almost as much shame about it as to take charity; somehow or other, the truly prudent family would have saved for a rainy day. Thus, when facing hardships, married women resorted to a series of stratagems to earn money without seeming to be working—and women's clubs encouraged and facilitated this kind of evasive response.

A spate of advice books informed the married woman of some of the techniques. "The average woman," suggested Ellen Church, in her aptly titled book *Money Making for Ladies*, "recognizes the value of money; if poor she wants to make it, and her anxiety to do this battles perpetually with her desire to do nothing which is strong minded and unladylike." Accordingly, Church told women to can fruits and make preserves, to find an outlet for fancy embroidery and needlepoint, or to do dressmaking at home. They might even pursue "one of the few means of money making in which a lady may engage without compromising her social standing"—to give music, art, embroidery, or cooking lessons to young girls. The secret was to remain behind closed doors.[48] A lady had to preserve the fiction that she did not work or that she only worked for pleasure. Neighbors were not to know of her situation.

To this end the clubs made their contribution. By the 1890s Womans Exchanges operated in some seventy-five cities, providing women with an outlet for their handiwork while preserving their anonymity. The exchanges sold bread, pastry, preserves, jams, needlework, and other handicrafts, so as to give an income to the "gentlewoman suddenly reduced to abject poverty." They only accepted high-quality merchandise—a woman had to submit samples of her work before Exchanges would place an order. In return, however, they kept the secret. At the Womans Exchange, all goods were marked only by number. So attuned were the middle-class organizers of the Exchanges to the stigma of work that they would often send their agent up the back stairs at night to receive the products in an unmarked bag.

The sponsors of the Exchange defined the enterprise as philanthropic. Their purpose was to relieve poverty, not to encourage women to earn money. They paid on a piece-by-piece basis—no woman could make a long-term contract with an Exchange—and they certainly did not pay well enough to allow anyone to maintain a decent standard of living through their sales. "The Exchange," argued Lucy Salmon, a rare critic of the system, "has encouraged the idea that women can work by stealth without being guilty of moral cowardice, and it has fostered the spirit that carries lunch in musicrolls, calls for laundry work only after dark and does not receive as boarders or lodgers wage-earning women." By allowing the masquerade to go on, by insisting that women should work "only when misfortune comes," the Exchange ultimately robbed women and their work of dignity and at the same time concealed a pressing social problem.* [49]

The fate of lower-class women in need was still more dismal—or, put another way, the critical failures of a policy toward poverty that emphasized the virtue, as opposed to the needs or rights of the individual, becomes all the more apparent as one moves down the social ladder. For all of Louisa Schuyler's determination, personal example was simply not a powerful enough mechanism to transform a municipal almshouse. The visits of a private corps of women inspectors might win some publicity for the abuses that inmates faced, but they were incapable of effecting change. The visitors lacked all authority.[51] The closest they came to the exercise of power was a regular audience with the city or state commissioner of charities and corrections, who undoubtedly had a pretty fair idea already of the deficiencies of his institutions.

Nor did the Bellevue Training School for Nurses have much impact on the quality of care given to the poor in municipal facilities. Very few graduates actually became hospital nurses. In 1898, 25 years after the school's founding, only 50 of the 550 graduates had taken up positions in public hospitals, while 208 of them entered the field of private nursing. This result reflected the school's criteria for accepting applicants; it would admit only the most refined girls, those with high standards of neatness and order. These women were just the ones who would not be eager to do hospital work. Their ambition was not to be matrons in charge of workhouse inmates, but to serve good

---

* Perhaps no example better reveals the stigma of work for married women than the inaccuracy of census reports. The returns do not provide an accurate breakdown of the number of married women engaged in nonagricultural occupations for the simple reason that married women were not eager to admit to the census-taker that they were working. Thus, the census figures in 1890 put married women at 12.1 percent of all those employed, in 1900 at 13.3 percent, in 1910 at 19.8 percent, and in 1920 at 21.2 percent. Although these calculations do point to a steady increase in the number of married women working, in fact the figure was probably always around 20.0 percent. The key to the change is the instructions given to census enumerators in 1910. For the first time they were specifically told to have women "state their occupation," that the mere presence of a married women at home was not itself to be an indication that she was a full-time housewife. "An entry should be made in this [occupation] column," the instructions read, "for *every* person enumerated. The occupation, if any, followed by a child, of any age, or by a woman is just as important for census purposes as the occupation followed by a man. Therefore, it must never be taken for granted, without inquiry, that a woman, or child, has no occupation." The dramatic rise in married women at work in the 1910 census stands as testimony to these guidelines.[50]

families. In fact, the Bellevue School maintained an alumnae association whose main purpose was to keep a register of graduates so that the well-to-do could know where to obtain trained nurses. Moreover, the few nurses who did work on the wards lacked the ability or the authority to enact reforms. Bellevue trained nurses to follow doctors' orders; they were "in all matters regarding management of the sick, absolutely under the orders of the medical men." [52] And until doctors themselves insisted upon raising the quality of care, Bellevue's condition would not change.

The relief that the women's organizations doled out was not much more satisfactory. If married women and widows solicited first one society and then another for aid, it was not because they were intent on committing fraud but because they were desperately trying to put enough private charity together to stay out of the almshouse. A few bags of coal and an occasional collection of groceries was simply not enough; and yet, as the records of the COS and comparable societies made eminently clear, this was typically the extent of support. Private charities did not have resources adequate to the job. But again, rather than publicize their limitations or lead a crusade to increase public welfare, the women made advice seem as helpful as cash. The COS records are also replete with examples of friendly visitors insisting that the family follow their way and their advice, regardless of the client's wishes. So, when one mother pleaded with the visitor that her daughter be allowed to attend secretarial school at her uncle's expense, the visitor refused, instructing her that the daughter was to go out to work, and if the mother persisted in thinking otherwise, the society would cut off her stipend (which is just what happened). The charities, too, were so obsessed by the fear of aiding one of the corrupt poor that hearsay became firm evidence. The woman accused by a neighbor of entertaining men soon enough found herself cut off from all assistance.[53]

In the end, married women in need had to find some employment or other, and it was almost always at the very bottom of the job ladder. The stores or mills that might have hired them when they were single assumed that mothers made irregular employees. The most readily available income came from doing piecework at home (a worker's irregularity, then, would cost *her* money, not the owner). Women could sew buttonholes or make suspenders or turn out artificial flowers, all the while keeping something of an eye on the children and even recruiting their help. Of course, the pay for piecework was considerably below even the levels of factory wages.

If not doing piecework, lower-class married women occupied the positions that no one else wanted, not even the immigrant women. Lacking skills and youth, they were forced to take the jobs that were left over. So they became the scrubwomen in the newly constructed office buildings, or domestics, servants, or laundresses in middle-class homes. Thus, in 1910 it was married women who made up fully 55 percent of all janitors, 51 percent of all laundresses, and 39 percent of all domestics.[54]

Somewhat aware of the desperate situation confronting these women, middle-class philanthropists, apart from giving minimal out-right aid, provided opportunities for domestic employment. A woman applicant to the New York COS, for example, first received a "Laundry Card" that entitled her to work in the agency's laundry and sewing room. There she would do her job, ostensibly improving her skills so as to become a better domestic. If she proved sufficiently diligent and worthy, the COS would find her outside employment. "I feel in a good many instances," insisted one representative, "that there is no more effective way of raising the standard of living in the family than letting the woman do day work in a family whose stan-dards are higher." [55] Once again, standards of morality were confused with standards of living.

In the 1880s and 1890s, some associations also began to establish day nurseries in working-class neighborhoods. Typically located in rented brownstones, the nurseries provided a place where the work-ing mother could safely leave her young children for a nominal fee, about 5¢ a day. And the nurseries, like the Missions and the homes for destitute women, mixed moral uplift with caretaker services. The children were to follow a well-ordered routine that inculcated habits of "neatness, order and healthfulness." The Bloomingdale Day Nursery of New York announced, with all condescension intended: "We received 1800 children. We gave many of them more abundant food and much better care than their poor homes could afford." The nurseries insisted that the children be brought to them spotlessly clean at 6:30 every morning, a difficult task for a woman who worked a 12-hour day and whose tenement lacked hot running water.[56] And they would agree to supervise the children only on the days the mother actually worked. If a mother was not on the job, she ought to be at home with her children.

Not surprisingly, the nurseries were not popular among working mothers. If the Bloomingdale Nursery enrolled a total of 1800 chil-dren, it generally had less than 50 in daily attendance. The Cleveland

Day Nursery had 142 children listed on its books in 1891, but only 25 were present on any given day. In fact, the nurseries generally received children from the woman who had no other option; they were, in every sense, a last resort. (Some nurseries were fearful that they might be taking in illegitimate children, but attendance was so poor that they would not often ask applicants to bring in a marriage certificate.)[57] The clientele was generally made up of destitute and deserted wives who were unable to turn to friends or relatives for aid. Lacking all choice, they were forced to accept the charity of the middle class.

Thus, married working women experienced the worst of both possible worlds. They not only lost the respectability that full-time motherhood afforded, but they had to take the positions that younger unmarried women did not want. They bore the stigma of working and the burden of long hours, hard labor, and very low wages. The well-meaning charitable societies not only failed to alleviate the problems but may well have, in their own way, exacerbated them. In sum, to be a working mother was as unfortunate a fate as any woman could suffer.

Single girls, particularly those with some freedom of choice, simply avoided the helping hand of the women's clubs. The YWCAs enjoyed little popularity among working girls, for the very good reason that in a city like New York there was no shortage of places to learn to type, and their employment bureaus were most active in placing domestics. In Baltimore, for example, 435 women applied to the local YWCA for jobs in 1887; 174 of them received positions, 165 in domestic service. By the same token, not many girls turned to them for rooms.[58] For one, the rates were not cheap, suitable only for those earning a steady income. More important, working girls wanted their privacy. The women who lived at the YWCA were almost invariably made up of the already convinced, those who were eager to listen to a woman superintendent inveigh against the perils that city life posed to virtuous conduct. Instead of serving as missionaries to the unconverted, the YWCA had middle-class women preaching to their own.

So intense was the desire of single girls for privacy in their living arrangements that during these years boardinghouses gave way to lodging houses. The "family-life" atmosphere of the one could not compete with the attractions of anonymity in the other. The old-fashioned boardinghouses of the pre-Civil War decades did have, as Arnold Wolfe explained with more than a touch of nostalgia, "something of the home element. Boarders knew each other; they met at table two or three times a day, and lingered a few moments in conversation after dinner in the evening. In summer they gathered on the front steps and piazzas, and in winter they often played euchre and whist in the landlady's parlor." The woman who ran such a house "took something of a personal interest, even if remote, in her boarders." In turn, the boarders, "found themselves becoming a part of the family even against their wills." But by the late nineteenth century, boardinghouse arrangements appeared unacceptable. The landlady, observers noted, supplied "board and room for five dollars a week and expected two girls to share one room, and one bath is considered sufficient for an entire household. . . . The food is plentiful, but ill prepared . . . the bedrooms are not tidy." More important, the houses did not allow for privacy. "Boarding-house life," even Wolfe conceded, "was no doubt often monotonous and the landlady oftentimes officiously zealous in taking care of the affairs of her boarders." [59]

The choice residence for single men and women became the lodging house, with its impersonal atmosphere. By the turn of the century, Wolfe estimated that 86 percent of the single population of Boston lived in lodging houses. These houses let rooms without board, and the rise of inexpensive restaurants and cafes gave the residents a choice of when to eat, what to eat, with whom to eat, and how much to pay. These new restaurants, noted Wolfe, represented "a powerful force tending to drive out of business hundreds of boarding-house keepers and to reduce them to the simpler employment of 'taking in lodgers.'" They also offered customers opportunities compatible with the "free spirit of the times." They became "favorable places for striking up a chance acquaintance," giving single men and women occasions to meet with each other on their own terms—not those of the women's clubs.[60]

It is not surprising, then, that Grace Dodge's working girls' clubs never achieved significant popularity. For all their comforts, the New York clubs had a total membership (at their own probably inflated estimate) of some 2,000 members, that, in any event, was only a small fraction of the female working population. And no wonder the numbers were low. The club leaders might extol the value of female friendship and cooperation, but they looked down on the girls as moral inferiors. To hear an occasional factory worker repeat their lines makes clear just how overbearing was the middle-class sense of superiority and smugness. "We work ten hours a day," one club girl told the ladies assembled at the National Convention in 1890. "How are we to get that development of mind and body that we need? . . . Our home influences are not of the best, always, and the atmosphere surrounding us is not a wholesome one. We must have an influence from outside that will strengthen our moral natures. . . . We need to be taught, both by precept and example, that there are higher aims in life than fun and flirtation. . . . We need to know how to take care of our bodies. We need to have our minds so filled with great and high and pure thoughts that while our hands are busy with our daily work our brains will be busier yet." [61] Such rhetoric canceled out what might have been the pleasures and conveniences of club life.

Working girls also refused to heed middle-class advice to avoid department store and factory work. In the post-Civil War decades, factory girls were well aware of middle-class disdain. "There is no impression more difficult to efface from the minds of well-intentioned women," wrote one woman journalist, "than that the entrance of girls into industrial pursuits lowers their moral standard." Nevertheless, the girls shunned domestic employment, preferring the greater autonomy of factory jobs. "Girls used to regular hours and prescribed duties," this journalist went on, "object to the irregular hours and desultory duties of the household. . . . Better scanty food, a hard bed, and personal freedom, than material comforts and only every other Sunday out." Again and again, the girls expressed these sentiments. "Some housekeepers do not know how to treat girls right," one worker explained to the factory inspectors in Minnesota. "They think that all a girl is good for is to drudge from morning till night and be driven around." Another echoed her view: "I would not do housework under any consideration. In the first place, I would not be anyone's servant. In the second place, I am not obliged to. In the third place, girls as a rule, are not treated properly." [62] Better the ten-hour discipline of the machine than the twenty-four-hour oversight of a middle-class housewife.

And the Florence Crittenton Homes, for even more obvious reasons, were nothing other than a last resort for a hapless few. Women entered the Mission when no other choice was available. Only 365 women took shelter in the Florence Crittenton New York Chapter in 1890—a bare fraction of the city's 60,000 women whom reformers estimated had to be rescued.[63] Unmarried mothers often preferred to raise their children alone or to abandon the infants to a foundling hospital. (The population of foundling hospitals was far greater than those of the Missions.) More, a potential Mission inmate knew she would pay dearly for her sins. She would have to undergo a lengthy penance and then become a domestic in an isolated rural community. So once again, the grim reality of life on the city streets seemed preferable to the helping hand of middle-class women reformers.

Thus, the definition of women's best interest that emerged from the concept of virtuous womanhood was, finally, a class-based definition. For all the notions of sisterhood, of one friendly female visitor helping another woman, of female visiting committees improving conditions in public charitable institutions, of female matrons rescuing the fallen, and of Grace Dodge's club ladies protecting the working girl and the country girl, the identity of sex was not as significant as the difference in class. When women reformers talked about the home going forth into the world, they meant the middle-class home going forth into the lower-class world. For all the assumptions that men were the common villains, it was the lower-class male who was, in the end, the most dangerous beast, and the lower-class woman who had to be lifted up to middle-class standards. Not for the last time would gender identity obscure class interests. Not for the last time would a policy based on the commonality of womanhood represent the efforts of the better sort to make their values everyone's values, to equate their interest with the public interest.

CHAPTER

3

The Ideology of Educated Motherhood

THE PROGRESSIVE ERA witnessed the triumph of a new ideal for womanhood that at once transformed the character of private and public duties and altered the tasks of mothers and the obligations of legislators. Appropriately labeled "educated motherhood," this definition set forth a series of postulates that were to guide the behavior of women and to set the direction for social reform. It took as its point of departure a novel sense of the needs of the child—who now seemed a particularly complicated and vulnerable creature. Within the family, the child required much more than affectionate care or a well-ordered routine. Child-rearing demanded very sophisticated skills of management; different types of responses and discipline were appropriate at different stages in the child's growth. Women had to be trained to the tasks of motherhood. A warm heart was simply not enough. "Everyone will concede, I am sure," one Progressive educator insisted, "that it is the mother's hand that moulds, but she greatly needs preparation for the process. She needs what many do not possess, the refinement which association brings, a broad outlook, a logical mind . . . qualities in which the average mother has little or no training. She must not rely too much on her natural instincts; the well-deserving but much-vaunted mother sense." [1] In essence, maternal impulses had to give way to maternal insights.

Social policy also had to reckon with this shift. Indeed, educated mothers had to bring their special sensitivity toward children directly into the public arena. Benevolent-minded women were to do more than carry out rescue operations, guarding country girls from temptation or lifting prostitutes from a life of sin. The Progressive agenda was at once more ambitious and more child-centered. Children required the attentive care of mothers, then of teachers, hence the appropriateness of laws prohibiting child labor, establishing kindergartens, and making school attendance compulsory. Children's health had to be carefully monitored, hence the need for maternal and child clinics in the cities (under municipal organization) and throughout the country (under a national program). While the Progressives were not the first to create special programs for children, no prior generation of reformers devoted as much attention or as much energy to their welfare. To an unprecedented degree, it became the charge of the mother and the state to pursue the best interests of the child.

From Instinct to Insight

So fundamental a shift in private and public orientation had deep roots in American society and reflected the judgments and concerns of widely diverse groups. The intense focus of attention on the child testified to an unprecedented professional and scientific interest in child study. No one person was more important to this movement than G. Stanley Hall. Remembered now mostly for having invited Sigmund Freud to deliver his first American lectures at Clark University, Hall was far more important in his time for inspiring a host of efforts to analyze the nature of child development.[2] Hall presented a highly dynamic view of this process, delineating distinct stages in growth and insisting that the parent (for Hall as well as for everyone else, this meant the mother) had to respond differently to the child at each particular stage. A ten-year-old, for example, required habit training. "Never again will there be such susceptibility to drill and discipline, such plasticity to habituation or such ready adjustment to new conditions." But to subject an adolescent to such a regimen would be inappropriate. "The drill methods of the preceding period must be slowly relaxed and new appeals made to freedom and interest. . . . Individuality must have a longer tether." [3] Child-rearing advice assumed a greater degree of age specificity. General maxims gave way to detailed instructions, so detailed that Hall insisted that women had to be specially trained to their responsibilities. "We must first of all distinctly . . . educate primarily and chiefly for motherhood." To this end, Hall argued that "coeducation should cease at the dawn of adolescence." And he was certainly prepared to evaluate how well women fulfilled the task of child-rearing: "The heart and soul of growing childhood is the criterion by which we judge the larger heart and soul of mature womanhood." [4] If the curriculum was child-rearing, the examination was the way that the child developed.

There was no mistaking the import of Hall's message, and his followers spelled it out in even greater detail. The educated mother had responsibility not so much for keeping a well-ordered household (as Catharine Beecher insisted), but for implementing the complicated rules of child development. "The mother who rocks the cradle," women learned, "is entrusted with a greater responsibility than merely caring for the physical requirements of her babe." She "has the privilege of witnessing the first burst of the bud of intelligence." She "must meet the demands of a newly awakened consciousness . . . must recognize the soul power in its restless activities, and must shape those activities into concentrated directed force. Has she wisdom enough to do this? Yes . . . she must read, think, study and apply what she learns." [5] The mother had to respond to the budding "intelligence" of the infant with more than affection; she had to study, read, and think to know precisely how to react. And as the child grew older, the problems grew more complex. If an infant required that mothers apply a special knowledge, an adolescent demanded still more sophisticated treatment.

No institution in the late nineteenth century was more determined to popularize and to fulfill the new ideas on childhood than the kindergarten, and its programs and sources of support help to clarify the origins and implications of the principles of educated motherhood. The kindergarten movement took its inspiration from work done in the 1840s and 1850s by the German pedagogue, Friedrich Froebel. But as is so often the case in the transfer of ideas or institutions, Froebel's innovations did not take hold in the United States until they fit particular needs and perceptions. In 1875 there were only some 95 American kindergartens in operation; in 1880, only 348. Then, decade by decade, the movement expanded: in 1890 there were 1,311 kindergartens; in 1900 there were 5,000; in 1910, 5,510; and in 1920, some 9,000, attended by roughly 10 percent of the nation's children. [6]

This rise in numbers reflected first the academic concern for childhood. Since the kindergarten brought young children together in one setting, it became an ideal place in which to analyze the child. As the United States Bureau of Education explained: "The child-study phase of psychology has turned the attention of educators increasingly to the necessity of providing opportunities for first-hand experiences with children. In 'laboratory' kindergartens, students of education may observe and then do practice-teaching, and thus learn how to interpret with scientific care significant expressions on the part of the children." [7] Appropriately, G. Stanley Hall endorsed the teachings of Froebel, or at least brought Froebel into his own intellectual framework. "He exhorted," declared Hall, "that every child should be at each stage of his life all that that stage called for. . . . The future should not dominate; and adult views and standards should not be prematurely enforced. Youth should not scorn boyhood, nor boyhood infancy." To Hall, Froebel taught (as Hall himself did) that "we must all live for and with the children. Indeed, what else is there in all this world worth living, working, dying for?" [8] Because kindergartens responded to the "stage" needs of the child and riveted attention on the child, Hall applauded and promoted the movement.

But support for the kindergarten extended well beyond academic circles to philanthropists and educators. Kindergartens were to teach and train many of the very young who had heretofore been neglected ("left fallow," treated like "wasting weeds," left to "play without supervision"). In fact, these supporters insisted, "much can be done when love, and scientific training and maternal aptitude encircle the child."

The child could be taught self-control, discipline, and good manners and habits without repressive means, without resort to a heavy-handed authority. The kindergarten, in the motto of its proponents, would instill "order without repression." Through play and other appropriate lessons, the young child would be trained to obedience, respect for work, and patriotism. It was a grand agenda, but one that seemed appropriate and manageable. The kindergarten children in their daily games would march—and learn that their marching was part of an allegiance to country. They would set out to make a clock or draw a calendar—and learn that "the clock helps us to be good." They would make Valentine's Day cards, not merely to express love to their parents but also to learn that the work of the ragman who carried rags to the mills to be ground into pulp was essential to the welfare of society. [9] Through the kindergarten, claimed Richard

Watson Gilder, editor of *Century*, "the children are brought into a new social order; they are taught to have regard for one another, and do acquire such regard—along with a new and highly valuable respect for law and order." [10]

Not surprisingly, public school administrators welcomed such a training of the young and helped to spread the kindergarten message. Now, the children who entered the first grade would be disciplined to the school routine. "In the kindergarten," declared one educator, "the child has learned that now means this minute, and not the next . . . he has learned self-control in the degree suited to his age . . . he had gained the power to distinguish—that first condition of clear knowing and thinking." Or, as another teacher insisted: "The kindergarten . . . should train the child in social habits, he should know when to subordinate himself for the good of the whole. . . . He should be trained in habits of obedience, attention, concentration, orderliness and the like." [11] So, too, not only did various businessmen applaud the kindergarten idea (an endorsement that would carry weight with a school board), but some even established kindergartens for their own workers' children. They were quite ready to support and popularize a program that takes children "at the most impressionable time of life and trains them in honesty, efficiency, and morality," a system where they would "learn patriotic songs and stories of the great men who have made America what she is." [12]

Much of the attraction of the kindergartens, in fact much of the reason for the new emphasis on child welfare, lay in reformers' eagerness to promote the assimilation of the hordes of immigrants that were flooding American shores. Through the intervention of the kindergarten, the children of the foreign-born could be removed at an early age from an alien and ghetto environment and be introduced to American values and practices. "The Kindergarten as an Americanizer," was a familiar refrain among proponents who were determined to make children "the basis of our program of Americanization." "Wherever the public kindergarten exists," argued one superintendent, "there the first opportunity presents itself to make the point of contact with the immigrant's home. The kindergartner seeks it out with a view to garnering the children of kindergarten age." [13] And not only could this institution directly influence children, but through them it could also influence the immigrant family, perhaps even the entire foreign-born community. "As soon as we reach the child, we reach the mother also," and therefore "systematic visiting in the homes of kindergarten children is a prime necessity." In this way, "the kindergartner can point out to the mothers in immigrant families the necessity of covering and destroying garbage . . . guarding milk and other food against contamination . . . clearing the yard, road, and neighborhood of broken glass. . . . She may urge them to apply for their naturalization papers. . . . The kindergarten teacher can render service to the immigrant mother in helping her plan for the education of her children . . . in keeping the children in school regularly, in keeping her informed of the kinds of employment available for her children, and in advising her in the care to be exercised in the choice of clear-thinking companions for her children." [14]

Organizations like the New York Kindergarten Association, a confederation of some forty private kindergartens in the city during the Progressive period, gave special attention to the immigrant child and family. Its leaders repeatedly asserted that kindergartens would transform slum children into law-abiding American citizens. "Every kindergarten," boasted the Association's president in 1904, "takes fifty children out of the streets, puts them into cheerful surroundings, in relations with refined women, and makes them feel the attractiveness of cleanliness, order and courtesy. . . . It is a delightful school for many children whose earliest education would otherwise be received on the streets." The kindergarten also taught the child "that work has dignity, and that there is a real pleasure in the doing of it. . . . It is the unskilled whose lives are monotonous, and to whom work becomes a drudgery. . . . When a little child holds up a piece of work and says triumphantly, 'I did that all myself,' the keynote of a productive life is struck." [15] The New York Kindergarten Association self-consciously attempted to extend its influence from the child to the home. It organized Mothers' Clubs, using the meetings as the occasion to teach the newcomers American ways. Moreover, "the kindergartner," as the Association explained, "has a reason for calling at the homes of the children, and is welcome as no other visitor would be. . . . 'In the name of children' has been a key to open all inhospitable doors." The results justified the efforts; the children were being treated better. One immigrant mother was reported to have told a kindergartner: "I am ashamed of my rough ways when I see how patient you are with the children. I did not know before that you could make children behave if you were gentle with them." [16] And, no less important, mothers were learning good habits. Another mother was said to have exclaimed: "Why, I have to have a place for everything now and keep tidied up, or Mary will speak of it." [17]

It was but a short step from these claims to the more general view that the kindergartens were a critical bastion of social order, a way to prevent crime and delinquency. "The kindergarten," one advocate explained, "is the great educational agent of this age, and is the only factor which will accomplish what all reformatory measures of the State have failed to do. . . . It is cheaper to support kindergartens than prisons." And were this not enough, others insisted: "No one could be an anarchist who had kindergarten training in his childhood. He knows and loves beauty and would never be a part of a revolutionary mob to tear down and destroy beautiful monuments of art." [18]

Despite the obvious appeal of this rhetoric, the kindergartens must not be understood exclusively in terms of their promise to assimilate and to discipline the immigrant. The movement shared broader goals, to bring its knowledge of child training to all American families, to become the great transmitter of the ideology of educated motherhood to all classes. The immigrant stood most in need of its lessons, but every mother had to practice its precepts. Elizabeth Harrison, one of the most active promoters of kindergartens, set out their wider mandate in *A Study of Child Nature from the Kindergarten Standpoint* (1895), a book that went through fifty editions and was translated into eight foreign languages. Froebel, she explained, invented "The Science of Motherhood," and established that "the destiny of the nations lies far more in the hands of women—the mothers—than in the hands of those who possess power." Mothers' tasks, Harrison went on, represent "one of the greatest lines of the world's work . . . the understanding of little children, in order that they may be properly trained." [19] The task demanded much more than doing what seemed natural. "The mother's loving guidance can be changed from uncertain instinct into unhesitating insight. . . . Instinct is often overruled by others; insight makes the mother stand invincible for her child's right to be properly brought up." [20] And in keeping with this judgment, Harrison gave educated motherhood the status of a profession. Motherhood "demands of woman her highest endeavor. . . . It demands of her that she become a physician, an artist, a teacher, a poet, a philosopher, a priest. In return, it gives her an insight into science, into history, into art, into literature, into human nature." [21] Training the child was a vocation—a fascinating, stimulating, and mutually educative one.

The National Congress of Mothers, a powerful network of Mothers' Clubs, took its inspiration from the kindergarten movement.

The organization was the immediate result of a conference that the Chicago Kindergarten College sponsored and of the determination of the Congress' first president, Mrs. Theodore (Alice McLellan) Birney, to educate women and the nation "to recognize the supreme importance of the child." Birney, a graduate of Mt. Holyoke College, was well versed in the writings of Hall and Froebel; and Hall spoke frequently to the organization, publicized its programs, and even wrote the introduction to Birney's own book, *Childhood*. Birney was also able to persuade Phoebe Apperson Hearst, then living in Washington while her wealthy husband George served as California's senator, to underwrite the cost of the Congress. The very first meeting, held in Washington in 1897, attracted 2,000 delegates; there was broad press coverage and even a White House reception for its organizers.[22] Enthusiastic about the collective ability of educated women to promote child health and well-being, the delegates returned home to organize state associations that, in turn, sponsored Mothers' Clubs in towns and cities across the nation. In 1900, Iowa's association boasted that it had clubs in every county of the state, and "in some counties as many as sixteen have definite organizations." By 1910, twenty-one states had systems of Mothers' Clubs with 50,000 members; by 1920, thirty-six states had a membership of 190,000 women. In 1924 the Congress changed its name to the Parents Teachers Association and continued to expand its influence.[23]

The Congress made its goal the "reconstruction of motherhood" for the benefit of child development. Specifically, it intended to use its organized efforts "to promote conferences (united action) on the part of parents concerning questions most vital to the welfare of the children, the manifest interest of the home, and, in general, the elevation of mankind." True to the precepts of educated motherhood, it sought "to inculcate the love of humanity and love of country, to encourage closer relations between home influences and school life, to promote kindergarten principles from cradle to college, to seek to create in all those characteristics which shall elevate and ennoble."[24] The Association turned logically to women to achieve these aims. "It is natural," declared Birney, "that women should lead in the awakening of mankind to a sense of responsibilities resting upon the race, to provide each newborn soul with an environment which will foster its highest development."[25]

The Congress hoped that the very pervasiveness of the clubs would promote success. "Any woman can organize a mothers' club," Birney assured the delegates. "She need not have either wealth, high social position or learning. She needs for her equipment only an earnest desire for knowledge herself and a maternal love which can embrace other children as well as her own." And the Congress encouraged the organization of clubs among a variety of women. There were to be clubs for mothers with children in school, so as to encourage communication between teachers and parents ("The school is but the broadening out of the home life; the home should be in the school and the school projected back again in the home"),[26] and clubs for women whose children had already left home ("They have time to devote to improving the general conditions affecting children . . . and can do it far better than those who have had no study of childhood and no experience with children"). Clubs for women living in cities would directly combat urban social evils ("One of the great reasons why more children go wrong in the city than in the country is because the natural avenues for their normal development are closed to them").[27] Clubs were also to bring in the immigrant mother ("The woman with leisure can do no greater missionary work than to organize mothers' clubs among her less favored sisters, the mothers who, while not lacking maternal love, are hampered through ignorance in the discharge of their duties").[28] Regardless, then, of social standing or locality, women were to work to create a better life for children and raise the quality of the citizenry of the nation.

While the rhetoric of the Congress may have seemed one more paean to motherhood, the organization was, in fact, an effective lobby for implementing social policy in accord with the precepts of educated motherhood. The Congress first set out to secure legislation giving mothers equal guardianship with their husbands over their children. It also supported the establishment of kindergartens in every school of the nation and playgrounds in every town and city. The Congress endorsed legislation on behalf of the dependent and deviant child. In place of orphan asylums, it advocated a system of foster homes, and in place of almshouses it lobbied for widow's pensions. So, too, the Congress worked to organize a network of juvenile courts, and local clubs collected funds to underwrite the salaries of probation officers and social workers.[29]

The founders of the Congress were so determined to educate women for motherhood that they advocated special courses for women college students. Not that they objected to a broad liberal education; rather, they wanted to establish chairs in child study (where Hall's students could spread his teachings) and courses in public schools and state universities on domestic science (to teach girls how best to fulfill their ultimate responsibility). "The higher branches of book learning are well enough for the girl or woman who has the inclination and time for them," declared Birney, "but they should be secondary in her education to the knowledge that shall fit her for motherhood." [30] Educated motherhood was to create "more ideal surroundings for its children; to purify the fountains of evil and render reform need-less." [31] The Congress was confident of fulfilling this extensive pro-gram. "One of the most hopeful signs of the times," concluded Birney, "is that evil of all kinds is now dragged fearlessly forth from its noisome dens into the light of day. . . . As soon as the men and women of America are fully awake to the dangers to which their ignorance gives rise, there will be such appreciation of the rights of children to be well born, wisely bred and trained, as will place parenthood where it justly belongs as the *highest of all vocations.*" [32]

Education for Reform

The ideology of educated motherhood had still another appeal and significance. It integrated two experiences that before the Progres-sive era appeared to be at odds with one another: the duties of mother-hood and the value of a college education. Educated motherhood made college training for women seem almost indispensable to the tasks of motherhood. This point was clear in the rhetorical flourishes of Eliza-beth Harrison. It emerged no less dramatically in the rationales for women's colleges.

The number of college-educated women climbed dramatically in the opening decades of the twentieth century. Some 85,000 women were enrolled in colleges in 1900; by 1920, the number reached a quarter of a million. In fact, the number of women graduates began to approximate the number of men graduates; 17 percent of all col-lege alumni in 1900 were women; by 1920, 40 percent. [33] Much of this rise did reflect the successful response of the women educators to the charges of late nineteenth-century doctors—clearly, a college education posed no peril to a woman's health; on the contrary, the regimen seemed to promote it. That fact alone helped to establish the legitimacy of the enterprise and to generate more applications. But then, as the notion that a college education was actually an advantage to would-be mothers gained popularity, it made even more sense (and became still more socially acceptable) for women to enter the university. "It seems to me," one editorial writer for the National Congress of Mothers declared in 1909, "that any sensible young man would place his happiness in the hands of a college girl. When children come to her, all the inherited instinct of motherhood is supplemented by a trained and disciplined mind. She will not ignorantly stupefy her infant with drugs . . . nor feed it with cake and ice-cream. . . . As the child grows older, she will keep pace with its education. No boy of hers will get to that sorrowful age when he feels that he knows a great deal more than his mother. She can be his companion and friend for all time." [34] No wonder, then, that young girls hearing this rhetoric moved easily to the campus.

The presidents of women's colleges were also comfortable with such a statement of principles. It provided them with a compelling, if by no means exclusive, rationale for women's education, and one that turned attention away from the fact that for women a bachelor of arts degree would not open up opportunities for post-graduate, professional education as it did for men. Although women made up 40 percent of the college graduates, they composed only 15 percent of the Ph.Ds. In 1920, about 53,000 men were enrolled in professional programs (law, medicine, and the like), but only 4,000 women. Indeed, between 1910 and 1930, women represented only 10 percent of the nation's doctors and only 2 percent of its lawyers.[35] Julia Lathrop, the chief of the Children's Bureau, noted that in a few professional schools "women have been more or less painfully admitted, but they remain men's schools for men's pursuits and the great foundations for original research are men's foundations." [36]

Under these circumstances, to have advertised a college education for women solely as a vehicle for upward occupational mobility would have been at once false and foolhardy. Accordingly, M. Carey Thomas, head of Bryn Mawr, warmly embraced and promoted the doctrines of educated motherhood as one justification for a college training. "Women cannot conceivably be given an education too broad, too high, or too deep to fit them to become the educated mothers of the future race of men and women born of educated parents. . . . They must think straight, judge wisely, reverence truth, and they must teach such clear and wise and reverent thinking to their children." The pity was that "we only have the four years of the college course to impart such knowledge to women who are to be mothers." [37] Alice Freeman Palmer, president of Wellesley, celebrated this same judgment. "The smallest village, the plainest home, give ample space for the resources of the trained college woman. And the reason why such homes and such villages are so often barren of grace and variety is just because these fine qualities have not ruled them. . . . Little children under five years of age die in needless thousands because of the dull, unimaginative women on whom they depend. Such women have been satisfied with just getting along, instead of packing everything they do with brains, instead of studying the best possible way of doing everything small or large; for there is always a best way, whether of setting a table, of trimming a hat, or teaching a child to read. And this taste for perfection can be cultivated; indeed, it must be cultivated, if our standards of living are to be raised." [38] One can hardly distinguish this rhetoric from that of the National Congress of Mothers.

In following this charge, some female students enrolled in humanities courses (English was one of the most popular majors in the women's colleges) and occasionally took a course in child study or home economics. They were ready to realize the benefits of a liberal education in running their own households, to fulfill the precepts of those educators who insisted that "the home offers an opportunity for the spending of every treasure and the use of every power. The well-trained mind finds in the home a chance for using its training." [39] But other female students discovered that the colleges were providing another series of courses that interested them still more, the new offerings in the social sciences. What they learned there was the public, as opposed to the private, message of educated motherhood—the notion that educated motherhood demanded community leadership from the college woman; or, in the words of M. Carey Thomas, "that practically all women . . . must look forward after leaving college to some form of public service." [40] It was a critical lesson for them and, indeed, for American society. Under its impact, as we shall soon see, female college graduates became a major force in shaping and implementing Progressive social policy.

During the closing decades of the nineteenth century, the social sciences began to enter many college curriculums. It was social science of a special sort, however—that is, an effort to investigate very specifically the nature of social problems, something very close to what we now consider to be social work. By 1888, Bryn Mawr was offering its students a course in "Charities and Corrections," and a few years later Vassar followed suit. By 1903, an undergraduate at Smith could choose from among such offerings as: Principles of Economics, Some Economic Problems, Recent Economic Changes, Charities and Corrections, Urban Social and Economic Conditions, Rural Social and Economic Conditions.[41] These courses, to be sure, were no less often taught at men's colleges, but they were undoubtedly more important to the women students precisely because the women would not be going on to professional schools. The social sciences for them were not the background to a career, but the career itself.

The career promised to be both worthy and useful. The approach of the social sciences to social problems was wonderfully energizing, filled with optimism and a sense of opportunity. The analysis was heavily structural—the causes of poverty, for example, almost always rested outside the individual, in the low wages received or the illnesses or industrial accidents needlessly suffered. As soon as society recognized the sources of these problems, as soon as it had the data at hand, then amelioration would come. As social reform abandoned its traditionally moralistic judgments on poverty and substituted an understanding of environmental causes, genuine social progress was certain. Hence the charge to the students was clear: abandon the emphasis on virtue that dominated their parents' generation, investigate social reality at first hand, compile the data, publicize it, and then lobby for legislation. In sum, use the principles of educated motherhood to improve not simply the well-being of one's own family but that of all society as well.

One of the clearest examples of the Progressive attitude toward social problems, one that captures the essence of the kinds of lessons that the college women were learning, is Robert Hunter's tract, *Poverty* (1904). Hunter himself was a college graduate and a product of a university training in the social sciences, and *Poverty* demonstrated the impact of that training. Hunter opened with a sophisticated description of the extent of poverty, coming to the then-startling conclusion that 14 percent of the population in good times and 20 percent in hard times were in distress; in absolute numbers, ten million Americans were in poverty.[42] Hunter went on to locate the causes of poverty very specifically in unemployment, sickness, injury, and excessively low wages that did not allow a worker to "maintain a state of physical efficiency." Dismissing the efficacy of the good housekeeping advice of friendly visitors, Hunter insisted that "there are also many, many thousand families who receive wages so inadequate that no care in spending, however wise it may be, will make them suffice for the family needs." [43]

Hunter broke away from the rigid dichotomy that had traditionally divided the poor into the worthy and unworthy, the moral and the immoral. To be sure, he could not escape the classification altogether —he did concede that there would always remain a group of paupers who should be punished rather than relieved. Yet, at his most innovative, Hunter set this group aside, treating the great majority of the poor as the deserving poor. He made eminently clear that poverty was not a fixed state (once poor, always poor), but rather a condition through which the lower classes moved regularly, sometimes climbing out of it, other times sinking back into it. Borrowing freely from the work of the English student of poverty, Seebohm Rowntree, Hunter described a life cycle of poverty—the typical unskilled laborer fared well right after marriage (when there were no children to support), worse as he started a family, better as the children grew up and entered the work force themselves, and then worse again in old age (when the children were gone and he was too feeble to earn decent wages). In all, Hunter made clear that objective conditions, and not personal habits, determined the fate of most working men.[44]

However grim and discouraging such an analysis might at first appear, contemporaries found the diagnosis liberating. "Those in poverty," asserted Hunter, "are fighting a losing struggle, because of the unnecessary burdens which we might lift from their shoulders." [45] As soon as social legislation improved tenement conditions, protected the worker against accidents, and improved his and his family's health, then the miseries of poverty would be alleviated. And then, of course, poor families would fare better and their children would have the right diets, the necessary attention, and the opportunity for schooling. Social reform was all one interlocked agenda—intervene where you would and the prospects for improvement were excellent.

This was an exciting, even heady, approach to social problems, and not surprisingly, college women pursued it diligently. Just how diligently is apparent in the appearance on almost every women's college campus of good government clubs, municipal leagues, and civic clubs. The Radcliffe Civics Club, for example, aimed "to prepare the undergraduates of Radcliffe to become active, intelligent, useful citizens, leaders in the community into which they are going after graduation." As one student member explained: "It unites in a single active body the undergraduate suffragist, anti-suffragist, and socialist chapters, college chapters of the Women's Municipal League of Boston and of the Women's Peace Party, and a debating committee." [46] To these same ends, student government appeared on the campuses offering, as in the case of the council at Barnard, "training in self-control, self-direction and democracy, and opening up horizons of usefulness and ability." Undergraduates also worked in settlement houses during their summer vacations. Bryn Mawr, for example, supported a settlement house in Long Branch, New Jersey where girls could live during their holidays. The colleges, too, began to administer community programs so that students would read to the blind or teach English to new immigrants. [47]

The knowledge acquired in the classroom, joined to the principles of educated motherhood, encouraged college graduates to confront the problems that industrialization, urbanization, and immigration posed. The new generation of women reformers were not overwhelmed by this trinity of social forces. To the contrary—one is struck by the exuberance and confidence with which they addressed the most wretched conditions. Theirs was to be a novel approach— they would not emulate their mothers' or grandmothers' programs —and the very originality of the design augured well for its success. No one made this point more forcefully than Florence Kelley, one of the three or four most energetic and skillful Progressive reformers. "For our grandmothers, at our age," argued Kelley, "philanthropic work was simple enough: neighborly help of those less comfortably placed." But times had changed: "For the thinking woman of our generation, the vital question is no longer between giving doles to street beggars on the one hand, or supporting the associated charities on the other." Moralism was an insufficient basis on which to do good. "Shall I preach temperance to men whose homes are vile tenements? . . . Shall I fritter away the days of my youth investigating the deservingness of this or that applicant for relief when the steady march of industrial development throws a million able-bodied workers out of employment?" [48] Instead Kelley proposed that college women "cast their lot with the workers" and aid them in organizing cooperative ventures (like labor unions) that would eliminate the miseries of poverty. We must, Kelley contended, "seek to understand the laws of social and industrial development in the midst of which we live, to spread this enlightenment among the men and women destined to contribute to the change to a higher social order, to hasten the day when all the good things of society shall be the good of the children or men, and our petty philanthropy of today superfluous. This is the true work for the elevation of the race, the true philanthropy." [49]

The College Dormitory in the Ghetto

All of these themes came together in the organization of the most Progressive of institutions, the settlement house. Although many ideas and impulses contributed to the movement, the experience of women in colleges and in clubs and the commitment of women to the ideology of educated motherhood were among the most important and creative sources for this highly unusual venture. The first settlement house began in London at Toynbee Hall, but it was Americans who most actively established these associations. By 1900, nearly one hundred settlement houses had opened in American cities, including Hull House in Chicago, Dennison House in Boston, and the Henry Street Settlement in New York. And it was college graduates, particularly women college graduates, who took up residence in the heart of the immigrant ghettos.[50]

It was an exciting prospect. Rather than remaining cloistered in their families' middle-class parlors, or even in college classrooms, the women would experience the reality of life, the "natural" as opposed to the "artificial." "Ever since my Oxford days," Vida Scudder, one of the founders of Boston's Dennison House, later recalled, "I had been beating my wings against the bars, the customs, the assumptions of my own class. I moved in a garden enclosed, if not in a hot-house, an enclosure of gracious manners, regular meals, comfort, security, good taste. I liked balmy air. Yet sometimes it suffocated me." Scudder was desperate for an adventure but had no urge to explore the "Gobi Desert or to seek the Pole." Hers was "a biting curiosity about the way the Other Half lived, and a strange hunger for friendship with them. Were not the workers, the poor, nearer perhaps than we to the reality I was always seeking?" [51]

The internal organization of the settlement houses was very reminiscent of the college. "It was startling," reported one visitor, "to find the atmosphere of a college dormitory in the center of the slums." [52] The building itself was typically a large, imposing, and well-maintained structure in the midst of an otherwise uninviting block of tenement houses; its living accommodations duplicated those of residence halls; the residents shared bedrooms and ate their meals together in a common dining room. Intellectual discourse was basic to the settlement house milieu. Guests frequently came from the up-town neighborhoods or from the university itself for dinner; lectures and formal discussions were frequent, good talk and hearty friend-ship in abundance. "Our fellowship was life giving," noted Scudder. "It pointed academic training to the finest ends of citizenship." [53] Henry Demerest Lloyd was probably not exaggerating when he called Hull House "the best club in Chicago." [54]

But the purposes of the settlement went beyond providing interest-ing company and conversation. The first ambition of the residents was to test—or, more properly, to apply—the theories that they had learned in their social science courses. "The city," declared Richard Mayo-Smith, one of the first university professors in sociology, "is the natural laboratory of social science, just as hospitals are of medi-cal science." [55] And the settlement house residents took this principle as their starting point. Scudder described the settlements as "a socio-logical laboratory where the patient, accurate and sympathetic ob-server may get at the truth." Living in the ghetto provided "the first-hand knowledge the college classroom cannot give," and the "actual experience of social and industrial conditions [was] a salutary correc-tive to theoretic study." Yet it was not knowledge for its own sake that the house residents sought. As Scudder explained: "He who would combat effectively the ills of our body politic: ignorance, poverty, crime, political corruption and moral disease—must see things as they are and reason from intimate and comprehensive knowl-edge as to cause and cure." [56]

Even this goal, however, was not sufficient. The settlement house founders aimed to do service while they studied and formulated social policies, to bring the principles of right living that they had learned to the ghetto. "The settlement resident," continued Scudder, "is not content with scientific generalizations, but quickly passes from im-personal observation to personal helpfulness." The residents were "social servants"—that is, servants of a special sort, not the "friendly visitors" that their mothers had been (making forays into the ghetto only to go back again); rather, they were "settlers," "actuated by the simple human desire to share—and to share their choicest possessions, those of mind and heart. . . . They were not only to teach but to learn; not only to give, but to get." [57] In this spirit, Helen Cheever, after her first day at Dennison, noted in the House Diary: "We have come here to be good citizens and good neighbors." [58]

The settlement house moved to carry out these commitments in ways that reflected the special experience of middle-class women in general and college-educated women in particular. First, they, like their mothers before them, were eager to influence and educate the poor through direct and personal encounters. But they altered the nature of the encounter—they were neighbors in the ghetto, not casual visitors to the slum—and the message—instruction in hygiene and child development took precedence over lessons in frugal housekeeping, virtue, and temperance. At the same time, the settlement house workers wished to formulate and enact structural legislative reforms. They wanted to bring their first-hand knowledge of the proper rules of hygiene not only to immigrant families but to state legislators; they looked to translate their first-hand knowledge of the conditions of poverty into a broad political program. Thus, the settlement house workers agitated to end child labor not so much because of the seeming immorality of the setting, but because of its threat to the physical growth and well-being of the child. The machine did not corrupt as much as it maimed and stunted. Progressive-minded women aimed to pass protective legislation for all female workers, defining them as potential mothers. Again, it was not their fear of vice but of ill health that was most acute. In sum, through settlement house activities, the women could use their particular insights to effect basic changes. "The Settlement," in Vida Scudder's summary, "aims to attain a permanency. . . . It aims to bring to bear on the seemingly hopeless misery of our great cities that spiritual help, that uplifting life, which comes through the power of a broad and organized effort. . . . The movement can . . . be the expression of great convictions; the conviction of our women of the new order." [59]

Some of the programs and activities that took place within the settlement house represented a self-conscious and even somewhat heavy-handed effort to make the immigrant over into the image of educated mothers. Appropriately, the house clubs were at the core of this enterprise, an almost direct translation of popular female associations into the special environment of the ghetto. The variety of clubs was incredible. The typical settlement house offered some twenty or more, but all of them had a pedagogical base: to teach the newcomers American values and practices. Some were modeled on the literary societies (studying American history or Shakespeare or English literature); others provided instruction in sewing or cooking (or carpentry for boys), and still others were devoted to drama and arts. Another range of clubs existed for the young, typically combining play with military drill. The Neighborhood Cadet Club, the Order Club, and the Improvement Club were parts of New York's University Settlement House offering, and their titles accurately represented their purposes.[60]

Predictably, many settlement houses organized a Mothers' Club. Henry Street, for example, created one in 1898, and it was still operating thirty years later. Its aim was to educate immigrant women to the doctrines of child welfare; the meetings consisted of lectures on child care, the necessity of play for building good muscles, the importance of regular habits to developing good character, and the significance of school attendance in promoting vocational advancement. The Mothers' Club also taught the value of giving growing children fresh milk, scheduling regular medical and dental check-ups, and keeping houses clean and sanitary—all to the end of preventing disease.[61]

Whatever the subject matter, the clubs were almost identical in structure. Every club elected its own officers, so that members received lessons in democratic processes. Every club collected dues (however nominal the sum), so that its members learned lessons in saving. Every club insisted on regular and prompt attendance, so its members acquired habits of punctuality. And the drill and exercise clubs for the young were even more obvious attempts to encourage orderly habits. In essence, the clubs aimed at character training. "Clubs and classes," insisted Mary Simkovitch, the head worker at Greenwich House, "mean that people learn right living through social relationships. If I learn to be fair, to play fair, to judge fairly when I am twelve years old in the club, I can see things straighter and act more squarely later on when I am thrown into those larger organizations of politics and trade unions." [62]

The settlements also used the clubs to promote American types of voluntary welfare organizations among the immigrants. At least one purpose of the annual outings that the settlement houses ran (beyond introducing the tenement dweller to the healthful air of the country) was to encourage a sense of mutuality of interests—and then to channel it into the formation of formal mechanisms for neighbors to assist neighbors. Thus the settlements established a cooperative loan fund; each member made a regular contribution, with the right to draw on it in times of need. A member would borrow five to ten dollars and return it in payments of twenty cents a week. In this way, her immediate needs would be met while she learned the lessons of mutual help, thrift, and responsibility. In a similar spirit, the settlement houses organized "visitation committees"; their members, as the Henry Street club explained, were "to call on those who are sick or in trouble and they take a present for friendship." [63] While one should properly note that the immigrants did not need such instruction (the church and synagogue poor funds knew about mutual help quite well), the settlement house workers were determined to recreate their own kind of organizations among the poor. Just as they visited the sick and brought gifts, so should the immigrant. Just as they saved money for hard times, so should the immigrant.

But settlement houses did not rest content with giving advice to the newcomers. They not only taught the immigrant women the rules of educated motherhood, but also provided them with some essential services for raising healthy children. The settlement houses often included a kindergarten in their activities so that mothers could bring children to these habit-training sessions; they ran playgrounds so that families could leave their older boys and girls at the House under supervision. They also distributed fresh milk and arranged appointments for medical and dental check-ups. Further, the settlement houses served as a critical intermediary between the immigrants and the institutions of the outside community. "We stand between the various organizations of the city and the people for whom they are intended," reported Katharine Davis, for a time headworker at the Philadelphia College Settlement. "We act as a bureau of information, often as an intelligence office. We look after the sanitary conditions of the neighborhood, report nuisances, try to have the streets properly cleaned, appeal to the Councils for more electric lights—and get them." [64]

Settlement house intervention frequently took on a still more specific character. The worker would refer a member to the appropriate charitable society for assistance and then vouch for her character when the society conducted an investigation. The worker was often the link between the school and the immigrant parent, frequently accompanying a nervous mother to a discussion with the principal or teacher. By the same token, the settlement workers invited the teachers to come to the House so that they could have a fresh and inside look at the community life of their pupils. [65]

The workers also assisted families in their dealings with the courts. They would accompany a mother to speak with a juvenile court judge, explaining the court's workings and decisions to the parent and at the same time giving the judge the kind of social information he wanted on the family. The workers might even become probation officers for youngsters deemed in need of supervision.[66]

Some settlement houses even attempted to create jobs for the unemployed as a form of work relief. Convinced of the significance of structural as opposed to moral causes for poverty, they were eager (in however limited a way, given their resources), to hire men out of work to paint or to repair the House. Their efforts, as they fully understood, were wholly inadequate to the scale of the problem, but they were self-consciously attempting to set a model for a new type of assistance: the dignity of a job would replace the charitable society's donation of a bag of groceries or coal. "The ordinary relief agencies," insisted Helena Dudley, headworker at Dennison House, "may be adequate in dealing with poverty resulting from incompetence, drunkenness, idleness, sickness or old age"; they did not, however, "have the machinery to help men and women thrown out of work by industrial depressions." [67] Not that the Settlement House possessed that machinery either—but at least its members would make the general point in practical terms: to give the poor jobs, not a dole.

The settlement house programs to train immigrants to citizenship and provide them with necessary services was part of a still grander goal: to make the immigrants a force for Progressive change. As educated mothers, they would join the ranks of reformers. The discussion clubs and mothers' clubs debated such issues as, "What is wrong with our tenements?" and "Should women have the vote?" Henry Street frankly encouraged its members to lobby for legislation to improve ghetto conditions. "Running New York," its *Bulletin* declared, "is just a big housekeeping job, just like your own home, only on a larger scale. Therefore you should be interested in city-wide affairs." Appropriately, the settlement organized a delegation of members to go to Albany "to ask the Governor for better housing for themselves and for all the people in the tenement." [68]

Indeed, settlement house organizers were persuaded that offering immigrant mothers child welfare services and teaching them social responsibilities would help to achieve a critical political reform: ridding the ghetto, and ultimately the polity, of the corruptions of the ward boss. This was no simple task. The ward boss ruled, as Jane Addams explained in her marvelously perceptive phrase, because he was a "stalking survival of village kindness." Her intimate knowledge of immigrant life made Addams fully aware of just how many and how vital were the functions that the boss fulfilled for his constituents. "Last Christmas," she recounted, "our Alderman distributed six tons of turkeys, and four or more tons of ducks and geese. . . . Inevitably some got three or four apiece, but what of that? He had none of the nagging rules of the charitable societies, nor was he ready to declare that because a man wanted two turkeys for Christmas, he was a scoundrel." Addams recognized that "the Alderman is really elected because he is a good friend and neighbor"—and it was the task of the settlement workers to become even better friends and neighbors if politics were to be freed of the machine.[69]

The campaign took many forms. The lectures on citizenship were part of it; so were the efforts to improve the delivery of municipal services. If the settlement house could get streets paved or cleaned or provide jobs or relief, then the boss would be that much less important. The settlement workers also launched a crusade against the saloon—not only because they, too, defined temperance as a worthy goal and preferred husbands to be at home with their families, but also because they recognized the close tie between the saloon and ward political life. "By attracting men from the saloon," declared Elizabeth Williams, the headworker of the New York College Settlement, the settlements "are removing them from the local headquarters of the organization"; more, by "providing opportunities for recreation, they cause them [the men] to cease looking to the political leaders for their pleasure." [70]

Some settlements moved directly into the political arena, putting up their own candidates, campaigning vigorously, and canvassing the neighborhood before election to get out the vote. In the 1890s, for example, Hull House workers took on the local boss, Johnny Powers. They charged that Powers was responsible for "incomparably filthy, ill-paved, and snowladen streets . . . scant public school accommodations, rapidly increasing tenements, lack of small parks and playgrounds. . . . taxation that favors the corrupt and oppresses the honest." They brought in speakers to campaign for their candidate, a forty-two-year-old Irish immigrant who belonged to their own Men's Club. Still, Powers won, and Addams knew why: "He is not elected because he is dishonest. He is elected because he is a friendly visitor." And as if to confirm her analysis, Powers went on to give a job to practically every member of Hull House's Men's Club.[71]

Finally, the settlement workers, in their direct encounter with the immigrants, attempted to encourage the formation of unions. Here they confronted not only the hostility of their own board members (whose companies might be the objects of such action), but sometimes even that of the labor organizers themselves. (Samuel Gompers once complained, "The workers are not bugs to be examined under the lens of a microscope by intellectuals on a sociological slumming tour.") [72] Nevertheless, at a moment when unionization was widely perceived as a radical and distinctly un-American scheme, the settlement residents played a significant role in defending and stimulating such ventures. Further, the unions exemplified the power of a cooperative enterprise, a variant of their own clubs and organizations. As Chicago settlement house leader Graham Taylor put it: "If the trade unions . . . were better understood . . . they would generally be regarded . . . as the most practical bond of brotherhood next to the Christian Church." [73] In more tangible terms, unions would obtain higher wages for their members, thereby enabling families to save for times of unemployment and illness. Higher wages would also mean that mothers would not have to go out to work, take in boarders, or sit and do piecework (with the children) in order to supplement a husband's meager income. Children would be able to attend school, receive nutritious food, grow up in more airy and clean apartments—in all, to live healthier and fuller lives under their mothers' close supervision.

Accordingly, settlement house loan funds were used to support their own members and outsiders who were on strike. Henry Street, for example, gave money to striking workers on the Lower East Side and in Passaic as well. And if the sums were nominal, the symbolic importance of the donation was not. Jane Addams, for her part, spoke frequently on the workers' need to organize and defended the right to strike even at the most heated moments, during the Pullman strike in 1894 and the Chicago building trade strike in 1900. The settlement houses also assisted in the formation of such unions as the National Women's Trade Union League and the Women's Clerk Benefit Association. They gave their rooms over as meeting halls, and the settlement residents assumed such positions as treasurer in the fledgling organizations. All of these activities fit neatly in the broader agenda of the settlement house: to the degree that unions helped men to earn a decent living, they allowed women to fulfill the precepts of educated motherhood. [74]

The second major strategy of the settlement house workers was to promote reform through legislative action. For all the value placed on personal interaction with the immigrant, they never lost sight of the need to effect social change through the expanded power of the state. There was just so much that the most well-intentioned immigrant mothers could accomplish on their own; many, perhaps even most, problems were beyond their control—and the state, therefore, had to intervene on their behalf, to correct the imbalances in power for their best interest.

And there was just so much that even the most energetic settlement house could do to improve conditions for the immigrant child and its family, even within its immediate district. If the settlement house residents were to raise up the standard of living not only for their own neighbors but for all of the poor, if they were to improve the life chances for the young not only in their ghetto but in all ghettos, structural change through state intervention had to be achieved. "We cannot change the heart of man by legislation," conceded Helena Dudley. "As long as it is full of wickedness, we can expect him to do evil. By legislation, however, where civic consciousness is aroused, we can tear down unsanitary houses, we can have more parks, we can have kindergartens and industrial training schools, libraries and museums. Work can be furnished for the unemployed and adequate provision can be made for the sick and aged without loss of self respect." [75] This judgment put settlement house residents in the forefront of Progressive ranks.

Although a panoply of reforms came together under the Progressive banner, the settlement house workers gave unprecedented attention to elevating the welfare of the child. And most significantly, they attempted to fulfill this mandate by expanding the responsibilities of the school. The school had to do much more than teach the three Rs. It was to promote physical, emotional, social, and occupational development of the child; it had to make him healthy, happy, and upwardly mobile. Mary Simkovitch, the headworker at Greenwich House, set out the credo in defining the "enlarged function" of the public school: "The work of the New York schools is not so much to create students as to make men, and this thought of developing the whole child and seeing him in relation to his family and his neighborhood and his industrial environment makes of the school a better and more important thing than it has ever been in the past." [76]

This novel definition of school activities reflected the reformers' commitment to the precepts of educated motherhood and their sense of the distance that prevented immigrant parents from realizing these precepts. The school was to compensate for and correct maternal ignorance. Since mothers were not attentive enough to child health, lessons in nutrition became part of the curriculum, and so did annual medical and dental examinations. Children needed exercise; hence playgrounds were added to the school facilities, and even occasionally a swimming pool. The school nurse came on to the staff, not only to look after the children and teach them the rules of hygiene, but to visit their homes and instruct their mothers as well.[77] Some schools added evening civic clubs to their programs, trying to make themselves into neighborhood centers. Indeed, the school almost seemed to be another kind of settlement house—and John Dewey, the leading Progressive educational reformer, made the comparison explicit. Dewey's ideal school looked much more like Hull House than the institution first imagined by Horace Mann.[78]

The Progressive school resembled the settlement house in still another way: it took as its agenda the narrowing of the gap between social classes. The presence of the college girls in the ghetto was one step in this direction. Dewey added another: the provision of manual training in the classroom, the teaching of workplace skills to the immigrant children so as to enable them to climb the American ladder of success. The school, as Dewey explained, was to remedy the "social deficiencies" in the outside society. Heretofore, Dewey argued, it had served only the needs of the intellectual and social elite, in effect widening the distance between social classes. "The old schools were not conducted to give equal opportunity to all, but for just the opposite purpose, to make more marked the line between classes, to give the leisure and moneyed classes something which everyone could not get, to cater to their desire for distinction." [79] The Progressive school, on the other hand, would democratize education—and thus democratize society—by making the curriculum more practical. "When schools were for people who did not earn their own living," whose major interest was "to be accomplished, polished and socially interesting," then "the material was abstract, purposely separated from the concrete and useful." Now that education was to serve everybody, the materials had to become relevant, "concrete, and useful." [80]

Manual training, or industrial training as it was known in the Progressive period, was to realize this new definition of purpose. Adding manual training to the curriculum placed the vocational needs of the lower-class children on the same plane as the intellectual knowledge sought by the upper classes. It provided children with the necessary skills to advance their careers. The point was not to train a child for one specific job, but to improve his dexterity and give him a practical knowledge that would enable him to fill many sorts of jobs. "Industrial education," as one proponent explained, "should not fit the child for any particular industrial work, but for any work to which, in the exigencies of life, he may be forced to turn his attention. It should expand and increase his resources and his confidence in himself." [81] Thus, the Gary, Indiana school system (that tried to become the model of Progressive education) employed "direct manual experience in construction work,"—that is, "giving the pupils the reasons for the methods employed, a knowledge of the more important properties of materials used, some idea as to where these materials come from and how they are manufactured, and how similar work is done under commercial conditions." [82]

These lessons would teach skills and good character. Dewey often equated manual training with an appreciation for old-fashioned artisan work. In quite nostalgic terms, he explained that when fathers worked at crafts at home, there were "factors of discipline and of character-building involved in this kind of life; training in habits of order and of industry, and in the idea of responsibility, an obligation to do something, to produce something in the world." [83] Now that fathers were in the factories, now that they were so typically immigrants and unskilled, some other institution would have to assume the function. For Dewey, and for the Progressives, that institution was the school. Character training and manual training were one and the same.

The Progressive school, attractive in and of itself, was also a highly desirable alternative to the factory. The practice that most shamefully violated the precepts of educated motherhood was child labor, and reformers unanimously concluded that its "evils . . . cannot well be exaggerated." [84] No environment was more noxious for a child than the factory: it was unhealthy and dangerous; it stunted growth; it robbed children of childhood. Doctors, like George Kober, testified that "a large percentage of children engaged in workshops, factories, or even at the . . . merchant counter, develop lateral curvature of the spine and other muscular deformities, not to mention their general weakness and predisposition to rickets, tuberculosis, and other pulmonary diseases. All of the bad effects are . . . intensified by unsanitary conditions . . . the inhalation of dust, impure air and injurious gases." [85] Factory inspectors, like Florence Kelley, recounted dismal stories such as that of a twelve-year-old boy forced to work in a box factory and constantly exposed to "excessive heat and to incessant damage from burns." When Kelley met this boy he was seventeen, already lame, and "undersized with big hands and feet, pinched features and the carriage of an old man." [86] In fact, the female inspectors whose original charge (in keeping with the notions of purity of the late nineteenth-century reformers) was to check upon the morals of the factory girls, soon took a leading part in the Progressive crusade to abolish child labor. "There is only one thing that must ultimately tend to raise the physical and even moral standard of our women operatives," argued one inspector in 1892, "and that is . . . to put an end to the employment of young children in mills and shops. . . . Whatever tends to keep our children for a longer period at school . . . and away from the harmful physical and moral influence of early labor, must one day result in an improved condition of the industrial classes." [87]

Given these horrors, why would immigrant parents consign their children to so awful a fate? Part of the answer, reformers believed, was the newcomer's ignorance of what constituted the child's best interest. But they understood that the problem had deeper roots. A desperate economic need compelled immigrant families to think in short-run as opposed to long-run interests. The wages that the twelve-year-old brought home immediately were more important than the future benefits of an education to his career or even his health. The immigrants, as Florence Kelley explained, did not understand the self-defeating character of their decisions. "Wage-earning children are an unmitigated injury to themselves, to the community upon which they will later be burdens, and to the trades which they demoralize. . . . They lower the standard of living of the adults with whom they compete." [88] In other words, were child labor abolished, the salaries of wage-earning adults would rise. The father alone would then earn what the father and son now earned together.

Under such circumstances, Progressives did not hesitate to turn to the state to enforce a policy that they believed to be in everyone's best interest—to empower the factory inspector to prohibit child labor and at the same time to empower the truant officer to compel school attendance. It was, in fact, preferable to move simultaneously on both fronts: to remove the child from the factory and place him in the classroom. "We must have compulsory education of the school children under 16 years of age," insisted Kelley. "No factory law is so good for the children as a law which keeps them not only negatively out of the factories but positively at work acquiring industrial efficiency and value. . . . Only when every child is known to be in school can there be any security against the tenement-house labor of children in our great cities." [89]

These same assumptions about child development underlay the playground movement, the effort to provide recreational space, equipment, and supervision to children in the cities.[90] The principle was not a simple one—that play was enjoyable and fun. Rather, reformers contended that play was critical to a child's health; growing muscles demanded exercise. And naturally, play had to be appropriate to each stage of growth; pails and shovels for small children, jump ropes for the slightly older, and march and drill for the older still. The playgrounds also were to organize children's activities after kindergarten and school hours, taking another occasion to train them to right habits (as the ghetto streets surely would not). The playgrounds were always enclosed by gates and fences and the activities conducted under the watchful eye of a director, for, as Jacob Riis explained, "We believe that the temptations of the street are a bad thing for the boys. Playgrounds untended and poorly supervised simply make the bad things of the street more extensive." [91] The sessions were to begin promptly: "To open and close with punctuality," explained the chairwoman of the Boston Association of Playgrounds, "lends an air of seriousness and importance, and the children enjoy and respect a certain amount of discipline." [92] The supervisor's first task was to organize the children to clean up the playground and to put the equipment out in its proper place, thereby teaching neatness, cleanliness, and responsibility. And the games themselves trained the children "to play fair, keep clean and speak the truth." The playground supervisors, like the kindergarten teachers, were "to study the nature of the child and to so conduct the play as to guide the children and not necessarily to restrain them." In other words, play was one more way of inculcating order without repression, of being sensitive to the needs of the child and serving the community as well.

The settlement house workers' concern for the child led them to agitate for the delivery of a new kind of health care. At their insistence, the municipal departments of health created a special division on child hygiene, with a particular mandate to reduce infant and maternal mortality. Lillian Wald, headworker at the Henry Street Settlement, led the campaign to establish the New York City Bureau of Child Hygiene, and its first director, Dr. Josephine Baker, summarized its principles in very Progressive terms: "Control of child life, is more of a socio-economic than a medical problem . . . more a question of environmental adjustment, industrial opportunities, living wage and civic cooperation than of medical and nursing care, per se." [93] The New York Bureau, therefore, sought to accomplish its aims through the education of the mother and the improvement of ghetto conditions; the Bureau would also refer the sick to medical doctors for treatment, but this was not its primary purpose. The Bureau's motto clearly expressed its means and ends: "Better mothers, better babies, and better homes." [94]

Consistent with this definition, the New York Bureau relied on women trained in the care of children to administer its programs. The public health nurses, graduates of the recently established nursing schools, were the key figures (not doctors). They worked directly in the community (not out of hospitals) in Baby Health Stations, opened first as milk depots, where women in the tenement districts could receive pasteurized, grade-A milk at prices cheaper than those of the neighborhood stores. The Stations were soon offering hygienic advice on baby and child care and teaching expectant mothers rules on personal hygiene. To Dr. Baker, the sixty-eight stations that the city was administering in 1920 were "educational preventoria or prophylactic centres, dedicated to [the] policy of keeping well-babies and children well, and emphasizing the preventive rather than the curative side of child hygiene work." [95]

The municipal public health nurses also visited the homes of expectant mothers before, during, and after childbirth to offer health instruction. The more these women understood about hygienic care, the greater their child's chance for survival and the lower their own risks of serious complications in pregnancy and delivery. The nurses offered "advice and instruction in diet, hygiene, clothing, fresh air, exercise, rest, care of the breasts, skin and teeth." They administered urinary examinations and made appointments at dispensaries (for tuberculin and venereal disease tests) and at hospitals (for those with serious medical problems). They also referred women in need of relief to social welfare agencies. Finally, the public health nurses sent a few women to hospitals for delivery—those presenting "suspicious signs and symptoms, or histories of previous prolonged or complicated labor." [96] Medical intervention was sometimes necessary to prevent death during childbirth, but such cases were exceptional.

Advice on nutrition was prominent among the Bureau's activities. Despite the availability of pure milk from the Baby Health Stations, the nurses encouraged mothers to breast-feed their babies. Pasteurized milk was for older children; the infant deserved the breast. Breast-feeding at once promoted and demonstrated a close maternal tie between mother and child. In this way a woman trained herself to meet the infant's needs, and later, the child's needs.[97] Moreover, the Bureau taught mothers that fat babies were healthy babies; it scheduled fat babies to come less frequently to the Health Station for checkups than puny, undernourished ones. The Bureau conducted "better baby" contests to educate the public in the importance of food, rest, and exercise for proper child development. In all, fat babies represented to the Bureau the right training of the immigrant parent. Here was a sign that she had learned the precepts of educated motherhood.

Rather than limiting their hygienic programs to correcting individual habits, the women reformers insisted that social and economic changes were necessary in order to raise the level of health in the community. In 1912 the federal government, responding to the intensive lobbying of women like Lillian Wald and Florence Kelley, established the Children's Bureau to promote the health and welfare of the nation's children. President Taft appointed Julia Lathrop, a resident of Hull House for 20 years and a close friend of Jane Addams, as its first chief. One of the Bureau's first projects was to conduct extensive investigations into the etiology of infant mortality. Discovering that different communities had different rates of infant deaths, the Bureau concluded that environmental conditions as well as maternal knowledge affected child health. "Babies died when parents did not know how to give them the scientific care needed to keep them in health," and equally important, when "wages were low, when the home was overcrowded, when the community supply of milk or water was contaminated, when the general sanitation of the home was low." A reduction in the mortality rate demanded an improvement in the standard of living.[98]

Settlement house workers used this finding to justify their reform programs. Promoting community health demanded more than enforcing pure milk and pure water standards. Rather, tenements had to be improved, wages raised, schools expanded. The infant mortality rate was not merely a statistic on morbidity but an accurate gauge of the level of social progress in the nation. "The infant mortality rate," declared Dr. Josephine Baker, "is the most sensitive index of municipal housekeeping of a community. It is more than that; it is an index of civic interest, cooperation, consciousness and worth." [99] A community with a low infant mortality rate had good sanitation, pure milk, and pure water and enforced both its child labor and compulsory schooling laws; its wage earners received a living wage and its families were stable. Mothers who did not have to work in order to supplement inadequate male wages could and would devote full time to child-rearing, and full-time mothering was a prerequisite of proper maternal watchfulness. In short, a low infant mortality rate represented the success of child welfare reform.

The Coalition for Suffrage

The political consequences of the concepts of educated motherhood were nowhere more evident than in the passage of the Nineteenth Amendment to the Constitution, the winning of female suffrage. The victory did not reflect the triumph of a concept of equal rights—for the most part, women did not agitate for the right to vote as citizens.[100] Women fought for suffrage in order to bring their special qualities to the ballot box. Women deserved the vote not because they were the same as men, but precisely because they were different. To be sure, in one form or another, the idea of special womanly qualities had pervaded the suffrage movement from its inception in 1848. Why was it, then, that victory finally came in 1919? Why did it take almost three-quarters of a century for the women's campaign to succeed? Why only in the Progressive period did the argument about the special contribution of women to politics prove effective? The answer to these questions rests in the ability of a new definition of womanhood to accomplish what an earlier ideology could not, that is, to bridge the gap between social classes and create a political alignment powerful enough to gain women the vote.

Throughout the nineteenth century, suffragists pressed their claims by denouncing a system that deprived refined and virtuous middle-class women of a right that was accorded to corrupt and lower-class men. The first official document of the movement, the Declaration of Sentiments issued at the Seneca Falls Convention of 1848, complained bitterly that women, the guardians of morality, had less political power than vicious immigrants. "He has withheld from her rights," argued the Declaration, "which are given to the most ignorant and degraded men—both natives and foreigners." And this theme became still more important to the agitation in the following decades.[101]

The Woman's Suffrage Association and the WCTU became close allies, linking the campaign for suffrage with temperance. Anna Howard Shaw, vice-president of the National American Woman Suffrage Association, was a close friend of Frances Willard, the moving spirit of the WCTU; Mary Livermore, one of the leading publicists for suffrage, was the founder of the Massachusetts WCTU. Further, both movements were committed to the notion that women should enter every place (including the polling booth) and purify every place they entered (the world of politics). As one suffragist told a Congressional committee in 1884: "When you debar from your councils and legislative halls the purity, the spirituality and the love of woman, then those councils are apt to become coarse and brutal. God gave us to you to help you in this little journey to a better land, and by our love and our intellect to help make our country pure and noble." Or, in the words of another: "You, gentlemen, by lifting the women of the nation into political equality, would simply place us where we could lift you where you never yet have stood—upon a moral equality with us." Julia Ward Howe used these same arguments to galvanize support among women themselves. "How are you to reconcile this moral superiority which you are held to represent," she would ask rhetorically, "with this political inferiority, in which you are bound to acquiesce?" [102]

Implicit in all these appeals was the notion that the middle classes were to refine the lower classes, that middle-class values had to triumph over lower-class ones. Temperance was one critical part of this effort. To abolish the saloon was to uphold the middle-class virtues of hard work, sobriety, and concern for family. Suffrage was another critical part, on an even grander scale. As soon as women had the vote, they would translate their moral standards into legislative codes. "To those who fear that our American institutions are threatened by this gigantic inroad of foreigners," one New York suffragist told Congress in the 1880s, "the best safeguard against any such preponderance of foreign influence is to put the ballot in the hands of the American-born woman." [103] Or as Carrie Chapman Catt, president of the National American Woman Suffrage Association, argued in 1894: "The government is menaced with great danger. . . . That danger lies in the votes possessed by the males in the slums of the cities, and the ignorant foreign vote which was sought to be bought up by each party to make political success." Catt was certain that "there is but one way to avert the danger—cut off the vote of the slums and give to woman . . . the power of protecting herself . . . the ballot." [104] Closing the saloon and winning the suffrage were, in effect, two campaigns in the American middle-class war against the immigrant.

Under these circumstances, the suffrage movement did not seek political support from the lower classes, neither from its men nor from its women. The suffrage conventions did express in a pro forma annual resolution a concern for the working girl, but this was not enough to make her feel welcome or comfortable within the suffrage ranks. As late as 1906, one speaker at the Convention of the National American Woman Suffrage Association (NAWSA), Mrs. Gertrude Barnum, chided her fellow delegates for not developing a political platform that was relevant to lower-class women. "A speaker should have been chosen from their ranks," she told the delegates. "We have been preaching to them, teaching them, 'rescuing' them, doing almost everything for them except knowing them and working with them for the good of our common country." [105] But even as Barnum spoke, the suffragists were breaking out of the traditional mold, forging a new kind of alliance, using the precepts of educated motherhood to join the concerns of the middle and lower classes.

One of the first signs of change was Florence Kelley's address to the NAWSA in 1905, an address that revealed the new perspectives and strategies of settlement house workers. It was time to stop thinking of improving the lot of the working classes through the likes of a temperance movement, Kelley argued. Poverty had much deeper roots; the issue was not so much morality as external social and economic conditions. Low wages, industrial accidents, and the premature entry of children into the working force were at the root of the problem, not a lack of virtue or an excess of drink. The suffrage movement had little support among wage-earners because it was still identified with the WCTU. To them, "woman suffrage meant chiefly 'prohibition' and an effort should be made to convince them that it includes assistance in their own legislative measures." [106] In the end, she urged the delegates to put the precepts of educated motherhood at the core of the movement, in this way uniting the classes in a common reform effort.

Kelley's arguments did win out, and after 1906 suffrage became an integral part of Progressivism. The campaign rhetoric for women's right to vote now echoed general Progressive principles, and the settlement house workers and the working girls themselves assumed a much more prominent place in the movement. Jane Addams urged the NAWSA delegates to win the vote, so as to accomplish the municipal reform that would promote child welfare. Choosing her words carefully, Addams insisted that "city housekeeping has failed partly because women, the traditional housekeepers, have not been consulted as to its multiform activities." Not only did the "complexity of a city government demand the help of minds accustomed to detail and variety of work" (Addams' stereotypic view of women's work), but more important, women had to bring to municipal affairs "a sense of obligation for the health and welfare of young children and a responsibility for the cleanliness and comfort of other people." [107] In very much the same language, Julia Lathrop told the Convention, "My purpose is to show that woman suffrage is a natural and inevitable step in the march of society forward; that instead of being incompatible with child welfare it leads toward it and is indeed the next great service to be rendered for the welfare and ennoblement of the home." [108]

Woman's suffrage would also promote the welfare of future mothers. Legislation would protect the working girl from ruinous exploitation. "The working women have much more need of the ballot than we of the so-called leisure class," Barnum told the NAWSA delegates. "We suffer from the insult of its refusal; we are denied the privilege of performing our obligations. . . . The working women have not only these insults and privations, but they have also the knowledge that they are being destroyed, literally destroyed, body and soul, by conditions which they cannot touch by law." [109] Only with the ballot could the working girl be protected against the greed of factory owners. Taking the Triangle Fire as her case in point, Mary Ware Dennett insisted that "it is enough to silence forever the selfish addle-headed drivel of the anti-suffragists who recently said at a legislative hearing that working women can safely trust their welfare to their 'natural protectors.' . . . We are *not* willing to consign unwilling women or helpless young girls to any such tender mercies. . . . The time has come when women should have the one efficient tool with which to make for themselves decent and safe working conditions—the ballot." [110] And Julia Lathrop made clear just how different this position was from the traditional posture of the suffragists, how far the movement had come from the views of Mrs. Catt. "The ignorant vote is not the working vote," she told the NAWSA delegates in 1912. "Working women in great organized factories have been having, since they began that work, an education for the suffrage. They are not ignorant voters, nor are the wives of workingmen; at least, they know in part what they need to safeguard themselves and their homes." [111]

The first result of these judgments was that working women began to appear at suffrage meetings, taking part in the annual meetings of the NAWSA. In 1913, Margaret Hinchey, a laundry worker, Rose Winslow, a stocking weaver, and Mary Anderson, a member of the executive board of the National Boot and Shoemakers' Union, delivered major convention addresses. "It was a comparatively new thing," recalled Ida Harper, the chronicler of the suffrage movement, "to have women wage-earners on the woman suffrage platform and their speeches made a deep impression." [112] In rhetorical and personal terms, the suffrage movement was broadening its appeal across class lines.

The alliance with the lower classes did not cost the suffrage camp the support of middle- or upper-class women. On the contrary: some of the same forces that helped to generate Progressive social reform also made suffrage seem all the more appropriate. How absurd it now appeared to deny women college graduates the vote. "In another generation or two," declared M. Carey Thomas, "one-half of all the people who have been to college in the United States will be women; and just as surely as the seasons of the year succeed one another or the law of gravitation works, just so surely will this great body of educated women wish to use their trained intelligence in making the towns, cities, and States of their country better places for themselves and their children to live in." The social science courses that the women had attended exerted their effect. "It is unthinkable that women who have learned to act for themselves in college and have become awakened there to civic duties should not care for the ballot to enforce their wishes." [113] So, too, in 1914 the General Federation of Women's Clubs, with a membership of almost two million women, endorsed the suffrage plank. Just as they united with settlement house workers to work to abolish child labor and to promote kindergartens, playgrounds, and juvenile courts, so they joined to win the vote. Dedicated to "civic advancement in America," they really could not do otherwise.

Thus, a powerful coalition of suffragists, child welfare reformers, club women, and working girls fought for suffrage. The union was visible not only to the delegates at suffrage conventions but also to the entire society. By 1912, the "handsome ladies" and the working girls had begun to parade together demonstrating their solidarity. "Women who usually see Fifth Avenue through the polished windows of their limousines," noted one reporter, "strode steadily side by side with the pale-faced, thin-bodied girls from the sweltering sweat shops of the East Side. Mrs. O. H. P. Belmont walked but a few steps ahead of Rebecca Goldstein, who runs a sewing machine in a shirtwaist shop. . . . The sight of the impressive column of women striding five abreast up the middle of the street stifled all thought of ridicule. They were typical womanly American women . . . women doctors, women lawyers, splendid in their array of academic robes; women architects, women artists, actresses and sculptors; women waitresses, domestics; a huge division of industrial workers; . . . all marched with an intensity and purpose that astonished the crowds that lined the streets." [114] With this alliance and common purpose, women were soon able to win the vote.

CHAPTER
4

The Politics of
Protection

THE IDEOLOGY of educated motherhood had an immediate and critical impact on social policy. Its rhetoric enjoyed a broad appeal, and the coalition that popularized it was at once effective and powerful. A national network of women's clubs and settlement houses made up an energetic and persuasive lobby, and over the course of the Progressive period, the women reformers were able to translate their views into legislation, particularly in the fields of health, work, and education. Yet, the outcome of all these efforts was generally disappointing. It was not simply that goals were so ambitious that reality had to fall short. It was not just that they aimed so high that dissatisfactions were inevitable. Rather, the results were more complex and more interesting, with consequences that were frequently unanticipated and at times counterproductive.

The new programs attempted to mobilize the power of the state to accomplish reform aims. That the settlement house attracted to its doors a relatively small proportion of the new immigrants is not particularly surprising. Any such enterprise would necessarily occupy only a narrow space within the broader boundaries of the ghetto. If immigrant parents did not flock to join the mothers' clubs, if their children did not rush to enroll in self-improvement clubs, that is in many ways to be expected.[1] More important were the efforts to transform public policy, to move from personal and private encounters to state action, to bring about compulsory legislation of one sort or another. It is most appropriate, therefore, to analyze three cases in women's reform: first, public policy and health, the implementation of the Sheppard-Towner Act; second, policy in the workplace, the effects of special protection laws for women; and third, changes in education, the fate of the enlarged public schools. Each of these programs represented the political implementation of the principles of educated motherhood, and each of them bore results remarkably different from their designers' expectations.

Promoting Maternal Health: The Passage of the Sheppard-Towner Act

In 1921, Congress enacted the Sheppard-Towner Act, the first federally funded health care program to be implemented in the United States.[2] Its mandate was clear: to reduce the infant and maternal mortality rate. So was its strategy: to provide states with matching federal funds in order to establish prenatal and child health centers. In these centers, women trained in the scientific care of children would teach expectant mothers the rules of personal hygiene and offer advice on how to maintain and improve the health of their children. The effort to reduce mortality was to be essentially educative. Advances in health care were to come not from the construction of hospitals, medical research, or the training of medical specialists—or even from new cures for disease. Rather, educated women were to instill in other women a broad knowledge of the rules of bodily hygiene and in this way prevent the onset of disease.

Sheppard-Towner was a stunning victory for women reformers, who saw in its passage the first result of female suffrage. "Of all the activities in which I have shared during more than forty years of striving," declared Florence Kelley, "none is, I am convinced, of such fundamental importance as the Sheppard-Towner Act." Here was compelling evidence that women could translate their political power into a special kind of effort to raise levels of health and welfare. For one, the Act gave women a primary, although not exclusive, role in the field of community health and welfare. For another, it expanded the responsibility of the state; the Act assumed that it was the obligation of the state to guard the health of its citizens. Finally, Sheppard-Towner was to offer a type of service that would not conflict with the practice of private physicians. The field of preventive health care was open; private doctors would cooperate with public clinics to improve the health of women and children. And each of these three assumptions reflected the ideas and experiences that women reformers had already learned and tested in their clubs and settlement houses during the heyday of Progressivism.

Educated women did not for a moment doubt their right to exercise leadership in the field of health. They had led the campaigns in their local communities and cities to establish municipal bureaus of child hygiene and baby health stations to educate parents about the rules of hygiene. And Sheppard-Towner incorporated these experiences into its programs. Part of its appropriation would underwrite the costs of sending public health nurses into the home to teach better health practices. It would also fund public clinics where mothers would bring children for physical examinations; mothers would be informed not only about special deficiencies that the child might have, but about the importance of maintaining a sanitary home, of buying pure milk, and of keeping the child in the school and out of the factory. Thus, Sheppard-Towner aimed to provide specific health services while promoting all the child welfare reforms.

Once women assumed that the prevention of illness had both a public and a private dimension, that infant mortality was not an immutable vital statistic but an index of the level of child welfare, they helped to establish the protection of health as a duty of the state. Sheppard-Towner incorporated this judgment. The Sheppard-Towner clinics were at one with the enlarged public school, the municipal bureaus of hygiene, and the playgrounds. "Well-baby clinics," declared Dr. Josephine Baker, "should be as free as the public schools, in either case the reservation being left to the parents to take their babies or children to private schools or private physicians . . . public health is not a special privilege but a birthright. . . . The infant welfare station is as much a part of the public function as the public baths, public playgrounds, libraries and schools."[3] Health was another obligation of the state to its citizens.

Finally, the sponsors of Sheppard-Towner assumed that no rival in the private sector had yet staked out the field of preventive health care. In assigning this task to women and the state, they assumed that physicians engaged in private practice were generally unwilling and often unable to offer this type of preventive health care to their individual patients. In fact, private doctors in 1920 used their skills to try to cure those already sick; medical schools were not training physicians to conduct preventive health examinations.[4] The Sheppard-Towner Act respected their domain. Its intervention was to the goal of *preventing* illness; it would not offer remedial medical services. "It is not the purpose of the child health conference to hold examinations or consultations for the obviously ill child or baby," reported the Children's Bureau. "Sick children, if brought to the conference, are referred to the family physician or other agencies for care and treatment." [5] By rigidly separating the role of the private doctor from the role of the public clinic, Sheppard-Towner proponents believed they could expand the responsibility of the state without antagonizing doctors or infringing on their territory. No conflict of interest seemed to impede the program's promise.

It was in another way, too, a reasonable expectation. The medical profession had already conceded to states and municipalities the right to intervene in the name of public health. Private physicians did not challenge the right of doctors working from municipal or state departments of public health to control communicable disease by purifying water, milk, and sewerage supplies. They were generally disinterested in public health campaigns, defining them as charitable and humanitarian, not a part of their workaday concern.

The depth of societal acknowledgment of this division of public and private roles is best illustrated by the apathy that the most conservative elements of the medical profession encountered when trying to defeat Sheppard-Towner in 1921. Wary of any state expansion in the field of health care, the American Medical Association (AMA) leadership worked to prevent the enactment of the measure. But they did not get very far. Part of the reason for their failure may well reflect Congressional fear of the new, and therefore unknown, power of female voters.[6] Perhaps more important, the AMA found little interest within the profession. Private physicians did not vigorously support the organization, because they did not believe that the programs offered by Sheppard-Towner would in any way compete with the services they offered to their private patients.[7] This was a public health program that belonged to women and the state, and hence it was not their concern.

Women reformers were convinced that these conservative physicians could not defeat their program. To the staff of the Children's Bureau, physicians were a "reactionary group of medical men who are not progressive and have no public health point of view." As such, they were that part of the citizenry that opposes "all public health which aims to make an enlightened community." [8] They had no special antagonism to Sheppard-Towner; they simply objected to everything. Clearly, as Progressive reforms took hold in more and more communities, narrow and self-interested groups like the American Medical Association would lose credibility.

For all this, the reformers did remain respectful of medical skills and territory. In setting up public child health and prenatal care centers, they insisted again and again that the state was supplying an essential service that could not and would not be delivered by private doctors. "When this prophylactic health service can be offered by private physicians to any extent," Dr. Baker went so far as to say, "there is little doubt that people who can afford to pay for such service will avail themselves of the opportunity." But this was not now the case; reformers were operating in an open field. The problem, as Dr. Baker explained, was not "how can we eliminate from our well-baby clinic those parents who could afford to pay for this service, but rather, how can we induce them to take advantage of this opportunity for the continued health of their babies?" [9]

Moreover, the child health center defined its intervention as very different from that of the average general practitioner. It would look to healthy children while the practitioner treated sick ones. Rather than focus on the symptoms of a disease already found in an ill child, the examiner in the center would measure the general physical condition of the well child.[10] Instead of dispensing prescriptions or doing surgery to cure a defined illness or physical defect, the center staff would advise on how to improve or to maintain health. It was to be as familiar with the developmental patterns of healthy children as the general practitioner was with the symptoms of disease.

The professionals who embodied this new attitude and generally staffed the centers were public health nurses and female physicians. In daily practice, the public health nurse was a combination nurse and social welfare worker, combining bedside care with hygienic advice. Appropriately enough, her training frequently came through courses offered in schools of social welfare and she was usually on the staff of a settlement house, a municipal department of child hygiene, or a public school, not a member of a hospital team. Her work in education and disease prevention made the public health nurse the ideal staff member for the Sheppard-Towner programs.

Similarly, it was female physicians who performed the straightforward medical tasks in the Sheppard-Towner clinics. This too was predictable—women doctors were prone to practice social medicine in a public setting.[11] No better trained to do it than their male counterparts or more knowledgeable (at least initially) about the fine points of illness prevention, nevertheless women doctors were more regularly providing preventive health services. They were disproportionately employed by bureaus of child hygiene and public health departments. And once Sheppard-Towner was enacted, they filled its staff and director positions.[12]

In part, this clustering may well reflect the bias of the male-dominated medical profession against female physicians, so deep that it closed hospital positions to them. And a general reluctance among men and women to use women doctors necessarily limited their ability to carry on a private practice. But no less important was a sense of a special commitment to the field of preventive health. In this way women physicians would further the goals of all educated women; their identification with reformers was at least as important as their identification as professionals. Accordingly, female medical societies were affiliated both with local medical societies and with the General Federation of Women's Clubs. And women physicians often led community campaigns to improve child health care. "Being women as well as physicians," Florence Brown Sherbon, president of the Iowa Society of Medical Women, reminded her colleagues, "we share with our sex in the actual and potential motherhood of the race. Being women we make common cause with all women as it is shown in our present affiliation with federate clubs, etc. And being women and mothers, our first and closest and dearest interest is the child." [13] By employing women physicians, the bureaus of child hygiene and the Sheppard-Towner clinics put on their staff those most sympathetic to their goals.

The implementation of Sheppard-Towner drew heavily on the experience of the New York City Bureau of Child Hygiene. Indeed, it enlarged and expanded the New York programs to fit the needs of children in all types of communities, small towns and rural areas as well as large cities.[14] The very size of the task compelled Sheppard-Towner to assign priorities. While the Bureau of Child Hygiene had focused primarily on providing services to immigrants and tenement house dwellers, Sheppard-Towner decided to focus first on families living in rural areas, and second, on those in small towns.[15]

Ever conscious of its national scope, Sheppard-Towner sought to create a series of permanent administrative units that would promote child welfare reforms. To receive federal funds, a state had not only to approve matching funds, but also to establish a state agency that would coordinate its health programs with the Children's Bureau. And this agency had to be a separate unit, a Bureau of Child Hygiene or Division of Child Welfare, within the state Department of Health.

Its concern for children could not be diluted with any other responsibility. Further, this agency had to spawn county agencies, minidepartments of child hygiene, to administer the funds. All of this was intended to bring into being a powerful and pervasive network of governmental bodies whose *exclusive* concern was child welfare. The reformers here had a firm grasp on how administrative organization might further social reforms.[16]

Sheppard-Towner also intended to encourage and rely upon the promotional activities of educated women. Before a local community could establish a Sheppard-Towner clinic, its members had to be sensitized to the need for preventive health care. The availability of federal funding would supply the impetus to begin the work. Urban women had already campaigned on this platform; now their more rural counterparts would agitate against polluted water and inadequate sewerage, unpurified milk and child labor. It was their turn to promote compulsory schooling laws, kindergartens, and playgrounds.[17]

Sheppard-Towner, like the New York Bureau, made public health nurses the mainstay of the program. Far outnumbering the physicians,[18] they were the ones who gave hygienic advice, who encouraged breast-feeding, who gave routine care to expectant mothers, and who instructed the midwives. In Sheppard-Towner, too, the education of mothers was the keynote of the enterprise. "Better baby" contests took place at county fairs; health clinics were frequently held in specially equipped mobile trucks named "the Child Welfare Special." The skills of the physician, while not ignored, were not central. A few full-time physicians assumed administrative responsibilities, generally heading state programs, and part-time and even volunteer physicians conducted the health conferences. But Sheppard-Towner essentially relied on the skills of women trained in the scientific care of children and female-led community reform campaigns to reduce infant and maternal mortality.

Finally, the Act respected the division of labor between the private physician and the clinic that the New York Bureau had established. "The principles to be adopted in administering these laws," announced the Children's Bureau, "are largely in the social and economic fields, and it is not a health measure in the sense [in] which the prevention or cure or treatment of disease is a health measure. . . . It belongs in its health aspect to that field of hygiene which doctors have long since discovered and turned over to the laity to practice."[19] When critics persisted in asking why a nonmedical organization had any responsibility in the field, reformers responded that health maintenance demanded more than doctors' skills alone could provide. "Prenatal and maternity care means more than good obstetrics; it means normal family life, freedom of the mother from industrial labor before and after childbirth, ability to nurse the child, above all, education in standards of care so that women and their husbands will demand good obstetrics and will no longer voluntarily run the risk of unnecessary child bed fever and similar preventable tragedies." [20] Medicine, in other words, was only a small part of a campaign for health.

Promoting Medical Expertise: The Defeat of Sheppard-Towner

For all the enthusiasm, successes, and political influence of its proponents, Sheppard-Towner was not destined to be the model under which generations of Americans would receive health services. By 1929, the medical profession had mounted a highly effective campaign that eliminated the program and made obsolete its assumptions about the proper methods of delivering health care. The defeat of Sheppard-Towner marked the end of female expertise in the field of health care and, at the same time, shifted the provision of preventive health services from the public to the private sector. Women trained in hygiene working in state-supported clinics gave way to physicians engaged in private practice.

Leaders of the medical profession successfully expanded the domain of the private doctor to encompass the role of women and the responsibility of the state. In essence, they helped to incorporate the services offered by the public clinics into the practice of the private physician. During the 1920s, it became appropriate and desirable for the first time for a private doctor to offer preventive health services and to give advice on personal hygiene. "Unquestionably, the greatest possibilities of usefulness of the physician to the public lie in the field of preventive medicine," John M. Dodson told his colleagues of the American Medical Association in 1923. "The family physician who seeks to render to his patients the service which will do them the most good is bound to enter the field of preventive medicine: to become in other words, the family health advisor as well as the family physician." [21] And his remarks were well heeded. By the end of the decade, not only children but also adults went to the family doctor for periodic health examinations. The doctor now judged both the progress of disease in the sick and the level of health in the normal and gave advice on personal habits as comfortably as dispensing drugs or recommending surgery.

The downfall of Sheppard-Towner directly reflected the willingness of physicians to assume these novel tasks. By including preventive health care in the services of the general practitioner, the AMA was able to persuade the federal government in 1927, as they had not been able to in 1921, that private doctors were the appropriate and the exclusive guardians of *all* matters of health—including, of course, the reduction of infant and maternal mortality rates. What is so startling, in retrospect, is how quickly even a modest program of preventive health service transformed the practice and image of the private physician.

By 1930, general practitioners had typically shifted the locus of their services from the sickroom to the office, from a reliance on emergency calls and bedroom care to a system of advance appointments and routine examinations of the healthy. Physicians began to keep detailed records of the past history and current state of health of their individual patients, to include charts on height and weight, and to measure each individual developmental change in light of the patient's past medical and social history. They investigated minor ailments and encouraged the correction of physical defects. In brief, they expanded their private practices to include the functions reformers had assigned to publicly funded clinics.

This shift does not reflect scientific advances. General practitioners did not suddenly discover new techniques that dramatically increased their diagnostic abilities. Nor did they obtain novel equipment that justified this change. Rather, the private doctor's take-over of public health services was a social, not a medical, phenomenon. It reflected, as its timing makes clear, a medical response to a political innovation.

It was the nationwide Sheppard-Towner program that was the catalyst transforming private medical practice. In fact, by organizing a Sheppard-Towner program, a community often took the first step towards altering the private practice of its local doctors. Sheppard-Towner services were set up only in communities that specifically asked for them, and the request itself revealed that at least some influential citizens were committed to preventive health care. "The local support of a center," reported the Children's Bureau, "indicates that the community desires the health of the mothers and babies conserved." [22] But the establishment of Sheppard-Towner clinics required the support not only of the lay community but of the resident medical professionals as well. Frequently, the state agency would not permit a community to act without the endorsement of its local medical society, a stipulation designed to prevent later conflict. Sheppard-Towner was not looking for a fight. But it also had the immediate effect of forcing local doctors to take an open stand on a public health issue; they could not remain, as they had before, neutral bystanders in a public health campaign. To resist a program that promised to save babies and mothers and to improve the health of children, cast them in an unattractive light. To accept the proposal was to agree to the importance of preventive health care. Further, the Sheppard-Towner clinics, particularly in small towns and isolated areas, had to rely on local physicians to conduct preventive health examinations—unlike the New York Bureau, they did not have a pre-existing core of physicians already active in the field of public health. So the local doctor who approved of Sheppard-Towner had, in fact, to be partly responsible for its administration. And once local doctors began to offer a popular service within a public clinic, they soon transferred preventive health care to their own offices.[23]

The very ambitious nature of Sheppard-Towner did contribute to private doctors' incorporation of its services. The demonstration prenatal conferences that it established, for example, extended beyond the giving of hygienic advice; the program was to become a model for an ideal type of complete health care. The clinics did try to maintain scrupulous relationships with private doctors. In Minnesota, for example, before a woman could be examined at a demonstration prenatal conference, the nurse had to ask her private doctor, if she had one, for permission; after the conference a record of the examination was sent to the physician.[24] Similar procedures were followed in other states, and all of them had the effect of placing the family doctors in a peculiar position. From their perspective, their patients were getting a medical service from a public clinic that they might be providing. No wonder, then, that many of them brought Sheppard-Towner techniques into their own practices.

An open and active campaign of the American Medical Association for the purpose of defeating Sheppard-Towner also encouraged general practitioners to alter their delivery of medical services. Beginning precisely in 1922, the first year that Sheppard-Towner operated, the AMA and local medical societies urged physicians to transform their practices, and the fact that this encouragement followed so exactly on Sheppard-Towner points to its major motivation: to remove the government from the business of health care. The drive was successful. Local medical societies offered instruction to all physicians (members or not) on the techniques of well-child and well-adult examinations and on the importance of routine prenatal care for expectant mothers. Medical schools also provided courses that would enable physicians already engaged in private practice to acquire these techniques.[25] And the physicians took the time to learn the lessons.*

The official journal of the AMA published instructions on how to conduct a preventive health examination. In 1922, the American Medical Association authorized its Council on Health and Public Instruction to "prepare forms suitable for use by private practitioners of medicine in carrying out the purposes of the periodic health examination." [26] In a lengthy and very specific article the next year, Haven Emerson, the chairman of the Council, described the necessary equipment and the best way to keep records. "The methods employed are those used in the diagnosis of disease," Emerson assured the doctors who found all this very new. "The attitude of mind, the point of view of physician and patient, is the chief distinguishing feature which makes the health examination sufficiently novel and important . . . to justify the following suggestions." [27] First, the physician was

---

* Periodic health examinations did precede the Sheppard-Towner Act. At the same time that the New York City Bureau of Child Hygiene was conducting routine examinations of infants in the baby health stations and of school children in the public schools, insurance companies were recommending periodic health examinations for their policy holders, and the United States Army was conducting them for its officers. Even a few industrial companies had begun to encourage their employees to undergo periodic examinations. But then, since these steps preceded Sheppard-Towner, why did the AMA wait to endorse periodic health examiniations until 1922, if not for the threat that it perceived in Sheppard-Towner? Moreover, although the links between the AMA campaign and Sheppard-Towner were not made explicitly and openly announced, there are references to the seriousness of the threat. "Thus far the medical profession has not attempted to correct the situation which caused the Sheppard-Towner legislation," Carl Henry Davis told the American Child Health Association in 1928. "What have we to offer as a substitute?" Two final points: first, the AMA is just one part of the story. The pages above explore how the personal experience of physicians made them responsive to the changeover. Second, Sheppard-Towner itself was not the only threat. During the 1920s, business organizations were beginning to hire their own doctors to conduct health examinations. "There are springing up all over the country," the American Medical Association warned its members in 1924, "commercial companies engaging physicians as employees to conduct periodic health examinations, anticipating a profitable business for their stockholders. It would be a reproach to the profession for a commercial company . . . to make a success in a field that is peculiarly professional."

to take a lengthy and highly detailed history of the patient. Filling out the forms (already in use in public clinics) demonstrated a private physician's commitment to health maintenance. "Even though inquiry as to the past illnesses of the patient and his ancestors," conceded Emerson, "does not directly contribute to the exact knowledge of his present bodily function and structure, the past personal and family history must be obtained because of the light they often throw on the patient's health." [28] But, Emerson assured physicians, if their schedules were too crowded, the patients themselves could complete the sheets before the examination.

Emerson also encouraged doctors to alter the style of their practice. "Health examinations," he insisted, "should be arranged for on an appointment basis and not merely as incidental to service for the sick at crowded office hours. An appointment is in every way desirable for both patient and physician, because of the necessity of spending not less than from three quarters of an hour to an hour with each patient." [29] Unlike the patient with a specific complaint or symptom, the healthy patient required a head-to-toe examination. Yet the new type of examination did not demand the purchase of costly items. Physicians already possessed most of the equipment—they just had to use it in a new way. "The tape measure, tongue depressors, spot light, stethoscope, blood pressure instrument, otoscope, laryngeal mirror, nose speculum, vision chart, rubber gloves, vaginal speculum, weight scales, simple urine test and a thermometer"—these were the necessary tools, and all doctors had them.[30]

The health examination, to be sure, did require a novel kind of skill and hygienic knowledge. "Physicians whose training and attention have been devoted almost exclusively to the treatment of serious or long-established disease processes," Emerson cautioned, "will not find themselves at once prepared to guide applicants for health service in the practices of personal hygiene." [31] Hence he encouraged them to review "the physiology of digestion and nutrition, and the effect and uses of physical exercise and development on the muscular, nervous, circulatory and respiratory system." [32] But sensing the formidability of this assignment, he went on to tell his colleagues that the task was not really so difficult. There were five common disorders to be detected among people in apparent good health: "sleeplessness, constipation, overweight, underweight and arterial hypertension." To alleviate these difficulties, "the physician should be prepared to give special instruction as to hygiene, manner of life, diet, etc. according to his own opinion in helping people, who think them-

The Well-Ordered Gymnasium   (ca. 1880)

Physical exercise classes were critical to the routine of the first women's colleges. These classes were an antidote to the dire consequences for women that doctors predicted would result from a rigorous intellectual education. *The Sophia Smith Collection, Smith College*

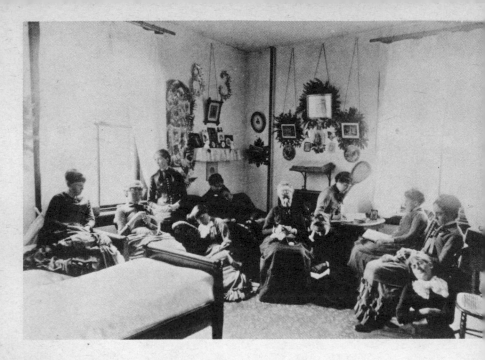

The George Eliot Club, Smith College   (ca. 1880)
Collegiate clubs were one of the most important models for the women's associations of the post-Civil War decades, providing the occasion both for intellectual discussion and sociability. *The Sophia Smith Collection, Smith College*

Organized Motherhood, New York City (ca. 1900)

As the crowded and businesslike atmosphere of this meeting of the General Federation of Women's Clubs suggests, women were eager and determined to translate feminine virtues into reform precepts. *Brown Brothers*

THE EFFECT
—OF—
ALCOHOL
—ON—
SEX LIFE

By Winfield Scott Hall, Ph.D., M.D.
Professor of Physiology, Northwestern University Medical School, Chicago

The sex life is dominated by a compelling instinct as natural as eating and drinking. The laws of custom and modern civilization demand that the sex life be under the control of reason, judgment and will.

Alcohol makes all natural instincts stronger, and weakens judgment and will, through which control must act.

Alcohol and all drinks of which alcohol forms even a small part are harmful and dangerous to the sex life for four reasons:

I. ALCOHOL INFLAMES THE PASSIONS, thus making the temptation to sex-sin unusually strong.

II. ALCOHOL DECREASES THE POWER OF CONTROL, thus making the resisting of temptation especially difficult.

III. ALCOHOL DECREASES THE RESISTANCE OF THE BODY TO DISEASE, thus causing the person who is under the influence of alcohol more likely to catch disease.

IV. ALCOHOL DECREASES THE POWER OF THE BODY TO RECOVER FROM DISEASE, thus making the result of disease more serious.

The influence of alcohol upon sex-life could hardly be worse.

AVOID ALL ALCOHOLIC DRINK ABSOLUTELY

The control of sex impulses will then be easy and disease, dishonor, disgrace and degradation will be avoided.

SERIES D. No. 10.

COPYRIGHT, 1913
BY AMERICAN ISSUE PUBLISHING CO.,
WESTERVILLE, OHIO

Price of this Poster, $2.00 per 100; one full set of 12 Posters, 40c.; three sets for $1.00.

THE AMERICAN ISSUE PUBLISHING CO.
WESTERVILLE, OHIO

Alcohol and Sex (1913)

As this temperance broadside makes clear, prohibition occupied an important place in women's reform. In the 1970s the fear is that alcoholic consumption might diminish the sex drive; in the 1890s the fear was that it would "inflame the passions." *Culver Pictures, Inc.*

Too Young to Suffer (1893)

Patent medicine companies, like Lydia Pinkham, popularized the notions of female frailty. The nostrums were to alleviate female suffering—and they may well have, since they were laced with opium. *The Schlesinger Library, Radcliffe College*

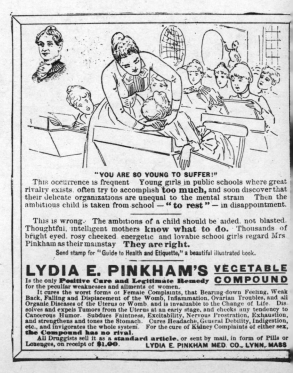

"YOU ARE SO YOUNG TO SUFFER!"
This occurrence is frequent. Young girls in public schools where great rivalry exists, often try to accomplish **too much**, and soon discover that their delicate organizations are unequal to the mental strain. Then the ambitious child is taken from school — "**to rest**" — in disappointment.

This is wrong. The ambitions of a child should be aided, not blasted. Thoughtful, intelligent mothers **know what to do.** Thousands of bright eyed, rosy cheeked energetic and lovable school girls regard Mrs Pinkham as their mainstay. **They are right.**

Send stamp for "Guide to Health and Etiquette," a beautiful illustrated book.

LYDIA E. PINKHAM'S VEGETABLE COMPOUND

Is the only **Positive Cure and Legitimate Remedy** for the peculiar weaknesses and ailments of women.

It cures the worst forms of Female Complaints, that Bearing-down Feeling, Weak Back, Falling and Displacement of the Womb, Inflammation, Ovarian Troubles, and all Organic Diseases of the Uterus or Womb, and is invaluable to the Change of Life. Dissolves and expels Tumors from the Uterus at an early stage, and checks any tendency to Cancerous Humor. Subdues Faintness, Excitability, Nervous Prostration, Exhaustion, and strengthens and tones the Stomach. Cures Headache, General Debility, Indigestion, etc., and invigorates the whole system. For the cure of Kidney Complaints of either sex, **the Compound has no rival.**

All Druggists sell it as a **standard article**, or sent by mail, in form of Pills or Lozenges, on receipt of **$1.00.**

LYDIA E. PINKHAM MED. CO., LYNN, MASS

The Miracle of Appliances (1910)
Technological innovations did relieve middle-class women of some of the burdens of housekeeping. The new vacuum cleaner, a marvel to behold, was far more efficient than a broom. *Brown Brothers*

The Glories of Department Stores (1903)

Department store owners did everything possible to make shopping an adventure. An opportunity to ride the new elevators, to try out the bicycles, or to view the fountain at Seigel and Cooper Company, made a trip downtown highly appealing to women—and profitable for the store owners. *Library of Congress*

The Typewriter (ca. 1900)

So linked were these machines to their operators, that both were known as typewriters. Typing became a woman's job. Middle-class, educated men found better opportunities for promotion elsewhere. *Culver Pictures, Inc.*

Sweatshop Labor (1910)

Women reformers consistently objected to factory employment for single girls. In the 1880s they denounced its corrupting influences—girls ought not to be working so intimately with men; and later they criticized its unhealthy influences—girls should not be working so many hours in such cramped quarters. *Brown Brothers*

The Triangle Fire   (1911)

The catastrophe of the Triangle Shirtwaist Factory fire and the photographs of its gruesome results (young, charred bodies in numbered coffins) made the Progressive crusade for protective legislation all the more appropriate.
Brown Brothers

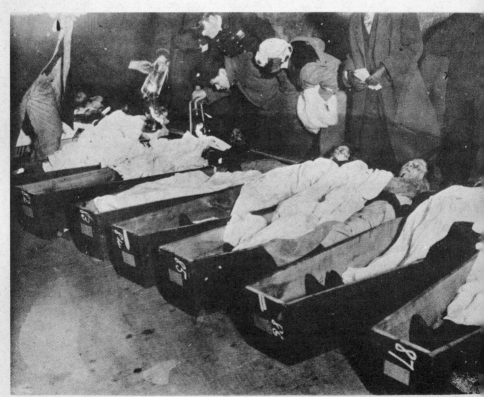

Grace in the Day Nursery   (ca. 1910)

The first day care centers were institutions of last resort, designed for the unfortunate children of working mothers. Accordingly, the centers took great pains to combine moral uplift with custodial care. *Brown Brothers*

Order Without Repression   (ca. 1910)

This motto of the kindergarten made its mission clear. It would inculcate "habits of obedience, attention, concentration, orderliness." The emphasis on order was realized; the degree of repression can be left to the imagination. *Brown Brothers*

Training to Domesticity (1912)

The public health nurse, a frequent visitor to immigrant families, taught rules of cleanliness and middle-class habits. The table and dishes were to be clean, and coincidentally properly set, with doilies and flowers included. *Brown Brothers*

The Well-Ordered Playground (ca. 1910)

The exercise classes that college girls attended in the 1880s, ghetto children took in the 1900s. The regimen that had been so health-giving to an earlier generation of frail women seemed appropriate for a later generation of immigrants. *Brown Brothers*

All Together Now (1910)

This Hull House club exemplified the settlement house program: a diverse group of immigrants joining together in a cooperative venture. *Lewis W. Hine, Culver Pictures, Inc.*

The Ideal Playground (ca. 1920)

The Gary system embodied John Dewey's Progressive educational views. The fence around the playground was to keep out contaminating influences; inside, the children learned rules of fair play and cooperation. *Brown Brothers*

Marching for Suffrage (ca. 1915)

Dressed in white, as if to symbolize their virtue, the suffragists marched to win the vote—not because they had a right to the ballot as citizens, but because they had a social duty to exercise as educated mothers. *Brown Brothers*

The Weigh-In (ca. 1922)

The first result of suffrage was the passage of the Sheppard-Towner Act, a program to promote maternal and child health. Public health nurses worked with doctors to teach the rules of illness prevention. With nutrition so much in mind, the baby scale took center stage. *Brown Brothers*

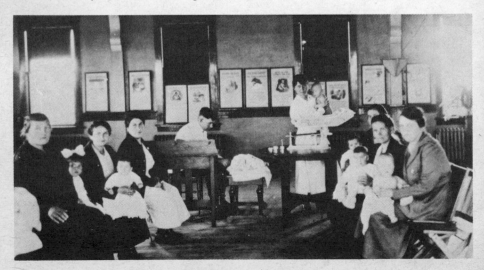

The Business of Glamour (1924)

When the wife-companion of the 1920s had to make romance and sexuality central to her marriage, the cosmetic industry boomed. By 1931, women's magazines carried more advertisements for beauty aids than for food. *Culver Pictures, Inc.*

The One True Couple (1928)

Sororities of the 1920s taught co-eds how to bob their hair, how to drink, smoke, and dance, and most important, how to catch a man. *University of Wisconsin Archives*

Women in the Navy Yard (1944)

Government propaganda to bring women into the work force was unrelenting —but it was always understood that when the men returned from the war front, women would return to the kitchen. *Culver Pictures, Inc.*

Suburban Streets (ca. 1960)

In the post-World War II years, Americans of all social classes looked to the suburb as the ideal community. At Levittown, New Jersey, the husband went off to work while the wife nested—and the only men around during the day delivered furniture, milk, and Dugan's cakes. *Leigh Photographs*

Vote ERA (1977)

Rights in Conflict (1977)

The contemporary women's movement often modeled itself on the civil rights movement. The protest march, the clenched fist, the appeal to the solidarity of sisters, all presupposed women's rights as person, not their duties as mothers. © *Bettye Lane*

The Hope of the Future (1976)
© *Bettye Lane*

selves quite well." [33] In other words, by assuming the task of preventive health examinations, the doctor made his understanding of the rules of hygiene the model for his patients. His idea of a good diet and of proper exercise would prevail. The viewpoint of the average physician now took precedence over the judgments of educated women and, as we shall see, the consequences of this change were far-reaching.

The AMA's instructions to physicians reappeared in many state journals of medicine, and state associations also mailed sample forms and lengthy instructions for conducting health examinations to their members. Indeed, this proliferation of advice and forms and directives protected the average doctor from charges of offering this service solely for private gain. "If it is sponsored by state, county, or district societies," Dr. Frank Billings told a meeting of the American Medical Association, "it relieves the family physician of any accusation that he is pushing this thing for his own benefit, because it is pushed by all organized medicine." [34] The Association's endorsement of periodic health examinations gave a legitimacy to this new medical role. The physician was reorganizing his practice to offer modern care.

General practitioners were under another pressure to incorporate this new role. Even before the passage of Sheppard-Towner, family doctors had begun to sense a loss of confidence among their own patients, and among the general public. As E. S. Levy, the president of the American Public Health Association, noted in 1923: "In spite of the fact that regular medical practice today is comparably superior to what it has ever been, there has never been a time when the people had less confidence in it." First, doctors were not identified with public health improvements; many of them did not even offer patients immunizations against disease.[35] More, the growing importance of medical specialists compounded the problems of the general practitioner. Specialists were becoming a dominant force within the profession during the 1920s, particularly in the case of obstetricians and pediatricians.[36] Specialists appeared to be the most scientific of doctors—and they were usually quite comfortable with the type of health care Sheppard-Towner advocated. "One of the most important measures to be developed is systematic periodical physical examinations," Dr. L. Emmett Holt told the American Pediatric Association. "This is fast becoming one of the most significant departments of public health. It makes possible the early recognition and correction of physical defects, the supervision of diet and inauguration of proper hygiene." [37] Accordingly, some specialists became allies of Sheppard-Towner, giving their approval and assistance to efforts to educate the public in preventive care.

The specialists' commitment to preventive health care reflected not only their concern for public welfare, but also their narrower professional interests. For one, an identification with preventive medical care allowed them to set themselves apart from general practitioners. While general practitioners relied on remedial medical treatment, they would focus on the importance of diagnostic skills. General practitioners could intervene only when illness occurred, but specialists promised to obviate the need for intervention. The specialists, then, by offering the public a "preventive" model for medical services were helping to increase the demand for their own services.

Without this orientation to preventive health care, it is doubtful whether the specialists would have attracted sufficient patients to sustain a practice. Few obstetricians could earn a living by only delivering babies; few pediatricians could keep a practice by treating sick children alone. By offering preventive care, however, the specialists expanded the opportunities for private practices devoted solely to obstetrical or pediatric services. The specialist easily justified assuming these new tasks. "The duty of the pediatrician," Holt insisted, "is not only to advance knowledge in all subjects related to the growth and health of children but to see that such knowledge is applied, for of what value is our knowledge unless it is used?" [38]

The Children's Bureau, as might be expected, was eager to work with the specialists. It appointed them lecturers and consultants; it used them to conduct demonstration health examinations, to encourage a county or town to accept a new program, to assist in writing pamphlets for nationwide distribution, and to instruct general practitioners on the best way to conduct a health examination. At the Bureau's annual Sheppard-Towner conferences, specialists played a major role in encouraging state directors to publicize the importance of periodic medical examinations for children and expectant mothers.

The specialists did help to legitimate the programs in many communities. Sheppard-Towner clinics in Minnesota, for example, not only employed obstetricians to conduct prenatal examinations but also gave local doctors the opportunity to consult with a prominent specialist. These encounters offered something to everyone in the community. The obstetrician had an opportunity to demonstrate to women "what constitutes a good obstetric examination" and to give a general talk on hygiene during pregnancy to which all the women of the community were invited. The general practitioner had the opportunity "to bring a complicated case for consultation to the specialist." And Sheppard-Towner programs gained prestige through this association. As the Minnesota director told the Children's Bureau: "The success of the conferences is due to the effective advance work of the nurse and the fact that the conferences are conducted by well-known obstetricians." [39]

The initial cordiality between child welfare reformers and pediatricians was apparent at the 1922 annual meeting of the American Medical Association. The Pediatric Section approved a resolution supporting the newly passed Sheppard-Towner Act, while at the very same convention, the House of Delegates of the organization condemned it. A highly emotional confrontation followed. "A committee of wrath was sent by the House of Delegates to reprimand the Pediatric section," reported one physician. "They were met with unrepentance and jeers." [40] Clearly the pediatricians, if not the AMA, were comfortable advocating a program that promoted preventive health care, despite its nonmedical sponsorship. (Following this event, the AMA prohibited sections from making their own recommendations.)

But the alliance between Sheppard-Towner and the specialists was short-lived. The specialists were soon defining the field of child and maternal health as exclusively the province of the medical profession and setting out to capture leadership from the women. "We must be teachers and leaders of the public in all these matters," Dr. Holt was already telling his colleagues in 1923. "This field we have neglected in the past; we have left the subject of popular health education too much to the nurse, the social worker and the nutrition teacher, and some of these groups largely owing to our neglect, have gotten somewhat out of hand." [41]

Over the course of the 1920s, more and more specialists established an alternate model for health delivery that shifted responsibility for the reduction of the infant and maternal mortality rate from public health nurses to the medical profession and its institutions. First, they converted the supervision of pregnancy into a physician's job, preferably an obstetrician's. They minimized the significance of the general rules of hygiene. Good diet and adequate sleep, however useful, could not guarantee an uneventful pregnancy. "We all appreciate that pregnancy is a physiological condition," Dr. Robert L. de Normandie told the directors of the Sheppard-Towner program, "but because of the fact that it may quickly become pathological, it is necessary to instruct each patient at her first visit to report to the physician any untoward symptoms." [42] The possibility of abnormality in a pregnancy was so great that the advice of public health nurses was almost irrelevant. Only a doctor who understood the complex bodily processes involved could determine each patient's needs, and these needs were not even necessarily consistent throughout a single pregnancy. "Prenatal care," Dr. de Normandie went on, "means medical supervision of the pregnant woman." [43] So women were to visit the physician's office frequently. Instead of one examination by a physician (as initially recommended by Sheppard-Towner) to separate out the "suspicious cases," the specialist demanded monthly visits at first, then, as the pregnancy progressed, bi-weekly and finally weekly visits. The obstetricians were not just to discover gross abnormality but to guard against any unforeseeable complications, which were, they insisted, ever so likely to occur.

As intensive medical oversight during pregnancy became appropriate, the nurse who gave hygienic instruction—while not removed from the office—lost all independent authority. "A properly qualified nurse may work in conjunction with the physician in the observation of a patient," declared Dr. L. de Normandie. "The nurse, however, must not assume any responsibility for her medical supervision; and her visits do not take the place of visits to the physician." [44] She could carry out a physician's instructions, but the two were hardly a team. The ultimate responsibility for all aspects of prenatal care lay with the doctor.

The profession's rhetoric was so powerful and compelling that, by the mid-1920s, the Children's Bureau itself was giving physicians primary, almost exclusive, authority to set standards for prenatal care. "Only by careful study of each case," reported the Bureau, "is it possible to determine whether a patient should be allowed to stay at home or be sent to a hospital." [45] So, too, in the field of child health, the Bureau linked the well-being of the patient to the physician's level of training. Educating a mother to the principles of child hygiene shrank in importance; neither the specialist nor any longer the Children's Bureau granted her a centrality in promoting child health. Regardless of her skill or dedication, they insisted, each child required intensive medical supervision. Thus, while still preferring the breast to bottle-feeding of infants, they did not endow the choice with its earlier significance. "It is important," stated the new 1926 Children's Bureau pamphlet on standards for child health examinations, "that the feeding of normal infants, whether breast- or artificially fed, be supervised regularly in order that serious disturbances may be prevented by remedying minor ones. Mothers who are nursing their infants often need simple advice quite as much as those whose infants are artificially fed." [46] Now the fat baby had to come to the clinic as often as the undernourished one. College training did not give women the complex medical understanding of child development that now seemed essential to raising healthy children.

Despite the shift in Children's Bureau views, the specialists in the late 1920s threw their weight against the continuation of Sheppard-Towner. The Congressional testimony of Dr. George Kosmak, a prominent obstetrician active in the New York Academy of Medicine, was one case in point. Kosmak defined pregnancy as a "medical problem," and therefore objected to a "strictly medical problem being turned over to lay organizations for a solution." [47] The correct way to reduce maternal mortality was to improve the training and facilities for obstetricians. Kosmak did not intend to eliminate the role of government in reducing maternal mortality but to alter it. He told the House committee hearings on extending Sheppard-Towner appropriations that he was "not opposed to the federal government participating in any movement to improve the care of pregnant women and their offspring"; rather, patients would best be served through federal support of medical education and research.[48]

Pregnant women, Kosmak argued, died primarily from sepsis infection and the toxemias of pregnancy. By understanding the etiology of these infections—which originated in individual pathology, not in social or economic environment—the physician would cure them. "Research is an entirely different matter," Kosmak contended, "from matching state appropriations to be expended in more or less unessential activities leaving the great problem untouched, namely the actual improved care of the pregnant woman. This cannot be accomplished by visiting nurses and social welfare workers—it depends on better medical attention. We are deluding ourselves as doctors as well as the public if we depend for relief on measures such as those deployed by the Sheppard-Towner and similar Acts." [49] Sheppard-Towner had become the "unessential activity." By emphasizing the pathology of pregnancy and the potential ability of medical oversight, research, and institutions to eliminate this pathology, the specialists made a convincing argument. With it they not only defeated Sheppard-Towner in 1929 but also channeled federal funds to suit their own priorities.

The defeat of the measure was not the exclusive work of the spe-

Also semi-professionals →

cialists. Not only did the skills of women have to be denigrated, but their efforts to deliver services with public funds had to be repudiated. The doctors had not only to sell the government on their superior training and the effectiveness of their institutions but to persuade it of the illegitimacy of community clinics. While the specialists discredited the abilites of women, the American Medical Association, along with other "liberty-minded" organizations, discredited their politics. The AMA engaged in a vicious smear campaign. Not only was Florence Kelley, one of the most ardent supporters of the measure, "the ablest legislative general communism had produced," but Sheppard-Towner was a "Bolshevik plot" inspired in Moscow. As reprehensible as the rhetoric was, so it was effective. Sheppard-Towner lost, the victim of the general practitioner's new style, the specialist's new authority, and the American Medical Association's new political power.[50]

The 1930 White House Conference on the Health and Protection of Children highlighted all these changes. The prominent role that child welfare reformers and educated women played in earlier White House Conferences on Children now went to the medical specialists. Grace Abbott, who had been in charge of the administration of Sheppard-Towner, took a minor part; the specialists who had lectured for her had the lead. And the notion that specialized medical skills could promote health dominated the proceedings.

Child welfare reformers had organized and controlled the first White House Conference in 1909 and the subsequent Conference in 1919. In both instances, delegates were optimistic about the ability of educated women to devise and execute social policies that would uplift the lower classes.[51] The rhetoric of the 1930 Conference was remarkably different. "Our country has a vast majority of competent mothers," President Herbert Hoover told the assembly. "But *what we are concerned with here are things that are beyond her power*. . . . She cannot count the bacteria in the milk; she cannot detect the typhoid which comes through the faucet, or the mumps that pass round the playground. . . . The questions of child health and protection are a complicated problem requiring much learning and much action." [52] Yet just a decade earlier Hoover had delivered a very different message. Then, he told the American Association of Child Hygiene, "I am one of those who hope much for these problems [of child care] from the enfranchisement of women. The major part of the progress to date has been due to the insistence of our women."

Over this period, as Hoover's shift made clear, the skills of educated mothers had become secondary, almost obsolete.[53]

The 1930 Conference broke with its predecessors in still another way. The earlier conferences had focused on the dependent and deviant child; the 1930 one took as its mandate the needs of *all* children, regardless of social class. This change too reflected the growing irrelevance of women's knowledge. Expert insight was as critical to the children of the middle class as to the children of the poor. Regardless of her education, a mother had to consult a pediatrician in order to raise a healthy child and, concomitantly, to go to an obstetrician in order to avoid complications during pregnancy. The hegemony of the medical expert had begun.

The First Equal Rights Amendment

The issue of women's work appeared relatively straightforward to the Progressives. Clearly, mothers did not belong in the labor force, since child-rearing demanded all of their attention. This view prompted women reformers to advocate widow-pension legislation during these years. Not only were institutions less desirable than the home (precisely because they could not possibly deliver the individual kind of care that the child required), but also needy widows deserved state support so that they and their children would not have to go out to work. As for single women, the principles of educated motherhood encouraged them to take up new types of positions in the labor force. Progressive ideas did help to create novel occupations, particularly in the field of child care, and women seemed the appropriate persons to hold them. Yet, once again, it was almost invariably the case that these jobs were of a very secondary sort—jobs with all kinds of restrictions that reduced, practically eliminated, the prospects for advancement, and jobs that almost inevitably kept women subservient to male superiors.

Perhaps the best starting point for understanding this curious dynamic is with the settlement house. Men and women together founded them, and men and women resided in them, together. (Jacob Schiff once objected to Lillian Wald that such an arrangement bordered on the immoral, but Wald was able to quiet his fears and not lose his financial support.) Most significantly, however, the men did not remain residents for very long; it was the women who stayed on. In many instances, the academic training that men received in the colleges, combined with the first-hand experience of the settlement house, led to a career in university teaching or sometimes in the law. The women enjoyed no such opportunities. Graduate programs in the universities kept strict quotas on the number of entering women, and the occasional woman Ph.D. usually found herself teaching at the college, as opposed to graduate school, level. "Women who expect to engage in college or university teaching," warned one woman professor in 1929, "should be aware of the reluctance of administrations to promote women or to pay them salaries equal to those paid men of similar attainments for similar work." Or, as another professor informed prospective female applicants to a graduate economics program: "The field for women with a Ph.D. in economics is decidedly limited. Women may be given minor positions, instructorships, etc. . . . in first-class colleges and universities, but would rarely be considered for one of major rank." [54] Thus, many women remained in the settlement houses because they had no place else to go.

Still, some new positions did open up in related areas, particularly social work and nursing. The move from the settlement house to the social work agency, the hospital, or outpatient facility was not particularly difficult. Women quickly dominated the field of social work —but the same process that operated in the nineteenth century to make women the typists and men the managers, to make women the salesclerks and men the supervisors, reappeared here as well. The social worker was usually the underling in the agency, and even more typically, in the hospital. According to Harriet Bartlett, a leader in the field of social work, a medical or psychiatric social worker, holding the most prestigious of jobs, was "a separate skilled agent, a specialist in the area of social problems." Nevertheless, such a social worker was not one among equals. Explained Bartlett: "The cooperative care of the patient by a group of specialists, which characterizes modern institutional medicine, is a process of teamwork. Since coordination is essential . . . the physician always remains the leader of the team." The doctors, of course, concurred: "It is the function of the physician," one of them declared, "to make the diagnosis and to prescribe the treatment to be followed, leaving the technician, be she nurse or social worker, the technique of its execution." [55] The male was the professional, the female the technician.

What was true for social work was even more true for nursing.

The ranks of female nurses did expand dramatically in the Progressive decades, reflecting the growing scientific character of the hospitals. In the post-Civil War decades, efforts to attract women to nursing and to establish special schools for nursing had not been particularly successful. When the hospital remained a kind of almshouse (despite the best efforts of Louisa Schuyler), and when attendants were generally other almshouse residents, women had little reason to pursue such an occupation, to register in nursing courses and then take up hospital positions. But as hospitals achieved their more modern status, a new style of physician attracted a new style of nurse. The number of training schools for nursing increased dramatically—by 1918 there were 1,129 such schools; by 1920 there were 1,755. And so did the number of trained nurses. By 1920, there were some 144,000 nurses, most of them women.[56] But the nurse was second to the doctor. "She is only the handmaiden," as one of them expressed it, "of that great and beautiful science in whose temple she may only serve minor parts, but nonetheless it is her duty to endeavor to grasp the importance of its teachings so that she may fulfill widely her share." [57]

With even greater support from the settlement house reformers, women assumed positions as public health nurses. Here was the opportunity to perform the tasks of educated motherhood in the community. At the health stations and later at the Sheppard-Towner clinics, the public health nurse gave advice. She also entered the public schools, "to treat children with minor diseases as far as possible in the school, to visit the homes to interest the parents in their future care, and to demonstrate any necessary treatment." Echoing the precepts of educated motherhood, one school nurse explained that "it is her duty to save children from deformity, disease and death, to lay a physical and moral foundation for splendid womanhood and capable manhood. If parents have failed to secure the necessary medical, surgical or dental treatment through ignorance, poverty or neglect, the nurse has the splendid opportunity to preserve and save child life." [58] But although her task was grandiose and her autonomy perhaps greater than that of the institutional nurse (courtesy of the physical distance that separated her from the doctor), still she remained, on the wider scale of things, second best. Women became public health nurses because men became doctors, and clearly, as in the case of Sheppard-Towner clinics, when they did their jobs well, doctors soon enough took over their major responsibilities. In short order, physicians were giving them orders, making them into technicians.

Finally, educated motherhood perpetuated the belief that women were the ideal teachers of the young—not only in public schools but in newly created kindergartens as well. The awareness and sensitivity that was vital to the proper training of children was very much a woman's task; not surprisingly, by 1930 fully 82 percent of all teachers were women. Indeed, by 1930, there were almost 8,000 public kindergarten teachers, and all of them were women.[59] But the triumph of the maternal model within the classroom did not mean the triumph of the maternal model in administrative positions. What was true before was still true now: the majority of school administrators, the principals and superintendents, were men. Women held the posts that men did not want.

The most important, and ultimately the most controversial, program that women reformers enacted in this field was protective legislation for working women. The reformers were certainly successful in getting the laws passed—but whether the laws actually operated to the benefit of women, to their best interests, is quite another matter. Between 1900 and 1920, the great majority of states restricted the number of hours that women could work: ten states, including New York and California, set an eight-hour maximum; another twenty states, including Massachusetts and Wisconsin, imposed a nine-hour limit; and still another seventeen, including Pennsylvania and Illinois, passed a ten-hour limit. Sixteen states outlawed night work (between 10 P.M. and 6 A.M.) in a number of occupations, and nine states established minimum wages for women (generally between $10 and $16 a week). Five states, including California, prohibited women from lifting heavy weights; six states, including New York, prohibited women from working immediately before or after childbirth. Many states outlawed women's work in certain occupations. Seventeen states, for example, did not permit women to work in mining; Ohio forbade women to work in shoeshine parlors, bowling alleys, and poolrooms. And several states passed blanket prohibitions against a woman working in any industry detrimental to her "health or welfare" or to her "morals" or to "her potential capacity for motherhood" or in "employment dangerous and prejudicial to her life, health, safety or welfare." [60]

What impact did these laws have on working women? Did the laws promote their welfare or impede their advancement and close off opportunities? These questions were at the center of a bitter (and highly relevant) debate in the 1920s between proponents and opponents of an equal rights amendment—and to follow this argument is not only to analyze an episode with many implications for the current ERA controversy but at the same time to understand the effects of protective legislation on the position of women in the labor force.

During the 1920s, a small but highly vocal group of women campaigned under the banner of the National Woman's Party (NWP) for equal rights.[61] They repeatedly petitioned Congress to pass a constitutional amendment "to secure for women complete equality with men under the law and in all human relationships." [62] To the NWP, the elimination of legal inequality was the logical outgrowth of the suffrage victory, a carrying forward of the original Seneca Falls Convention platform that demanded full social and economic equality for women. "There is not a single state in the union," argued Doris Stevens, a leader of the party, "in which men and women live under equal protection of the law. . . . Woman is still conceived to be in subjugation to, and under the control of the husband, if married; or the male members of the family, if unmarried." [63] An equal rights amendment would put an end to all such discrimination.

To fulfill this goal, the NWP was forced to repudiate much of the legislation that Progressive reformers had enacted. It strongly objected to protective legislation for women workers, insisting that any laws that viewed women as a special class violated their rights. Women ought not to be lumped with children as a group in need of paternalistic intervention; legislation that defined women exclusively in terms of their roles as mothers denied them freedom of choice. "The pleas of special protection for women only," declared an editorial in *Equal Rights*, the party's official publication, "is based on the assumption that the maternal function incapacitates women from free competition in the industrial field. This takes for granted motherhood as a constant corollary for womanhood." [64] Such a judgment restricted opportunities for those who for one reason or another chose to enter the world beyond the home. "Motherhood is the most glorious advantage women can enjoy, but all women do not enjoy this privilege," Mary A. Murray, chairperson of the Industrial Council of the NWP, told a New York legislative committee. "There are women who never marry, women beyond the childbearing age. How cruelly unjust to handicap all women at all times under the guise of protecting motherhood." [65]

So, too, the NWP denounced that most favored piece of Progressive legislation, the Sheppard-Towner Act. Once again, the law singled out women as a class for special protection, defining them—regardless of their individual talents or aspirations—as mothers, not persons.

The NWP did not want to abolish Sheppard-Towner but to reorient its goals. All women did not require special education to become effective mothers. And not all women would become mothers. Some women, it was true, were unable for physical or other reasons to cope with pregnancy and motherhood, and they might require assistance. But then, the NWP said, define them as a separate category instead of making them prototypically female. "That group of women," contended Doris Stevens, "will still be protected by such special legislation, just as workmen's compensation, written to cover special groups of men, and soldiers' bonuses and funds for invalid soldiers are written to protect them." [66] Make maternity benefits, like workmen's compensation and veterans' benefits, available for the disabled and the exceptional case. Do not set women apart as frail, weakly, and therefore in particular need of health care.

By the same token, the NWP criticized the widow pension acts—they, too, presented women as a special class and treated them exclusively in terms of motherhood. The party did agree with the ultimate goals of the legislation; the state should support children at home rather than in orphan asylums or almshouses. But they disagreed with the provision that made only mothers eligible for benefits. If the bill really intended to aid children, as its sponsors contended, then why could not worthy widowers receive stipends to keep their children at home? "Is there any reason to believe," asked Doris Stevens, "that a needy widower should not have the same protection for the child that a deserving widow has?" [67] The NWP, in other words, was not challenging the Progressive assumption that the state ought to promote the health and welfare of children. They were objecting to a law that made women, and women only, responsible for the duties of child care.

In similar terms, the NWP insisted that to single out working women for protective treatment was ill-advised, because it deprived working men of important benefits and at the same time was counterproductive to women. The NWP was very much a part of the Progressive tradition, in the sense that it looked to the state to intervene on behalf of the working classes. The difference was that it urged that social class, and not gender, provided the only legitimate basis for such laws. "The objection to special legislation," argued Harriot Stanton Blatch, a staunch suffragist and the daughter of Elizabeth Cady Stanton, "is not on the grounds that no protection is necessary, but because partial laws have not protected men and have thrown women out of employment or crowded them into the lower grades of work." [68] Insisted Stevens, "Protection, no matter how benevolent in motive, unless applied alike to both sexes, amounts to actual penalization." [69] An equal rights amendment would compel the state to protect all workers, both men and women.

This position of the NWP in favor of class-based protective legislation also reflected the view that the vulnerability of the laboring classes was not tied to gender but to work environments. Working men were just as often the victims of ill health as working women. "Welfare workers," continued Harriot Stanton Blatch in a stinging attack on special protection, "always seem to think of industrial women as spavined, broken-backed creatures, and the sons of Adam as tireless, self-reliant, unionized supermen. Neither estimate is correct. Both need the protective aegis of the state." [70] To buttress her argument, Blatch presented health statistics to demonstrate that men succumbed to tuberculosis more frequently than women; that male children died in infancy more frequently than female children. Clearly, whatever special protection was appropriate, was appropriate for both sexes.

The point of the NWP's data on men's health was not to suggest that all working people were broken and in ill health. On the contrary, the party was eager to demonstrate that the illness of some workers ought not to become the pretext for defining all workers as sickly. The working woman that NWP had in mind was healthy, vigorous, adult, and competent. Protective legislation had confined her all too often to the most low-paying and necessarily overcrowded jobs. An equal rights amendment would liberate her. If women in the work force were allowed the same opportunities as men, vigorous and highly skilled women would no longer be required to "set their pace with the weakest of their sex." Women were not children and ought not to be treated as such.

In keeping with this judgment, the NWP demanded the abolition of legislation regulating night work for women. "When night work is in operation," insisted Mary A. Murray, "adult women should have the same rights as adult men to engage in it if they so choose. It is for them and not for others to decide if their earnings will compensate for changing from night to day. It is for them and not for others to decide whether their private arrangements are better served by working at night." [71] Women did not need the legislature to make up their minds for them. They could decide full well what arrangements were in their own best interest.

The propriety of an equal rights amendment split the suffrage coalition. Settlement house workers and child welfare reformers vigorously opposed its passage. To them, suffrage was not one victory in the long struggle for female equality; it was the opportunity for women to fulfill their particular political mission. Equal rights directly contradicted the concepts inherent in that mission, and they reacted fiercely to what they considered a wrong-headed and mischievous concept.

Throughout the 1920s these Progressive reformers demanded that social policy recognize and take into account gender distinctions. "The political rights of citizens are not properly dependent upon sex," Florence Kelley insisted, "but social and domestic relations and industrial activities are." Kelley ridiculed attempts to pass an equal rights amendment: "Women cannot be made men by act of the legislature or by amendment to the Federal Constitution. The inherent differences are permanent. Women will always need many laws different from those needed by men." [72] To Kelley, social legislation had to acknowledge and compensate for these differences, not ignore them.

To Progressives, the NWP's demand for social and legal equality represented the revival of a cruder Social Darwinist view of society. "The amendment looks backward to the days when 'equality' was conceived to be absolute and rigid in nature," declared one pamphleteer for the National League of Women Voters. "These were the days also of the cruel and unsocial doctrine of 'laissez faire'." [73] In effect, to support an equal rights amendment was to restrict government intervention, to turn the clock back to the time when property rights took precedence over community welfare.

Progressivism, as its defenders in the 1920s insisted, was more concerned with equal protection under the law than with formal legal equality before the law. An equal rights amendment would reverse this judgment, necessarily promoting the interests of an upper class against a lower class. "Equal rights between large groups," argued Ethel Smith, president of the National Women's Trade Union League, in opposition to the amendment, "may be more important to society than equal rights of the individuals within these groups." [74] To protect all women might not be in the best interests of a few particular women—but in the case of such conflict, the rights of the talented few had to give way to the needs of the masses. Indeed, the women reformers did not hesitate to identify the NWP with more traditional opponents of Progressivism, those who would exploit the working classes. Just as robber barons placed profit before health, income before safety, and property before welfare, so the NWP elevated its demands for higher-paying jobs and advancement for middle-class women over the needs of the immigrant women. "The Woman's Party," noted Felix Frankfurter, then Professor of Law at Harvard, "is concentrating upon reforms and upon sentiments of special concern to a comparative handful of professional and leisure-class women, who seem either indifferent to or ignorant of the consequences they will bring upon millions of wage-earning women. The proposed amendment threatens the well-being, even the life of these millions." [75] The amendment was the latest manifestation of greed and self-interest in combat with the common welfare.

Progressives presented an analysis of the actual position of women in the labor force that was designed to buttress the case for protective legislation. Viewing the world through the windows of the settlement house, they made the vast majority of women workers seem indistinguishable from the child laborers. Dr. Alice Hamilton, in a lengthy critique of the equal rights amendment, declared: "I must, as a practical person, familiar with the great, inarticulate body of working women, reiterate my belief that they are largely helpless, that they have very special needs which unaided they cannot attain." [76] Clara Beyer, a researcher for the Women's Bureau, drew a similar picture: "Women are an unstable factor in industry, that the majority enter industry to fill the gap between school and marriage." [77] They were disproportionately young: in a "typical manufacturing establishment, 33 percent of women workers were under 20 and only 14 percent of working men." And they were unhealthy: "Working girls in mills succumbed more frequently than men to tuberculosis." [78]

Moreover, Progressives contended that women workers were still more at risk for being unable to organize to improve working conditions in the ways that men did. As a more stable and skilled group in the labor force, men were able to form unions and battle (at least in some of the crafts, successfully) for minimum wages and decent working conditions through collective bargaining. But the young ages, transiency, and lack of training among the great majority of women workers precluded such action. Citing figures from New York State in 1920 (where only 11 percent of women workers belonged to unions), Clara Beyer argued that "because of their lack of skills and their extreme youth, trade unions among women have been of slow growth, far slower than [among] men." Under these circumstances, the abolition of protective legislation would be disastrous. Proponents of the equal rights amendment might depict women workers as competent to make their own decisions and arrangements, but they were ignoring the basic facts about the character of working women. "While the masses of women workers are so far down on the industrial scale," concluded Beyer, "it is ludicrous to talk of their freedom to choose their occupations, to bargain freely for their wages and hours of work. It would be more to the point to talk of the freedom of employers to exploit their workers." [79] And Hamilton concurred: "It would be a crime for the country to pass legislation which would not only make it impossible to better their lot in the near future, but would even deprive them of the small measure of protection they now enjoy." [80]

Finally, these opponents of the amendment could not understand why the elite of the women's working force (and it was the elite, they were convinced, who were behind the amendment) should be so disturbed by special legislation. After all, since they worked outside the factories and did not work at night, the laws did not restrict their freedom of action. "Why should an organization composed chiefly of highly paid professional or semi-professional women," demanded Florence Kelley, "some of whom have worked themselves out of the wage-earning group, devote itself to defeating the efforts of the wage earners to gain by legislation such leisure as the more favored, self-supporting women already enjoy?" [81] The better-placed had no reason to deprive the lesser-placed of vital protections.

This rhetoric, appealing and persuasive, helped to defeat all attempts to enact an equal rights amendment. But the arguments, it should be clear, were often less than valid; they did not present an accurate portrait of women in the work force or of the disadvantages that all women suffered from protective legislation. The majority of women workers were not the young, helpless girls Progressives described. Only one-fifth of the working women in 1920 were under the age of twenty—this even in a large, industrial, and immigrant-populated state like New York. Nor were all types of women workers as transient as Progressives believed. Several Labor Department studies of clerical workers in large corporations revealed that women remained in these positions longer than men.[82] But most important, by 1924 it was apparent that protective legislation could be counterproductive for unskilled workers, and even the Progressives had to confront, however reluctantly, the negative aspects of their program.

The major distinction that must be drawn to understand the effects of protective legislation is not between skilled and unskilled jobs, but between occupations in which women made up the majority of the workers and occupations in which they were the minority. In the first instance, special laws could often improve conditions, as in the case of department store employment. In the second, however, the situation was often the reverse. Manufacturing plants that used successive shifts of workers dismissed women when night work laws were enacted. Unable to take a rotation, the women became less valuable employees. In the printing industries, where so much of the work was done at night, women again lost out. So, too, protective legislation forced women out of their posts as streetcar conductors (the work was too hard) and out of the buffing, grinding, and polishing trades (which seemed too unsafe).[83] As Elizabeth Baker accurately concluded in the mid-1920s: "In occupations or industries where men greatly predominate, protective laws for women are likely to prohibit rather than protect their employment, or, in other words, to relieve men of the competition of women."[84] Put another way, one major result of protective legislation was to encourage, even compel, women to remain in those occupations that were already filled with women.

The Progressives did attempt to fashion a counterargument to these facts. The Women's Bureau, the government agency established to investigate and report on the conditions of working women and, not surprisingly, staffed by Progressive-minded women reformers, in 1928 examined the effects of protective legislation. The findings made up a rather odd document, at once acknowledging the hardships that the laws imposed and trying to minimize their significance. The study did bring to light some genuine conflict of interest among different types of women workers. But rather than addressing this conflict, the Women's Bureau, as Progressives were often prone to do, preferred to ignore it.

The core issue was whether the innovation on behalf of some workers did or did not deprive others of the opportunity to earn a decent wage or advance their careers. Clearly, some industries subjected to protective regulations experienced a drop in the number of women in their ranks (factories with shifts, polishing and grinding, and the like). Moreover, it was simply not true that professional or semi-professional women were unaffected by protective legislation. The Bureau conceded that night work prohibitions, "when applied indiscriminately to special occupations that are professional or semi-professional in type, [have] resulted in restrictions of women's employment."[85]

But, then, how justify these laws? On what grounds was a system that harmed some women workers to be defended? The answers were, in fact, quite lame: only a minority of women, it was claimed, actually lost their jobs because of these laws, since most women were employed in female-type occupations. But such a response was obviously circular: it was no answer to the charge that protective legislation forced women into a few occupations to say that women were actually working in only a few occupations. Another tactic was to insist that a "natural fit" existed between women's special talents or inherent frailty and certain types of work. Yes, protective legislation allowed women to work only passenger elevators and not freight elevators, but this restriction ostensibly played only "a small part in limiting women's employment." Women, maintained the Bureau, would "naturally" have preferred to operate passenger elevators. "There are well-defined lines between the types of services required of men and of women operators, and between the types of services at which the sexes excel." [86] The Bureau did not go on to try to define what made men innately more suitable to the one kind of service and women to the other—what was "natural" did not stand in need of explication. Most important, the "natural fit" removed any onus from protective legislation. Since this kind of selectivity would have gone on in all events, protective legislation could not be blamed for the outcome. The Bureau also insisted that "modes of production" or "public opinion" determined women's occupational choices—but once again, beyond a retreat to a stereotypic view of women, little evidence was offered to defend such a position. The critical point for the Women's Bureau was that the protective legislation had in no way affected the forces that determined occupational choice.

The Progressive drive to ameliorate the conditions for working women was, in the end, of mixed value. Undoubtedly it did encourage the grouping of women in only a few occupations—at the least, it did nothing to help disperse them through the labor force, to expand freedom of choice, to open up opportunities. At the same time, it certainly helped to perpetuate the idea that women were frail, weak, and in a phrase, childlike. Probably some women workers did gain a few advantages from the legislation—the workplace was made somewhat more comfortable and the routine of work less grueling. Nevertheless, protective legislation certainly proved no answer to the discrimination that women found on the job, to the restrictions that bound them in, to the dynamic that forced them to accept those positions that men did not want. The Progressives did not let these considerations dampen their enthusiasm for protective legislation or reduce their opposition to an equal rights amendment. A very different set of assumptions and a very different ideology than educated motherhood would have to take hold before the linkage of women with children would break down, before an equal rights amendment would seem the appropriate policy to pursue.

The Expanded Public School

The most appropriate test case for evaluating Progressive child welfare programs is the attempt to organize and administer an expanded public school system. It would not be a difficult exercise to demonstrate the limited accomplishments of the playground movement. All too often the equipment was poor, the supervisors ill-trained, the children put to drill more than to play. It is also a simple matter to describe the inadequacies of the kindergartens. Such a champion of the movement as G. Stanley Hall was anything but enthusiastic about their actual practices. The facilities were not pleasant or even healthy; typically, the lighting was poor and the ventilation inadequate, and the children shared drinking cups and towels. Their routines, Hall discovered, did not encourage spontaneity or creative play; to the contrary, the kindergarten seemed so rigid a place as to warrant being described as "a little school factory." [87] But however poorly these programs turned out, the reform agenda has to be judged on the basis of its grander and more critical effort to substitute school attendance for factory work. Could Progressives accomplish this aim? What were the costs? What were the results, both intended and unintended, of their intervention?

That the reformers did manage to get their legislation enacted, and that child labor declined while school attendance rose, is eminently clear. The great majority of states, including all the major industrial ones, expanded the scope of their child labor laws and provided mechanisms for effective enforcement. Even allowing for some false reporting and inadequate policing, the shift is impressive. In 1900, in nonagricultural pursuits, the number of children between the ages of 10 and 13 in the labor force was 186,000. Between the ages of 14 and 15, there were 502,000. Twenty years later, 50,000 children between 10 and 13 were at work and another 367,000 between 14 and 15; by 1930, the number had declined still further to only 30,000 between 10 and 13 and 168,000 between 14 and 15. Including agricultural work in the calculations does not reduce the impact of the movement. In 1910, 12.3 percent of all children below 13 were in the labor force; by 1920, 4.4 percent; by 1930, 2.4 percent. Indeed, by 1920, in such states as New York, Massachusetts, Connecticut, Ohio, Pennsylvania, and Illinois, less than 1 percent of children under 14 were employed.[88]

So, too, by the early 1920s, stringent compulsory education laws operated in every state, requiring school attendance until the age of 14 or 15 or 16, depending upon the jurisdiction. Appropriately, school expenditures swelled, doubling between 1900 and 1910, slightly more than doubling between 1910 and 1920, and still gaining between 1920 and 1930. The length of the average school term increased from 135 days in 1890 to 162 days in 1920; then to 173 days in 1930 (approximating the present term of 179 days). And school attendance kept pace. In 1890, on the average, pupils attended school for 86 days a year; by 1920, for 121 days; by 1930, for 143 days (again close to the present average of 162 days).[89] The factory inspector and the truant officer were doing their jobs.

But what happened to the children who were now compelled by law to enter and remain in school? It may be fair enough to conclude that no matter how dismal the experience, children were better off at the desk than at the machine; however inadequate the program, it was still preferable to send them to classes than to factories. But reformers did set higher sights, in part because they were determined to fulfill the ambitious precepts of educated motherhood, and in part too because they faced a very immediate and pressing problem: no sooner did they coerce school attendance than they had to make school sessions relevant to a new, and probably recalcitrant, student body. How should the school treat its captive audience—what kind of program should administrators design for students? What kind of program would keep them from truancy?

The system that many looked to for an answer was first put into practice at Gary, Indiana. John Dewey applauded the Gary plan as representing "a synthesis of the best aspects of the Progressive 'schools of tomorrow.'" Randolph Bourne, so active in all sorts of Progressive reforms, devoted an entire volume to *The Gary Schools*. They were "the most ingenious attempt yet made to meet the formidable problems of congested urban life and modern vocational demands which are presented to the administrators of the city schools." To

Bourne, Gary represented "a fundamental reorganization of the public school to meet changing social and industrial conditions." [90]

In many ways, Gary seemed the right place for implementing a Progressive model. Its population was composed of unskilled immigrant labor (in 1908, 56 percent of the town was foreign-born), who worked in the prototypical heavy industry, steel (it was U.S. Steel, of course, that founded Gary); and the town had all the social problems that any Progressive could imagine—"all the problems," as Bourne described it, "of congestion and bad housing and sanitation that curse the large industrial cities. . . . Communal problems have all been thrown upon the people themselves to solve." [91] And Gary had one more advantage: it had elected a Progressive mayor who, in turn, appointed William Wirt, an admirer of Dewey, to organize its new school system. Here, then, was the chance to start from scratch and yet confront all the ongoing dilemmas of reform in an industrial society.

If it was the function of the Lowell boardinghouses to create a moral and disciplined work force, it was the goal of the Gary schools to create an efficient and healthy work force.[92] Dewey's manual training program was to be the means to the first end; the Gary schools made extensive provision for shops so that students would have "substantial opportunity to participate in numerous forms of industrial work." [93] The shop was not to train to specific employments; its lessons had "only incidental bearing upon preparation for a wage-earning vocation for pupils below sixteen years of age. Its primary purpose is to contribute to the general experience, general intelligence and general development of the pupil." [94] Wirt, who described himself as a "scientific manager" of school "plants," echoed the Dewey rhetoric faithfully: "Formerly the school plus the home and small shop educated the children. The small shop has been generally eliminated and the home has lost most of its former opportunities." Therefore, "a much greater part of the education of the child must be assumed by the school. . . . The school must do what the school, home and small shop formerly did together." [95] Gary's manual training answered that need most directly.

Wirt was also very attentive to the school's obligation to promote the children's health. The Gary schools built elaborate playgrounds, indoor gymnasiums, and even swimming pools. Physical fitness was so central to the routine that it was the doctor and not the teacher who decided on each pupil's particular schedule. Every child underwent a physical examination, and with the results at hand, the doctor prescribed so much classroom activity, so much gymnasium activity. As Dewey described it, those "not strong enough for the strain of classroom work are not sent home, but are kept in school and given a program suited to their strength; their classroom time is cut down to a minimum and they spend most of the day in the playground or in the gymnasium doing the sorts of things the doctor says they need to get strong." [96] Thus, the shops, the gym, crafts, and exercise—not the classroom or the three Rs—dominated the Gary routine.

The Gary schools, like so many other Progressive institutions, also attempted to reach into the community. The playgrounds and gymnasium facilities operated after school hours, on Sundays, and during summer vacations. "In most sections of the city," declared Wirt, "the greatest problem of the school is to counteract and overcome the demoralizing influences of the child's life in the streets and alleys and, unfortunately, in many homes, so-called." [97] The school sponsored pure milk campaigns—the children brought in milk from home to test its purity; students made posters to explain the value of sanitation in preventing disease and drew maps of their neighborhoods to keep track of community improvements. "From time to time," reported Dewey, "an auditorium period is devoted to showing these maps and pointing out the good and bad features of blocks and neighborhoods." [98] Civic responsibility was taught in still other ways. Shop time went to mending clothing for fellow pupils. "One year," Bourne recounted, "the shoeless condition of some of the children set a demand for a shoe shop, in which old shoes were made over into wearable new ones." [99] Finally, the children learned about efficient family management. "On more than one occasion," boasted Dewey, "some newly arrived family has moved from an overcrowded rear shack to a comfortable flat with the same rent because through the children they found out their bad quarters were unnecessary." [100] Just as the settlement house trained mothers to become Progressive reformers, so the Gary schools trained children.

Judged by the most relevant school statistic, the Gary system appeared to be doing exceptionally well: attendance was up, truancy down. "The freedom of the Gary schools," concluded Randolph Bourne, "does not seem to make for truancy. The percentage of attendance in November 1914, was for boys 92.9 percent; for girls, 91.6—a remarkable record when it is considered that boy truancy in most city schools is much the greater." [101] And other observers agreed that Gary ran an appealing program. "There is an air of hap-

piness about the children which is marked in both work and play. . . .
Play and work are merged into interesting activity." [102] In all, the
innovation seemed a Progressive dream come true, a reform that was
in everyone's best interest. The children liked it, the community
benefited, and the directors of the U.S. Steel plant could look forward
to employing healthy and productive workers.

Yet, the Gary model did not take hold, and its program was
adopted in only a handful of municipalities. The reasons for its lack
of popularity can be put succinctly: for some, Gary offered too
much manual and physical education; for others it offered too little.
Thus, many educators insisted that Gary's emphasis on occupational
training and exercise led to a gross neglect of the basics; its students
could not read or spell or do arithmetic as well as others. As one
evaluation sponsored in 1919 by the General Board of Education for
the Rockefeller Foundation concluded, Gary might offer an "en-
riched curriculum," but the "final levels of achievement reached are
comparatively low. . . . The entire investigation reveals many and
consistent evidences of careless work, imperfectly developed habits
and marked lack of achievement." [103] So, too, many parents, particularly immigrant parents, protested vehemently against the implementation of a Gary-like program. Certain that education ought to
provide mobility into white collar jobs, they were convinced that
Gary's curriculum undermined their ambitions. The plan actually
became the focal point of the New York City mayoralty campaign
in 1917. The incumbent, fusionist party mayor, John P. Mitchell,
endorsed it, only to lose to the democrat John Hylan, who opposed
it—and while other issues certainly played their part (the Mitchell
coalition was splintering just as Tammany was reviving in strength),
the Gary issue was prominent. Parents charged that a Gary-like system amounted to "enslaving the youth of this city, fitting them to be
the tools and slaves of the aristocracy." [104] The plan, after all, came
out of a company town dominated by U.S. Steel and named after
the steel magnate Elbert Gary; and the Gary plan, Hylan's platform
charged, "aims to make our public schools an annex of the mill and
the factory." As one parents' meeting resolved: "We are not demanding luxuries. We merely want our children raised as free and
independent citizens, and we are going to have that if we have to
fight for it, even if we have to resort to the methods of 1776." [105]
Defeating Gary seemed worth a revolution.

Gary also disappointed those who were impatient with so general
and broad a program of manual training, who wanted a very specific,

practical type of vocational training. Wirt himself (who remained superintendent at Gary until 1939) was flatly opposed to vocational education, convinced, like Dewey, that the function of the school was to educate the "whole child," not to fit him or her to a given occupation. "If you believe," commented one observer, "that vocational education is confined to specific training for a trade and that this must be carried out in a separate trade school, and that general education has no relation to it except as it may add a fringe of culture, then you will think that there is no vocational education in Gary." And this is precisely what critics did think.

At the very time that Wirt and Dewey were establishing the Gary program, the Massachusetts Commission on Industrial Education was advocating a system of vocational training. The Commission dismissed manual education as the equivalent of "general education," a preparation for "higher training in some college or engineering school." Its aim, on the contrary, was to found a separate system of vocational schools to be "parallel to existing public high schools but independent from them" that would provide "preparation for some life pursuit." [106] By 1910, the National Association of Education also supported this type of training, noting that it provided "not motor training, but specific motor abilities. . . . not preparation for life—any life —but preparation for a specific kind of life." A specialized society demanded specialized education, "special preparation for a vocation." [107]

Vocational education brought together a varied and powerful coalition of supporters, so powerful that by 1918 the federal government, through the Smith-Hughes Act, was making funds available for public schools to implement the program. The National Association of Manufacturers (NAM) delighted in education along "intensely practical lines." From its perspective, vocational education would increase the supply of skilled labor without much on-the-job training and without the restrictive control of the labor unions. "To authorize and found and organize trade schools," agreed the NAM, "is the most important issue before the American people today. It is this way only that we can undo the monstrous crime which organized labor has committed. . . . In none of the professions . . . is there any attempt made to limit the number of people who may desire to engage in them. It is only in skilled and manual labor that the attempt is made to monopolize the opportunity of life. . . . The absurd doctrine that we as a nation can have too many skilled mechanics . . . is, as we say, unaccountable." [108]

Despite the charges of the NAM, the craft unions themselves supported vocational education. To be sure, they were somewhat ambivalent about the program, fearful of an anti-union bias in the schools; but in the end they believed that the more skills the workers possessed, the greater the union leverage against business, indeed, the greater the propensity to join a union.

So, too, many (but not all) child labor reformers endorsed vocational education. If the school were immediately relevant to a career, children were far more likely to remain in the classroom and out of the factory, at least until the age of sixteen. Convinced that many children dropped out of school not because of the avarice or ignorance of their parents but because of the dullness and seeming irrelevance of the curriculum, reformers anticipated, along with the Massachusetts Commission, that "large numbers of these children would be in school if the school promised some preparation for some life pursuit." As Owen Lovejoy, one of the leading child labor reformers, argued: "Our problem is to supply the attractive power in our educational system that will prove the complement of prohibitive legislation and compulsory elementary education." That complement was vocational education: "Anything is admirable, that will make our schools a part of real life." Others like Grace Abbott and Sophonisba Breckenridge agreed: it was far better to have children aged fourteen to sixteen learning vocational skills than entering the factories in the ranks of the unskilled.[109]

Vocational training did have its opponents. Those who disliked manual training and found it coercive had even less patience for vocational education. And to John Dewey, the system represented the "greatest evil now threatening the interests of democracy in education," promising to widen rather than to narrow the gap between classes.[110] The result of all the controversy was that public school education remained broad and general (without any concessions to the Gary plan); but the high schools, night schools, and newly created "continuation schools" (afternoon classes for those between fourteen and sixteen who were at work) did provide vocational training. In this way, the students seemingly had a choice that the Gary system did not provide—only those who wanted to pursue vocational training would have to do so. No one would be forced into factory work.

But even this compromise did not fulfill reformers' expectations. Federal and state vocational education expenditures expanded (from $8.5 million in 1920 to $30.0 million in 1930). However, the bulk of the money did not go into establishing separate, full-time day programs. (Only 4 percent of the students in urban settings were actually enrolled in a purely vocational education institution.) Instead, most of the funds—and most of the students—went into part-time and evening classes.[111] Vocational education became not a parallel track to the regular schools, but a diversion; not a fully legitimate and popular program, but an aside. When students and administrators voted with their feet, they did not give vocational education a vote of confidence. Further, the Progressive reform program ran up against more problems than just low attendance. In practice, the system came close to fulfilling Dewey's worst fears.

The disappointing record of vocational education programs emerged vividly in the 1936 staff report to President Franklin Roosevelt's Advisory Committee on Education. Conducted by John Dale Russell, professor of education at the University of Chicago, the study was "the first attempt at an extensive outside appraisal of the federally reimbursed program of vocational education in the United States," [112] and its findings, on the whole, were discouraging —almost grim. Vocational instruction was, as intended, "very specific and narrowly related to the occupational skills it seeks to develop." But the committee found that it was too specific for an industrial system that was in the midst of "rapid technological change." As a result, "it is entirely possible that the specific processes learned in the training period may be obsolete before the trainee has an opportunity to enter employment." [113] The Committee noted that "representatives of organized labor and of industrial management are critical of the inadequate preparation for skilled trades. . . . In general, the highly specific training in the all-day program of many vocational schools has been of little value to boys intending to enter trades and industrial occupations." Not only were the machines used for teaching purposes all too typically obsolete and methods of instruction outdated, but also "vocational education in trades and industries has tended to produce a supply of labor without reference to the demands for it or the possibility of absorbing it into employment." [114] Worse yet, the programs held out false promises to the students. "Pupils are lured into the trade and industrial classes under the pretense that they will be given training completely equipping them as skilled mechanics or craftsmen." But the promises were false and "the inability of pupils who have completed the requirements in the skilled trades is a source of bitter disappointment." [115]

Vocational training may even have reduced students' opportunities in the labor market. "Many employers state," reported Russell, "that they prefer to employ boys who have had only a good general high school education, rather than those who have had trade courses. This preference on the part of employers, however, may frequently arise from the desire to obtain the more intelligent individuals as employees." In other words, the employers understood precisely how recruitment worked. "A general high school education usually serves as a selective device to weed out those of lower intellectual ability." Who was encouraged to enter vocational training? The weaker students—and in short order, vocational education had an unmistakable stigma about it.

Were all this not discouraging enough, the Russell survey reported instances of rank exploitation of those enrolled in vocational programs. Some school courses were run in conjunction with actual factory production, "plant training" it was called, with foremen serving as teachers. But then "beginning workers in the plant have been classified as 'pupils' long after they have mastered the fundamentals of the process, and have been paid only low wages or no wages at all for a long period of time even though they were engaged in regular production." [116] Union representatives also complained that at times "the production of trade-training classes is sold on the open market in competition with merchandise produced in regular industrial enterprises. . . . This type of arrangement has been specially prevalent in the textile industry, frequently through cooperation with a factory in the local community which agrees to furnish the necessary machinery and raw materials to the school in return for the finished product." [117] In these instances, vocational education literally transformed the school into a factory, which was certainly not what the reformers had in mind.

In the end, the Progressives' agenda for the school could not be fulfilled, partly because of the difficulty of what they were attempting. The schools were simply not institutions well-suited to deliver vocational education. Technology changed too rapidly. The machines were antiques. The teaching staff was inadequate to the job. And no wonder; if one had the skills to teach a trade, those skills were more profitably used in the marketplace. As Russell found: "The teaching of vocational subjects does not appeal to enough young people who are making a choice of a career. . . . Many persons trained for teaching the vocational subjects have found that their avenues for advancement are chiefly outside the school system." [118]

Even more important, reformers were trying to devise a program that was supposed to be in the best interests of others, but the others wanted very little of it. Vocational education was supposed to keep students in school and out of the factory, because reformers—but not necessarily the students—defined school as being in their best interest. Just as in the case of protective legislation for working women, the effort to abridge freedom of action and to substitute preferences turned out in many ways to be counterproductive. It took little insight on students' part to recognize that vocational education would not advance their careers. After a handful of incidents they would know that the general high school track was the preferred track, not only in office work but in factory work. After a few broken promises (an inability, for example, of graduates to satisfy requirements for entering a skilled trade), they would understand that vocational education could not substitute for direct, on-the-job training. After a few cases of exploitation they would recognize that it was better to work for wages than for grades. So it should not be surprising that the schools were unable to integrate such a program into their curriculum or that the students should have avoided it—either by following the general education track, or by trying to get into the work force as quickly as possible.

In sum, the fate of the social policies that emerged from the principles of educated motherhood gave reformers little cause for satisfaction. In some instances, the results were astonishing. Who would have imagined that maternal health programs would not only be scuttled but, in fact, be moved so emphatically from the public to the private sector? Whatever the Progressives first had in mind, they did not envision expanding the prerogatives and powers of the medical profession. By the same token, protective legislation, whether in the name of women or child laborers, turned out to be far more controversial than its designers had imagined and far more complicated in its actual workings. Who could have expected that the laws might well injure some women workers—or that such a proposal as an equal rights amendment would split the suffrage ranks? Neither had reformers intended to set up a two-track system, to penalize, through exploitation or closed-off opportunities, those now compelled to stay in school. Taken together, these unanticipated developments, not surprisingly, helped to set off a retreat on the part of women from the public arena.

CHAPTER

5

From the Nursery
to the Bedroom

HOWEVER TEMPTING it may be to describe a unitary, static, and invariably subservient role for women, definitions of proper womanhood have changed dramatically over the past one hundred years. Just as the concept of virtuous womanhood in the post-Civil War decades gave way to ideas on educated motherhood in the Progressive era, so in turn did the ideal of educated motherhood give way in the 1920s to a view of woman as wife-companion. The essential components of this new model were at once romantic and sexual. The primary relationship in a woman's life was no longer to be with her children but with her husband; a highly affective and emotive tie between them was now at the core of family life. "Marriage," declared critic and writer Ludwig Lewisohn, "should be created by love and sustained by love . . . that precise blending of passion and spiritual harmony and solid friendship without which . . . the close association of a man and a woman is as disgusting as it is degrading." [1] And while there was certainly nothing unusual in speaking of spiritual harmony and friendship, the priority that Lewisohn gave to passion and the stinging terms with which he described its absence ("disgusting and degrading") make clear the novelty of the 1920s' perspective. The proper role for the woman shifted from mother to wife. She still remained in the home, but she moved from the nursery to the bedroom.

Popular advice books in the 1920s for the first time began to suggest that the birth of a child might complicate and even disrupt marital ties. The baby's demand for a mother's time and attention would interfere with the intense relationship between husband and wife. "If children come," warned Lydia Commander in one tract for women, "the wife cannot share her husband's pleasures, attend theaters, lectures or concerts with him; nor can she read books or even the papers as he can. He goes on growing mentally and she falls behind. Presently the finer side of the marriage has disappeared and both are unhappy." [2] In the literature of the 1880s, only a frivolous woman worried about not attending the theater after her baby arrived; in the 1920s, all women might share such a concern. So, too, when "modern marriage" and "romantic marriage" became synonymous, advice books counseled young women to commit what late nineteenth-century minds considered a gross breach of morality, that is, to enjoy at least some forms of premarital sexual activity. "The girl who makes use of the new opportunities for sex freedom," declared two prominent sociologists, "is likely to find her experiences have been wholesome . . . she may be better prepared for marriage by her playful activities than if she had clung to a passive role of waiting for marriage before giving any expression to her sex impulses." [3] Indeed, it is difficult to imagine a more shocking piece of advice to a generation trained to the precepts of virtuous womanhood.

The feminists of the Progressive period were highly critical of these developments. Charlotte Perkins Gilman, writing in 1923, had few kind words for "The New Generation of Women": "A generation of white-nosed women who wear furs in Summer cannot lay claim to any real progress." Romantic sexuality meant that "women have shown an unmistakable tendency to imitate the vices of men. In this they are not only as bad as, but worse than, men, because anything injurious to the race is more harmful and more reprehensible as it affects the mother. The behavior of women in this matter is precisely that of any servile class set free. Indulgences previously enjoyed by the master and denied to the slave are eagerly seized upon." To Gilman, substituting wifehood for educated motherhood represented "women's abuse of new freedom." [4]

Marriage for Love and Sex

To understand both the causes and implications of this change, it is again appropriate to look first to the colleges. The campus was one of the most important breeding grounds for the new ideology, and one of its most powerful popularizers. Just as the courses and extracurricular activities of the colleges had trained one generation to the mission of educated motherhood, now the large coeducational public universities taught their undergraduates, in and out of the classroom, the new role of wife-companion. The changing content of the courses in the social sciences clarifies the shift in orientation. Women in 1900 learned about the curability of poverty through environmental manipulation; their successors in the 1920s learned about the crisis in family life that could be resolved only through a new kind of marital relationship.

As the sociologists described it, the modern American family was in a state of collapse, having lost its traditional functions and inherited sources of legitimacy. Looking back, rather nostalgically and simplistically, to the preindustrial family, they argued that the family had once been the center of production; working together on the farm or at the artisan's bench had ensured family solidarity. At the same time, the father-husband had ruled as a patriarch over his wife and children, commanding obedience to his will. Then, industrialization and democracy intervened, diminishing the father's control over property (by making the family into a unit of consumption) and reducing his control over the family (by encouraging wives and children to pursue their own interests). Under these altered conditions, the traditional family could not survive. Only new types of arrangements could prevent disintegration.[5]

The situation was not altogether bleak, because the sociologists had found an answer to the crisis. A new style family seemed to be emerging, its members bound not by financial ties and autocratic rule, but by affection. Romantic love and sexuality would provide the cohesive force, and, accordingly, the sociologists, unlike the Progressive-minded feminists, celebrated romantic love. "The fact that there are so few motives for marrying at all except this desire to join in the fellowship of love," maintained Ernest Groves and William Ogburn, probably the most influential students of the family, "makes modern matrimony as it now exists . . . predominantly an expression of the profound need of men and women to find their highest happiness in the close character-developing experiences of marriage and the family." [6] Here was the key to the family's survival. "The distinguishing feature of the modern family," they insisted, "will be affection. The new family will be more difficult, maintaining higher standards that test character more severely but it will offer richer fruit for satisfying human needs." [7] Love and affection, in other words, were the contemporary equivalents of economic dependence.

This new definition tied the perpetuation of the family directly to the romantic and sexual quality of the husband-wife relationship. Ernest Burgess explained that three principles "have shaped and will in all probability continue to mold the sexual and familial behavior of our people": first, "that the highest personal happiness comes from marriage based on romantic love"; second, "that love and marriage are essentially personal and private and are, perhaps, even more than other aspects of life to be controlled by the individual himself"; and finally, "that, in consequence, sex and marriage are not to be taken lightly, but seriously in their import for personal and social welfare." Charlotte Gilman notwithstanding, there was nothing frivolous or indulgent about this new ethic. Romance and sexuality brought the "highest personal happiness"; they were the finest, perhaps the only, mode of expressing individuality in industrial society. In sum, the sociologists promoted the new ideology and gave it a profound legitimacy.[8]

Romantic marriage, everyone agreed, did place more of a burden on wives than on husbands. The woman had to assume primary responsibility for keeping the flame of romance alive. As Robert Lynd, an incredibly astute observer of American mores in the 1920s, remarked, woman's "status must be won and rewon by personality and attractiveness if she is to get and keep a husband under the dissolving bans of modern marriage." More cynically another sociologist, Clifford Kirkpatrick, described the wife's obligations as "the preservation of beauty under the penalty of marital insecurity, the rendering of ego and libido satisfaction to the husband, the cultivation of social contacts advantageous to him, the maintenance of intellectual alertness, the responsibility for exorcising the demon of boredom." Both partners were to find happiness within the family, but it was the wife's ultimate duty to make the marriage rewarding.[9]

The extracurricular activities of the colleges trained the coeds to fulfill the requirements for successful marriage that the sociology courses established. "Marriages do not fail," noted one woman college official, "because American women are ineffective mothers [so much for the Progressives], nor because they are poor homemakers [so much for Catharine Beecher], but because they are uninteresting wives. It is that failure that should be averted by college training. . . . If college is going to train for marriage, not only the immediate and necessary knowledge concerning sex adjustment must be given, but the type of training and direction that will keep woman as interesting as she was before marriage." [10] In the 1890s Elizabeth

Harrison had insisted that motherhood required a woman to be doctor, artist, teacher, poet, and philosopher. Now wifehood demanded the same sort of virtuosity; only a philosopher, artist, poet, and teacher could keep a husband satisfied, could be as interesting after marriage as she was before.

Almost every observer of the college scene recognized that the reform activities of an earlier generation of students no longer commanded interest. Even at the prestigious Eastern women's colleges, the civic societies lost their appeal. "The debating club is rather an elusive affair," remarked one Bryn Mawr student in 1929. "One can never be quite sure whether this is the year when it is alive or not." Nor did the social service programs attract large numbers of eager workers. In 1927, the diverse charitable groups at Bryn Mawr merged into one small club. "The majority of the college," noted another undergraduate, "is apt to forget these responsibilities except when it signs a pledge which gives them financial support." And the Bryn Mawr students hardly looked forward to a stay at the settlement house in Long Branch. "The work is arduous," they complained, not "the ideal way of spending even part of a summer vacation." [11]

The Progressive campus associations and activities were the victims of a new kind of organization, the sorority house. The sorority's dominance over the extracurricular life of the college pointed first to an explosion in the number of women students attending Midwestern coeducational schools (while enrollments at the Eastern women's colleges remained constant). That the state colleges had not often constructed dormitories for women made the growth of the sorority that much simpler; numerous girls did require places of residence. Thus, before 1920, only an occasional sorority house appeared on a campus; then during the 1920s the chapters proliferated, with some fifteen to twenty of them to be found at every coeducational college. At Indiana University, for example, by the middle 1920s, two dormitories housed some 220 girls while seventeen sororities housed 600 girls. [12]

The popularity of the sorority testified to more than convenience. It had a broader and more appealing program to offer. Perhaps the best way to understand the novel character of the sorority is to compare it with the clubs of the Progressive period. The older organizations had been democratic in membership: anyone interested in joining was welcome. The sororities, to the contrary, limited their membership—not only did the girls have to compete for places, but the sororities themselves were usually restricted, most glaringly on the basis of color or religion but no less importantly on the basis of social requirements. One had to be of the right background, manner, and style. More, the clubs had frankly public and political goals, to train the girls to become leaders in reform movements. The sororities were almost exclusively concerned with private ends, to mold a winning personality. "The outstanding attitude of modern youth," claimed Ernest Burgess, "is one of self-consciousness and sophistication about sex. Youth in this day and generation are rated in terms of sex appeal." [13] And nowhere was this rating more consistently made and perpetuated than in the sororities.

It is not claiming too much to assert that the sorority's primary aim was to train its members to become ideal wife-companions, to translate the dictates of the family sociologists into a code of behavior. The sororities taught the girls about good appearance—how to apply cosmetics, how to bob hair, how much to shorten skirts. They instructed the girls in the talents of being good hostesses (later girls would know how to entertain their husband's friends and business associates). They gave practical lessons in playing bridge, in drinking, in smoking (all of which would fit the girls well for membership in the country clubs); they also defined the standards of sexual permissiveness—how far to go to interest a man (petting), without going too far (premarital intercourse). Perhaps most important of all, the sororities organized dances and socials so that a member would meet the right kind of man; she could then make the marriage that would be so central to her life. "Four nights a week in most co-educational colleges," commented one woman dean on sorority life, "men may call. Even this amount of time is felt by some girls to be too limited! These girls come to college to get a fraternity pin as well as a sorority pin! The college age is the mating age and many fine friendships ripen into love and marriage follows." [14]

With the stakes so high, "rushing" for a sorority often became the focus of a girl's freshman year, so all-consuming that she would "select 'snap courses' in order to 'make grades' to be installed." And the sororities, for their part, screened applicants carefully with their purposes well in mind. "A very deplorable practice in sororities," observed one woman dean, "is to select girls who dress well and rate well with men." In this way, the girl would not only be a credit to the organization but also help to swell the pool of available men that all the members would meet. And of course, failure to get an invitation to the sorority was a personal calamity. "On those campuses having sororities . . . where membership is invitational," reported one college official, "there are terrible disappointments in store for those girls who are socially crude or who for some other reason do not 'make' a sorority. In many cases this has led girls to leave college." Accordingly, this official advised girls to become as attractive as possible to a sorority: "If a girl wants to 'make' a sorority she must have something to contribute to that group. It may be music, art, dramatics . . . but there must be something which picks her out of the throng and makes her an individual that stands out with a larger promise of success than some others." [15] Clearly, the effort was worth it. Rushing a sorority was not at all unlike catching a man.

The female chaperons in the sororities were as different from the traditional dormitory "mothers" as the sororities were from the Progressive clubs. The stout matron who enforced strict curfews did not belong in this new setting. "The chaperon's place is not for an old lady who wants a nice home," sorority girls would explain to a college administration, "but for a woman who takes her calling as a profession and treats it as such." (After all, the girls were about to take wifehood for their profession.) More, "she should be attractive personally. . . . The ideal chaperon should dress with taste, be neat in all personal things, and always appear well-groomed for any occasion." So, too, "she should have charm and personality in order to make a good hostess and create the hospitable atmosphere found in the real home." [16] In essence, the chaperon was the proper ideal wife-companion, the model that the girls had to mind for themselves.

Just how neat the fit was between the findings of the sociologists and the practices of the sorority is apparent in the generally favorable and supportive attitudes that most college administrators adopted toward the sororities. In the 1920s the state universities often created a new position, dean of women, whose major concern was with the social experiences and adjustments of the female students. And these new deans, probably as much by choice as by necessity, found themselves working very closely with the sorority. "The actual spirit and conduct of these groups," declared one of them, "is more important than any other influence in determining the moral character of our colleges." While the deans might regret one excess or another, on the whole they were remarkably content with the results of this influence. The sororities fostered the right kind of college spirit; they "put over" most of the big projects launched by the administration. "Loyalty to their alma mater ought not to be greater among organized students . . . but, in general, it seems to be so." [17]

The sororities also enabled the colleges to impart social as well as intellectual skills, and the deans defended the task as a legitimate, even critical university function. "It is in these laboratory situations," explained a dean of women, "that an understanding of human nature is acquired and that habits of tolerance for the views of others, habits of being at ease with fellow students, instructors, and strangers, habits of taking and sharing responsibility are cultivated." The sorority cultivated "the art of living" in almost all imaginable aspects. "It can demonstrate the meaning of friendship by cultivating confidence, loyalty and democracy in a small group; it can teach tolerance in human relations; it can stand for good taste in social affairs, restraint in politics and discretion in expenditures; it can develop initiative and leadership in its members." [18] Seemingly, then, the sororities would instill leadership and responsibility. But as the dean's own rhetoric made clear, the premium was on friendship, not social reform; on being at ease with students, not investigating poverty; on the art of living, not on the grim reality of the slums. The deans' conclusion that the sororities gave their members "the power to lead the community" may have been correct. But the question remained: leadership in what direction?

As soon as one turns from the colleges to the larger society the answer becomes eminently clear: leadership in popularizing the woman's role as wife-companion. Advice books that were once filled with recipes and child care suggestions now gave wives helpful hints on how to keep romance in marriage alive. "Life seems so dull when couples forget honeymoon days," warned the new-style Lydia Pinkham pamphlets (selling, if you will, sexuality as much as good health). "The secret of being happily married is simple. Have lots of pleasure that both husband and wife enjoy . . . and above all, be good friends." [19] The advice-to-women columns in the daily newspapers spread these notions to Middletown (Muncie, Indiana, as made famous in the study of Robert and Helen Lynd). "The old idea used to be," wrote one syndicated columnist, Dorothy Dix, "that the way for a woman to help her husband was by being thrifty and industrious by . . . making over her old hats and frocks. . . . But the woman who makes of herself nothing but a domestic drudge is not a help to her husband. She is a hindrance. . . . The woman who cultivates a circle of worth-while people, who belongs to clubs, who makes herself interesting and agreeable . . . is a help to her husband." [20] Those who disregarded this advice ran the risk of divorce. The woman who stopped being an interesting and attractive friend might well discover that her husband was looking elsewhere for sex and companionship. So the Lydia Pinkham pamphlets instructed the wife to "make her home and herself as attractive as possible," to "be as sweet and as loving as before they were married." [21] The courtship and honeymoon stage was now supposed to set the tone for the entire marriage.

Almost everywhere a woman in the 1920s looked, the same message reappeared. Advertisements that once had presented full-bosomed mothers holding their babies and proclaiming the sanitary marvels of a particular soap gave way to pictures of slim and attractive young girls praising deodorizing qualities of the product. Washing machines promoted in 1910 for washing clothes cleaner now were sold with the slogan: "She washes most of the morning, then dances half of the night." Or, "A big wash in the morning yet a bridge party at night." (The lower lines of the advertisement would even include a "bridge tip" to make the woman that much better a player.) Polished floors, once a sign of a meticulous housewife, were linked to sociability: "Let them dance on your floors—it's easy to repolish them to gleaming beauty." Even the kitchen was to express a winning personality: "Nine times out of ten, before the evening is over your guests have been out in your kitchen. Is it modern and up-to-date— full of color and cheer and conveniences?" [22]

"National advertising," commented Ernest Burgess, "utilizes sex as perhaps its most enticing lure in baiting the attention of the buying public to its wares." [23] And advertisements for mouthwash, deodorants, and sanitary napkins were all cases in point. Women had to avoid the "social handicaps" of bad breath, perspiration, and body odor, or risk loss of popularity and sex appeal. "In her life there was no romance," announced one advertisement for Listerine. "Why was she still single? Halitosis (unpleasant breath) is the damning unforgivable social fault." And what could be less romantic than body odor? "Sweet as a rose the first dance," ran one line. But then, perspiration during the second dance, and "though she was one of the best-looking girls in the room, he certainly wasn't enjoying it." Stains ruined clothing and reputations: "The woman of the world allows no fears or uneasiness as to her own personal irreproachableness to intrude on her busiest day, her most important evenings. Only with an underarm dry at all times can she be sure . . . she will be immaculate in low-cut evening gowns." The Palmolive soap advertisements taught: "Beauty, charm, youth may not be the fundamentals of romance but they *help*. . . . Keep that schoolgirl complexion." Asked another advertisement: "Embarrassed by dishpan hands?" The drawing showed two well-dressed couples eating by candlelight—with the hostess distraught. "I was pouring coffee," she confessed, "and for the fraction of a second his glance rested on my hands. I knew my hands looked red and rough from housework and dishes. . . . I felt the evening was a failure." And a similar appeal ran through the advertisements for sanitary napkins. "In a gloomier age," a Modess promotion declared, "women were resigned to drudgery. Today, young womanhood does not permit drudgery to cloud her joy of living. . . . It is this eagerness for youth which has won for Modess, in so short a time, a nation-wide popularity." [24] Although one can only guess at how seriously women took these messages, it is not coincidental that the sales of mouthwashes, deodorants, lotions, and sanitary napkins all rose dramatically through the 1920s.

The decade also witnessed the growth of the cosmetic industry and the proliferation of beauty parlors. In 1931, as Robert Lynd noted, the *Ladies Home Journal* for the first time carried more advertisements for cosmetics than for food. What had once been disreputable (the "painted" woman) was standard and acceptable. "Charm classes," remarked another sociologist, "are popular and are sponsored even by the Young Women's Christian Association." [25] As late as 1900, only an occasional cosmetician or stylist visited the home of a wealthy patron to do her hair; by the 1920s these services were in demand among almost all middle-class women. Beauty parlors became commonplace in large cities and small towns. Beauty care, "once considered a luxury," commented the trade journal *Beauty Culture*, is "now deemed a necessary and people in all stations of life . . . are becoming regular patrons." New York City in 1922 had 750 beauty parlors; five years later it had 3,500. Not one beauty parlor operated in Middletown in 1900; seven were open by 1928. [26] Indeed, by then, some 30,000 beauty parlors operated in the country (the number rose to 40,000 in 1930), and the National School of Cosmeticians estimated that 80 percent of American women were "investing in good looks." Anyone who doubted the fact could ponder the "national total bill for manicures, face lifts, massages, hair dyeing, cosmetics and all, the sum of $1,825,000,000. This is more than Uncle Sam spends on his navy." [27]

These developments inevitably reshaped the character of women's club life. It was not that attendance or membership dropped sharply; rather, here—as on the campus—a basic shift in style and activity took place from political and literary discussions to bridge and athletics. "Things have changed in our clubhouse," complained one old-fashioned leader. "Once the auditorium echoed with brilliant speeches. Now it rings with such terms as 'no trump' and 'grand slam.' " One journalist who set out to investigate "Is the woman's club dying?" reported a curious transformation. "The woman of to-day wants to grow slender. . . . The desire to be slender has drawn women to the tennis court, golf links, and swimming pool. The desire to be 'smart' has drawn them to the country-club veranda." [28] Crusades for the juvenile court and the widow's pension were a thing of the past. The wife-companion had little time left for political activity.

In fact, the ideal wife-companion had little time left for anything apart from her marital relationship. Leaving aside for the moment the matter of child-rearing, the new definition of proper womanhood was extraordinarily private. Bridge clubs were not only nonpolitical but nonintimate. The close ties that bound women together in the settlement houses or the mothers' clubs were now relaxed, almost severed. As one observer, Dorothy Bromley, expressed it in what was intended as a defense of the change: "Feminist-New Style professes no loyalty to women *en masse*. . . . Surveying her sex as a whole, she finds their actions petty, their range of interests narrow, their talk trivial and repetitious. As for those who set themselves up as leaders of the sex, they are either strident creatures of so little ability and balance . . . or they are brilliant, restless individuals who so often battle for women's rights for the sake of personal glory." [29] So, too, the Lynds discovered in Middletown "the growing tendency to engage in leisure time pursuits by couples . . . the unattached man or woman being more 'out of it' in the highly organized paired social life of today." Female fellowship was a victim of romantic marriage.

It is difficult to describe this shift without falling into tones of sarcasm. The flapper image, the notion of woman as sex object, the "retreat" from public to private life all seem now like retrogressive steps. And yet, to understand the nature of the change in its own terms, it is best to see it not from the 1970s back, but from the 1890s forward. In part, the triumph of an ideal of wife-companion does testify, in the women's world as in the men's, to a broad disillusionment with reform activities in the post-World War I period. The 1920s was not a decade conducive to continued political action. Opponents effectively smeared Sheppard-Towner programs as "communistic." One WCTU leader noted: "This isn't the organization it used to be. It isn't popular you know. The public thinks of us—let's face it—as a bunch of old women, as frowzy fanatics. I've been viewed as queer, as an old fogey, for belonging to the WCTU. . . .

This attitude was not true thirty years ago." Small wonder, then, if feminism new-style found bridge-playing more rewarding than political agitation.[30]

But the causes do go deeper. However little empathy one may have for the choices that women made in the 1920s, it is critical to appreciate just how liberating the role of wife-companion appeared to be. Here was a way for daughters to assert individuality, to carry on their own particular type of crusade. If their grandmothers, in WCTU fashion, had violated sensibilities by storming into the saloons, if their mothers had defied norms by marching for suffrage, they would in their day break tradition and smoke, dance, pet, bob their hair, and raise their skirts. In Bromley's terms, the new-style feminist "is intensely self-conscious." If all this took the form of admiring the "chic," of trying to "set off feminine charms," it still had a daring and exciting quality.

Remember, too, that in a very important way, the accomplishments of the Progressive period did not enhance opportunities for women in structural ways. University graduate programs were still not open; the professional job market was shut tightly. Even more critical, the suffrage campaign had not been fought on the grounds of equality or equal opportunity—and the few efforts, such as those of the National Woman's Party, to move the legacy in that direction ran into the bitter and successful opposition of the Progressives themselves. It is all the more predictable, then, that in the absence of such an ideology women in the 1920s expressed themselves in personal and private terms. Flaunting conventions on the dance floor was a good deal more feasible than battling quota systems.

Margaret Sanger: The Panacea of Birth Control

No person or movement better illuminates the origins of women's new role in the 1920s than Margaret Sanger and birth control. Sanger's program, in the first instance, sharply divided the Progressives from their successors, the women of the pre-War from the women of the post-War generation. Sanger was convinced that birth control not only fulfilled but extended the entire Progressive agenda; the Progressives, however, remained convinced that birth control violated their most fundamental precepts. Moreover, the popularity that birth control enjoyed among middle-class women both reflected and promoted the ideal of a romantic and sexual marriage. The wife-companion eagerly adopted birth control, and the availability of birth control made the precepts of wife-companion all the more practical and appealing.

Margaret Sanger began her career as a public health nurse on Manhattan's Lower East Side. Her ghetto experiences made her, like other women reformers, keenly aware of the disastrous effects of poverty on immigrants' lives. But unlike the majority of feminists, Sanger believed that the elimination of poverty would come only from a reduction in family size. "The most serious evil of our times," she declared, "is that of encouraging the bringing into the world of large families. The most immoral practice of the day is breeding too many children." [31] Not the tenement or the sweatshop but the inability of the poor to regulate the size of their families was at the root of the problem. Hence, Sanger sympathized with suffrage, yet she was not active in the movement; nor did she join the public health campaign to save babies by teaching women the importance of hygiene in pregnancy; and she did not work to encourage the formation of labor unions among the working classes or to transform schools or to build parks or to improve neighborhoods. To Sanger, the panacea was the education of every woman to the use of birth control. By faithfully using contraception, every family would necessarily assume a higher standard of living.

The underpinnings for Sanger's program came not from courses in sociology and economics but from a personal and intimate relationship with the noted British psychologist, Havelock Ellis. In 1914 (after fleeing the United States to avoid prosecution for illegally distributing birth control information), Sanger traveled to England where she met Ellis; and she proceeded to gain from him an understanding of how "selective reproduction" could alter the family and society. Ellis had recently published *The Task of Social Hygiene*, and Sanger's own views, to a large degree, were drawn from it. To Ellis first, and to Sanger later, the programs in vogue in Europe and America offered some immediate relief but did not reach to the heart of the issue. The work of the reformers, Ellis wrote, was "exclusively concerned with the improvement of life." Their effort had "accepted the stream of life as it found it, and while working to cleanse the banks of the stream, it made no attempt to purify the stream itself." Accordingly, Ellis set out an alternate design in *The*

Task of Social Hygiene to effect "a transformation of what was formerly known as social reform." [32]

There were two components in Ellis's proposal, which at first seemed oddly juxtaposed, the one almost irrelevant to the other. First, he urged a program of selective reproduction to promote racial purity and to reduce the actual numbers of the poor. "The control of reproduction," he maintained, "renders possible and leads on to a wise selection in reproduction. It is only by such a selection of children to be born that we can balance our indiscriminate care in the preservation of all children that are born, a care that would otherwise become an intolerable burden." But Ellis elaborated a second theme, a new relationship between men and women. "It is the task of this hygiene," he exuberantly declared, "not only to make sewers but to remake love. . . . At one end social hygiene may be regarded as simply the extension of an elementary sanitary code; at the other end it seems to have in it the glorious freedom of a new religion." The freedom in this new religion was for women and men to enjoy sexual love. "In love," Ellis insisted, "the demand for each sex alike must not be primarily for a mere anatomical purity, but for passion and sincerity." [33] What linked these two pronouncements, or more important, the ways by which these two perspectives were to effect the practical implementation of social policy, Ellis did not explain. But in some manner or other, selective reproduction, eugenics, and sexuality were to build a new and better society.

However puzzling Ellis's assumptions, Sanger knew just what to make of them. The movement for birth control that she led in the United States was to realize all of Ellis's goals. If anything, Sanger was not only more pragmatic but also more dogmatic than Ellis, and birth control became the solution for an incredibly wide range of social, economic, and sexual problems. It was the "very pivot of civilization," the method to create a new race, to eliminate poverty and bring a new freedom and satisfaction to women.

As Sanger set out to promote birth control, she made a more or less comfortable alliance with eugenicists. While many of them did remain aloof from the birth control movement, nervous about a program that had an economic rather than a biological underpinning and that might limit the reproduction of the middle rather than the lower classes, a large number of prominent eugenicists did support Sanger. "The efforts of eugenics and of birth control," declared one of them, "are tending more and more to work for the common end." And Sanger, although not eager to promote larger families among the middle classes, did support eugenics for the poor. She too favored restrictions on immigration and the sterilization of the unfit. In fact, she advocated a policy of sterilization for "cases where birth control is likely to fail." [34]

More central to Sanger's campaign was the promise that birth control would reduce poverty, or, to put it more broadly, that it would accomplish in one grand sweep all that the assorted items of Progressive legislation sought to achieve piecemeal. Still more than Ellis, Sanger anticipated such a result from the widespread use of contraception; a reduction in family size would automatically produce a dramatic improvement in standards of living. Family size, not low wages, was the curse of the poor; in effect, she blamed the victims, not the economic organization of society, for their plight. Since poverty had its source in the internal structure of the individual family, its solution was within the control of the wife.[35] The woman who practiced contraception obviated the need for environmental change. Birth control enabled her to manage the job of reform alone.

Not only did too many mouths to feed deplete the laborer's income, but also, by having so many children, the poor were in effect breeding their own competition, creating too many unskilled laborers in an already overcrowded market. "Labor is oppressed," Sanger contended, "because it is too plentiful; wages go up and conditions improve when labor is scarce." [36] Small families would eliminate child labor and even make compulsory schooling legislation less critical.

Sanger believed that Progressives' protective legislation might well exacerbate existing problems. To Sanger, the Sheppard-Towner Act taught "a poor woman how to have her seventh child, when what she wants to know is how to avoid bringing into the world her eighth." [37] It was birth control that promised to improve women's health. Mothers of small families were generally more vigorous than those with broods of children. "Excessive child bearing," Sanger argued, "is now recognized by the medical profession as one of the most prolific causes of ill health in women." And she quoted William J. Robinson to substantiate the point: "Every physician knows that too frequent childbirth, nursing and the sleepless nights that are required in bringing up a child exhaust the vitality of thousands of mothers, make them prematurely old, or turn them into chronic invalids." [38]

Sanger urged women to agitate for the legalization of birth control as they had battled for suffrage. Birth control, even more than suffrage, gave women "the key to the temple of liberty." Now women must "fight for the right to have, without legal interference, all knowledge pertaining to her sex nature." Sanger turned to the suffragists for assistance: "Every woman interested in the welfare of women in general, should make it her business to agitate for such a change in the obscenity laws." The freedom for women to decide "when they shall become a mother, under what conditions" was the most precious of all freedoms.[39]

But Sanger could never forge this alliance, and the causes for her failure bring us to the second element in Ellis's program and to the notions of wife-companion. Sanger believed that birth control would both change the lower-class family and produce a profound alteration in the middle-class family as well, specifically in the private lives of women. Sanger preached Ellis's novel views on female sexuality. "We can hope for no advance," she insisted, "until we attain a new conception of sex not merely as a propagative act, not merely as a biological necessity for the perpetuation of the race, but as a psychic and spiritual avenue of expression." Birth control would "free the mind from sexual prejudice and taboo, by demanding the frankest and most unflinching reexamination of sex in relation to human nature and the bases of human society."[40]

One of Sanger's fullest statements on sexuality appeared in her 1926 manual, *Happiness in Marriage*. (It is no accident that birth control advocates wrote some of the most popular marital advice books in the 1920s and 1930s, from Paul Popenoe, *Modern Marriage: A Handbook* to Drs. Abraham and Hannah Stone, *A Marriage Manual*.) Contraception, as Sanger made eminently clear, was not merely a mechanism for reducing family size but also for intensifying the sexual relationship between husband and wife. *Happiness in Marriage* opened with a statement of this principle: "Husbands as well as wives today realize the importance of complete fulfillment of love through the expression of sex. . . . Sex expression is not merely a propagative function, nor the satisfaction of an animal appetite. . . . Sex expression, rightly understood, is the consummation of love, its completion and its consecration." Thus, Sanger declared: "Before reading the chapters which follow, cleanse your mind of prurience and shame. Never be ashamed of passion. If you are strongly sexed, you are richly endowed." And the rest of the book's chapters were variations on the theme of how to build up and preserve such an endowment.[41]

The critical moment was courtship. The style of behavior set in this stage was to persist throughout the marriage. "The period of wooing," insisted Sanger, "is therefore the most beautiful, as well as the most important in the lives of the young man and young woman." The man's "early experiences . . . form the basis of his experience in the all-important role of marriage." Accordingly she instructed him to "Dramatize your love . . . be aggressive. It is the role of love to act."

As for the woman, she had to respond with exquisite sensibility: "Many a possible romance and marriage have been thwarted by too passive an attitude or too hasty an acceptance on the part of the girl. . . . For the woman as well as the man the period of courtship or wooing demands a distinct technique." Sanger wanted the woman "to be playfully elusive. She must respond to the advances of the man of her choice, but she must not respond too rapidly. . . . She must remember that adventurous primitive man does not value highly an easy capture." Then, when marriage did take place, the couple had to prevent "this intimate and thrilling relationship from sinking to the level of the commonplace." As Sanger explained, "Sex-love and happiness in marriage, I repeat, do not just happen. . . . Eternal vigilance is the price of marital happiness. . . . The nuptial relation must be kept romantic. When either feels that fatigue or monotony is beginning to enter the relation, he or she must take the initiative of intensifying and rejuvenating it. . . . Do not be afraid to take the brakes off your heart, to surrender yourself to love. . . . Unclamp this emotion; let it have full, healthy exercise." Here, in other words, was the credo of the wife-companion: marriage based on passion, sexuality, and, of course, birth control.[42]

While few writers could match Sanger's raw enthusiasm, other authors did link romantic sexuality with marital happiness and birth control. "The couple must have a safe, efficient, and unobstructive method of preventing births," insisted Dr. G. V. Hamilton of the Rockefeller Foundation's Bureau of Social Hygiene, "or they must so limit their physical relations as to cause serious frustrations and harmful emotional tensions, which are bound to lead to unhappiness and perhaps to the destruction of their love and their marriage." As Groves and Ogburn phrased it, "Unless sex is carried to a high level of psychic response, her relationship becomes disappointing and she is no longer passive in her dissatisfaction." And they immediately noted that the modern woman "is unwilling to pay too high a price for sex pleasures. . . . She has a definite idea of how many children she is willing to have. . . . In many cases she is unwilling to accept even the coming of one child as the price of sex experiences."[43] Another supporter of Sanger, Paul Popenoe, distinguishing the new view of sexuality from the old, urged couples to have frequent sexual intercourse. "The idea that frequent coitus may result in the production of an inferior child, and that if the parents would remain continent for some weeks before conception they would thereby store up some mysterious virtue that would be passed on to their offspring, seems to be wholly imaginary." Virtue now rested in the expression of sexuality: "The art of love is the greatest of all arts, alike in the satisfaction which it brings to the artist and the benefit which it confers on the world." [44]

Sanger was not only convinced that sexual continence was a "psychological liability, an absolute danger to female health," but also that a highly romantic and sexual marriage was in the best interests of children. Once again, she aimed to incorporate the entire Progressive agenda into her own platform, including its concern for the child. The wife-companion would as a matter of course produce exceptional offspring. "The child thus born is indeed a flower of love and tremendous joy," Sanger declared. "It has within it the seeds of courage and of power. This child will have the greatest strength to surmount hardships, to withstand tyrannies, to set still higher the mark of human achievement." Sanger, in fact, coined the popular slogan, "Every child a wanted child," a phrase to which she attached the most vivid details. The "unwanted child" was conceived by a woman fearful of pregnancy, who at best practiced coitus interruptus, and who loathed sex. "Can a mother," she asked rhetorically, "who brings the creation of the little life in disgust and in disgust brings it to birth, bequeath to her baby the strength, the mental vigor or the disposition to happiness that is his inherent right?" Moreover, the "unwanted child" was typically a street waif, an illegitimate child, an exploited child laborer, an eventual entry in the statistics of infant mortality; a mother suffering in poverty could not love her offspring. "We forget," Sanger noted, "that under the stress of caring for many children, under the strain of helping to earn bread for hungry mouths and clothing for bodies clothed in rags, the strongest mother love may turn bitter and cruel." [45]

In contrast stood the "wanted child," conceived in love, planned for, and eagerly anticipated, ready to be schooled and trained to a productive life. "Each and every unwanted child," Sanger contended, "is likely to be in some way a social liability. It is only the wanted child who is likely to be a social asset." The availability of birth control, she assured her audiences, made the difference. In effect, Sanger subsumed all the nightmarish images of the dependent, the delinquent, and the defective child under the category of "contraceptive ignorance and failure." All the bright images of children of a new and higher race looked to love and sexuality.[46]

Margaret Sanger's trip to Europe also provided her with practical knowledge of a safe and effective contraceptive technique. In Holland, Dr. Johannes Rutgers of the Dutch Neo-Malthusian League taught her the method for fitting women with pessaries. Upon completing his course she, like the midwives he trained, became an expert "in the hygienic methods of family limitation." [47] With the pessary, Sanger had a device that would at once allow women to limit family size and, by separating the sexual act from the reproductive act, to take pleasure in sexual relations.

Before a woman could use the pessary, she would have to become knowledgeable about and comfortable with her own body. The woman's use of the pessary, unlike the man's use of the condom, required a thorough understanding of the female sexual organs, and even more a woman's willingness to insert the device deep into her vagina. Here, then, was another consideration that linked lessons in sexuality to contraception. Despite Sanger's enthusiasm for the pessary, she knew well that most women had a very limited sense of their own generative organs or of their physiology and "that many were even afraid of their own bodies." Women held a variety of fantasies about the pessary, believing "it could go up too far, or that it could get lost, etc., etc." Sanger's pamphlet on *Family Limitation* tried to allay the fears in blunt terms: "It cannot get into the womb, neither can it get lost. The only thing it can do is come out." [48]

Sanger understood that the douche and the condom, the most common contraceptives of the time, were "less trouble for women." Nevertheless, she advised them to learn to use the pessary, for it alone, she insisted, allowed sexual pleasure. The other methods "deprive [women] of that great sacred closeness which the full play of magnetism gives when not checked by fears as in withdrawal, or interfered with as in the use of the condom." [49] To Sanger, sex was so "health-giving" that the pessary had to be the contraceptive of choice.

The Dutch system trained women to become experts in sexual hygiene. Johannes Rutgers believed that fitting a pessary and dispensing contraceptive advice was a woman's job, not a physician's. The task required a knowledge of rules of hygiene and a sensitivity to women's needs, not an ability to treat disease. The Dutch midwife was to instruct her women clients in "cleanliness, the uselessness of drugs and the non-necessity of abortion." [50] Sanger, in turn, hoped to give American public health nurses a similar kind of training. This new female expert would, she hoped, become integral to child and maternal health clinics.

But Sanger's proposals never became part of the Progressive programs, and in retrospect it seems surprising that she could have imagined that Progressive reformers would embrace her views. By defining reduction in family size as the single best way to eradicate poverty, Sanger slighted the entire movement for protective legislation. Similarly, by making a deep and passionate husband-wife relationship the prerequisite for conceiving and raising healthy children, she violated the precepts of educated motherhood.

To child welfare reformers, Sanger grossly exaggerated the benefits of family limitation. "It would be too much to claim that freedom for birth control would at once do away with child labor," insisted Owen Lovejoy. "There are other influences as potent as poverty, the greed of employers and the overcrowding of homes." Worse yet, Sanger had the equation reversed. There was nothing intrinsically wrong with large families; they were only a problem because society was unwilling to protect the children of the poor. It was not family size, then, but social attitudes that mattered most. "Any argument for birth control," insisted Lovejoy, "based on a fear of over-population or on the fear that the individual families will be financially unable to support their offspring is vicious because it started from a false premise." In true Progressive fashion, Lovejoy concluded: "The world is big enough and rich enough to furnish a foothold for all the children that can be born under decent health conditions." [51]

Perhaps even more important, the sexual implications of birth control repelled women reformers. In 1920, Sanger solicited the support of Carey Chapman Catt, a leading suffragist, claiming that the legalization of birth control was logically the next campaign for suffragists. Catt could not agree. She told Sanger that she would not oppose her, but neither would she endorse her. "In my judgment," responded Catt, "you claim too much as a result of one thing. Most reformers do that. Your reform is too narrow to appeal to me and too sordid." To Catt, birth control would encourage the perpetuation of a society based on male superiority and standards. It urged women to embrace sexuality instead of telling men to emulate the moral virtues of women. "When the advocacy of contraceptives," Catt continued, "is combined with as strong a propaganda for continence, (not to prevent conception) but in the interest of common decency, you will find me a more willing sponsor. That is, a million years of male control over the sustenance of women has made them sex slaves which has produced two results: an oversexualizing of women and an oversexualizing of men. No animal is so uncontrolled as the mass of men." Thus Catt concluded: "Now merely to make indulgence safe does not do enough." Whatever social gain would be provided by birth control would be offset by "some increase in immorality through safety." [52]

Just as Charlotte Perkins Gilman would not support an equal rights amendment, neither would she join a birth control movement. While Gilman believed that some good might be accomplished by bringing birth control to the lower classes, she remained nervous about its effect on the family and on the mother-child relationship. Defining woman first, last, and always as "a dutiful and affectionate mother," she admired a movement that advocated free choice for women but could not tolerate its demand for a highly sexual relationship between husband and wife. Marriage was primarily "for the advance of their young and secondarily for the pleasure of companionship." A marriage without children was "a continuous license for barren indulgence." Although in some cases "we find married lovers maintaining a honeymoon basis of enjoyment, in most we see a weary disillusionment, an unromantic dutiful submission to an unromantic physical indulgence." Gilman also insisted, Sanger notwithstanding, that sexual freedom was no guarantor of health. "Some doctors point to the number of nervous wrecks made by suppressed desires. Have they counted them and compared them with other wrecks, mental and physical, made by indulged desires? Besides, there is this to be said for the ill health of the suppressed—it is neither contagious nor hereditary." [53]

Sanger was also frustrated in her attempts to win the support of women's clubs. In 1916, for example, she was denied an opportunity to speak before the influential Woman's City Club of Chicago, and her attempts to meet and convert working-class women in that city were no more successful. "Chicago," she recalled in her autobiography, "was so well organized by social workers, through the influence of Jane Addams of Hull House, that it was extremely difficult for me to reach these women without the sanction of a woman prominent in social work who was 'not interested in birth control.'" [54]

Jane Addams would not support the movement either. While both

Sanger and Addams assigned women the task of working for a better society, Addams had little empathy with Sanger's crusade to expand women's sense of sexuality. Like Catt, Addams was committed to an ideal of the virtuous, and very clearly nonsexual, female, whose mission was not to emulate the bestial male but to curb and refine him. "As woman fulfills her civic obligations while still guarding her chastity," insisted Addams, "she will be in a position as never before to uphold the 'single standard,' demanding that men shall add personal virtues to public duties." This new relationship was to be "virtue between equals," promising to "make women freer, nobler, less timid . . . and more humane, and will also inevitably modify the standards of men." [55] Given these views, Addams was hardly likely to give Sanger a cordial welcome in Chicago.

Sanger also received a hostile reception from the Children's Bureau. While the Bureau informed women requesting contraceptive aid to write directly to the Bureau of Social Hygiene, it would not itself provide birth control information. Even more important, it would not allow the Sheppard-Towner programs to do so either. "The purpose [of] the Sheppard-Towner Act," Grace Abbott declared, "is not to prevent children from coming into the world but to save the lives of babies and mothers." [56] The birth control movement did not receive any support from the federal agency set up to guard the welfare of the nation's children.

For all the hostility of Progressive reformers to birth control, it was Sanger's views, and not theirs, that won acceptance in the 1920s —acceptance, that is, in the private choices that middle-class families made. Indeed, the close fit between Sanger's rhetoric and the ideology of the wife-companion is apparent in the speed with which middle-class women followed her advice. As every survey of contraception in the 1920s demonstrated, middle-class women were not only using birth control in greater numbers but were also using Sanger's preferred method, the diaphragm.

The sex histories of different birth cohorts that Alfred Kinsey and his associates compiled (disproportionately from urban, well-educated, and Protestant groups) point to the dramatic changes in private practices. Although only 12 percent of white women born before 1899 reported that they had never practiced contraception, 23 percent said that they relied primarily upon "withdrawal" and another 24 percent upon the douche. For the women born between 1900 and 1909 (entering marriage in the 1920s), or born between 1910 and 1919 (entering marriage in the 1930s), the number who never practiced contraception dropped (7 and 8 percent respectively), as did the number relying upon the douche (15 percent and 8 percent), and still more dramatically, the number practicing withdrawal (15 percent and 7 percent). The diaphragm became the preferred method of contraception, used by 42 percent of Kinsey's respondents in the 1900–1909 group, and 53 percent in the 1910–1919 group.[57] The surveys of Katharine B. Davis, and Phyllis Blanchard and Carlyn Manasses, as well as public opinion polls conducted among college students, all confirm Kinsey's findings.[58] In the 1920s and 1930s among the upper echelons of society, contraception, with a preference for the diaphragm, became standard.

But private practices, particularly among the middle classes, and public policy, especially as it affected the lower classes, were two very different things. Sanger had sought to influence both arenas, to produce a new kind of love and a new kind of social order. But her successes were only partial. Working-class women were much less prone to practice contraception or to use the diaphragm. As the Lynds, for example, reported from Middletown, all of the twenty-seven women of the business class that they interviewed took the use of birth control "for granted." Yet, "of the 77 wives of workers . . . only 34 said that they used any means of birth control," and only half of those, it appeared, were using the diaphragm.[59] Moreover, Sanger's effort to establish public birth control clinics ran into opposition from the Catholic Church (as Sanger phrased it, "the machinations of the hierarchy of the Roman Catholic Church"); the clinics were also held in violation of the Comstock laws, making the distribution of contraception at one with that of pornographic material (a link that had appeared self-evident to the generation of the 1880s, caught up in notions of virtuous womanhood).[60] And Sanger's efforts to enlist the support of Progressive reformers against the Church and against Comstockery met with little success.

The implementaton of Sanger's program in the public arena was a complicated and curious affair. Her ability to shape middle-class attitudes and practices was greater than her influence over the lower classes—and a good part, but not all, of the difference reflected her failure to establish a network of public birth control clinics. These clinics were supposed to bring contraception to the poor. How did Sanger attempt to overcome opposition and open the clinics? Why was her effort to found them not more successful? What became of her goal of making public health nurses, as in the Dutch model, the primary dispensers of contraceptives? The outcome of Sanger's program bears a striking resemblance to the fate of the Sheppard-Towner Act. For all the dissimilarities in assumptions, the results of the two movements in terms of medical practices, the position of women, and the delivery of services to the lower classes were very much the same.

The Doctor as Sexual Counselor

After 1920, Sanger's inability to win the support of prominent Progressives no longer troubled her. The turning point for her came in 1918, when the New York State Court of Appeals ruled that only licensed physicians, and not nurses in birth control clinics, could prescribe or provide information on contraceptives, and then exclusively for the purpose of curing or preventing disease.[61] Birth control devices were legal only for use by the sick or as a way to reduce the spread of venereal disease, and in both instances, distribution had to remain under the physician's control and authority. Sanger, instead of continuing a lengthy and perhaps futile battle to allow for the free and unrestricted distribution of contraception as a right under the First Amendment (as was her original intention), decided to work within the boundaries set by the court ruling. And in doing so, she ceased to be the "woman rebel" and became first and foremost a birth controller.

The decision reflected Sanger's intense faith in the value of contraception. She placed the movement's progress, no matter under whose auspices, above all other considerations. If the diaphragm was more easily dispensed by doctors as a health measure than by women as part of their right to free speech, then so be it. Distribution came first, and Sanger was determined to give women what they needed most—the device. Her task then appeared to become more manageable. Rather than convincing recalcitrant women reformers of the value of contraception and persuading legislators and judges to abolish rigid obscenity laws, she now had to teach physicians the value of the pessary, and they, in turn, would popularize it. After 1920, Sanger worked to broaden doctors' right to dispense contraception, that is, to amend obscenity laws so that physicians could prescribe contraception for healthy as well as sick women. "In this country," she wrote in 1929 to her associate, Dr. S. Adolphus Knopf, "it was I who switched the birth control movement from the channels of free speech where I had first claimed it belonged, into the realm of the medical profession. . . . Upon my return to the U.S.A. I sought with all my voice and the power of my pen to get the medical profession to consider birth control one of its jobs—the techniques of contraception its main study." [62]

By making medical distribution of the pessary the primary goal of the birth control movement, Sanger minimized the role of the public health nurses trained in sexual hygiene. Educated women were no longer needed to teach the ignorant about anatomy or sexuality. The doctor, not the public health nurse, now held the key to the liberation of women. And once it became a medical decision to prescribe the device, it also became the doctor's task to offer sexual counseling. The knowledge women acquired about their bodies was to be learned in the office. The doctor became the arbiter of standards of normal and abnormal sexual behavior.

Thus, in the 1920s, at the same time that Grace Abbott was encouraging the medical control of health care so as to ensure the success of Sheppard-Towner, Sanger was encouraging the medical control of contraception and sexuality to ensure the success of birth control. In both instances, the implementation of an ambitious reform agenda assumed precedence over a female-directed program; the private physician took on the novel tasks of caring for the healthy and providing sexual counseling. Moreover, the Sheppard-Towner and the birth control movements, both of which had set out to raise the level of health and well-being of the lower classes, ended up by promoting a new type of care for private patients that neglected the poor. By promoting the distribution of contraception primarily through private physicians, Sanger made certain that this technology would first and foremost reach the middle classes.

Sanger's decision to follow the courts and give contraception over to the doctors prompted opposition from some among her original supporters. They continued to agitate for the unrestricted distribution of contraception. They scorned her efforts to enact "doctors only" bills, defining them as "special privilege class legislation," more convinced that physicians would effect the distribution of contraception among the middle classes and not the poor. As Mary Ware Dennett, one of Sanger's earliest allies, declared in 1926: "The former policy was one of vehement scorn of the indecent laws and the object was to get contraceptive information directly to the people in the quickest way possible by published information and clinical service—regardless of the law; a striking contrast to the propositions of the last two years for laws to keep the subject of contraception still classed with obscenity laws and to let no one give it except physicians." Dennett did not agree that distributing the pessary to physicians would promote women's health. Such an "extraordinary swing of the pendulum from revolutionary defiance of all law to advocacy of special privilege class legislation" was, she felt, the ruin of the movement.[63]

Sanger was not moved by the attack. Mrs. Dennett, she told Dr. Knopf, "has always espoused the cause of liberty of speech and press, whereas the movement has evolved itself into a plea for scientifically teaching a knowledge of physiology and anatomy and research. In my estimation, it is not at all a question of 'freedom of press,' but it is a question of getting the individual woman suitable information through the channels of the medical profession." [64] This really was no answer to Dennett's charges, just an indication that Sanger was determined to follow her new medical strategy.

Sanger, however, did try to respond to Dennett's and her own concern for the poor through an effort to establish public birth control clinics. Sanger confidently set out to organize a nationwide network of such clinics, to be financed by philanthropic members of the community and served by local physicians. During the 1920s, Sanger sent agents all over the country to become acquainted with community leaders, to inform them of the options for action in obscenity laws, to encourage them to set up clinics, and to tell them how they could most easily obtain birth control devices. The agents, like Sanger herself, had another task as well. They were to visit the offices of private physicians and persuade them of the safety and effectiveness of the pessary. If the physicians were interested, the agents promised to send them a ready supply for their patients. Given Sanger's own willingness to allow a medical monopoly over contraceptive distribution, it is not surprising that she was more successful in persuading doctors to distribute the device than in establishing clinics. The number of physicians willing to prescribe contraception for private patients far exceeded the number willing to work in clinics and serve the poor.

The few birth control clinics that were established in the 1920s were generally organized by a handful of dedicated women, together with an occasional Protestant minister and a liberal-minded and, typically, female doctor. But few of these organizers could persuade local hospitals, charitable organizations, or the public health service to support or incorporate the work of the clinics. The clinics remained dependent upon the largesse of a few middle-class individuals, not on substantial middle-class institutions.[65] In fact, the movement was so weak that Sanger encouraged anyone who felt the slightest inclination to go ahead and set up a clinic—perhaps the enthusiasm would be contagious. "You ask what you can do to help," she responded to an old friend from Schenectady, New York. "There is, of course, always the possibility of opening and starting clinics. Why not do that as a local venture? It is the only way to get activity. The laws in New York State will never be changed while the R.C.'s [Roman Catholics] have so much influence in Albany, but you can open a clinic and run it for 'the cure and prevention of disease' and do a marvelous amount of good." [66] During the 1920s a number of birth control clinics did open, but many of them closed just as quickly. By 1930, there were only 30 clinics functioning long enough and efficiently enough to present records for study.[67]

A few dedicated birth controllers did manage to administer successful clinics. Sanger was able to obtain sufficient funds and medical staff to keep her New York Clinic alive, and a few others, particularly women doctors, could match her feat. But on the whole, the motives of the various founders were often idiosyncratic, even at cross-purposes. Sanger herself paid little attention to this—the importance of birth control was so great that any ally was welcome. Thus, in Chicago, Dr. Rachelle Yarros, a child welfare reformer and long-time resident of Hull House, set up clinics to offer birth control advice as a way, to her mind, of reducing the rate of abortions, the number of prostitutes, and the spread of venereal disease. "I realized even then," Yarros recalled, "that the only way to do away with the [abortion] evil was to substitute something safe and better that would supply the need for limitation and regulation of families." [68] So, too, Yarros believed prostitution was more a "menace to health and welfare" than a "moral question"; and "it is through better sex education and higher sex ideals," she contended, "that we may hope effectively to attack immorality and promiscuity." Thus, Yarros looked to the clinics to provide contraception and to "dispel ignorance of men and women in sex matters, to teach them frankly and earnestly how to retain and foster love in marriage." [69]

At the same time that Yarros was opening clinics in Chicago, Dr. Lydia De Vilbiss, a passionate eugenicist, was starting one in Florida to curb indiscriminate breeding among the lower classes. De Vilbiss, an early and active supporter of Sanger, staunchly objected to any type of protective legislation that might increase the family size of the poor. In opposing Sheppard-Towner, for example, she maintained: "The women physicians who attend baby welfare clinics, are usually women of uncommonly fine attainments . . . often unmarried and practically childless, [who] find more lucrative employment in keeping alive the children of the slums or the devastated regions of the world than using their strength, energy and ability to bear and rear children of their own." [70] So intent was De Vilbiss on limiting lower-class families that she was not at all reluctant to compel them to use contraception or lose welfare support. She was also prepared to identify the uneducable poor so as to sterilize them. "Our only hope as I see it," De Vilbiss told Sanger in 1932, "is a strong countercampaign to enlist the support and cooperation of official and voluntary health and welfare agencies and get them to work taking this information to the pauper sick and holding the 'big stick' of further non-support unless they conform." And she assured Sanger: "I have seen this done." [71]

De Vilbiss instructed her staff to visit the poor in their homes, to offer them contraceptive techniques, and to arrange physicians' examinations for possible sterilization. "We are completely sold on the idea," she calmly noted, "of sending sympathetic, experienced lay women . . . into the poorest homes and there giving the women a contraceptive and teaching them how to use it. Also, they fill out a careful case record which in each instance should be reviewed by the physician, and where eugenic sterilization is indicated we go to work on the case. I now have more than a dozen of the best doctors on our staff and all I have to do is call one of them up whenever I want an operation done without cost, or for a very nominal sum which the patient is able to pay, 'sometimes a chicken.'" De Vilbiss despaired of "these women [who] are so dumb that they get pregnant rather than send us word that they are out of jelly or come to the office to get it." [72] To her, such a woman was an appropriate candidate for sterilization.

Whatever one might think of these different goals, the clinics remained few in number. Most observers were far less confident than Sanger of anyone's ability to maintain a clinic when enthusiasm had to compensate for limited funding and little community support. "It is a mistake," warned Caroline Robinson after examining these clinics, "to think that birth control centers can be started on a slight foundation if only legal difficulties can be gotten out of the way." [73]

A clinic could open with volunteer services from one or more physicians, but it took a salaried doctor and social worker to keep it functioning. Further, the indifference and sometimes outright antagonism of many prominent individuals and groups in the community hampered the efforts of both the staff and the directors. Although lack of cooperation or hostility from the local Catholic Church, private charities, physicians, and traditional women's clubs could not prevent a group from starting a clinic, they could often affect the clinic's prospects for survival. Without substantial backing or institutional connections, a clinic could be assured neither of adequate funds nor of a sufficient number of referrals, and for both these reasons, clinics frequently closed down.[74]

Sanger's efforts to distribute birth control through private physicians met with greater success. Over the 1920s and 1930s, more and more physicians became willing to prescribe contraception to their private patients. Before 1920, few doctors were ready to lead a campaign or to test their authority to dispense birth control for the cure of disease. Like everyone else, they associated contraception with prostitution and immorality. Only when women began to agitate for an unrestricted right to distribute contraception did physicians move to expand their own activity. The medical profession entered the field of birth control just as they entered the field of preventive health care: soon after women mounted their campaigns, doctors enlarged their services to include the routine care of the sexually and physically normal.[75]

The attitude of individual physicians toward Sanger and her allies was consistent with their attitude towards the women reformers supporting Sheppard-Towner. George Kosmak, a prominent obstetrician, was outspoken in his disdain for both groups. He objected not to their goals but to women assuming tasks that belonged to doctors. Kosmak, a practicing and devout Catholic, personally favored continence over birth control. But his own preferences did not prevent him from campaigning to expand doctors' distribution of contraception. "Would it not be more dignified and appropriate," he insisted, "if we as physicians both individually and collectively divorce ourselves from this sensational propaganda, and when called upon for advice by our patients in these matters, study the conditions carefully in each case and counsel them as the occasion demands, freeing their minds at the same time from the nauseating slush that now characterizes this subject?" [76] Kosmak believed that educated women should encourage the ignorant to practice continence, leaving to physicians the more professional and complicated task of prescribing contraception and offering sexual counseling.

Similarly, the Sub-Committee of Public Health of the New York Academy of Medicine promoted birth control, but again, only on its own terms. This highly prestigious group of physicians was eager to expand the authority of the individual doctor in dispensing birth control and educating the public about sexuality. It would not, however, advocate birth control on First Amendment grounds. In 1921, the Committee informed Mary Dennett that it would not support her amendment to revise the penal code: "Such an amendment would remove every obstacle to the indiscriminate distribution of information relating to and advertisement of methods for prevention of conception from both lay and professional sources." But this refusal was not tantamount to a lack of support for birth control. The Committee favored amending existing laws in one particular way: "Nothing in the obscenity law shall apply to duly licensed physicians, licensed dispensaries, and to the public health authorities in connection with the discharge of their respective duties in protecting the health of patients and the community." [77] Throughout the decade, the Committee consistently agitated for nothing more and nothing less than a medical monopoly.

In the birth control movement, as in Sheppard-Towner, the self-interest of the specialist played a critical role in shaping the medical profession's response. Just as obstetricians' and pediatricians' readiness to perform prenatal and routine health examinations enlarged their authority over pregnant women and well children (and not coincidentally, allowed them to carry on a financially rewarding practice), so gynecologists' readiness to offer contraception and sexual counseling expanded their authority over female patients (and underwrote their practice as well). Normal sexual functioning became part of the doctor's domain; the gynecologist moved from treating the diseased and the deviant to regulating the lives of the healthy. It was Robert Dickinson, a prominent Brooklyn gynecologist, who provided the model for his colleagues and helped to make the new cult of romantic sexuality in the 1920s an appropriate medical concern.

Dickinson was among the first supporters of the medical distribution of contraception, defining it as a privilege inherent in the doctor-patient relationship. Yet, like so many other physicians, Dickinson had little patience for female reformers and their First Amendment goals. As early as 1916 he urged doctors "to take hold of this matter, and not leave it to the radicals and let it receive harm by being pushed in any undignified or improper manner." [78] In fact, Dickinson hoped that his own speciality, gynecology, would practice preventive medicine and guide patients' sexual practices. "We have trained students and interns," he told his colleagues, "with an outlook on laparatomy and pathology rather than on physiology, life adjustments and pelvic social problems." (Perhaps no phrase better expresses what the medicalization of sex meant than "pelvic social problems.") After all, argued Dickinson, "considering the incorrigible marriage habit of the race, it is not unreasonable to demand of preventive medicine a place for a little section on conjugal hygiene that might do its part to invest with dignity certain processes of love and begetting." [79] Realizing this goal became the focus of his career.

As "conjugal hygiene" became part of gynecology, the ability of the physician to prescribe birth control took on an added importance. "In all marriages," Dickinson asserted, "except a marriage where both partners are ascetic, sterile or impotent, birth control and the mechanisms of love loom large as techniques of happiness. Honoring all honorable acts of love means teaching them." [80] By prescribing contraception, the doctor actually promoted marital happiness.

In 1923, the same year that Sanger opened her first medically supervised clinic, Dickinson established the Committee on Maternal Health, to oversee "a scientific investigation of contraception, sterilization and problems of sterility and fertility from a medical and public health point of view." [81] The Committee's aims were to research *all* problems of sexuality, underfertility as well as overfertility, normal as well as abnormal sexuality. So while Sanger devoted her efforts to the distribution of contraceptives, Dickinson and his Committee worked to collect clinical data on sexual and contraceptive practices, and—eventually and logically—on marital adjustments.

This medical turn of attention to sexuality seemed to be liberating. Dickinson very self-consciously wanted to free sexuality from traditional constraints. "Sexual desire is not a sin," he declared. "The sex parts are not shame parts and autoeroticism is apparently natural and rarely physically harmful." To Dickinson, as later to Kinsey, the natural was the normal. If the great majority (Dickinson estimated around 85 percent) of women had at one time or another practiced masturbation, it was, by definition, an acceptable practice for everyone. "It would seem to be so general an experience as to warrant calling it a natural phenomena." [82]

Dickinson's very ability to take statistical findings and turn them into precepts made the role of doctor as sexual counselor seem all the more appropriate and legitimate. "The removal of taboos on sex writing and sex curiosity," contended Dickinson, "has disclosed to the young woman that autoerotism is quite general, and that petting arouses thrills or passions in others besides herself. She is therefore ready to try to give voice to her puzzlement, and talk freely to a non-censorious advisor who is thought to be trustworthy." [83] Dickinson took pride in the fact that patients who came regularly to his office no longer went to the priest. "In the confessional, I formulate my statement in respectful and careful language," one patient told him. "I can talk to you more freely than I could to the priest." [84] In other words, the gynecologist had now established his hegemony over sexuality.

Clearly, Dickinson's advice was not so radical as it was supportive of the new ideology of the wife-companion. "There are many instances," he maintained, "where marriage is the only complete solution [to masturbation]. The most difficult of our problems, *cherchez l'homme*, the seeking and securing of the right man or the near right man, is the most effective prescription. It is physical therapy as well as psychology." For Dickinson, marriage remained the most natural of all sexual practices; nothing, he claimed, equaled the joys of sex with the same partner. The well-adjusted woman was a married woman. "Non-marriage and non-mating are social and biological thwarting," he insisted. "They constitute the frustration of love-comradeship, childrearing, and homemaking." [85] Dickinson's precepts effectively confirmed the prevailing social ideology.

Just how neat the fit was emerges in Dickinson's perception of the changes in gynecological practice. In 1895, his single female patients arrived because of "something terrible." They were "dressed in Victorian clothes, reluctant to disclose the existence of pelvic trouble or the pelvis." They came for "delivery, pregnancy, abortion, syphilis, gonorrhea and what used to be called 'betrayal,' frigidity in coitus and autosexuality." His patients, in short, were seeking treatment for a serious condition or illness. In the late 1920s, on the other hand, Dickinson's single female patients made appointments for sexual check-ups. His typical single patient was "a pretty, well-educated girl of good social status, usually coming for a premarital examination, marrying her first love, intending to learn the physical mechanics of coitus and to control fertility." [86] This contrast pointed to a revolution both in the style of medical care and in sexual mores.

Dickinson, in fact, believed that these transformations would reduce dramatically the prevalence of women's diseases. The widespread use of safe and effective contraceptives would lessen the need for abortion; the rise of early "love" marriages would effect a decline in venereal disease, frigidity, and masturbation. A woman's willingness to talk to her doctor about sexual problems would prompt her to seek preventive medical care, enabling her to get assistance before radical medical intervention became necessary.

While the new gynecological practice may have encouraged an expansion of sexual freedom among some women and made still others more knowledgeable about and comfortable with their bodies, the medicalization of sex had important negative effects. For one, only a bare minority of doctors met Dickinson's ideal. Some remained altogether uncomfortable with the subject of female sexuality, incapable of open and frank discussions with their patients; others delivered rounds of homilies. More, the public role for women first envisioned by Sanger disappeared. Instead of training women as instructors in bodily health and sexuality, the birth controllers told women to "ask their physicians." Finally, the private physicians' dominance in the field of contraception assured its uneven distribution (at least insofar as any female devices were concerned). For a woman to "ask her physician" for a safe and effective contraceptive presupposed that she had a physician, that she could afford a contraceptive, and that the physician would be willing to give it to her, regardless of her marital status. The type of medical services that doctors were offering middle-class married or about-to-be-married women were not available for the poor or for the single woman. Clearly, not all women had equal access to a contraceptive that enabled them to control family size or to enhance sexual satisfactions. Once again, a program that promised widespread benefits ended up being very class-bound.

Training Children to Happiness

An appreciation of the ideology and practice of romantic sexuality and the expansion of the domain of the expert provide the necessary ingredients for taking up the final and critical consideration: the new definitions of proper child-rearing and the institutions created to meet them. In significant ways, the novel conceptions of child care in the 1920s actually reinforced the ideal of the wife-companion. One more reason why women took to the bedroom and the bridge club was that the experts moved them, firmly and insistently, out of the nursery. To an unprecedented degree (even bearing in mind the Jacksonians' insistence on obedience training), mothering appeared to be a dangerous pursuit—dangerous, that is, to the welfare of the child. It was almost as if the best thing that a mother could do for her child was to devote herself still more completely to her husband.

The importance that G. Stanley Hall had to the generation of the 1890s was enjoyed by the behavioral psychologist John Watson in the 1920s. Both men exerted a major influence on the styles of child-rearing, but there were few other resemblances between them. Hall had urged women to respond to every signal that the child emitted; Watson wanted them to leave the child in peace—to reduce, not to increase, their commitment. The best statement of Watsonian principles appeared in *The Psychological Care of Infant and Child* (1928). Sarcastic in tone and heavy-handed in making its points, the book's dedication warned the reader of what was to come: "To the First Mother Who Brings Up a Happy Child." One quickly learned why such an admirable creature had not yet appeared. Ignorance about child-rearing was widespread. If mothers had once assumed that their instincts or their education might equip them to rear children, Watson disabused them of the notion: "*No one today knows enough to raise a child.*" [87]

The situation was even worse than that. Mothers were on the wrong track. They had no understanding of "the dangers of too much mother love." If the Progressives had worried about the neglected child, Watson despaired of "the overkissed child." He recounted how he went riding "with two boys, aged four and two, their mother, grandmother, and nurse." In the course of the two-hour ride, "one of the children was kissed 32 times. . . . The other child was almost equally smothered in love." [88] Watson went on to trace "the adult effects of too much coddling in infancy," all of which were disastrous. "How does it show? It shows as *invalidism.*" Because he was smothered in love as a child, the adult complains incessantly that " 'my digestion is poor; I have a constant headache; my muscles

ache like fire; I am all tired out; I don't feel young any more' . . .
and so on through the whole gamut of ills." Further, such an adult
was incapable of functioning in society because "no one is there to
baby us." Consequently, he retreated, took to bed, to be in "a secure
position to demand constant coddling." Why should a mother indulge
in such damaging practices? Watson had a ready answer: "She is
starved for love—affection, as she prefers to call it. It is at bottom a
sex-seeking response in her, else she would never kiss the child on
the lips." [89] In other words, Watson was advising women to express
their sex-starved impulses to their husbands, not to their children.

However strident the rhetoric or seemingly idiosyncratic the position, the Watson message, in fact, dominated the child-rearing literature of the 1920s, particularly the various pamphlets that the
Children's Bureau distributed nationwide. "Child Management,"
(written for the Bureau by Dr. Douglas Thom), informed the mother
that "interest and love alone on her part are not enough to assure
success. . . . The very love of the mother for her child may be the
'stumbling block'. . . . This love is invariably [not sometimes, but
invariably] associated with excessive worry, anxiety, and, at times,
definite fear which prevent the most intelligent approach to many
problems of childhood." [90] To Thom, the "oversolicitous parent"
was as bad as the "stern, cold, forbidding parent"; if the latter pro-
voked emotional "hunger pains" in the children, the former "nause-
ated [them] by overstimulation." There was an image for the mother
to ponder: her love as nauseating.

She would not get much relief by turning to one of the Bureau's
most popular pamphlets, "Infant Care." Here the Watsonian position
was translated into specifics:

A few minutes of gentle play now and then is good for the baby. However, all babies need a great deal of rest and quiet, and much of the
play that is commonly indulged in is too exciting.

Rocking the baby, jumping him up and down on the parent's knee, tossing
him and shaking his bed or carriage form bad habits, as they make the
baby dependent on attention.

Do not hold him nor rock him to stop his crying, and do not nurse him
until the exact hour for the feeding comes. It will not hurt the baby,
even the tiny baby, to cry.[91]

The same points recurred in the Bureau's "Are You Training Your
Child to be Happy?" In the Watsonian world there was nothing in-
congruous about "training" to "happiness." The pamphlet declared

that "to be a good father or mother is one of the hardest jobs on earth" and went on to list the common mistakes that parents committed. Every one of them involved a mother's over-attention and smothering concern:

Are you so afraid the children will get hurt that you will not let them run and play and climb outdoors? You keep them from learning to be strong and independent.

Do you boss your child too much? How can he learn then to think things out for himself?

Do you say, 'Don't' or 'Stop,' every time your child starts to do something? How can tied hands ever learn to be useful?

Do you want to keep your child's love for yourself? That is very selfish. It keeps the child from making friends.

Do you 'baby' and pet your child too much? You are being good to *yourself*, because you like to take care of him. But you are being bad to *him*.[92]

The affectionate mother was, in effect, selfish, satisfying her own needs but crippling her child.

These same lessons reappeared in the sociologists' tracts on marriage and the family. Although most of their attention went to the husband-wife relationship, there was room enough to present the perils of mother love. "The mother," contended Gladys and Ernest Groves, "has had the opportunity to impress herself too much upon the child. Her influence has been excessive." Acutely concerned about "the dangers in the mother-child association," they went on to fault the mother for "too strong an attachment . . . which she has unconsciously used to hamper the child's natural tendency towards independence. She has evoked the power of love, she has created it to hold the child captive to her attitudes and desires." The Groveses recognized the novelty of these statements. "Such ideas are staggering blows to the complacency and idealism that has so long gathered about the role of mothers." Still, there was no ignoring them: they represented the recent truths "made by science and sociology." [93]

Just as these books and pamphlets reduced the competence of the mother to the point where she almost seemed a criminal figure, stunting and warping her child's development, so they went on to elevate the skills of the expert. The primacy that doctors enjoyed in preventive health care they now also assumed in child-rearing. Thus, "Are You Training Your Child to be Happy" gave mothers suggestions to discourage the child from masturbating (keep his clothes loose, make sure he is busy); but if none of these worked, "if he keeps on doing these things after you have tried to make him forget, ask the doctor to examine him." And then it added, in one of the clearest statements of medical omniscience: "Perhaps there is something not quite right with the child's body. The doctor will make it right." So, too, mothers learned that "your own doctor or the doctor at the clinic will give you a plan for your baby. The plan will tell you at what time your baby should sleep each day. It will also tell you how much food to give him and at what time to feed him. The doctor will also tell you how to change the plan as your baby grows older." [94] And a new kind of cautionary tale reinforced these precepts:

MRS. GUERRA AND HER TWO BABIES

Mrs. Guerra had her first baby at home.
A neighbor came in to help her.
A doctor told her to feed the baby every four hours.
The baby cried.
Mrs. Guerra and her friend said, 'The baby is hungry; we must feed him.'
The baby cried soon again. Mrs. Guerra fed him again.
She fed him many times.
Soon the baby got sick and cross.

Mrs. Guerra had her second baby at the hospital.
The nurses took care of him.
They fed him every four hours.
They did not pick him up when he cried.
They knew that babies get exercise when they cry.
Babies need exercise.
This baby was well and happy.
The nurses said to Mrs. Guerra, 'When you go home, do as we do. Then your baby will be well and happy and good.'
Mrs. Guerra went home in two weeks. She did what the nurses told her.
The baby was always good and happy. He was always well.
She said: 'I made a mistake before. The nurses are right. Now I will see what I can do with my big baby to keep him well too.' [95]

The moral was clear: doctors and nurses knew what was best to make the child good, happy, and well. The medical experts guaranteed not only health but right conduct and even happiness.

The preeminence of the expert over the mother found institutional expression in two major innovations of the 1920s, the nursery school and the child guidance clinic. In both cases, psychologists, psychiatrists, and social workers extended their influence in ways that duplicated, rather precisely, the new importance of the pediatrician, the obstetrician, and the gynecologist. In contrast to the Progressive period, when the lower-class child practically monopolized reformist attention, the decade of the 1920s gave its concern to the middle-class child—and the shift occurred as the importance of mental adjustment began to rival, perhaps even to surpass, physical well-being. A new roster of symptoms demanded attention. As Dr. Arnold Gesell, one of the leading child psychologists of the period, explained, the new expert was no longer so concerned about "pupils with discharging ears and deteriorating molars," but rather about "the child with night terrors, the nail biter, the over-tearful child, the over-silent child, the stammering child, the extremely indifferent child . . . and a whole host of suffering, frustrated and unhealthily-constituted growing minds." [96] Once personality development became at least as significant as bone development, the psychiatric social worker and the guidance counselor had the same right to intervene in the life of an apartment-house family as the settlement house workers had to intervene in the life of a tenement family. In fact, personality training was so complex that the new professionals were duty-bound to intervene more thoroughly than their predecessors. It was one thing to tell mothers to feed their children or to run better baby contests where the prize went to the fattest; it was quite another to raise well-adjusted children, particularly when mothers were so prone to overprotection.

The first institution that the experts designed to cope with the problem was the nursery school. The process of raising the well-adjusted child had to be started early, surely by the age of two or three. "It has been found," reported Gladys and Ernest Groves, "that from whatever quarter the scientist comes to a study of human behavior, whether as a psychologist, sociologist, mental hygienist, or educator, he finds that the unwise behavior of the mother has had much to do with the wrong starting of the personality trend. . . . It may be said that the mother has had the first influence and has not wisely used it. The fault has not been lack of interest, as a rule, but lack of understanding." [97] The nursery school, organized by psychologists (not—as in the case of kindergartens—by well-meaning women), and placed in university laboratories (not in settlement houses), would detect and correct abnormal development before it warped the child's personality. The nursery, as one prospectus explained, "deals with children from 16 months to 4 years, when the child's emotional reactions are becoming fixed, and consequently the most important period in his life." The nursery school teacher herself was trained in education and psychology; she knew that "the child who needs the teacher's attention constantly in order to feel herself adequate, shows an emotional lack. The child who plays happily until he sights his mother and then . . . becomes hysterical . . . likewise evidences emotional disturbance." [98] And having once spotted such symptoms, she would try to alleviate them through conferences with parents or through referrals to psychologists on the school staff or in the community. In short, the nursery school was something of a diagnostic clinic.

A nursery school experience offered another critical advantage —it would loosen the mother-child tie by involving the youngster more intensively with teachers and peer group. The kindergarten had looked to strengthen the mother-child relationship; the nursery school wanted to relax it. The explanation came right out of Watson and the Children's Bureau pamphlets. As John Anderson, chairman of the 1930 White House Conference section on the pre-school child, observed: "Freed by labor-saving devices from many of the tasks which formerly kept her occupied, living in a small apartment, she [the mother] has little to do except to exercise close supervision over the children's affairs. As a result, the mother is likely to form such a close attachment to the child that he is robbed of his initiative or spontaneity. Or she is so concerned over minor and insignificant elements of behavior that she becomes unduly tense and excited." [99] By contrast, the nursery school teacher was "impartial and impersonal," encouraging the child's independence. "There is no ever-present parent," boasted one school report, "to see that they eat on time. . . . Whatever the children lose in the feeling of security, they gain in self-confidence and assurance of their own ability." [100]

Schoolmates also provided critical lessons in real-life adjustment. "No matter how broad the attitude of parents, and no matter how wise the training within the home," insisted the promotional literature, "children do not learn the reality of the world unless they have been allowed to have many experiences outside the home." The nursery "counteracts the evil of being an only child, providing children of the same age to whose will the child must bend, in a manner acceptable to them." So keen were the nursery schools on taking over the child that their first preference was for a nine-to-three o'clock day (morning sessions were a compromise). Indeed, some of the schools were so possessive that they were soon defending themselves against the charge that because of the nursery school, "home life is being impoverished," that "mothers are giving up their children to the care of so-called experts." [101]

The nursery school orientation to the child reappeared in the child guidance clinics that sprang up in every major urban center in the 1920s. What few clinics there were in the Progressive era had devoted their attention exclusively to wayward youth, to those who came before the juvenile court or were incarcerated in reform schools. In the post-World War I decades, the clinics not only proliferated, but they also extended their domain to include all children who appeared in need of adjustment. As one proponent declared, the clinics were "organized to assist the individual adjustment of children presenting problems in personality and behavior, employing to this end the techniques of psychiatry, psychology, medicine and casework." [102] Such a program paid no regard to divisions of social class; symptoms, not incomes, mattered. "It has a responsibility," insisted another mental hygiene expert, "in regard to the mental health of children of the well-to-do family, who never reach the community social work institutions, as well as the children who come in contact with courts and social service organizations." [103]

The Watsonian distrust of the overbearing mother reappeared in the case histories that child guidance professionals compiled. William and Dorothy Thomas's *The Child in America* (1928), perhaps the most important statement of the principles of the movement, presented some eighty pages of case records and then concluded, "This study makes it plain also that the attitudes of the parents are largely responsible for the bad habits of the children." More specifically, they reported that from all the disciplines—from anthropology, psychology, psychiatry, and sociology—"the home is coming in for criticism as the point at which the child is spoiled." [104] The root problem in one case was that "the mother has apparently never had the time or the urge to develop any interests outside of the household and her own bodily sensations," so that "under a regime of petting, nagging, scolding, and utter lack of training in habits of living or behavior, the children grew up into a band of individualists who were constantly at odds with the school." In another case: "Here are two boys who have in common a history of long-standing hypochondriacal complaints in a setting of parental spoiling." [105] Scratch a problem child and you discovered an overbearing mother.

The magnitude of the problem was almost staggering—in two senses. For one, the range of symptoms that demanded treatment was extensive. There were "latent and secret maladjustments," as the Yale Guidance Clinic put it, that had to be corrected. There were overt problems as well. The list included, according to the University of Minnesota Institute of Child Welfare, temper tantrums, day-dreaming, destructiveness, excitability, feeling of inferiority, indifference, impulsiveness, extreme inhibition, irritability, self-consciousness, shyness, improper language, poor attitude toward authority, hair-chewing, listlessness, meticulousness, petty stealing, and on and on.[106] Further, if it took the Thomases one chapter to discuss the "varieties of maladjustment," it required another to describe the battery of personality tests that psychologists were employing in the 1920s; and, obviously, a poor score on any of them became the occasion for intervention. No wonder, then, to make the second point, that the estimates of the number of children in need of guidance was very high. As the Thomases concluded: "The recent work in the child guidance clinics and the nursery schools [properly linking the two] has disclosed the fact that behavior troubles in small children, bad habits and emotional instability, are widely prevalent in the whole population." [107]

All of this, of course, put the mother in an unenviable position. The child guidance experts agreed on her ineptitude and "the increasing helplessness of the family." (This very helplessness was what made the clinics such vital institutions.) But at the same time, the experts who criticized the overinvolvement of the mother did not in any significant ways encourage her to leave the family setting and make a genuine commitment to a career or a task outside the home. A hobby? Yes. Anything more serious or full-time? No. "Society," as one professional explained, "has adapted itself to the right of the father to go on with his profession, but when the mother goes out, the young generation stands in danger of being neglected." [108] So the mother was, in effect, in a terrible trap. Her devotion to the child would warp his growth; her ignoring the child would foster neglect. Thus the new child-rearing experts made the mother into a shadowy figure—hovering in the background, distrustful of her impulses, wary of her emotions. Or, to return to the theme of wife-companion, a woman's rewards had to come primarily from her relationship with her husband. Seemingly he could cope with and satisfy her deep emotionality.

Clearly, there was an untenable quality about such a definition of a woman's roles—not only because her wants and needs were consistently being defined in terms of the interests of others, but also because her own freedom within and without the family was narrowly circumscribed: the world outside remained closed off while the world inside was shrinking. It would take some time before all this became apparent—the Great Depression and World War II intervened to interrupt the process. But the ideal of the 1920s was resurrected enthusiastically in the post-1945 period, and then, when women tried to fulfill the precepts of wife-companion, their frustration and anger mounted. The results would be the women's revolution of the 1960s.

CHAPTER
6

Woman as Person

No SOONER did the model of wife-companion take hold than two catastrophes, the Great Depression and World War II, brought two remarkably contradictory experiences to American women. The Depression drove them out of the job market, the war propelled them back—and in unprecedented numbers. But women and policy makers alike understood that both experiences were atypical, departures from the regular course of things. Normality returned in 1945, and then the conceptions of the 1920s reemerged and took on a second life. For the next fifteen years women attempted to realize the precepts of wife-companion, an effort that turned out to be, in many cases, acutely frustrating and embittering.

The Interregnum of Depression and War

To a country struggling with the most massive unemployment rates in its history, the notion that any woman might wish to work outside the home, or that single women who had traditionally been employed in schools, offices, stores, and factories might want to continue to work promoted widespread objections. The point was to "Get the Men Back to Work," as the slogan went, to spread the few available jobs as widely as possible. Official policies tended to discriminate rather openly against women in the labor force. Already in 1932, a "married persons" clause affected all federal civil service workers; whenever a reduction in personnel was necessary, the first employees to be dismissed were those who had spouses holding another federal position. Although the law did not specify that the husband was to keep his job and the wife to lose hers, more than three-quarters of those dismissed under the act were women. New Deal legislation perpetuated these practices. Men received preferences for Works Progress Administration (WPA) jobs; single women, even those lacking all other resources, were at the bottom of the lists. Women in other positions, such as teaching, did no better. It seemed patently unfair to allow the wife and daughter of an employed man to work while an unemployed man could not feed his family.[1]

During the 1930s, the federal government funded day care centers for the first time. But these institutions certainly did not intend to bring women into the job market. Administered by the WPA in very ad hoc fashion (the centers were typically located in the basements of public schools), they represented a limited effort to employ a few of the women teachers that school boards had dismissed and, even more important, to provide some of the children of the poor with hot meals. Day care under the New Deal maintained its traditional reputation as a last resort, an appropriate setting only for those in need.[2]

If the Depression kept most women at home, World War II sent them into the factories. With men on the front lines and war supplies in acute demand, the nation had little choice but to employ women in all sorts of positions that had never before (and perhaps never since) been conceived of as appropriate for women. In Republic Steel, for example, the women were in the front offices typing, and in the foundry, next to the furnaces, rolling the steel. (In one government-sponsored propaganda film, "Women of Steel," a reporter asked a worker if the heat were intense, to which she replied, ever so quaintly, yes, but not much hotter than in the kitchen.) Yet at the very same time that the federal government pleaded with women to take war jobs, it made eminently clear that work for them was an emergency measure and a temporary expedient. When peace returned, they were to return to their homes. (Thus, the Women of Steel told reporters in one breath that they loved the jobs, and then, in the next, that they would give them up as soon as the men came back from the war.) In all events, wages climbed, patriotic duty called, and work, as one federal agency concluded, was "tempting to even the most home-loving mother."

Once large numbers of women with children entered the labor

force, agitation for some kind of day care program mounted. The War Manpower Commission told employers that women with young children should be hired only "at such hours and on such shifts that will cause the least disruption of family life." The guidelines, however, were impossible to enforce, and hard-pressed manufacturers were not likely to ask women about their household situations. The Roosevelt administration next looked to local communities to provide facilities for the care of children, but few of them wanted to incur the expense. Finally, in 1943, the federal government did intervene. Under the provisions of the Lanham Act (for funding construction of wartime facilities), it provided appropriations for day care; yet, in every way this was a stop-gap measure. The actual administration of the program became enmeshed in bureaucratic warfare, with different agencies battling for control. The Federal Works Administration (concerned only with construction) won out over the Federal Security Agency (dominated by the Children's Bureau), but little good came of that result. It was not only that the FWA ignored altogether the quality of the programs, but in addition the number of centers actually built remained very low. As of February 1944, only some 66,000 children were enrolled in federally-supported facilities, and by the spring of 1945, the number just reached 100,000. The centers met less than 10 percent of the need.[3]

That the centers were so scarce and so poorly run reflected and promoted a sense of their temporary character. Social attitudes towards day care reinforced these judgments. The Children's Bureau, for example, was not at all eager to see day care become a permanent program. Its 1942 Conference quickly decided that day care facilities should not be constructed immediately adjoining defense plants—for then they might become *too* convenient, outlive the emergency, and encourage women to stay at work. So, too, wartime conferences on the family were filled with complaints not about the paucity of day care centers, but about the fact that mothers were actually using them. Readers of one of the most prestigious social science publications, *The Annals*, learned that mothers who resorted to day care "forget what it may mean to take little children from their beds in the early morning and hurry them off. They forget that there are many children who have a dangerous feeling of insecurity when they are away from their mothers from dawn to dark. . . . In this tug of war between children and jobs, the children are losing." Critics charged mothers with being "war work deserters," for neglecting their children and not providing "adequate care and supervision."

There were even fears that desertion might become habit-forming: "Once having left the children to their own devices, and finding that it can be done over and over again, the mother may develop much satisfaction . . . from evading her accustomed responsibility." [4] Given these judgments, it is not surprising that federal funds for day care were cut off as soon as hostilities ended, another piece of legislation that, fortunately, no longer seemed necessary.

With the war's end, traditional occupational patterns among women reasserted themselves. Of course, working women did not disappear from the labor force; in fact, between 1940 and 1950 their numbers rose slightly, from 27 percent to 31 percent of all women. But the major increase came in spheres of work that were stereotypically women's (particularly office work) and not in manufacturing (where dramatic gains had been made during the war) or in the professions (which remained closed to women).[5] No less important, older ideas about women's work were not challenged (as they really had not been during the war, either). The post-World War II period did not witness agitation for equal pay or equal rights; there was no sense that married women with children should be working. The war was not so much a transforming experience as an interruption, after which women returned to pursue an inherited role.

Undermining the Model of Wife-Companion

Immediately after 1945, a massive increase took place in suburban developments. Although such communities had been planned and promoted ever since the 1850s, in the late 1940s an unusually large number of Americans began to put a suburban home at the core of their preferred life style. Between 1950 and 1960, nearly two-thirds of the increase in population in the United States occurred in the suburbs; over this decade, the population in 225 major cities rose 8.7 percent and in their suburbs, 47 percent. Some very practical considerations helped to promote this change. The federal government, fearful of a return to depression conditions, underwrote the construction of homes in the suburbs. Low-interest mortgages were generally available, and veterans had added inducements—until 1972 they could

purchase homes with a $1 down payment. At the same time, the fed-
eral government undertook a massive highway construction program, thus enabling people to commute to work from communities
lacking adequate public transportation networks.[6] But these points
merely explain why it was possible for families to live in suburbs.
They do not clarify why a suburban home became the first choice
for the American family.

In fact, the appeal of suburbia to women was intimately linked to
the ideology of the wife-companion. By opting for the comfort,
roominess, and seclusion of a suburban home, a woman announced
her preference for an essentially private existence. The very distance
of the suburbs from the city isolated her from the problems of urban
life, the very problems that had so involved the Progressives. Promoters advertised their developments as "escapes" and retreats from
the crime, noise, and dirt of the city—and most of those who made
the retreat were content to give up a public commitment.

Sociological studies of the suburbs point to the highly self-
conscious character of this decision. In carrying out his research on
Levittown, New Jersey in the early 1960s, Herbert Gans asked
women to list their "principal aspiration" for moving to this new
community. The overwhelming majority (78 percent) told him of
their desire to enhance the conveniences and the qualities of family
life. They had come for "comfort and roominess for family members
in a new home"; for "privacy and freedom of action in an owned
home"; for "furnishing and decorating the home"; for "better family
life," or, simply, for carrying out the "normal family role, being a
homemaker." Only a handful of women anticipated a more active life
of any sort outside the home. Only 8.0 percent came for a "better
social life"; less than 1.0 percent came to be "active in civic affairs";
and less than 0.5 percent looked to involvements "in churches or
clubs." [7] To move to Levittown was to make a commitment to the
family, not the community.

Just as an intense concern for the quality of family life brought
these women to the suburbs, so this attitude organized their day-to-
day world there. Suburban houses looked inward; architects noted
that the typical design focused the home within "its own private
garden with service facilities (kitchen, etc.) facing the road." The
privacy promised to encourage a close and deeply emotive tie between husband and wife. The spacious master bedroom, generally
set apart from the rooms of the children, was well-suited to a highly

sexual relationship. And wives anticipated spending many evenings alone with their husbands, not with family or friends; in Levittown a woman would often not visit a neighbor whose husband was at home, probably, as Gans concluded, "because of the belief that a husband has first call on his wife's companionship." [8] Social life tended to consist of couples visiting each other informally. If bridge was invented in the 1920s, it reached new popularity in the 1950s. So, too, the suburbs promised to offer children their own private space. Each child would have its own bedroom, in accordance with the best psychological principles; and it seemed safe to play unsupervised in a suburban development. Ostensibly there was no need for an iron fence and a trained matron to keep out corrupt street influences.

Public life in the suburbs represented a variation on the 1920s theme of country clubs and bridge clubs. The women of Levittown organized associations to facilitate casual contact with like-minded people, to pass the time in pleasant and congenial fashion. The clubs did not set out to provide a new community with facilities, to establish a neighborhood center or a library or a teenage athletic team. It was the local lawyer, and not the women, who saw to it that a library was built in Levittown; it was the school superintendent who organized the PTA, and the chief of police who led the drive for a Levittown Youth Sports Association. The women did not even bother to investigate Levittown's public schools. "They were sure," Gans reported, "that the new schools would be as satisfactory as their new neighbors." [9] Suburban women did not share the commitments of their Progressive predecessors. They had much more in common with the feminists new-style of the 1920s than the reformers of the 1900s.

For all the rewards and personal satisfactions that the suburbs promised, some women were soon discovering that the other side of privacy was loneliness and isolation. Gans detected some of this at Levittown. It was only women (albeit a minority of women) who reported loneliness; women suffered disproportionately from emotional illnesses and committed all the suicides. [10] But what was hinted at in Levittown was dramatically articulated and confirmed in the encounters between Betty Friedan and a group of her former Smith College classmates. Friedan was better able than any other critic to uncover and to express the malaise that all too frequently existed for suburban women. She interviewed her 1942 Smith classmates 15 years after graduation and then, "like a reporter on the trail of a story," supplemented their accounts. The story that then emerged in *The Feminine Mystique* (1963) was the gap between the rhetoric of the wife-companion and a reality that was empty and frustrating.

Friedan discovered that the wife-companion ideal appealed to women in all social classes. "The suburban housewife," she wrote, "was the dream image of the young American woman and the envy, it was said, of women all over the world. . . . She was healthy, beautiful, educated, concerned only about her husband, her children, her home. She had found true feminine fulfillment. As a housewife and mother, she was respected as a full and equal partner to man in his world." [11] But Friedan was just as certain that the image was a sham. Translating the precepts into practice had disastrous consequences.

Point by point, Friedan exploded the myth of "the feminine mystique." Her informants, she reported, found suburban life a nightmare. "A film made of any typical morning in my house would look like an old Marx Brothers' comedy," recounted one woman. "I wash the dishes, run the older children off to school, dash out in the yard to cultivate the chrysanthemums . . . help the youngest child build a blockhouse, spend fifteen minutes skimming the newspapers so I can be well-informed. . . . By noon I'm ready for a padded cell." Suburban housewives had become prisoners in their own homes, not enjoying privacy but suffering solitary confinement. "Many women," Friedan informed her readers, "no longer left their homes except to shop, chauffeur their children, or attend social engagements with their husbands." Preoccupied by an endless routine of household chores, they had lost self-respect. "The problem," as one woman put it, "is always being the children's mommy, the minister's wife and never being myself." [12] As a wife-companion she could only find fulfillment vicariously, through the achievements of others.

On the basis of these responses, Friedan launched a two-pronged attack: the suburban housewife was both an inadequate mother and an inadequate wife. Devoid of purpose in her own life, she was incapable of giving her children a sense of competency and autonomy. The young, charged Friedan in tones reminiscent of Watson, were not only infantile but "incapable of the effort, the endurance of pain and frustration, the discipline needed to compete on the baseball field or get into college." And she predicted a dismal future for them; an endless number of emotional difficulties would plague them throughout adulthood.[13] The curse of a lack of self-direction and self-satisfaction in the mother would be visited on the children.

The wife-companion was a failure not only in the nursery but also in the bedroom. Friedan's respondents regularly reported that sex was the only thing that made them feel alive and gave them an identity. And she took that to mean that lacking any other outlet, they attached disproportionate importance to sexual intimacy. Their emphasis on sexual fulfillment was destructive. Men, able to achieve satisfaction through careers, found sex a diversion; for wives, sex was a vocation. Under these circumstances, women made sex into a "strangely joyless national compulsion." Friedan quoted one marriage counselor to confirm her point: suburban wives "made such heavy demands on love and marriage [that] . . . sometimes literally almost nothing happens." Their all-consuming passion disturbed their husbands, the proof to be found in the increase in male-initiated divorce actions. The rise reflected "the growing aversion and hostility that men have for the feminine millstones hanging around their necks." [14]

The villains ultimately responsible for so grim a state of affairs, argued Friedan, were the experts who had foisted this role on women. The psychologists and Freudian analysts had misled women. Without much understanding of either Watson or Freud, and without any sense whatsoever of the historical antecedents of the role of wife-companion, she insisted that "the feminine mystique derived its power from Freudian thought." In terms that were far less novel than she imagined, Frieden declared: "It is time to stop exhorting mothers to love their children more, and face . . . the fact that most of the problems now being treated in the child guidance clinics are solved when mothers . . . no longer need to fill their emotional needs through their children. It is time to stop exhorting women to be more feminine when it . . . depersonalizes sex and imposes an impossible burden on their husbands." [15] Children would not require psychological and psychiatric counseling if their mothers were happy. Sex would prove fulfilling if women made it one of many sources of pleasure.

But then Friedan did go on to make a new point, new at least to the world of Watson and Freud. The way for women to escape their predicament was not for them to devote themselves more fully to their husbands (as Watson intimated), or to bring their children and themselves still more quickly to a child guidance clinic and therapist's office (as psychiatrists suggested), but to gain satisfaction in work. "The only way for a woman, as for a man, to find her-

self, to know herself as a person is by creative work of her own.
There is no other way." Indeed, since Friedan was speaking to college graduates and college students, she urged them not merely to
take a job (for earning money or killing time) but to pursue a
career (for finding fulfillment). Work was no longer a tactic to improve women's marital choices or an insurance policy to protect her
in widowhood. Rather, it was to be at the center of a woman's
existence, her primary source of identity. With little notion of the
implications of such a message to women who had not passed through
Smith, Friedan concluded that a career was "a new life plan for
women"—the answer to *all* problems confronting *all* women.[16]

Even as Friedan was writing, married women, particularly those
with children, were entering the job market in unprecedented numbers. In 1940, only one-quarter of American women worked; by
1974, 46 percent worked. And the increase was not the result of more
single or divorced women joining the labor force, but of more married women, and married women with children, entering it. "In
1940," as two Bureau of Labor statisticians calculated, "almost half
the women in the labor force were single and only 30 percent were
married; in 1970, about 20 percent were single and 60 percent were
married." In 1948 (when such statistics were first collected), one-
quarter of women with school-age children (between 6 and 17)
were employed; by 1972, over one-half of them held jobs. Even more
dramatic was the rise in employment among women with preschool
children (below the age of 5). In 1948, mothers of preschool children
made up 10 percent of all women workers; in 1960 they were 19
percent. In fact, by 1974, one out of every three mothers with a preschool child was at work.[17]

For all their consistency, these statistics must still be interpreted
cautiously. Just as the census may have understated the numbers of
married women working in 1900, it may well be exaggerating the
number now. The problem rests, of course, with the census taker's
reliance on the individual respondent for information. Hence, the
statistics may demonstrate not changing habits but changing norms.
Since mothers with preschool children now believe that they *should*
be working, they may be telling the census taker that they *are* working. Also, many more women than men are employed part-time; only
41 percent of women workers in 1970 were full-time workers.
Nevertheless, it remains the case that the composition of the labor
force is undergoing a fundamental, even revolutionary, change. Be-

fore very long, the overwhelming majority of women, whatever their family situation or household responsibilities, will be at a job.

How are we to understand this new situation? What was it that brought married women with children into the labor force in such large numbers? One critical element was the rapid post-war growth of service industries that dramatically expanded the number of white-collar jobs. If men quickly assumed the best-paying managerial positions, still numerous clerical and office posts became available for women. In 1950, women held only 4.3 percent of all managerial positions; in 1973, after more than 20 years of job expansion, they held 4.9 percent. Yet during the same time the number of women in clerical and office jobs increased. In 1950 women held 27 percent of these positions; by 1974, 34 percent.[18] So there were more openings for women, albeit of a very special sort. While men had greater opportunity to enjoy careers, women had greater opportunity to take jobs.

Labor analysts in the post-war period not only perceived existing vacancies in service industries but also predicted critical labor shortages in the future. To ward off this coming crisis, they adopted a very novel stance; they urged employers to hire and train women for managerial positions. At the same time, they encouraged women with college degrees to return to the labor force and assume these jobs. Thus, the women's magazines that had traditionally carried articles by psychologists declaring that woman's place was in the home were now carrying articles by labor experts insisting that woman's place was in the office. Arthur Fleming, at one time Secretary of Health, Education and Welfare, was in 1962 a contributing editor to *Good Housekeeping*, and he used his position to publicize the new message. "The number of trained women workers," he contended, "must increase 25 percent between now and 1970 as compared with 15 percent of men—if we are to capitalize on our opportunities for economic growth."[19] Given the low birth rate of the Depression years, the earlier age at which women now married, and the increased length of time that they spent in school, many of the vacancies in the labor force would have to be filled by married women with growing children. Therefore, Fleming, like Friedan, urged mothers not merely to go to work but to pursue careers. He paid lip service to the needs of the family but was far more concerned with the needs of an expanding post-war economy. Thus, in the early 1960s educated women received the same advice from two very different sources: whether for reasons of personal fulfillment (as in Friedan) or for public well-being (as in Fleming), they were to join the work force. Leaving the home took on an altogether novel legitimacy.

Women as a Minority

Just when the isolation of suburban life and expanded opportunities in the labor force were beginning to undermine the model of the wife-companion, a new definition of proper womanhood, a notion of woman as person, began to filter through American society. This was a view of woman as autonomous, energetic, and competent. Woman was not to be defined by her household role, by her responsibilities as wife or mother; she was in no way to be limited by any special gender characteristics. This new definition of womanhood emphasized the similarities between the sexes, not the differences. It rendered the notion of special protection outmoded and irrelevant. In brief, woman as person was fully capable of defining and acting in her own best interest.

This ideal showed surprisingly little continuity with a feminist past. The movement for female suffrage, with its insistence on women's special roles and responsibilities, was irrelevant. Even the 1920s National Woman's Party, which survived to introduce an equal rights amendment into Congress almost every year, offered little in the way of appropriate rhetoric or leadership. New feminist organizations, without ties to traditional women's clubs or women's political organizations, were to set forth the new model and establish its relevance to social policy.

Part of the impetus to a definition of woman as person may have come from an acute dissatisfaction with the narrow and frustrating quality of life as a wife-companion and from a sense of the new options within the labor market. But part of it also came from the civil rights movement. Although it is commonplace to observe that women's protest followed on blacks' protest, that one effort to advance the position of an oppressed group stimulated another, neither the conceptual nor the political links between the two movements are as obvious or as simple as they may first appear. In fact, there is little historical basis for making such a connection. White middle-class women were not involuntarily wrenched from a native culture and transplanted to an alien society to suffer the degradations of slavery. More, the civil rights movement itself was unwilling to see women's problems as identical to its own. Stokely Carmichael's remarks on the appropriate position for women in the movement—on their backs—is now legendary. But other men in more polite ways said almost the same thing. "Women are not a civil rights issue," the leaders of the NAACP Legal Defense Fund told Muriel Fox and Betty Friedan, when they were soliciting support for the National Organization of Women. Nor did feminist recruiters receive substantial backing from black middle-class activist women. " 'We don't want anything to do with that bag,' " Friedan remembers them saying. " 'The important thing for black women was for black men to get ahead. And when the black men got the rights they had been denied so long, they would give black women all the equality they desired.' " Sexual discrimination may have been the key issue for white women, but it was not for black women.[20]

Feminists themselves for a long time did not perceive the need for a civil rights organization for women. They did not, for example, take the lead in demanding national legislation that would combat the discrimination that women suffered as it combatted the discrimination that blacks suffered. Curiously, the demand came to be embodied in the law before it was self-consciously advanced by feminist leaders. The federal law that treated the two forms of discrimination in similar fashion was the product of a series of fortuitous circumstances, not of a skillful lobbying campaign. In 1964, Title VII of the Civil Rights Act, outlawing racial discrimination in hiring practices, was the subject of a bitter Congressional battle; conservative Senators were attempting to defeat or to dilute the bill in every possible manner. Howard Smith, a senator from Virginia, in an effort to demonstrate just how ridiculous legislation governing hiring practices was, added an amendment to Title VII forbidding sexual as well as racial discrimination. But the Johnson administration was so determined to see the law enacted that when Congresswoman Martha Griffiths and Senator Margaret Chase Smith threatened to raise a fuss if the Smith clause were omitted, the administration threw its weight into keeping the prohibition against sexual discrimination. While feminists were certainly pleased at this accident of drafting, they had nothing to do with it and they really did not expect very much to come from it.[21] As a result, the clause was not taken seriously by the Congress that passed it, the president who signed it, the administrators who were to enforce it, or the employers who were to obey it.

Although employers dutifully posted signs announcing that their hiring and promotion policies did not discriminate either on the basis of race or of sex, corporations did not in practice treat blacks and women in the same way. Given the power of the civil rights movement at this time, employers did make some effort to alter policies toward blacks. But women did not make gains. Women filed numerous complaints with the Equal Employment Opportunity Commission (EEOC), the enforcement arm of Title VII, protesting unfair treatment. Indeed, it is striking just how quickly individual women turned to the Commission to redress their grievances. (No rhetoric may have linked sexual and racial discrimination, but the women knew at first hand about bias.) Nevertheless, these complaints went unanswered. With no organization ready to pressure the administrative agency, Title VII was meaningless as far as women were concerned.

But not altogether meaningless, for the very presence of the clause in Title VII did inspire a group of "underground" feminists to pursue the issue of sex discrimination. One EEOC staff member did begin to encourage such traditional women's groups as the League of Women Voters and the American Association of University Women to protest the agency's lack of activity on behalf of women. But the organizations ignored him, and Title VII too. They were unable to see any connection between racial and sexual discrimination; middle-class women in salaried positions seemingly had nothing in common with unskilled black laborers. Many of the leaders undoubtedly were reluctant to confront the issue, still believing that women belonged at home.[22] In all events, the established women's organizations did not concern themselves with sexual discrimination. Some of them would catch up and come along later, but they did not lead the movement.

Their reluctance to act was really not surprising. Even Friedan, so aware of the problems of middle-class women, was unwilling until 1966 to form a civil rights-type of organization. At first she was convinced that women did not have "to organize anything as radical as a civil rights movement, like the blacks." It was all a matter of will and energy; once women were committed to careers, employers would recognize their skills and determination and end discriminatory practices. But as Friedan learned more about the unfair treatment that women encountered in the labor force, as more cases filed with

EEOC came to her attention, she shifted ground. She began to worry about a "feminist backlash"—if enough women entered the job market, only to be treated as second-class citizens, they would soon beat a retreat to the family and find the same problems all over again.[23] Perhaps a women's civil rights organization was not inappropriate after all.

Dissatisfaction with the EEOC initially prompted Friedan and other feminists to look to the Citizen's Advisory Council on the Status of Women for corrective action. Originally established by President Kennedy in 1961, the Council had the broad mandate to "examine the needs and changing position of American women to make recommendations to eliminate barriers to their full participation in the economic, social, civil and political affairs of the nation." By the middle of the 1960s, the national Council, and the state Councils that it spawned, had collected voluminous material documenting sexual discrimination; the Council knew well the unwillingness of the EEOC to enforce the sex discrimination clause. The feminists expected support from the Council. Traditionally, federal agencies like the Children's Bureau had drawn up model codes and lobbied for the passage of legislation to correct injustices. But to the feminists' surprise, the Council, at its Third Annual Conference in 1966, refused to allow a public resolution demanding that EEOC treat sexual discrimination like racial discrimination to come to the floor. The Conference officials ruled that the sponsors of the resolution were not official delegates to the meeting and, hence, were out of order.[24]

Behind the Council's refusal to press the issue, to do battle against barriers to women's "full participation" in American society, lay a critical difference between this organization and others like the Children's Bureau or the Women's Bureau. The older bodies were the products of an already-existing coalition; they were the culmination of reform efforts, not their initial sponsors, and they worked to fulfill an agenda that their creators had long before established. Feminists, on the other hand, were trying to capture an already-existing agency and turn it to their own purposes, which was a futile effort. The Council, for all the language of the mandate, was very traditional-minded. Its members came from long-standing women's organizations, service clubs, and religious associations. Not that any of them favored discrimination against women, but the Council was going to move carefully, cautiously, and behind the scenes. Faced with the indisputable fact of massive discrimination against women, it preferred to respond in a low-key manner. So instead of calling in the media and going for the headlines, the Council would petition the EEOC to alter its policies. And when the EEOC ignored its resolutions and refused to give discrimination against women the same attention that it gave discrimination against blacks, the Council did nothing. In effect, the Council disagreed not so much with the aims of the feminists as with their methods—which was another way of saying that the Council would not be a driving force in creating a vigorous public protest movement among women.

It was fitting, then, that the Council's rebuff became the occasion in 1966 for the new feminists to establish their own association. The National Organization for Women (NOW), as the group was called, pledged to "take action to bring women into full participation in the mainstream of American society now," but not the sort of action that the Council took. There was no reason, NOW argued, to "examine conditions"; the extent of discrimination was already documented. Nor was there any cause for merely "encouraging" women's participation in the work force; large numbers of women were already employed and they needed immediate assistance to get better-paying jobs and long-overdue promotions. NOW believed that only by publicizing both the extent of discrimination against women and the unwillingness of government agencies to take corrective action could they generate reform. By moving from politics to the media, from compromise to confrontation, NOW became the first civil rights organization for women.

NOW also found the rhetoric of the civil rights movement to be particularly appropriate and useful. "The time has come," declared NOW's Statement of Purpose, "to confront with concrete action, the conditions which now prevent women from enjoying the equality of opportunity and freedom of choice which is their right as individual Americans, and as human beings." Women in the labor force had to date received "token" appointments; businesses made no "serious effort to advance and recruit" them. "Working women are becoming increasingly—not less—concentrated on the bottom of the job ladder. As a consequence, full-time women workers today earn on the average only 60 percent of what men earn." So, too, women were the victims of inequality in the educational system. They, like blacks, were denied admission to prestigious colleges and professional schools. As a result, "women comprise less than 1 percent of federal judges; less than 4 percent of all lawyers; 7 percent of doctors.

Yet women represent 53 percent of the U.S. population." Further, the media, the textbooks, and the law—indeed, all social institutions —portrayed women in stereotypic fashion and presented a "false image." Finally, NOW proclaimed its opposition to "all policies and practices—in church, state, college, factory, or office—which, in the guise of protectiveness, not only deny opportunities but foster in women self-denigration, dependence, and evasion of responsibility." [25]

One must remember that in 1966 the civil rights rhetoric had a very optimisic and Progressive quality that the organizers of NOW found highly appealing. Under the leadership of Martin Luther King, Jr., the movement spoke fervently about cooperation and brother-hood. "My dream," declared King in his 1963 speech from the steps of the Lincoln Memorial, "is a dream deeply rooted in the American Dream. I have a dream that one day on the red hills of Georgia sons of former slaves and the sons of former slaveowners will be able to sit down together at the table of brotherhood." And the women who formed NOW shared a similar vision. Their ambition was to create for American women "an active, self-respecting partnership with men." NOW had no "enmity toward men, who are also victims of the current half-equality between the sexes." Hence in NOW's dream, "a true partnership between the sexes demands a different concept of marriage, an equitable sharing of the responsibilities of home and children and of the economic burdens of their support." In all, NOW assumed that its program would eliminate the causes of "much unnecessary hostility between the sexes." [26]

It would not take very long before this rhetoric would have a naïve ring. Just as the civil rights movement would move from brotherhood to black power, so the women's movement too would shift from partnership to a war between the sexes. But in their origins, both movements believed that their demands were just and in everyone's best interest, and that their success was therefore assured. Whites of good reason and men of good reason would sooner or later promote a new social justice.

Such an identification with the blacks invigorated the women's movement. NOW declared its willingness to offer "active support to the common cause of equal rights for all those who struggle against discrimination and deprivation." [27] This proclamation gave the feminists a very solid sense of purpose. Imagine how it felt for a middle-class woman to have a part in the "world-wide revolution for human rights." This orientation also seemed to reverse some of the traditional lines of influence between middle-class women reformers and the poor, giving feminists a further sense of their own novelty. If the Progressive women had set out to mold the poor in their own image, NOW supporters in the 1960s claimed to be ready to learn from the poor. They adopted their rhetoric and strategy, and predictably, at least some of them began to affect their style of dress and manners. Blue jeans came into fashion, women became "sisters," and first names became the appropriate form of address. And although they had no way of knowing it, women's groups and black groups shared still another similarity—they both became the target of undercover FBI investigations.

But this similarity in style had an even more important consequence for the first feminists. It led them to believe (mistakenly, as we shall see later), that social policies implemented on behalf of middle-class women would, by their very nature, also favor lower-class women. Since feminists viewed themselves as one more oppressed minority, they inevitably assumed that policies designed to improve their own lot would improve everyone's lot. Rather than believing that social class differences would create conflict, they thought that gender similarity promised unity. Identity of sex seemed more important than class divergences. So central was this assumption to the new feminists that they could not imagine a time when the best interest of middle-class women would not fit with the best interest of lower-class women. Their sense of identity with the groups below gave them the self-confidence, deceptive to its core, that social policy could be restructured to the advantage of all women.

The civil rights movement had yet another impact on the women's movement. The drive for school desegregation prompted a major reexamination of learning patterns in American children, a reexamination that would soon alter the understanding of learning patterns among women as well. The proponents of desegregation had not only to overturn the constitutionality of a separate-but-equal doctrine as it applied to school facilities, but also to repudiate a traditional system of classification in the schools that labeled blacks as slow learners. Immediately after the 1954 Supreme Court victory in *Brown*, a group of psychologists (who had successfully pressed the view that the stigma of separateness made it inherently unequal) began to attack established methods of classification. Stereotypes about low levels of academic achievement among black children had to be eliminated before communities would actually go about desegregating their schools. And so psychologists began to reevaluate the accuracy and reliability of the procedure that was at the core of classification systems, the IQ test.

These psychologists maintained that the IQ examination was culturally biased in favor of middle-class children. It tested primarily for "cognitive skills"—in which middle-class children excelled—and did not measure "adaptive behavior" skills—an ability to survive in a difficult and hostile environment in which black children excelled. This limitation was critical because the test was unable to predict which children would succeed in the world beyond the classroom. In fact, this group of psychologists argued that success in adult life had so little to do with a person's IQ that the examination should be altogether abolished.[28]

This was not the first reconsideration of the dependability of the IQ test. It had been under scrutiny ever since its widespread use in the United States beginning in the 1920s. Before the 1950s, however, analyses of the IQ had the purpose of refining the test. They presupposed the value of the procedure, looking only to make the measurement still more accurate and discriminating. Both psychologists and educators had assumed that the ideal school was made up of a series of "special classes," and that the model classroom contained a student body that was homogeneous in intelligence. The ultimate purpose of the IQ was to match the child to the right setting, and the better the test, the more appropriate the classification.

The new psychologists brought altogether different assumptions to the field. They were seeking a mix of heterogeneous children. In their ideal classroom, learning occurred as frequently from social interaction as from books; an unclassified school, therefore, would benefit both the child and the wider society. The IQ, as their novel experiments demonstrated, was a barrier to implementing such a program. The test scores appeared to be self-fulfilling prophecies; teachers who were told that a child "showed great promise" subsequently paid him more attention and graded him higher. In other words, social expectation was the major variable determining a child's level of achievement in school.[29]

This new type of psychological research had a serendipitous effect on the women's movement. While some researchers were examining the differences in school performance between blacks and whites, others began to look at the differences between boys and girls. Again,

it seemed that social expectation was the critical element in determining outcomes. The intellectual capacities of the sexes were identical, but their patterns of learning were not. Girls achieved more than
boys in elementary school but began to slip behind in high school;
by college, women were not only achieving less than men but were
even rating men's potential to achieve higher than their own. The
key to the puzzle was societal values. As girls matured, they fell
victim to cultural judgments that brains and beauty did not mix, that
learning was a man's business, that a woman who was too smart
would become an old maid.

One set of experiments that psychologist Matina Horner carried
out revealed that women tended to fear success precisely because it
did not fit with a properly feminine image. "The high, if anything
increasing, incidence of fear of success imagery found in our
studies," reported Horner, "indicates the extent to which women
have incorporated society's attitudes . . . that competition, success,
competence, and intellectual achievements are basically inconsistent
with femininity." Rather than contradict the norm, women tended to
"compromise by disguising their ability and abdicating from competition in the outside world." [30] The implication of Horner's research
for the women's movement was clear: to promote a new image that
made success compatible with womanhood.

The primary target of the ensuing campaign was not the IQ test
but psychoanalytic doctrines—the writings of Erik Erikson, Bruno
Bettelheim, Helene Deutsch, and Freud himself. All of them, feminists
argued, had elevated socially determined roles into biological truths;
all of them had cloaked myth in the garb of science. Thus, they
quoted Erik Erikson's dictum that a mature woman's fulfillment had
to take account of the fact that "somatic design harbors an 'inner
space' destined to bear the offspring of chosen men, and with it, a
biological, psychological and ethical commitment to take care of
human infancy"; and they then asked how Erikson knew this. So,
too, they quoted Bettelheim's contention that "we must start with
the realization that, as much as women want to be good scientists or
engineers, they want first and foremost to be womanly companions of
men and to be mothers." And they wondered what made him so certain
of this. Such notions, the feminists insisted, reflected not scientific findings but "the cultural consensus." To psychoanalysts, one feminist
noted, "a woman's *true* nature is that of a happy servant . . . and
they back it up with psychosexual incantation and biological ritual

causes." In similar fashion, "psychologists and psychiatrists embrace these sexist norms of our culture . . . [and] do not see beyond the most superficial and stultifying conceptions of female nature." [31]

The Freudian idea of woman as an inherently passive mother and companion received its fullest expression in the writings of Helene Deutsch. Her immensely influential two-volume work, *The Psychology of Women*, was almost a twentieth-century restatement of the nineteenth-century view that God first made a uterus and then built woman around it. Deutsch linked psychology to sexuality and sexuality to social functioning. Women, she argued, defined their lack of a penis as a psychological and sexual defect and, in an effort at compensation, tried to substitute the clitoris. But the clitoris was merely an "inferior organ," one "so rudimentary that it can barely be considered an organ"; clitoral masturbation inevitably proved unsatisfactory, incapable of gratifying "the active and aggressive instinctual impulses." The result of this sexual frustration was an abdication—the normal woman gave up aggressive drives and turned instead to a feminine—that is, passive—role. In one of the clearest statements of the view that anatomy was destiny, Deutsch concluded, "Thus the inadequacy of the organ can be considered a biologic and physiologic cause of psychological sex differences." [32] Neurotic women, obsessed by the lack of an organ, became aggressive and homosexual. The well-adjusted woman, at peace with her biology, became passive, receptive, and masochistic.

The critical attack on Deutsch came from the laboratory. The experiments of Dr. William Masters and Virginia Johnson demonstrated the absurdity of defining women's role as inherently passive in a sexual sense. The primary contribution of Masters and Johnson was to present an altogether new image of female sexuality. The title of their book, *Human Sexual Response*, conveys the principal finding that basic similarities marked the anatomy and physiology of male and female sexuality, "that direct parallels in human sexual response . . . exist to a degree never previously appreciated." With the aid of sensors and cameras, they measured and photographed women's, and men's, responses to sexual stimulation; and their findings, from changes in heartbeats to color flushes, informed a startlingly ignorant medical profession of the most elementary facts. There was no difference between vaginal and clitoral orgasm; female sexual responses were at least as intense as the male's, perhaps even more. A normally functioning woman, they reported, "within a short period after her first climax, will in most instances be capable of having a second, third, fourth and even fifth and sixth orgasm before she is fully satisfied." Under these circumstances, it was absurd to describe a clitoris as an inadequate organ.[33] And it was equally absurd to label men sexually active and women sexually passive.

At least one woman psychiatrist skillfully explored the implications that Masters and Johnson's findings had for psychoanalytic theory. Dr. Mary Jane Sherfey dedicated *The Nature and Evolution of Female Sexuality* to Masters and Johnson, and the book was a world apart from Deutsch's *Psychology of Women*. Combining new findings in biology (which demonstrated that insofar as embryonic growth was concerned, males developed from females and not the other way around) with the new data on sexual responsiveness, Sherfey presented a woman who was anatomically whole and sexually active. While carefully noting that an "Adam from Eve" view did not establish female "superiority," she did destroy the notion that anatomy dictated men's dominance in the marketplace and women's passivity in the home. Sherfey also suggested that a conflict of interest marked the relationship between men and women as, indeed, it marked the relationship between women's self-expression and social order. The act of intercourse, for example, was not necessarily the most satisfying form of sexual stimulation for the woman. More, the woman's multiorgasmic capability might well have to be tamed, indeed repressed, in order for society to cohere.[34] Sherfey, still very much within the psychoanalytic framework, was adding another dimension to the discontents in civilization.

The findings of Masters and Johnson also helped to expand the concept of sexual normality. A wide range of stimuli, it seemed, produced satisfying sexual responses. And this premise was critical to the viewpoint of the latest, and incredibly popular, addition to the shelf of sexual advice books, Alex Comfort's *The Joy of Sex*. The title's play on *The Joy of Cooking* and the book's organization into main courses, relishes, and condiments reflected the notion that one can follow instructions in the bedroom to achieve gourmet sex as easily as one can follow instructions in the kitchen to achieve gourmet cuisine.[35] Everyone has the necessary equipment, and the recipes, while important, are easy to follow. No barriers need block the attainment of sexual pleasure.

In sum, all of these elements, from suburban and workplace realities to the diverse influences of the civil rights movements, contributed to the formulation of a new definition of woman. They not only rendered the concept of the wife-companion obsolete but offered another one in its stead: woman as active, energetic, fully competent, and capable of self-definition as a person in sexual and in social terms. Woman's essence was no longer to be found in a household role but in her own achievements.

Family Life as a Zero-Sum Game

The first appearance of the new definition of woman was not intended to disrupt family life. The writing of Betty Friedan, the first Statement of Purpose of NOW, the findings of Masters and Johnson, and even the recipes in *The Joy of Sex* did not imagine that an active and liberated woman would war on her husband or her children. On the contrary, they all believed that woman as person would be a better wife and mother. Her energy and activity would make the home a more interesting, more exciting, and more satisfying place.

To Friedan, the ideal feminist was both a working wife and a mother. Liberated women were "not battleaxes or manhaters," and she noted with pride that "there are men in our own ranks." Indeed, Friedan's new woman would command a respect from men that her predecessors had not. "The officials we interviewed," she reported, "treated us as attractive women, but without the glint of contempt that so often belies men's flattery of women. Because we were and are serious about real equality . . . they treated us with real respect." [36] The relevant "other" for Friedan remained the man. The goal was to gain equality with him.

So, too, Masters and Johnson translated their laboratory findings into a sex therapy program in order to enhance marital life. They offered their treatment only to couples who had agreed in advance to remain together for five years. Alex Comfort's books also insisted that a variety of techniques would help keep sexual interest alive over a long married life. In fact, married couples enjoyed the best sex: "One needs a steady basic diet of quiet, night-and-morning matrimonial intercourse. . . . The more regular sex a couple has, the higher the deliberately contrived peaks—just as the more you cook routinely, the better and the more reliable banquets you can stage." [37] Even the unconventional section on "foursomes and moresomes" urged readers to share sex only with other couples committed to maintaining their own marriages.

But despite this initial conservatism, the women's movement was soon issuing far more radical proposals. Amazing as it may seem more than ten years later, the organizers of NOW in 1966 believed that ending sexual discrimination in the work force and establishing a national network of day care centers would immediately accomplish the social and economic equality of American women. Their facile optimism reflected a very limited experience. And no sooner did a national organization for women come into being than their education began. NOW's existence prompted women from all over the country to recount the discriminations that they had experienced. NOW became a sounding board for grievances that went deeper than anyone had ever imagined or could even immediately comprehend. Constituents, in other words, taught the NOW leaders about the real nature of women's experience in the world, and constituents then went on to radicalize the reform agenda.

Unable to anticipate the complexity of a program that would bring equality to women, NOW's first leaders were unable to control the rank and file. Once constituent pressure began to direct organizational policy, the women's movement became (and to this day has remained) essentially leaderless. Some of NOW's founders withdrew when new goals conflicted with their personal beliefs. The others who stayed, like Friedan herself, were forced to accept policies that they had never anticipated or even favored. In fact, the very passive title of Friedan's autobiography, *It Changed My Life*, is an honest indication that she was swept up in the current created by the movement—that in NOW, members directed leaders.

Through this dynamic, NOW's list of demands rapidly expanded. Within a few years it was spearheading the fight for the passage of the Equal Rights Amendment to the Constitution, leading an attack on abortion laws, organizing specific programs to equalize educational opportunities for women, demanding important changes in marriage, divorce, and rape laws, and agitating to end discrimination against lesbians.[38] In each instance, it was constituent pressure that brought the organization into these issues.

In 1967, just one year after NOW's founding, the priority that organizers had first given to the enforcement of Title VII gave way to a commitment to pass an equal rights amendment. It was by no means a universally approved strategy. To some labor union officials,

particularly the United Auto Workers (who were actually helping to pay NOW's mailing costs), an equal rights amendment would
abolish special protective legislation that they, like the Progressives
before them, believed to be in the best interests of blue-collar workers. For others, an equal rights amendment raised the prospects of
NOW becoming identified with the National Woman's Party—and
they wanted to keep the new feminist organization distinct from an
old, tired, and ineffectual one. But these views did not carry; pressure from NOW constituents overrode the objections. "As I listened
and watched the women all over the hall who spoke," recalled
Friedan, "I saw that very few were opposed to taking a stand on
the ERA." The old-line National Woman's Party members made a
quick alliance with younger delegates. "When those very old suf-
fragettes sitting in the front row got up to speak on the Equal Rights
Amendment," continued Friedan, "I saw that they *spoke to* those
very young women who had never heard of it before and were
kindled by it as they had not been by narrow job issues."

And no wonder. An equal rights amendment promised in one
grand sweep to eliminate not only job discrimination but *all* discrimination. The younger women in NOW had little desire for special protection. Committed to a view of woman as competent—fully
capable of acting in her own best interest—they were far more comfortable with equal rights than with particular privileges. Better to
have an amendment that would offer a legal basis for abolishing all
forms of discrimination than to perpetuate a system that treated
women as children.

NOW's decision at the same 1967 convention to campaign on
behalf of abortion on demand also took the organization in a direction
that its founders had not anticipated. Perhaps the social class and
income of the Smith alumnae allowed them easier access to medical
abortions than most women had; or perhaps it was a dirty secret that
they would not share with an interviewer. But Friedan, along with
other NOW officers, seemed amazed at the diverse types of women
who enthusiastically advocated a liberalized abortion policy. "The
women speaking up passionately for it," Friedan noted, "were not
only the young women from everywhere, but the square, middle-aged
housewife types from Indiana and points south." [39] Once again, the
first-hand knowledge of NOW's members, and not the ideas of its
leaders, wrote the platform.

And so it was with lesbian rights. Friedan, always intent on keeping
the organization at least within range of middle-American values,

Affirmative action?

feared that the "lavender menace" would wreck NOW. Convinced that lesbians were trying to capture NOW for their own purposes, Friedan did manage to force many of them out of the organization. Nevertheless, the determination of most members to speak for the rights of all women in all situations overrode Friedan's objections. Although few NOW members were homosexual (in a recent survey, 8 percent reported themselves homosexual and 9 percent bisexual), they empathized with the discriminations that these women suffered. Thus, NOW resolved at its 1971 convention that a "woman's right to her own person included the right to define and express her own sexuality and to choose her own life style; therefore, we acknowledge the oppression of lesbians as a legitimate concern of feminism." [40]

Around the issues of equal rights, day care, abortion, and discrimination against lesbians, NOW left the precepts of educated motherhood and wife-companion for a model of woman as her own person. In a very short time, it rejected and renounced as harmful to women the social policies built on these inherited assumptions. Progressive special protection was one more form of discrimination. Even Sanger's version of "voluntary motherhood" had merely given to women the option to space their children; the feminists of the 1960s demanded that women have the freedom to choose *not* to become mothers—or even wives. The new women reformers had a wider tolerance for various forms of sexual expression. Behavior that before had been labeled as sick or corrupting was now protected and sanctioned under a right to privacy. Only women themselves, and no one else, could define and implement their own best interest.

The adoption of these planks not only marked off the feminists of the 1960s from their predecessors but also pointed to a critical shift in the women's movement itself. NOW had begun in 1966 as a civil rights organization; by 1971, it was a women's liberation organization. This shift altered both its agenda and underlying assumptions, particularly its notion that the interests of men and women were ultimately compatible. Friedan and her allies had never thought in terms of competing interests or trade-offs. Ostensibly, programs that benefited women would benefit men. But as such issues as abortion and lesbian rights became prominent, and as the efforts to implement them began, the old view gave way. Friedan complained in 1970 that Kate Millett's *Sexual Politics*, which made sexual warfare the moving force in history, was "genuinely dangerous to the movement." Friedan was convinced that "no serious, meaningful action emerges from a sexual emphasis. There is simply talk, anger, and wallowing. It is also based on a highly distorted, oversimplified view of our society, men and women, family relations, relations to children." [41] But Friedan notwithstanding, beginning in the 1970s a conflict model, not a consensus model, pervaded the women's movement.

The issue of liberalized abortion most dramatically revealed how competing interests affected family relationships. Abortion on demand might be in the best interest and within the rights of women, but it was not necessarily in the best interest of husbands or of society in general. Even its most passionate supporters recognized that a pro-abortion policy did entail benefits to some at costs to others, that trade-offs were inevitably involved. If a woman had the right to abortion, did her decision require the consent of her spouse? What about those cases where the woman's desire to abort a fetus conflicted with her husband's desire to have a child? Did the fetus have rights apart from the mother's? When, if ever, did a fetus take on a life of its own—after three months? six months? only after delivery? Did society have an interest in preventing abortion? Would the right to abortion inevitably lead to infanticide for deformed babies or euthanasia for the senile? Conversely, did the poor have the same right to abortions as they had to medical treatment? The federal courts resolved some of these issues, generally dismissing husbands' claims and those of the poor but disallowing all restrictions on women's prerogatives before the fetus was three months old. The very language and passion of the debate, however, illustrated all too vividly the deep character of the controversy. For the first time, it appeared that women's interests, family interests, and societal interests were in conflict.

The debate over abortion provided one context for the emergence of the children's rights movement. The doctrine of woman as person implicitly suggested that maternal roles might not be consistent with women's needs—and then the case of abortion made the conflict explicit. An early and important statement on children's rights appeared in a small book written by three psychoanalysts: Joseph Goldstein, also a professor of law at Yale, Anna Freud, the director of the Hampstead Child Therapy Clinic in London, and Albert Solnit, a professor of pediatrics and psychiatry at Yale. Aptly entitled *Beyond the Best Interest of the Child*, the tract contended that the traditional notion that courts should promote the child's best interest had been a masquerade, cloaking policy decisions that were ultimately made in the parents' best interest. Just when the women's movement was asserting that the role of mother could conflict with the welfare of women, these authors were arguing that the natural mother—or, for that matter, the father—would not necessarily promote the welfare of the child. Moreover, just when the movement was insisting that women's rights should be enhanced regardless of the costs to others, these authors were insisting that children's rights should be enhanced regardless of the costs to others.

Goldstein, Freud, and Solnit argued the case in only one aspect— child custody proceedings. Previously, custody decisions had automatically favored the biological parent: the right of a mother to her child was almost always held paramount over that of foster parents and usually over that of a father. It was time, declared Goldstein and the others, to revise this policy; a genuine concern for the child should promote custody decisions that favored the "psychological" parent. Carefully avoiding the use of the term "mother," they referred only to the parent, and in their definition, the fit parent was the one who was actually satisfying the child's psychological needs. "Whether any adult becomes the psychological parent of a child," they announced, "is based on the day-to-day interaction, companionship, and shared experiences. The role can be fulfilled by a biological parent or by an adoptive parent or by any caring adult—but never by an absent, inactive adult, whatever his biological and legal relationship to the child." The critical consideration was to respect the child's attachment to his psychological parents. "An absent biological parent," the authors maintained, "will remain or tend to become a stranger." [42]

Thus, in that terrible and tragic case when Dutch Jews returned at the end of World War II to reclaim children left for safekeeping in non-Jewish households, the children's rights doctrine would have reversed the Dutch Parliament's flat decree in favor of the biological parents and instead upheld the psychological parents. "More interests will tilt the scale toward leaving well enough alone, than toward allowing the biological parents to prevail." [43] What seemed cruel and heartless from the perspective of the parent was, in fact, in the best interest of the child.

In more general terms Goldstein, Freud, and Solnit questioned earlier assumptions about the meaning of a "wanted" or "unwanted" child. As formulated by Margaret Sanger, these terms reflected the sentiments of the biological parent—if the natural mother did not want the child, the child was unwanted. But by viewing the concept from the perspective of the child, the authors could contend that a child who was unwanted by the parent might well be wanted by someone else. So in the first instance, they wanted to upgrade the prerogatives of foster parents, giving them first rights to adopt a child already in their care. They also favored speedy adoption procedures, compelling a biological parent to decide quickly on custody; and they urged that a decision once made by the biological parent in favor of adoption be irreversible. Nor would they allow child welfare agencies to remove a child from the psychological parent except in cases where the child's interest, and not those of the agency or of the biological parent, dictated it. Finally, they strongly advocated state adoption subsidies, so that the psychological parents would have full rights to the child without forfeiting financial compensation.

Psychoanalytic doctrines provided one foundation for the recommendations of Goldstein, Freud, and Solnit. Defining the child as one who changes "constantly, from one state of growth to another," who perceives the world in "an egocentric manner," who cannot maintain "positive emotional ties with a number of different individuals," who can "freely love more than one adult only if the individuals in question feel positively to one another," they elevated, predictably, psychological ties over biological ones.[44] Relying also on the laboratory experiments of John Bowlby, they stressed the special nature of time to children and the detrimental consequences of prolonged separation. A six-month absence might seem short to a parent, while to a two-year-old it was interminable and had devastating effects.

But why were psychoanalytic doctrines, which for decades had been used to tighten the link between mother and child, now suddenly put into the context of children's rights? The answer rests first in the new awareness of the distinction between the interest of the biological parent and that of the child. When one could no longer assume that a woman was primarily a mother, that her needs were identical with and indistinguishable from the child's, then child advocacy took on a novel meaning. In essence, these authors were saying that if there were an adult ready and willing to care for the child, do not disturb the relationship.

If child advocates like Goldstein, Freud, and Solnit shared a sense of pessimism, others like Selma Fraiberg evinced a deep anger. Although Fraiberg agreed with Goldstein, Freud, and Solnit that social policy should favor psychological parents over biological parents in custody battles, she was much more intent on diagnosing the "diseases of non-attachment," or the ill effects on children when women go out to work and abandon the role of mother. Her book, *Every Child's Birthright: In Defense of Mothering* was intended "for all those radicals, like myself, who think that our survival as a human community may depend as much upon our nurture of love in infancy and childhood as upon the protection of our society from external threats." And that survival, Fraiberg argued (along the lines of Bowlby) depended upon "the human qualities of enduring love and commitment to love [that] are forged during the first two years of life." [45]

Fraiberg insisted that the child from birth to the age of three could not tolerate "the care of a succession of anonymous sitters." At the least, "parents who understand these [distress] reactions as signs of love take special pains to see that a sitter employed for the parents' night out, or the mother's afternoon away, will be a person known to the child and trusted by them and their child." From the ages of three to six, "most children can tolerate separation from the mother for a half day . . . without distress when a good and stable substitute care plan is provided." Nowhere did Fraiberg actually come out and tell women to stay at home and not go to work—but ideal substitute mothers, she noted, are not to be found; mothers of children below six could only take "an afternoon away" or "half a day away." In other words, a career choice was in basic conflict with child development. For a working woman "there are almost no good solutions open to her—at least so far—which serve the needs of her child." Either the child is neglected "and so may learn that the world outside of the home is an indifferent world, or even a hostile world," or it is passed from one sitter to another and so "may learn that all adults are interchangeable, that love is capricious, that human attachment is a perilous investment." [46] Thus women's liberation, when examined from the perspective of the child, seemed a dangerous doctrine. If the woman gained independence, the child lost love and stability.

Given such disparities, it becomes less difficult to understand the steady decline in the American birth rate over the past decade. It was not merely that the technology of birth control (through the advent of the Pill) facilitated family limitation; rather, more women were reluctant to assume the responsibility for rearing several children. In the mid-1970s the birth rate reached an all-time low of 1.8 children per family (and there is every indication that the figure will not climb substantially higher in the near future). This did not mean that more women were choosing to remain childless; instead, women were postponing having children until later in life and then having fewer children than ever before. This pattern was perfectly consistent with career or job interests—with getting a start in a position, interrupting work for a brief stint at motherhood, and then returning sooner rather than later to the work force. As these figures (and Fraiberg's laments) make clear, women's decisions no longer gave mothering its traditional primacy.

By the same token, the individual needs of women no longer seemed compatible with one lifelong marital relationship. Not that women stopped or were supposed to stop marrying; although the divorce rate climbed (doubling over the past ten years), so did the number of remarriages. Rather, an expectation of impermanence now seemed normal within a marriage. If the experts of the 1920s counseled women to find fulfillment in an intensive and all-consuming intellectual and sexual relationship with one man, their counterparts in the 1970s told them that fulfillment was not a unitary, once achieved-always achieved state, that different stages demanded new relationships. In the 1950s, as in the 1920s, diamonds were "forever." In the 1970s, diamonds were "for now."

Several recent best-selling books (with paperback sales of over two million copies) have attempted to spread this message, to put to rest any lingering notion that the marital contract ought to be permanent. One of the first books in this genre was George and Nena O'Neill's *Open Marriage*, which appeared in 1972, sold several million copies, and five years later was still a staple on the paperback book racks. *Open Marriage* set new standards for marital relationships and simultaneously prepared the couple for their impending divorce. (The *New Yorker* cartoonist who had beau on bending knee asking belle please to be "his first wife" must have read it.) The O'Neills contrasted the closed marriage—with lifelong monogamy ultimately for the sake of the children—with an open marriage, dedicated to "exploring new and different relationships for the sake of individual fulfillment and growth." Not ones to shirk the issue of just how open an open marriage should be, they insisted: "We have no intention, of course, of denying that some people can be sexually monogamous for life . . . in which [case] neither one ever has or even wants extra-marital liaisons. But they are rare and becoming rarer." The essence of the open marriage was its temporary quality, and hence the O'Neills warned the reader: "Nor will your wife necessarily be the mother of your children. She may be, but don't count on it. . . . This is not negativism, only realism." [47]

Implicit throughout their book is the notion that an open marriage is preferably a childless one. After all, it is one thing to caution a husband that his current wife may not be the mother of his children— but it is another thing to warn children that their mother of today may not be their mother of tomorrow. The O'Neills, understandably, preferred to ignore this dilemma; given the complexity of what an open marriage means to children, they were unwilling to address it. In occasional asides they applauded the fact that more couples were deciding not to have children, and they did ask that husband and wife share equally in child-rearing responsibilities. But fundamentally, an open marriage was a childless one, a temporary liaison between two persons to satisfy individual needs.

So, too, Gail Sheehy's immensely popular *Passages: The Predictable Crises of Adult Life* insisted that creative adulthood demanded a succession of marital partners. Sheehy's beginning point was to characterize stages of adulthood as others, like Hall in the 1890s and Erikson in the 1950s, characterized childhood. Adult life, she argued, was marked by an inevitable series of crises (the "trying twenties," the "forlorn forties"), and the successful resolution of each of them represented creative development. "Predictable" adult bouts of "stagnation and equilibrium and depression" were part of the normal growth process. To be sure, not all "people who suffer the most severe crises always come through with the most inspired rebirth." Nevertheless, "people who allow themselves to be stopped, seized by the real issues, shaken into reexamination—these are the people who find their validity and thrive." [48]

Sheehy painstakingly traced the implications of her stages of development for marital relationships. Older ideas of permanence in marriage presumed a static view of adulthood. If our adult identities and possibilities were once and for all secure by the age of twenty or twenty-five, then an initial choice of mate could be presumed to be a permanent choice. But once growth and instability marked adulthood, once it was composed of a series of stages, then such expectations were unrealistic—in fact, severely limiting. "Even in a relatively static society," Sheehy declared, "the odds are minimal that any couple can enjoy matched development." In so fluid a society as the United States, the ideal of "one true couple" had to be obsolete.[49]

Sheehy was still more pessimistic about the prospects for or the desirability of marital stability, because men and women of the same chronological age experienced very different developmental crises.

Each partner moved through essentially incompatible stages, making it impossible for a relationship to satisfy the needs of one partner without sacrificing the needs of the other. "Men and women are rarely in the same place struggling with the same questions at the same time," contended Sheehy. Thus, if Dick and Jane married when they were both in their twenties, their "developmental rhythms" would be in continuous conflict. A man in his twenties was gaining "confidence by leaps and bounds," but his wife of the same age was "usually losing the superior assurance she once had as an adolescent." Then during the thirties when a man "wanted to settle down," his wife was "becoming restless." At forty, when a man "feels himself to be standing on a precipice, his strength, power, dreams, and illusions slipping away," his wife "is brimming with ambition to climb her own mountain." Sheehy was certain that marital instability must result from these discrepancies: "Because the adult world is not in the mental health business," she told her readers, "it rarely presents the young couple with opportunities that serve equally each one's readiness to individuate and need to feel secure." Occasionally, she conceded, "there will be the perfect compromise." [50] But a couple that weathered the first crisis should not anticipate a second success. Upon finishing *Passages*, one is surprised that only 40 percent of first marriages end in divorce.

Like the O'Neills, Sheehy chose to ignore the implications of her findings for child-rearing. She favored later marriages; women who waited until the age of thirty to marry were less restless than those who married earlier. But since the majority of Americans traditionally did marry in their twenties and had children soon thereafter, Sheehy's stages posed an inevitable conflict between adult growth and the needs of a child. When women, during their early thirties, were "becoming restless," they were also raising children. In fact, both men and women at this age were to be making new choices and altering commitments. To pass successfully from the twenties to the thirties necessarily "involves great change, turmoil . . . a simultaneous feeling of rock bottom and the urge to break out. . . . It often means divorce or at least a serious review of marriage." Obviously this turmoil left little time or emotional energy available for the child.

Sheehy's own commitment to individual adult needs as against familial responsibilities finally made her a champion of divorce. For women in their thirties, divorce was "a rite de passage." "Is this ritual necessary before anyone, above all herself, will take a woman's need for expansion seriously?" [51] The answer was an unequivocal yes. The divorcee was an attractive and vital person, not a stagnant mother or unfulfilled wife.

Running through all this literature, from Goldstein to Fraiberg to Sheehy, is a contemporary definition of family life as a battleground among members, each trying to gain his or her own personal victory. It is an unusual perspective, one that is particular to our own times. For generations social critics predicted the demise of the family, but their predictions were by way of a lament, an effort to recall family members to their proper duties, to enhance maternal, paternal, and filial responsibility. Many contemporary social critics also predict the demise of the family, but they are far from certain as to how to rescue it, even whether to rescue it. A few observers like Fraiberg have attempted to revive a traditional ethic, to remind mothers that their grandmothers knew best, that folk wisdom has its strengths. But others insist upon the futility of such an endeavor; grandmothers do not set (and never really have set) the fashion. The more popular response is to take up the cause of one or another family member and set out the strategy that will most effectively realize that member's best interest. Since the family is a battleground, every member should have, and now does have, its own Clausewitz. Hence, women should anticipate divorce as a rite of passage; men should know that when they want to settle down their wives will want to climb mountains; children should understand, or at least have lawyers who understand, that their own interests will not necessarily be furthered by parental decisions.

Whatever the precise nature of the advice, one assumption is common to all of it: family life is a zero-sum game. Some interests must be sacrificed to others. What is good for wives is not necessarily good for husbands and what is good for mothers is not necessarily good for children. Where our predecessors saw harmony, we see discord. Where they saw mutuality of interest, we see conflict of interest. And as we move from the private sphere to the public, the sounds of discord grow more intense. The political arena does not take second place to the family as a battleground for competing interests.

CHAPTER

7

Liberation Politics

FEMINIST EFFORTS to translate the new definition of womanhood into social policy have sparked intense antagonism and conflicts. To the women's movement, equality in employment, provisions for day care, and reproductive freedom are all logical and appropriate programs; competent and energetic women have the same rights as men to privileges and opportunities in the labor force; federal assistance for day care could facilitate working and mothering. And certainly women have the right to control their own bodies, to decide for themselves when to bear children and whether a pregnancy should or should not be terminated. But to others, each of these demands represents a challenge. Will women's entrance into the work force cost men jobs? Who exactly will control day care and pay the bill? Does a right to an abortion mean that women can command a doctor to perform the procedure? What of the moral sensibilities of the Catholic Church and other religious groups? In effect, proposals designed to advance the interests of women do threaten other vested interests—the interests of males, experts, professionals, union leaders, clergymen, and all who feel a personal stake in the perpetuation of older values.

None of these developments ought to have been particularly surprising, for in unmistakable fashion, the fate of the women's movement recapitulated the fate of the civil rights movement. Martin Luther King's dream of cooperation between the races and the hope of black leaders for a rapid desegregation of schools and other facilities were among the last major efforts to achieve social change within a Progressive framework—that is, with the assumption that one group's demands for equality would not conflict with another's; that all Americans had a stake in an equitable system; that people could be partners, not adversaries, in the march for justice. But by 1966 this dream had faded, replaced by the much harsher and combative doctrines of black power. Progress, it seemed, was coming too slowly; opposition to civil rights was far more entrenched and powerful than had been imagined. It was time to talk not of brotherhood but of group interests, not of equality but of rights, not of a balance of interests but of competing claims. In many ways, black power advocates were the first to assert the primacy of a rights model, to attack a whole network of American institutions as fundamentally corrupt (in their terms, "racist"), and to denigrate the professionals and the experts who bolstered them. And black power set the tone and became the model for the protest movements of other minority groups. In short order, prisoners' rights, mental patients' rights, students' rights, and gay rights organizations were challenging the prerogatives of administrative experts—be they psychiatrists, wardens, college presidents, deans, or high school principals—and the legitimacy of their institutions—be they mental hospitals, prisons, or universities.

The women's movement became part of this reaction. By the 1970s it, too, asserted self-interest as vigorously as possible; it, too, organized to lobby, to sue, to agitate, to put pressure on the legislature, to influence the media—and to try to do all of this more systematically, more energetically, and more effectively than its adversaries were. If Progressive reformers appealed to the national interest, feminists now appealed to women's interests. To be sure, one could still hear rhetorical flourishes that the ERA would "symbolize and effect a new era of humanhood," that it would benefit men as well as women. But when it came down to the core of things—to realizing women's equality in the work force—the strategy was to advance women's interest first and last, to obtain for women their share of the positions, pay, and promotions, no matter how costly their effort was to other claimants. The question was, and remains, whether the women's movement will be sufficiently professional, cohesive, and organized to win not only the first round but also, when the counterattacks inevitably come, the second and the third as well. This is what it means to treat politics as a zero-sum game.

Equal Rights in the Workplace

One of the first political bodies to feel the effects of the women's movement was the Ninety-Second Congress (1971–1973). Lobbyists for NOW and other women's groups worked vigorously to accomplish their priorities. First, to promote sexual equality, they persuaded Congress to approve the passage of an equal rights amendment to the Constitution and at the same time to amend specific federal laws so as to prohibit discrimination on the basis of sex in Health Manpower Training Programs and in educational institutions receiving federal funds. Then, to facilitate women's advancement in the labor force, they were able to effect legislation that not only revised the tax codes to permit families earning under $18,000 a year to deduct child care costs but that also provided federal funds under the Comprehensive Child Development Act for the construction of day care centers. It was a good beginning, made even better by the fact that the initial reception among the states to the ERA was highly favorable. Within two years of Congressional passage, thirty-three states ratified the amendment. The ERA represented to its proponents "the culmination of the 'women rights' segment of the Movement, which works for normative changes in society through legal and institutional means," and even more, it embodied "the 'liberation' issue, for in denying that sex is a valid legal classification of persons, it implicitly denies societal values based on biological differences between the sexes and recognizes that social roles are learned, and therefore relative." It seemed not at all fanciful to imagine that sexism would die a quick death, that a new "era of humanhood" was about to be ushered in.[1]

Before very long, however, a far grimmer reality intruded. Opposition to the ERA coalesced, attacking both its symbolic and institutional character, protesting its effort to implement new kinds of "societal values" and "normative changes." The symbolic objections were not very complicated—although they certainly were intense and effective enough to stall the amendment's passage. A group of women, supported with funds from the most conservative organizations in the country, were able to mount a campaign that carried broad appeal. They defined the amendment, appropriately enough, as an attack upon the primacy of domestic roles for women. The ERA threatened to undermine "some of those precious necessary rights particularly affecting women who wish to be full-time wives and mothers." Not that they could ever frame the character of this challenge in very specific terms, for what was at stake was not law but values. So, when pressed, the groups tried to argue (altogether incorrectly) that the ERA would abolish alimony payments (or, conversely, compel women to support lazy men) or prohibit separate-sex restrooms. But what the opposition was really concerned about was that the ERA elevated a new definition of womanhood to a national norm. It legitimated the idea that married women should work—that women had to find fulfillment in their own accomplishments, not in their husbands' or childrens'. And that message was one that a good number of housewives did not want to hear or to countenance. "We feel the family is under attack in America," declared one of them, "and we feel the Equal Rights Amendment could be the turning point on whether family life as we know it will survive." At stake was woman's proper role. "Personally," this woman went on, "nothing makes me happier than when my little boy comes home from school and says, 'Is my mother home?' and I'm there." [2] Thus, just as Americans had once insisted that a constitutional amendment enshrine temperance as a national norm, these women were saying that a constitutional amendment should *not* establish feminism as a national norm. Status in the office should not be elevated over status in the home. Housework should not be a stigmatized calling. Full-time mothers and wives should not become obsolete.

A backlash movement was bound to come when the full implications of the ERA premises were understood. The ERA does at the least carry enormous symbolic significance. Its passage would signal the triumph of a novel definition of woman as person, putting to rest both Progressive notions that women needed special protection and the 1920s notions that women were first and foremost their husbands' helpers. But this opposition, even if successful in the short run, even if capable of blocking or preventing passage of the ERA, is ultimately not very important. The ERA has pitted the professional woman against the volunteer, the working mother against the housewife—but it has also pitted the present life style of the mother against the future life choices of her daughter. In 1975 and 1976, the victory went to the mother, but it will very likely be a temporary one. There is every indication that the preferences expressed in the ERA are going to have a much firmer hold on the coming generation than they enjoy in the passing generation. (Indeed, proponents of the amendment probably missed a critical point in strategy by not making an open appeal to mothers to vote on behalf of their daughters. The movement might well have gained far more grass-roots strength by asking: "Do you want your daughter kept out of college because of a quota on women? Do you want your daughter passed over for promotion because she is a woman?") For women as well as for men, prestige is more and more going to be distributed on the basis of personal, not surrogate, achievements. No matter what the outcome of this ERA battle, the feminists are likely to win the symbolic war.

The evidence supporting such a statement is pervasive. There is no mistaking that consciousness has been raised, at least in the upper middle classes, with a ripple effect downward already evident. Advertisements have begun to lose some of their sexist characteristics (women, too, need life insurance and should buy Adidas sneakers for jogging). Dolls now show women as doctors as well as nurses (even if they do not yet present men as nurses). "Ms." as a form of address is no longer a joke; "chairperson" has lost its awkwardness. Some newspapers think it is even news, and worthy of Sunday supplement coverage, when a woman decides to quit her job and raise her baby. Indeed, that some people find it necessary to argue (and the *New York Times* on its "Op-Ed" page finds it fit to print) that women should be free to be mothers as well as office workers testifies to the fact that the new norm is competing well with the old— although it is highly doubtful whether the women's movement has, or will, become so powerful as to justify fears of its tyranny.

But the most important evidence of the substantial differences between daughters' and mothers' life styles comes from the admissions rates to professional schools. In recent years the number of women attending law schools and medical schools has climbed dramatically. In 1973, there were three and one-half times the number of women enrolled in law schools (16,760) than there were in 1969 (4,715). So, too, the number of women in medical school has almost doubled. In 1969, there were 3,392 women who made up 9 percent of the students; by 1973, women had increased to 7,824, or 15 percent of the group. More women also entered traditionally male white-collar occupations. Between 1960 and 1970, the number of women accountants rose from 80,400 to 183,000; the number of engineers climbed from 7,000 in 1960 to 19,600 in 1973. The number of female real estate sales agents jumped from 46,000 to 83,600, and the number of female insurance agents and brokers rose from 35,300 (or almost 10 percent of the group) to 56,600 (or almost 12.4 percent). As the image of the working woman has changed, women have entered occupations that Progressive protective legislation had closed off. Over the 1960s, the number of women guards and bus drivers tripled; the number of policewomen doubled. Women entered the skilled trades too in unprecedented force. The percentage of women carpenters rose from 0.4 to 1.3, the percentage of electricians from 0.7 to 1.8, and the percentage of auto mechanics from 0.5 to 1.4.[3] Clearly, women were leaping traditional barriers, and in many cases traditional barriers were coming down.

But the conflict over values and the inroads that the younger generation has made into positions that were once exclusively male is only one part of the story—and not necessarily the most significant part. When one turns to institutional change, from the achievements of a few pioneers in the man's world to a structural analysis of the position of women in the labor force, the gains become far less notable and the clash of competing claims far more intense. It may only be tokenism that is marking women's progress. Even more disturbing, the efforts to enforce rules against sexual discrimination have been neither wholehearted nor effective. The passage of the ERA may well represent a victory for the values of the women's movement, but whether it will help to advance their actual position is acutely problematic.

For one, a reduction of sex stereotyping in jobs at the very moment when unemployment in the economy has been rising has had the effect of bringing more men into positions that were once exclusively women's. Although an absence of discrimination on grounds of sex properly cuts both ways, it does mean that the gains that women have made in some occupations is offset by losses in others. Thus, the number of male elementary school teachers rose from 140,000 (or 14 percent of the total) in 1960 to 231,000 (or 16 percent of the total) in 1970—counterbalancing advances made among women carpenters and electricians. So, too, between 1972 and 1976, the attempts to end job stereotyping in the Bell Telephone System led to an increase in the number of women in managerial positions as well as a decrease in the total number of women working for the company. The number of male telephone operators has climbed far more rapidly than the number of female operators. In all, Bell now employs 15,000 women—four years ago it employed 25,000 women.[4]

More important, the disparity in wages between men and women did not decline over the past decade—in fact, it widened! In 1963, the median earnings of full-time, year-round women workers were 63 percent of those of men workers. In 1973 the figure dropped to 57 percent. To be sure, the gap varied from occupation to occupation. Among clerical workers, women in 1965 earned 72 percent of the salaries of the men; in 1973 they earned 61 percent. Women in professional and technical work earned 66 percent of men's salaries in 1962 and 63.6 percent in 1973. These figures, it should be noted, do not indicate in any simple fashion that employers were biased against women. Market forces were at play: the number of women entering the work force, particularly in the less skilled positions, has been so great as to depress the pay scale; women with higher educational achievements are in greater demand for skilled positions and hence have fared better. Yet, as Caroline Shaw Bell explains, if one cause "of the worsening position of women's work in terms of earned income has been the influx of women into the labor force," the other cause is "stringent occupational barriers." [5] Sex stereotyping of jobs remains strong enough to crowd women into a few occupations and thus to reduce their wages. A very rigid sense of what constitutes women's work still dominates in the work force and in the society, and the consequences of that rigidity are apparent in the lower earning power of women.

But then what of the efforts of government agencies and federal legislation to reduce job discrimination against women? More precisely, what has become of the Equal Employment Opportunity Commission? Why has the agency not performed better? In fact, insofar as women are concerned, no one doubts that it has performed poorly. Practically every observer, whether from a feminist organization or the Government Accounting Office, agrees that the EEOC is not doing its job adequately, or even competently. The problem does not rest in the EEOC's formal powers. In 1972, the Equal Employment Act expanded its jurisdiction to cover more than 75 percent of the work force (including everyone employed by federal and state government, by public and private educational institutions, and by employers and unions with fifteen or more members). The Act also gave the EEOC the authority to sue those agencies or companies it found practicing sexual discrimination. Rather than merely serving as a watchdog agency, the EEOC had the right to go to the courts in order to compel compliance. Nor do the EEOC's failures reflect an absence of compelling precedents, either in the courts or in the administrative agencies, with which to buttress its litigation. The difficulties go deeper, raising the fundamental issue of whether statutory regulations must inevitably remain dead letters, and whether practice will ever conform to law.

The EEOC has been remarkably inefficient, displaying "bureaucratic inadequacies" which are staggering. Feminists may be correct in charging that the record of accomplishment is so bad as to "only be explained by a deliberate policy of nonenforcement." By 1975, the EEOC had a backlog of over 100,000 cases; in 1978 it stands at 130,000. The agency never filled vacant staff positions in order to be able to handle the cases. Instead, it adopted a series of stratagems to reduce its docket without fulfilling its mandate. At least 10,000 complaints before the EEOC were "resolved," because, as investigators discovered, "people gave up, moved, or were not available." Since the EEOC took so long to act, the plaintiffs lost energy or contact. Another 30,000 cases were simply lost, the papers misfiled or otherwise neglected. Further, the agency conducted inadequate examinations of the facts in the cases brought to its attention. One Government Accounting Office report described the EEOC's field work as "very poor, often resulting in unsuccessful conciliation and certainly contributing to the 90 percent rejection rate [by its own attorneys] of cases for litigation." Some of the complaints may have been unjustified, but clearly the EEOC procedures were also at fault. The EEOC chairperson did not dispute the conclusion. "The investigation of the charges," he conceded before a Congressional committee in 1975, "is not the investigation you and I would want for litigation." [6]

More, the EEOC has pursued a policy that one law professor has labeled "clear the docket at any cost." This policy permits a field office representative to settle a case "on any terms acceptable to the charging party prior to investigation." It also allows the field office to issue a "right to sue" letter to the charging party, which terminates the Commission's responsibility and leaves enforcement to the complainant. Finally, the EEOC frequently consolidates cases and thereby issues an annual report with fewer cases on hand—not because it has acted, but because it has juggled numbers. Such policies either accomplish nothing, or merely shift the burden of enforcement directly to the parties and the federal courts, or "represent a significant retreat from the Commission's formerly perceived role as a guardian of a fundamental public interest." Thus feminists are convinced that the EEOC has turned the body of anti-discrimination statutes into a "paper tiger which need not be obeyed." Independent investigations concur in this verdict. After computing returns from almost 50,000

firms that reported to the EEOC in both 1965 and 1970, two researchers concluded that "the occupational distribution of white
women had changed very little relative to the occupational distribution of white males." [7] Companies could perpetuate traditional practices with little fear for the consequences.

The EEOC generally has not managed to implement the occasional
orders and decrees it does impose. "Without a vigorous monitoring,"
as two feminists have charged, "these decrees and agreements are
obviously not worth the paper upon which they are printed." The
EEOC lacks the capability to do a thorough job, and, recognizing its
limits, one investigatory commission asked it to review "at least 25
percent of its conciliation agreements," not a very considerable
percentage. Other recommendations are not much more satisfactory.
In 1977, the Department of Labor held public hearings on whether
the EEOC should monitor only the practices of the largest corporations that held federal contracts (a policy that the new commissioner,
Eleanor Holmes Norton, seems about to adopt). But many feminists
objected that such an approach might give a free hand to professional
organizations and universities to practice discrimination.[8] The EEOC,
by appearing to be abandoning the field, would trigger a backlash
response.

Even the occasional EEOC success story has its darker underside.
In 1973, the EEOC entered into what appeared to be a precedent-
setting agreement with American Telephone and Telegraph Corporation. AT&T agreed to "an affirmative action plan incorporating goals
for achieving full utilization of women and minorities at all levels of
management and nonmanagement," to be implemented over a six-year
period. It consented to award back pay not only to the litigants in the
case but even to many women and minority workers who had never
sought promotion because they "were aware of the company's discriminatory practices." But the AT&T decree did not set a pattern for
other settlements. A subsequent agreement between the EEOC and
the steel companies was not nearly so advantageous to women, and
NOW and other civil rights organizations actually brought suit against
the EEOC, taking to court the very agency that was supposed to defend their interests. The effects of the AT&T decree itself also clarify
some of the most troubling aspects of compliance decrees. By 1976,
four and a half years after the agreement, the number of women holding positions with salaries of $30,000 or more rose from 382 to 888.
Yet, the total number of women that AT&T employed declined at a
rate twice as great as that of men.[9] In sum, the implementation of an

EEOC decree to end sex stereotyping led to a decline in opportunity for the average woman worker.

Another of the barriers to equality for working women is the sluggish state of the economy. A contraction in the job market does hurt newcomers, be they women or blacks or members of other minority groups. Some feminists fear that a persistent recession will not only impede progress but also cancel gains already made. "The economic environment," notes one analyst, "may prove to be the major determinant of women's role in 1980. . . . Scarcity of jobs in the next decade [will] produce a greater competition in the labor market and a tremendous backlash against women." [10]

Despite the persistence of these problems, ample room does exist for optimism about future prospects. The economist Victor Fuchs argues persuasively that the very fact that women did not *lose* considerable ground in their earning powers during a period of marked expansion of participation in the work force augurs very well. "Able to hold their own . . . the long-run prospects for women must be viewed as favorable." [11] Nor is it naïve to believe that token advances can encourage real ones. The publicity that accompanies the advancement of a few secretaries into higher-paying and more responsible administrative positions may well prompt others to compete for these jobs. The delight with which the media covers "the first woman who . . ." is probably helping to raise women's expectations and to alter sexist images. The token woman may turn out to be a model for the young.

The prospect for change through federal agencies is not altogether bleak, either. The presence of a large pool of women in the law schools today may mean that the EEOC will be staffed tomorrow by a group far more sympathetic to enforcing compliance. Reformers understand quite clearly the need to "capture" federal bureaucracies through a variety of stratagems. Thus, Jo Freeman, a political scientist and feminist, has counseled women's organizations not only to carry out more litigation and public education campaigns but also to make certain that an agency knows full well what women clients want of it. "Government agencies are subject to a sufficient number of demands to effectively prevent them from looking for any problems they don't already have." [12] Women activists recognize that one of their tasks is to keep administrators alert to their problems.

The ease with which progress can be measured in this field simplifies such efforts. The difficult task is not to define what constitutes discrimination but to implement corrective actions. The response of a corporation or a university that the available pool of qualified women is too small to permit promotions is already suspect, and it is very likely to become still more so in the future. For all the debate about whether affirmative action programs constitute just or unjust practices, whether quotas and goals are identical, and whether measurement should be based on equality of outcome or equality of opportunity, there remains a fundamental agreement on the principle that equal pay and equal rights are fair, that women should not suffer discrimination. Indeed, as compared to the blacks, women enjoy some considerable advantages. The abolition of sexual discrimination in the work force likely requires less social engineering and less intrusive policies than, for example, the desegregation of the schools. Sexism is probably less virulent than racism. A busing program inevitably generates more heat and controversy than an AT&T compliance order.

Thus, sooner rather than later women will enjoy equal pay and equal opportunity. Advances may well come first in the professions and filter down more slowly into blue-collar positions. But the gap between rhetoric and reality is bound to be closed, for the next generation of women if not for this one.

Who Cares for the Child?

The concept of woman as person has also redirected the course of social policy toward the family. If women's career choices are to be enhanced, discrimination by sex is only one of the problems, and perhaps not even the thorniest one at that. Much more complicated and controversial is the potential redistribution of domestic responsibilities, particularly in the realm of child care. If women are going to enter the work force, who is going to be at home with the child? Here the broader sense of a conflict of interest within the family takes on an immediacy that is as troubling as it is unavoidable. The issue has divided groups in terms both of strategy and of goals. There is no agreement on whether child development will necessarily suffer if substitutes for full-time mothering, such as day care programs, are implemented. Nor is there consensus on which organizations should control the delivery of day care, or what the content of the program should be, or who should staff the centers.

The 1970 White House Conference on Children illustrates all too well the difficulties of formulating social policy under such circumstances. At earlier White House conferences, the delegates shared a prior consensus on what constituted an ideal family and what direction social policy should take. At the first of the conferences in 1909, settlement house workers and child welfare reformers insisted that optimal child development demanded full-time mothering. To this end, they proposed the first widow pension program (what we know as Aid to Dependent Children), to enable the worthy but poor mother to stay at home and care for her children. Confident that the middle-class family exemplified the ideal, the delegates looked to reshape the lower-class family in its image. By the same token, at the White House Conference of 1930, specialists in child health contended (to a man) that women, even the college-educated among them, were unable to fulfill the complex tasks of child development. "It is beyond the capacity of the individual parent," noted one participant, "to train her child to fit into the intricate, interwoven, interdependent social and economic system we have developed." [13] The legitimacy of the nuclear family was not in doubt, only the way its proper functioning could be enhanced. Accordingly, the delegates proposed that social policy buttress the skills and institutions of the expert. They called for federal funding of medical research, pediatric programs, hospitals, and clinics, all to improve professional skills.

The White House Conference of 1970, however, differed from its predecessors on almost every count. For the first time, delegates were not social workers or professional child welfare experts but more political types (chosen directly by governors, members of congress, and the White House staff) with a special concern for minority representation, particularly from the black community. There was also more conflict than consensus among the views of the delegates, so a complicated and weighted voting system reported sixteen "overriding concerns" and twenty-five specific recommendations. Most important, rather than trying to resolve issues and make highly specific proposals, the Conference formula was to include a bit of everything. What was the ideal family? Blacks, eager to repudiate the Moynihan Report with its implication that female-headed households reared deviant children, could not agree with clerics who continued to celebrate the traditional two-parent nuclear family. The result was not to condemn the nuclear family but to make each variety of family organization equal to the other (a formulation that minority groups favored). We "do not favor any particular family form," the delegates declared. "Children can and do flourish under many other family forms than the traditional nuclear structure." [14]

Conference participants agreed that massive federal intervention was necessary to aid America's children. "We must act now," the chairperson insisted, "if our society is to flourish." This sense of urgency, however, could not be translated into specific programs. Unwilling to define any one family structure as desirable, the delegates were unable to define any one political approach as best. A "uniform policy and human service program," the Report noted, "which will cover all individuals is virtually impossible because so many different forms of family exist in this country." Accordingly, it advocated "comprehensive child care programs," but the word "comprehensive" had to substitute for well-designed and exact recommendations. The minority groups were able to insert a plea for programs that would be "family centered, locally controlled and universally available with initial priority to those whose needs are the greatest." But what local control meant and how a universal program was to give preference to the needs of the poor was hardly addressed, let alone resolved.

A sense of discontent with existing institutions did pervade the Conference. Schools, it was charged, were not operating in satisfactory fashion. But the delegates could only call for a new kind of system without ever becoming more precise. They asked that "optimal alternate forms of public education be created which are entirely independent of all present local and state regulations." Yet there was no blueprint or even a hint of what these alternate systems should be, beyond the statement that they should emanate from the community. So, too, the health system was criticized as patently inadequate, but the recommendations could do little more than propose a "new delivery system" that was to be "organized under a variety of auspices." [15] Federal assistance was necessary and change should come, but the delegates left unanswered the critical questions of what should constitute the change.

The very generality of these aims had one major political advantage. A discontent with current policy toward the family and the child enabled middle-class feminists and black activists to form an initial alliance. Both groups wanted to win federal support for new child care policies, particularly for preschoolers. And both groups looked to the precedent of Head Start, enacted by the Kennedy Administration, for encouragement and guidance. To civil rights activists, Head Start represented the first federal recognition of the special need of economically disadvantaged preschool children for compensatory services. And it was all the more appealing a precedent because local communities had administered the program. Marian Wright Edelman, director of the Children's Defense Fund, told a Congressional Committee that Head Start was "the first time low income and minority group parents were told, 'you have a stake in your child's development and you have a right to make decisions about the way this program runs.' " [16] For middle-class feminists, Head Start represented a novel alternative to the exclusive reliance on home care for preschoolers. They delighted in the fact that a nonfamilial setting was offering a quality program. Thus, the two groups came together to urge massive federal funding for child development facilities, a network of day care centers.

To some supporters, the fact that the centers would supply basic nutritional and physical care to preschoolers was reason enough to back them. Shirley Chisholm, for example, championed day care in Congress because she was certain that it was the only way the federal government would give black children hot meals and medical checkups. Others were concerned about the growing numbers of children in poor families whose mothers had no choice but to work.[17] Day care would at least put a roof over the heads of these "latch key" children who otherwise would be left on their own. But these were minimal considerations. Most supporters of day care shared grander goals. The new child development centers would provide more than a last resort service to those in urgent need. They promised to begin the complicated task of restructuring American social and political institutions to eliminate sexism and racism and to redistribute power.

Feminists and civil rights activists saw day care as a way to liberate women to carry on their own careers and at the same time to socialize children to tolerance. Day care made it not irresponsible for a woman to work or for a single parent to rear a child. The facility could deliver quality services as fine as those given in any family. "The *place* where care is given is not the most significant dimension for the child," argued the White House Conference. "The issue is the kind of care given, how he is handled, what abilities are nurtured, what values are learned, and what attitudes toward people are acquired." [18] If the day care staff performed well, the mother could safely give over her child.

The use of day care would also have distinct social benefits. The program promised to unite the social classes. "Think for a moment what this would mean," declared Congresswoman Bella Abzug. "It would let local groups of parents and women set up child care centers for children from all socio-economic backgrounds. It would let community groups create the models for that universal kind of child care we are all talking about—a child care system that would accommodate rich and poor alike, that would let our kids grow up with a chance to know each other and to learn that they can bridge the racial and economic gap that divides their parents." [19] By creating high-quality institutions that would serve all children, society could achieve the goals of the civil rights movement and the women's movement.

Day care offered still another advantage. The centers would not only supervise the preschooler but also become a focus of family activity. This aim was very much in the mind of one of the most active supporters of day care, Marian Wright Edelman. She hoped that the facilities would provide the entire family with comprehensive health and counseling services. Further, "as many activities as possible should involve families in the life of the Center. Siblings and other young people should be employed to work with the younger children. Different kinds of parents will need different kinds of options for participation, ranging from working in centers on a paid or volunteer basis or simply dropping in." Linking the family to the center would not be easy, but Edelman was determined to see the attempt made. "Building up participation is a hard and long-term effort. Child care workers must establish a relationship of trust and a basis for continuing outreach." [20]

The ultimate goal of such outreach to Edelman, as to Jane Addams before her, was to promote a new kind of politics. But while Addams had looked to replacing the ward boss with municipal managers, Edelman looked to replacing a central bureaucracy with community control. The involvement of parents in the administration of day care was to become the basis for their involvement in the administration of all institutions that affected their lives. Day care was the first step in a long-range program that would reallocate power from the city hall to the neighborhood, not to build a new kind of ward boss but to expand the authority of the citizenry. Thus it was critical to Edelman that child development centers be run by "local policy committees with parents comprising half of the committees with a veto of major staff and policy decisions." The lessons that parents learned in running the day care center could then be extended to controlling other agencies. [21]

However grand the hopes of the proponents of day care, the record of implementation is one of almost unrelieved failure. State and federal programs, and most private ones as well, have been dismal, providing inadequate services that do not benefit either the child or the mother or society at large. A 1972 study by the National Council of Jewish Women of 500 centers, selected at random from all parts of the country, concluded that the level of care everywhere was grossly inadequate. Of public, nonprofit day care centers, 62 percent provided strictly custodial care; of proprietary, privately run centers, 85 percent were custodial. Only 10 percent of the public centers and 1 percent of the proprietary centers gave "superior" care, that is, the kind of care that supporters' rhetoric had promised. A recent survey of New York's 240 licensed centers reported that 52 were "inadequate," not meeting the minimum standards for health, sanitation, and safety.[22]

It is not difficult to locate the major reason for this dismal performance. Day care policy has been inextricably tied to welfare policy, so that its first and last consideration has been to reduce relief rolls. Programs are simply not concerned with the delivery of quality care, but with taxpayers' costs, particuarly with welfare costs.

One of the first federal programs to support day care facilities was, appropriately enough, the 1967 Work Incentive Program (WIN). WIN, part of the Johnson administration "war on poverty," was to provide AFDC recipients (mothers and fathers of dependent children) with job training and skills, thus enabling them to go off the rolls and become self-supporting. In order to free the parent to undergo this training, some kind of supervision had to be provided for the child, and so WIN was ready to appropriate funds to cover the bulk of the costs of child care programs, including day care. All the pieces seemed to fit together well. The welfare recipient would obtain, as the Congressional legislation phrased it, "a sense of dignity, self-worth, and confidence which will flow from being recognized as a wage-earning member of society." The children would benefit too. Not only would they receive quality day care, but "the example of a working adult in these families will have a beneficial effect on child development." [23]

None of these promises have been kept. Admittedly, it is difficult to teach AFDC mothers (of whom almost half have not gone beyond an eighth-grade education) marketable skills, and especially difficult to find them jobs in a contracting economy. But WIN never really tried. It had the short-term goal of reducing welfare, not the long-term one of enhancing employability. As one WIN official told a Senate committee: "The WIN system was designed not to keep people off welfare. It was designed to take people off welfare once they got on." What mattered was not how many people acquired new skills but how many dropped off the rolls. Further, an old-fashioned disdain for the poor reinforced WIN's focus on the relief rolls. "WIN," declared its Sixth Annual Report, "introduces a discipline into the welfare system—that those supported by public funds and able to work must accept employment, preparation for employment when offered, rather than passively subsisting with public support." [24] Once again the issue was resolving itself into how to discipline the lazy poor.

Whatever advantages there were to WIN's training programs (even if there were not many) went first to men. The original legislation provided that employed fathers had to receive priority in training programs, and WIN followed these instructions scrupulously. Perhaps it was because men might find jobs quicker than women and so get off the rolls sooner; or perhaps it was simple sexism, so that if skills were being taught, it was better to teach them to men first. In all events, women made few gains. Congresswoman Martha Griffiths complained in 1974 that women were not being brought into the WIN program in proportion to their representation on the AFDC rolls. More, "although women's rates of dropout are less than men's, women are less likely to be placed in employment after they complete job training." Both Griffiths and the Civil Rights Commission protested that "even when women are placed, they end up with the lowest paid and most demeaning work with little chance of significant salary increments." WIN also perpetuated sex-stereotyping in jobs. "Women were rarely enrolled," charged the Civil Rights Commission, "in training programs generally considered traditionally male." [25] Instead of becoming a model agency that might have expanded women's options, WIN used whatever means it had to perpetuate traditional forms of discrimination against women in the work force.

Children fared no better than their mothers, and for many of the same reasons. WIN did have funds for subsidizing day care (contributing 90 percent to a state's 10 percent), but it had little interest in providing quality day care. If any child care service was available, the WIN participant had to accept it—and more often than not, the service was casual. "Child care arrangements under WIN are extremely informal," reported the Child Welfare League of America. The head of the Women's Bureau also complained to Congress that "care in centers for eligible children is rare and most mothers in the program have been forced to make their own arrangements. These have proven to be haphazard and subject to frequent changes, interruptions and breakdown." Thus, in 1974 of the 56,000 children under the age of six with a parent enrolled in WIN, only 20 percent were in centers. Fully 53 percent were cared for in their own or a relative's home.[26]

This reliance on informal care was appropriate to a program with short-term goals. WIN, in fact, only took responsibility for providing child care during the period of training and for ninety days after employment began. Accordingly, the turnover among the children was quite high and the agency refused to worry about "ideal" placements. With its eye always on the relief rolls, WIN was not going to dally over the quality of a child care facility. And, of course, once the mother was employed and off the rolls, child care was her problem.

The second major federal program funding day care also began in 1967 with the Johnson "war on poverty." Title IV, as an amendment to the Social Security Act, removed all ceilings on the amount of money that the federal government would appropriate to match the purchase of social services; if a state or local government or even a private agency would put up 25 percent of the cost of obtaining the service, the federal government would supply 75 percent. Not surprisingly, under this arrangement federal expenditures mounted. In 1967 it spent $282 million under Title IV; in 1972, it expended $1.6 billion. And not surprisingly, reaction soon set in. In 1974, under a Republican administration, Title XX superseded Title IV, setting a ceiling—and a low one at that—for federal matching expenditures.[27]

Under both Title IV and Title XX, local welfare departments could fund child care services for their clients. The expectation was that such services would allow welfare mothers to go out to work or would give deprived children of a lower-class "problem" family the advantage of day care. But the programs did not fulfill the mandate. For one, quality care is very expensive, even on a matching basis, and the sums expended were never sufficient. Most child development experts estimate the costs of delivering quality day care per child to be about $3,000 a year; expenditures under Title IV were less than half of that. For another, supervision was always inadequate, not only because of the inherent difficulty of oversight but because no one wanted to close down a center that might be allowing a lower-class mother to be at work and off welfare. Although federal licensing standards enacted in 1968 were rigorous, few centers met them—and yet loss of license was a rare occurrence. A 1973 Department of Health, Education and Welfare (HEW) audit of conditions in 522 facilities revealed that four-fifths did not meet federal requirements "even in basic health and safety areas." Imagine, then, how inadequate they were in meeting child development criteria.

Moreover, once day care support became a welfare program and assistance went only to the lowest income families, the public centers became ghetto institutions. In New York, angry parents charged that day care centers were "concentration camps for the poorest black and Puerto Rican families." And the New York experience was not at all unusual. The survey of the National Council of Jewish Women reported that fully 75 percent of the 500 centers were essentially segregated, serving either whites or blacks exclusively. This was a far cry from the day care center as "the meeting ground of rich and poor, black and white." The Executive Director of the Child Welfare League summarized the problem well in Congressional testimony: "When it is imperative to hold down costs and at the same time to keep spaces open in order to encourage welfare recipients to take jobs or training [licensing] surveillance and [client] advocacy suffer." [28]

The shortcomings that were endemic to federal day care programs did not lessen the enthusiasm of proponents. They have remained convinced that if only the centers could be adequately funded, if admission were not vested in welfare departments, and if child development and not relief rolls were to dominate policy thinking, then quality facilities could be created and administered. Thus, a broad coalition of civil rights, feminist, child welfare, and labor organizations joined to move the Child Development Act of 1971 through Congress. The bill's "special emphasis" was to provide child care services free for children whose families earned up to $4,320, and to provide them on a sliding scale of payment for children in families earning up to $6,960. The appropriation was to total $2 billion—a sum that might appear to be substantial but was actually far below the costs of giving the services that the bill pledged. As Gilbert Steiner of Brookings Institution has calculated: "In the case of families with incomes under $7,000 . . . the annual cost of the proposed child development program could amount to $17 billion. . . . Every version of the child developmental legislation promised more than the money it authorized could buy." [29]

Some awareness of this disparity must have filtered through to the bill's proponents, for before long they were battling among themselves for a slice of a too-small pie. Would day care be equally available to the well-to-do and the poor? Did middle-class families have as much right to the service as lower-class families? "During the drafting session, we fought fiercely over priorities," recalled Marian Wright Edelman, the bill's chief architect. "Welfare mothers almost came to blows with some of the middle-class women liberationists who thought they should have equal access to day care if they wanted time to go to an art gallery. But welfare mothers who have no choice but to work wanted their kinds of needs to come first." [30] Edelman's sarcasm about middle-class feminists was one striking indication that the day care coalition would not survive for very long.

In all events, the welfare mothers won this first battle—perhaps because the costs of federal funding for all children would have been astronomical. The victory, however, was futile. President Nixon vetoed the Child Development Act, claiming that funding day care centers would "commit the vast moral authority of the National Government to the side of communal approaches to child rearing over [and] against the family-centered approach." By raising the specter of day care as communistic (which Steiner contends was quite intentional with "communal" as a code word), Nixon not only put this bill to death but also ended agitation for expanded federal support for several years. Congressional supporters may well have known that the charge was "sheer nonsense," but when the mail supporting the president poured in and they could not muster a majority in the House, day care moved off the agenda.[31]

It moved back on in 1975 when Walter Mondale, who had tried to keep the issue alive in Congress during the Nixon and Ford terms, arranged for his Subcommittee on Children and Youth to hold extensive public hearings on federal support for family and child services. Their focus was a bill modeled on the 1971 Child Development Act, and Mondale anticipated (perhaps because a national election was coming up) that the time was ripe for reconstituting a broad base of support. After all, as he observed: "There are about one million spaces available in licensed day care programs for the six million pre-school children whose mothers are working." And since the number of working mothers was climbing rapidly, surely it was appropriate to "increase the resources available to families and children who need this kind of help." [32]

Although the need for child care services had increased between 1971 and 1975, so had the disagreements among the program's original sponsors. Mondale had assumed when the hearings opened that a diverse and energetic coalition would once again favor a day care bill. But as the testimony went on, he grew far less confident of such an outcome. Although proponents continued to urge federal funding, they could not agree on issues of implementation: who should control and administer the centers and who should staff them. It was not the question of priorities that now divided them. Rather, the controversy went deeper, at least in a political sense. As Mondale himself soon noted: "We have a problem deciding how to proceed with this bill."

In 1971, "this legislation had the support of a broad coalition of educational, religious, and community, and other groups. . . . Four years later . . . we have the coalition facing turf disputes." [33] The difficulty was not primarily the prospect of another presidential veto, but how to hold together an alliance that was fast splintering.

The dispute came down to a confrontation between Marian Wright Edelman, head of the Children's Defense Fund, and Albert Shanker, president of the American Federation of Teachers (AFT), a branch union of the AFL-CIO. Edelman felt that the basic principles she had written into the 1971 bill still applied. As one of the foremost advocates of the needs of black and other minority children, she forcefully described the continuing state of neglect. "The waiting lines for decent child care are not disappearing," she told the Subcommittee. Federal support was critical to expand the delivery of services, but, as she carefully explained, the support had to be forthcoming in a very particular way: funds must be channeled from a new federal agency directly to the community. Only agencies and institutions with no history of prejudice could meet the needs of minority children. In effect, Edelman wanted federal funding to bypass the state and local government bureaucracy and go straight to the community. In the language of the debate, the "prime sponsors" of facilities eligible for federal support would be community groups of 5,000, not elected officials. "We maintain," declared Edelman, "the same very deep reservations we have always had about the capacity and willingness of many state governments to support the kind of community institutions and to allow the degree of parental participation this legislation envisions." [34] Day care appropriations were not to increase the patronage available to downtown politicians, but to expand the powers of the local community.

Just as Edelman was eager to avoid established political networks, so was she determined to have day care services housed and administered in new and distinct settings. Despite the availability of space in public schools and a growing pool of unemployed teachers, she argued that the needs of minority children could not be met if day care were to become a part of the schools, with a staff hired on the basis of educational credentials. For one, Edelman did not believe that administrators trained primarily to teach children would be comfortable or responsible in overseeing programs whose goals were not essentially cognitive. Too many school boards, she predicted, would undercut day care, and "simply put those funds where they can spend them most easily and with the fewest adjustments in the regular school program." Furthermore, people from the community who had a long-term commitment to minority youngsters ought to be in charge of the facilities. Child care work was "a separate and distinct profession," requiring "men and women with warmth, openness and demonstrated effectiveness in dealing with young children." These traits had no connection with professional degrees. "Academic credentials," Edelman insisted, "by themselves do not measure those kinds of skills." [35]

Behind this distrust of administrators and teachers was an even more fundamental suspicion of the schools. The schools' track record with minority children was so disappointing that they could not be allowed to control day care. Edelman reminded the Subcommittee that "2 million school-age children are out of school." Worse yet, "millions more are in schools but are not learning because the schools do not have the flexibility, the sensitivity and, some argue, the resources to deal with their special problems and needs." Given these inadequacies, Edelman could not "justify sending even younger children into that atmosphere, particularly when it is precisely the children who are most in need of child care services whom the schools most often exclude or otherwise disserve." [36] Public schools could not and would not help her constituents.

Although Edelman spoke primarily for the disadvantaged, she had been able in 1971 to muster the support of the women's movement. Despite the debate on priorities, a perceived similarity of interest between middle-class and lower-class women remained. By 1975, however, this sense of identity had weakened. The women's movement had decided to focus its resources on ending sexual discrimination in the work force and passing the ERA. The feminists may also have concluded that in light of the politics and costs of day care, it was highly unlikely that federal funds would ever underwrite services for middle-class children. So while women's organizations continued to give rhetorical support to day care and to set up "task forces on child care," the issue did not have priority. They were not going to spearhead a lobbying or public education drive.

The 1971 coalition that supported day care had included national trade unions, and given the growing disinterest of the women's movement, their support in 1975 was all the more critical. But now, more clearly than before, the unions had a very particular stake of their own, a stake that became the core of the "turf" dispute. Albert Shanker was the leading advocate for the unions. As a newcomer who had played no part in framing the 1971 bill, he told the Mondale

Subcommittee that he was bringing "a brand new source of community support" to an essentially sagging coalition. He had no patience for the earlier approach. "I feel very strongly," Shanker insisted "that programs which are essentially aimed at, let us say, the poor, only turn out to be poor programs. These programs are generally inadequately funded. . . . The poor do not have, in this country, an adequate base from which to expand or maintain these programs." Day care demanded a very different and enlarged base, in essence, a tie to the public school system. Only "when the school system is unwilling or unable to undertake this responsibility," declared the AFL-CIO Executive Council resolution that Shanker read to the Subcommittee, "some other appropriate public or non-profit community organization should be eligible." [37] In other words, the primary sponsors for day care should be the public schools.

Shanker made his case by contrasting the impermanence and ad hoc quality of Edelman's community groups with the well-rooted and traditional strength of the public schools. Perhaps the major impetus to Shanker's discovery of day care was shrinking school budgets and the consequent lay-offs of teachers. His aim may well have been to bring the largesse of federal funds for day care to his unemployed union members. But whatever the motives, he presented his position well. The school system that he described bore no resemblance to the inefficient and incompetent organization that Edelman had criticized. "We feel," Shanker declared, "that prime sponsorship should rest within the public schools, because we have within the public schools a national system of governance which has already developed expertise in terms of the administration of programs, in terms of coordination with other city agencies, in terms of development of certification, standards of personnel, in terms of many facilities, in terms of space." [38] Furthermore, linking day care to the schools would bring a new corps of experts with appropriate skills into the enterprise. It might not always be appropriate to hire unemployed teachers, Shanker conceded. It would always be right, however, to hire professionals with credentials. Again, Shanker probably was looking to enlarge his own membership—community-based workers would not join the AFT but "professionals" undoubtedly would. Yet again, he had a good argument at hand: the schools could see to it that only the most qualified and well-trained people assumed responsibility for child care.

Shanker even had an answer to Edelman's devastating attack on the unresponsiveness of the public schools to minority children. The schools had not only mended their ways but had learned from experience as well. They were different institutions in 1975 than they had been in 1965. "We believe," he testified, "that critics have greatly distorted the state of education today. A resurgence of in-service and pre-service reforms has occurred. Alternate schools, work study, and community-as-school programs, open education—all exist within the public schools. . . . The fact is where the public wants change and works for change, the schools have responded." Shanker's schools were, ostensibly, innovative and, unlike Edelman's community groups, a known commodity. It was true, Shanker allowed, that Edelman's strategy might benefit minority children, but the risk was too great. "I think," he concluded, "that instead of setting up an alternative institution with no evidence at this point as to whether it will be better, worse, or the same—we might do much better in our concern for the child if we are to turn to what is there, use its experience, and bring about the development of new services." [39] In effect, Shanker wanted the schools to incorporate the programs of the civil rights activists and so regain the centrality and the legitimacy that they had lost in the 1960s.

The enactment of comprehensive child development programs has become caught in the quagmire of adversarial politics. The Mondale hearings did not produce legislation; the distance that separates Edelman from Shanker cannot be easily bridged. A high-quality child service program may be in the public interest, but advocates are unable to agree on how to implement it. Civil rights groups do not want child care in the hands of the professionals, fearing that they will be white upper-middle class, and without the right values and sense of commitment. The unions, for their part, are unwilling to have community groups assume a task they believe is rightly theirs. Lay groups ought not to supersede the school or the teacher in providing services to children. It is difficult enough to conceive of a compromise between these two schemes; the deep commitment of each side to its own position renders a settlement almost impossible.

The problem goes beyond the specifics of this issue. Day care is only a single instance of the confrontation between two conflicting social ideologies. To one group, traditional and established institutions will inevitably ignore a minority's best interests; day care, like welfare, will turn out to be a boon for the middle-class professionals, not for the poor. It will improve the lot of those who administer the program, not its clients. And if minority groups cannot capture and control the organizations and institutions that are ostensibly designed to serve them, how will they ever manage to increase their power in the larger society? To the other side, minority group advocates are attempting to change the rules of the game in midstream. The promise was that credentials would be rewarded in this society, that degrees and qualifications would count for most. Minority groups also seem to them to be violating every principle of social cohesion, trying to promote their own particular values and control their own particular institutions as though they were a nation apart. To make matters worse, the first victories in the 1960s went to the minorities, so that the opposition now believes that it must launch a vigorous counter-attack to recapture lost ground. Its stance will be uncompromising, for fear that any further losses will cost it dearly in the job market and in the political arena.

So on the narrow front of day care, the prospects for immediate accomplishment are not very favorable. On the broader issue of comity in the political arena, there seems to be little bend, little trust, little room for maneuver. Perhaps the traditionally powerful forces in society will in the end dominate. Day care, for example, would not be the first instance of a group of professionals taking over a program that others designed. The precedents of Sheppard-Towner and birth control seem particularly relevant: a group of advocates enters an essentially empty field, calls for a novel program under its own direction, convinces the society of its value, and then witnesses a group of experts, using credentials that may not be at all relevant, taking it over. But there are now strong indications that such an outcome would not end the controversy. Activists are very much aware of conflict of interest and far more anti-professional in their orientation. To them, it is a question not of better service but of a different kind of service; it is a matter not of expertise but of values. So if vested groups capture the programs, they will probably find not only a continuing series of challenges to their authority, but also a bitterness and even an air of illegitimacy surrounding the victory.

One More Round: Women and Their Doctors

The adversarial quality of politics emerges even more vividly in the third and final social policy concern of the new feminists, the field of health. It was inevitable that a definition of woman as person would open another round in the ongoing confrontation between women and physicians. Every generation, it seems, has to reformulate the relationship, and the post-1960s era proved no exception. In the past, collegiate education, Sheppard-Towner, and the birth control movement were the occasions for dispute and compromise; now feminists have set out to liberate themselves from inherited roles and traditional authorities. They have raised the most basic questions about women's right to control their bodies, or as the title of one book so aptly put it, *Our Bodies, Ourselves*. The issues were varied but all interrelated, ranging from the definition of disease (is pregnancy an illness?) to the nature of reproductive freedom (is there any limit to women's control over their bodies, whether pregnant or not?). In fact, the policy implications of a commitment to reproductive freedom have raised controversies that make the ERA and day care battles seem mild in comparison.

The first goal of the women's campaign has been to restrict the domain of the physician, to move away from the alliances that Sheppard-Towner and birth control advocates made. The prime targets were the obstetricians and gynecologists. *Our Bodies, Ourselves* labeled their care "condescending, paternalistic, judgmental and noninformative." These doctors not only treated women with an acute lack of sensitivity but even worse, exercised an "imperialism of knowledge." And medical imperialism subjugated women. "This kind of ignorance about our bodies, and particularly those parts related to reproduction and sexuality, is connected with the alienation and shame and fear that have been imposed upon us as women." [40]

Accordingly, feminists started programs to educate women about their bodies: to demystify health care would liberate them from doctors' control. The efforts have taken many forms, from those that the press has sensationalized (such as teaching women to use a speculum) to those that were obvious and long overdue (instructing them in breast examination and the choice and use of contraceptives). Education in sexuality also assumed a new significance. Medical training no longer entitled a gynecologist to serve as a sexual counselor (a practice that Sanger had helped to create and to perpetuate). "Just because a doctor is certified ob-gyn," noted one tract, "doesn't mean that he is qualified or trained or prepared in any way to give advice or counsel or any other sort of help in any human relations area of a woman's life." The occasional courses in psychology or human behavior that he might take could bolster his confidence, "but these are simply not enough to qualify him for the delicate work of therapy or counseling about sexual adjustment." The goal of all these feminist efforts was not only to make women healthier but also to alter their self-image, to give them, in the way Vassar did in its time, new confidence and energy. "For us," declared *Our Bodies, Ourselves,* "body education is core education. . . . Picture a woman trying to do work and to enter into equal and satisfying relationships with other people—when she feels physically weak . . . when her internal bodily processes are a mystery to her . . . when she does not understand nor enjoy sex." Only by taking responsibility "for our physical selves" will women "start to use our untapped energies. . . . We can be better friends, and better lovers, better *people*, more self-confident, more autonomous, stronger, and more whole." [41] In brief, bodily knowledge would promote, almost guarantee, the realization of the ideology of woman as person.

The institution that many women reformers looked to for accomplishing this transformation was the new-style clinic. It would offer, explained one feminist doctor, "cooperative care: one in which health is a common concern to patient and professional alike; where self-knowledge replaces mystery, where orders bow to instructions; where self-help is regarded as a matter of common pride and not as stubbornness; where decisions are made by all involved and not passed down from on high." The ideal clinic would mix lay with professional staff; more important, the staff would be primarily female. As one clinic reported: "Although male physicians and counselors were seen as technically competent, many women felt that a female staff would be more aware of their special needs, and could relate more effectively to their questions, concerns and attitudes." The clinics would also be community-based and community-administered. "We envision," declared *Our Bodies, Ourselves,* "medical clearinghouses in each community, run by and composed of community people, doctors, medical students and nurses . . . to educate community people from childhood up in preventive commonsense medicine, to fight for equal medical care, and finally, to keep doctors and nurses really in touch with the people they are caring for." [42] This design for health care was strikingly similar to Marian Wright Edelman's design for day care. In both instances, community control would be the antidote to professional authority.

The day care analogy cannot be pursued very far, however, because the health reform program has enjoyed even less success. Minority groups did ally with feminists to advocate a clinic approach to the delivery of medical services (the pediatrician is to them what the gynecologist is to women). Even so, the alliance has not been effective. It is one thing to try to build up a program in an open field, as was the case with day care; it is quite another to come up against one of the most well-organized and prestigious professions, which has the added advantage of a history of skillful and effective lobbying. Any federal program that looked to fund community clinics under lay control would bring to the fore medical spokesmen whose opposition would be even fiercer than that of an Albert Shanker. Moreover, the health reform movement does depend upon the cooperation of the physician. Its advocates are not medical abolitionists. They are aware of the need to use doctors' skills to treat disease; what they object to is the way in which these skills have been exercised, in scope and in manner. But their pleas all too often fall on deaf ears—and there is really little that reformers can do about it until, perhaps, women and minority group members now completing medical school offer alternative styles of medical care.

The medical profession is, in fact, attempting to accomplish something akin to Shanker's proposal—to take over the programs of women and minority groups by adding new services to its own programs. Doctors are placing nurse practitioners and physicians' assistants on their own office and hospital staffs. The new paraprofessionals are generally women, and they are, in their ideal form, to "bridge the gap between the highly skilled technical care which physicians can provide for sick patients, and the comprehensive personalized care they sometimes fall short of providing to well patients." [43] The nurse or assistant is to conduct routine physical examinations and give advice, calling upon the doctor when she detects a significant physical abnormality. But it is doubtful whether the addition of a paraprofessional will alter the style of medical services. The most significant effect may be financial; the patient will pay a doctor's price for being examined by a nurse practitioner—who, in most matters, is likely to echo the doctor's personal views or the hospital's policy. If the doctor or the institution has little respect for patients' rights, it is doubtful whether the paraprofessional will be any more sensitive. If anything, paraprofessionals may find themselves compensating for their lack of medical credentials through social counseling, thereby extending still further the domain in which medical expertise rules. All of this may represent the aura of change without its substance.

The movement for "reproductive freedom" has brought more accomplishments and generated deeper controversy. In the area of contraception, law finally did catch up to practice. By 1965, the number of Protestant families using some form of birth control had reached 87 percent, and the number of Catholic families was not far behind at 78 percent. That same year the Supreme Court ruled in the Griswold case that dispensing contraceptive "information, instruction and medical advice to *married persons*" was protected by "the zone of privacy created by several constitutional decrees." Its 1972 decision in *Eisenstadt v. Baird* dispelled whatever lingering doubts remained by expanding the Griswold precedent to include unmarried persons. "If the right of privacy means anything, it is the right of the *individual,* married or single to be free from unwarranted governmental intrusion into matters so fundamentally affecting a person as the decision whether to bear or beget a child." Indeed, by the time of the Eisenstadt decision, Congress had approved the Family Planning Act, providing birth control information without cost to anyone who wanted it and federal subsidies to underwrite the establishment of family planning clinics. There was so little opposition to the Act that one Senator felt compelled to remark that the committee holding hearings could not find any group to speak out against the concept of planned parenthood.[44]

Predictably, the expanded view of women's rights came into conflict with state prohibitions on abortion. During the late 1960s a handful of states, including New York, broadened the grounds for which a woman could obtain an abortion. But the breakthrough came in January 1973, when the Supreme Court decided that a woman in her first trimester of pregnancy, in consultation with her physician, had the right to obtain an abortion; state interference in that privilege was unconstitutional. In including the woman's right to terminate pregnancy under the right to privacy, the Court cited first the potential medical dangers to the woman. But it quickly left these traditional grounds, noting: "Maternity, or additional offspring, may force upon the woman a distressful life and future. Psychological harm may be imminent. Mental and physical health may be taxed by child-care. There is also the distress for all concerned, associated with the unwanted child." And hence the woman's right to an abortion.[45]

The merits of the decision aside, the opinion itself was neither brilliant nor consistent. It did not persuasively demonstrate why states could not attempt to resolve so murky a question as when life begins. It did not establish abortion as a "right" in the sense that the poor had a claim on the government to pay for the procedure. But whatever its weaknesses, the decision had major consequences, both intended and unintended, for social policy.

The number and type of women who underwent abortions, and their experiences, effectively put to rest some long-standing objections. For one, it became immediately obvious that abortion was a very safe procedure. In New York State, from mid-1970 to mid-1972, about 402,000 abortions took place with only 16 deaths. In the country as a whole between 1972 and 1974, there were 3.4 deaths per 100,000 legal abortions, as compared to a maternal mortality rate of 14.8 per 100,000 live births. For another, abortion on an outpatient basis (relying upon the vacuum aspiration technique instead of on surgery), proved to be a very practical and low-risk technique for women in their first trimester of pregnancy; it was also simple and inexpensive to administer. Moreover, the number of women who took advantage of the liberalization in the abortion law was staggering. In 1973, there were 747,000 abortions; in 1974 there were 900,000; in 1975, more than 1,000,000. And most women seemed to suffer none of the acute guilt that some psychiatrists had predicted; they were not filling hospital beds with post-abortion depression. Finally, public health officials noted not only a decrease in deaths from legal abortion as compared to illegal abortion, but also "lower out-of-wedlock birth rates and improved infant health." [46]

The change in law prompted a change in public opinion. Before 1973, public opinion polls revealed that less than a majority of the population was in favor of abortion. After 1973, polls reported a majority in favor of the Supreme Court's liberalization of abortion (52 to 54 percent of the respondents to various Gallup polls). So, too, NBC polls indicated that a majority would keep abortion laws as they are now or further liberalize them. It was also evident that women used abortion for sound reasons. In most cases they were unmarried (in New York City in 1974, two-thirds of the women undergoing abortion were single) and very young (in New York, 51 percent were under twenty-five). [47] Taken together, these findings pointed to a massive and safe reliance on abortion by women who seemed to be making sane and sensible decisions.

Yet the victories for the pro-abortion forces have been less than complete, and the controversies marking the policy have become more acute. Resistance to providing women with the option of abortion increases as one moves farther from urban centers. In non-metropolitan areas, only 15 percent of private hospitals and 11 percent of public hospitals delivered abortion services in 1974 and 1975; indeed, in metropolitan areas, fewer than half the private hospitals (46 percent) and about one-third of the public hospitals carried out abortions. The low percentage of abortions in public facilities is all the more critical because they traditionally service the poor. In effect, and abortion clinics. Hence, for women who live at some distance of a state, and then not typically in public but in private hospitals and abortion clinics. Hence, for women who live at some distance from a city or who are poor, an abortion (even before the recently imposed Congressional restrictions) has not been available on demand.[48]

A hospital's failure to deliver abortion services indicates not a lack of demand but an unwillingness to meet it. In New Jersey, for example, a Health Department survey in 1974 revealed that of the sixty-nine hospitals in the state, thirty-nine would perform an abortion only to save the mother's life—in clear disregard of the Supreme Court ruling. In a city like Milwaukee, doctors in one public hospital refused to perform abortions except where the life of the mother was in danger, and moreover, they refused to allow the hospital to hire doctors willing to perform abortions in compliance with the law. A suit finally did force the hospital to alter its policies, but the litigation process took two years.

The refusal of many hospitals to carry out abortions obviously reflects the pressure exerted by Catholic doctors and the Catholic church. (Milwaukee, for example, has a population that is 40 percent Catholic.) But the hospitals are responding to more than just Catholic sentiments. Religion quite apart, many doctors, for personal or professional reasons, remain ambivalent about or opposed to abortion. One hundred medical school professors in 1972 did urge their colleagues to recognize "that abortion has become a predominantly social as well as medical responsibility. For the first time, except perhaps for cosmetic surgery, doctors will be expected to do an operation simply because the patient asks that it be done." They accepted this change in order to serve "the new society in which they live."[49] Many others, however, are reluctant to grant their patients this kind of authority.

Physicians' objections to abortion in the Milwaukee case revealed how much more than Catholic doctrine was at stake. (Indeed, since polls report that some 46 percent of Catholics favor legalized abortion, this is to be expected.) Some doctors argued that abortion was "a waste of valuable medical effort." As one of them put it, "Performance of an abortion is bad medicine. . . . If I were to do an act that I consider bad medicine it would be unethical on my part." Others frankly objected "to being ordered to perform any medical service." Still others insisted that "I cannot approve of the use of surgical approach for solution of a social problem." Given the fact that in the nation as a whole "only one-fourth of [all] hospitals, and fewer than one-fifth of public hospitals, provide any abortion services," clearly, doctors' social views are shaping institutional practices.[50]

Opposition to abortion has come too from Right to Life groups where again, Catholic efforts have been prominent but not exclusive. The president of the National Right to Life Committee in 1976 was a black, Methodist woman surgeon. And for all the charges that she was a figurehead for an essentially Catholic movement, in fact, there was constituent support for her anti-abortion position in every one of her diverse identifications. Blacks have claimed that abortion constitutes genocide, the newest white man's technique to reduce their numbers in the population. Methodists have been joined by fundamentalist Protestant groups and Orthodox Jews in condemning abortion. Traditional-minded women link the ERA with abortion because neither gives primacy to domestic and maternal obligations. And surgeons do object to being told to perform an operation.

The result of the staunch pro- and anti-abortion sentiments has been to make the controversy, in the political jargon, a "bullet" issue, that is, no matter how a representative or senator votes on all other matters, a "wrong" vote on abortion (be it yes or no) will cost constituent support. Congress may well have exaggerated the strength of the anti-abortion forces because they have been so active and energetic; and first evidence suggests that "congressmen who took a consistent, favorable position with regard to legalized abortion appeared to have a slight edge in the 1974 election over those with an anti-abortion record." [51] In all events, the conflicts have been fierce and quintessentially adversarial. The 1977 stalemate in Congress on whether Medicaid funds could be used to cover the costs of abortion (the program had been funding 300,000 abortions a year at the cost of $50 million) was one indication of the volatility of the issue. And the resolution, taken months later, was objectionable to both sides: Medicaid funds would pay for an abortion when the mother would suffer "severe and long-lasting physical health damage" as certified to by two doctors, or for "medical procedures" in the case of rape or incest that was "promptly" reported. Anti-abortion forces found these provisions far too liberal. Pro-abortion forces were no less disturbed at being back in the all-too-familiar position of having to rely upon medical determinations. Once again, the doctor held the key, which meant that the poor would be subjected to inconsistent and varying decisions.

One final incident conveys the bitter quality of the confrontation. Secretary of Health, Education and Welfare Joseph Califano, in light of his own and President Carter's opposition to abortion, set up a special committee, chaired by a woman, to explore "alternatives to abortion." The committee's report concluded that "the literal alternatives to it are suicide, motherhood, and some would add, madness. Consequently, there is some confusion, discomfort, and cynicism greeting efforts to 'find' or 'emphasize' or 'identify' alternatives to abortion." [52] Upon receiving the report, Califano disbanded the committee.

Thus in abortion, as in so many other cases, the attempt to implement a social policy reflecting the concept of woman as person has brought some benefits to the middle class but not to the lower class. As we have seen, at AT&T, the EEOC has helped educated women to rise in the ranks, but the less educated now find fewer jobs; the new legitimacy of day care affords greater options for the middle-class but does not provide the lower-class with services. So, too, middle-class women can rather easily obtain an abortion; lower-class women will be lucky to do so. This outcome may in part reflect the fact that American politics, especially when there are costs involved, is not responsive to the needs or the rights of the poor. But something deeper emerges too: women have not been able to unite in a movement that would allow the identity of sex to override the differences in class. Despite the reformers' belief that sisters would act together in an effective alliance, the results have not been satisfying. In the end, lower-class women receive little or nothing from WIN or day care or liberalized abortion. The women's movement has not managed to do much better for the lower classes than any of its predecessors.

There is, then, nothing altogether novel in the consequences of current social policies. However disappointing the present record of the EEOC or the WIN program, the performance of the Charity Organization Society or the child welfare reformers or the Sanger group was no more satisfying. The current conflicts over policy have a familiar ring. Not for the first time have the interests of women clashed with the interests of professionals. Day care and abortion do in some ways repeat the experiences of Shepard-Towner and birth control.

Yet, something novel and encouraging does appear, if only faintly, in the present state of reform, and it emerges from this very recognition that interests and values are in conflict. Feminists and, not coincidentally, other advocates of minority rights share a new determination to advance their own interests as they, and not experts or surrogates, define them. They are acutely aware that a call to the common welfare, whether it be to the well-being of children, or to the future of the family, or to the stability of society, has all too often abridged women's freedom of action. If some women have been and remain eager to respond to this appeal, that is their prerogative. But others who may wish to reallocate the burden or avoid it altogether are asserting their right to choice. They now have a very clear, even raw, sense of what constitutes cooptation as opposed to real gains, where compromise becomes capitulation, and when trade-offs become surrender. One cannot be certain of the consequences of this orientation; an understanding of past and present developments does not chart future directions. Nevertheless, two observations and one small item of comfort are worth noting.

First, this new sense of the rules of the game may help to promote women's interests, at least middle-class women's interests. The willingness of activists to do battle in a second, a third, and a fourth round may well promote their ambitions. The women's movement is becoming another—and not altogether weak—vested interest group, and this transformation is likely to bear results in the American political system. Second, this approach to social policy is likely to exacerbate tensions, to make an appeal to the common welfare still more obsolete. Pressures will generate counterpressures, sharp disputes over "turf," and an unwillingness to make concessions. One need only look to the political activities of blacks, professionals, children's advocates, and labor unions to appreciate the strength of this dynamic. We are likely to live with lawsuits and challenges and an overheated political rhetoric for some time to come. Given the assumptions and the stakes, not only women but other groups as well are going to be ready for successive rounds.

The solace? As others have discovered before us, it is difficult to be king when the gods are changing.

Notes

Chapter 1

1. David Potter, *People of Plenty* (Chicago, 1954); Robert Wiebe, *The Search for Order 1877–1920* (New York, 1967); and Stephen Thernstrom, *Poverty and Progress* (Cambridge, Mass., 1964).
2. Daniel Boorstein, *The Americans: the Democratic Experience* (New York, 1973), p. 352.
3. Marion Harland, *The Housekeeper's Week* (Indianapolis, Ind., 1908), p. 13.
4. Boorstein, *The Americans*, p. 254.
5. Ibid., pp. 530–535.
6. P. R. Moses, "Some Data on Electricity in Apartment Houses," *Architectural Review* 10 (1903), p. 11.
7. Sam B. Warner, Jr., *Streetcar Suburbs* (Cambridge, Mass., 1962).
8. A. C. David, "A Cooperative Studio Building," *Architectural Record* 14 (October 1903), p. 243. David notes that while in 1870 the island of Manhattan was dominated by single-family homes and tenements, by 1900 this had changed. That year only ten single-family homes were built and apartment buildings were dotting the skyline.
9. Ibid., p. 242; T. Richardson, "New Homes of New York," *Scribner's Monthly* 8 (1874), p. 68.
10. O. F. Semsch, "The Heating, Plumbing, and Refrigerating in Apartment Houses," *Architectural Review* 10 (1903), p. 106.
11. Ernest Flagg, "Planning of Apartment Houses and Tenements," *Architectural Review* 10 (1903), p. 89.
12. Moses, "Some Data," p. 11.
13. D. N. B. Sturgis, "The Planning and Furnishing of the Kitchen in the Modern Residence," *Architectural Record*, 16 (1904), p. 391.
14. Edward Stratton Holloway, "Apartments and How to Furnish Them," *House Beautiful*, 56 (1924), p. 130; I. M. Rubinow, "Discussion," Third Annual Meeting of the American Sociological Society *Papers and Proceedings* (1908), p. 38.
15. Frank Presbrey, *The History and Development of Advertising* (New York, 1929), pp. 379, 417, 421–422; Boorstein, *The Americans*, pp. 318–321.
16. Harland, *Housekeeper's Week*, p. 74.
17. Edward Marshall, "The Woman of the Future," *Good Housekeeping*, 55 (October 1912), p. 436.
18. Ralph M. Hower, *History of Macy's of New York, 1858–1919* (Cambridge, Mass., 1943), pp. 271–272.
19. Ibid., p. 163.
20. Ibid., p. 104.
21. William H. Taft, "The Dedication of Wanamaker's 1911," *Golden Book of the Wanamaker Store Jubilee Year, 1861–1911* (Philadelphia, 1911), Vol. 2, p. 3.
22. Hower, *Macy's*, pp. 280, 235.
23. Ibid., p. 164.
24. *Golden Book*, pp. 150–151.
25. Hower, *Macy's*, p. 284.
26. Ibid., p. 166; *Golden Book*, p. 285.
27. Hower, *Macy's*, p. 273.
28. Boorstein, *The Americans*, pp. 536 and 103; Hower, *Macy's*, p. 166.
29. Hower, *Macy's*, pp. 160, 325.

30. Agnes S. Donham, "History of Woman's Educational & Industrial Union" (Boston, 1955), typewritten manuscript. Papers of the Boston Woman's Educational and Industrial Union. Schlesinger Library, Radcliffe College.

31. Marion Talbot, *The Education of Women* (Chicago, 1910), p. 46.

32. Over the past few years, this subject has received extensive attention from historians. Some of the work I found most helpful was: Charles E. Rosenberg and Carroll Smith-Rosenberg, "The Female Animal: Medical and Biological Views of Women," in Charles E. Rosenberg, *No Other Gods: On Science and American Thought* (Baltimore, 1976), pp. 54–70; G. J. Barker-Benfield, *The Horrors of the Half-Known Life* (New York, 1976); John S. Haller, Jr. and Robin M. Haller, *The Physician and Sexuality in Victorian America* (Urbana, Ill., 1974); Carroll Smith-Rosenberg, "The Hysterical Woman: Sex Roles and Role Conflict in Nineteenth Century America," *Social Research*, 39 (1972), pp. 652–78.

33. Alexander H. Bullock, "The Centennial Situation of Women." Address at the Commencement Anniversary of Mount Holyoke Seminary, Worcester, Mass. (1876), pp. 31–32; Catharine E. Beecher, "On the Needs and Claims of Women Teachers," First Women's Congress of Association for Advancement of Women, 1873, *Letters and Papers*, p. 159.

34. Mrs. Frank Malleson, *Notes on the Early Training of Children*, 3rd ed. (Boston, 1892), pp. 39; 91–92.

35. Newton Riddell, *Our Little Ones* (Raymond, Neb., 1895), p. 14.

36. Quoted in Haller and Haller, *The Physician and Sexuality*, p. 90.

37. Dean Briggs, "Remarks," Smith College Quarter Centennial Anniversary *Proceedings* (Northampton, Mass., 1900), p. 151; Frances Power Cobbe, *The Duties of Women* (New York, 1898), p. 138. Cobbe was an English suffragist whose lectures were first delivered and published in England and then went through many American editions.

38. Dr. Charles Meigs quoted in Barker-Benfield, *The Horrors*, p. 83.

39. Quoted in Rosenberg, "The Female Animal," p. 56.

40. A statement found in the N.Y. State Medical Assn. *Transactions* (1875). Quoted in Mary Putnam Jacobi, *The Question of Rest For Women During Menstruation* (New York, 1877), p. 4.

41. Mary Wood-Allen, *Ideal Married Life* (New York, 1901), p. 117.

42. Ibid.

43. The Mary Putnam Jacobi quotation can be found in Barbara Ehrenreich and Deidre English, *Complaints and Disorders* (New York, 1973), p. 19.

44. Wood-Allen, *Ideal Married Life* p. 118.

45. One of the most famous tracts that describe neurasthenia is George M. Beard, *Sexual Neurasthenia, its Hygiene, Causes, Symptoms and Treatment* (New York, 1884). See also the writing of S. Weir Mitchell, particularly *Fat and Blood* (New York, 1878). An interesting analysis of the type of treatments doctors offered female neurasthenics can be found in Ann Douglas Wood, "The Fashionable Diseases: Women's Complaints and Their Treatment in 19th Century America," *Journal of Interdisciplinary History*, 4 (1973), pp. 25–52. See also, Haller and Haller, *The Physician*, p. 15. Barker-Benfield, *The Horrors*, pp. 83–84, notes the differences between the etiology of disease in the sexes.

46. Lydia Pinkham, *Guide for Women* (1893), p. 2. The Lydia Pinkham Manuscript Collection at the Schlesinger Library, Radcliffe College, has numerous relevant pamphlets.

47. Quoted in Jacobi, *The Question*, p. 5.

48. Barker-Benfield, *The Horrors*, p. 83.

49. Quoted in Jacobi, "The Question.," p. 5.

50. Vassar College, *First Meeting of the Trustees*, Feb. 26, 1861, p. 13.

51. The best-known work was by Edward H. Clarke, *Sex in Education, or a Fair Chance for Girls* (Boston, 1874).

52. John H. Raymond, *Vassar College: Its Foundation Aims, Resources and Course of Study* (1873), p. 76; James Harris Fairchild, *Oberlin, the Colony and the College 1833–1883* (Oberlin, 1883), p. 176; Elizabeth M. Farrand, *History of the University*

of Michigan (Ann Arbor, 1885), pp. 202, 203; James E. Pollard, *History of The Ohio State University* (Columbus, 1953), pp. 63, 64.

53. Raymond, *Vassar College*, p. 17.

54. James Orton, *The Liberal Education of Women* (New York, 1873), pp. 197–198.

55. Raymond, *Vassar College*, p. 21.

56. Vassar Female College, *Prospectus 1865*, p. 17. For their views on vocational training, see pp. 23–24.

57. For a discussion of moral treatment, see David J. Rothman, *The Discovery of the Asylum* (Boston, 1971).

58. Vassar, Wellesley, and Bryn Mawr followed this plan. Smith used a series of domitories instead.

59. Raymond, *Vassar College*, p. 13.

60. Frances A. Wood, *Earliest Years at Vassar* (Poughkeepsie, N.Y., 1909), p. 45.

61. Vassar Female College, *Report on Its Organization*, p. 7.

62. *Prospectus,* p. 3.

63. Wood, *Earliest Years at Vassar*, p. 29; Vassar Female College, *Report on Its Organization*, p. 35.

64. Maria Mitchell, "The Collegiate Education of Girls," Congress of the Association for the Advancement of Women, *Proceedings 1880,* p. 67.

65. Jacobi, *The Question*, pp. 225, 227.

66. Mary Putnam Jacobi, "Mental Action and Physical Health," is quoted in Marion Harland, *Eve's Daughters* (New York, 1882), p. 233.

67. Mary Taylor Bissell, "Physical Training as a Factor in Liberal Education," in the Association of Collegiate Alumnae *Papers*, Pamphlet 14 (1886), pp. 2–3, Sophia Smith Collection, Smith College.

68. Ibid., pp. 2–4.

69. Ibid., p. 4.

70. Carroll D. Wright, "Health Statistics of Female College Graduates," Massachusetts Bureau of Statistics of Labor, *Sixteenth Annual Report*, 1884, p. 1.

71. Annie G. Howe, *Health Statistics of Women College Graduates: Report of a Special Committee of the Association of Collegiate Alumnae* (Boston, 1885), pp. 10, 12.

72. Ibid., p. 14.

73. "Addresses at the Inauguration of Bryn Mawr College" (1885), p. 18.

74. Smith College, *Official Circular* No. 14 (October 1887), p. 29.

75. Bissell, "Physical Training," p. 1.

76. Elizabeth Lawrence Clarke, "Alumnae Responses," *Smith College Quarter Centennial Anniversary 1875–1900*, p. 60.

77. [Anonymous] "Smith College," *Scribner's Monthly* 9 (May 1877), p. 9.

78. Clarke, "Alumnae Responses," p. 61.

79. *Official Circular* No. 14, pp. 28–29. Throughout these decades women physicians produced a body of literature explaining their own position on how to prevent ill health in women. See the many articles in the *Woman's Medical Journal.* For an analysis of the careers and practices of women physicians see Mary Roth Walsh, *Doctors Wanted: No Women Need Apply* (New Haven, 1977).

80. Bissell, "Physical Training," pp. 5–6.

81. S. Weir Mitchell, *Fat and Blood* (Philadelphia, 1878).

82. Ibid., pp. 42–45.

83. Ibid., p. 96.

84. S. Weir Mitchell, *Lectures on Diseases of the Nervous System Especially in Women* (Philadelphia, 1885), p. 269. He also notes, "It is a plan never, in my opinion, to be used where exercise, outdoor life tonics, or change have not been thoroughly tested" (pp. 282–283).

85. S. Weir Mitchell, *Doctor and Patient* (Philadelphia, 1887), pp. 141, 146.

86. Ibid., pp. 153, 13.

87. Ibid., p. 153.

88. Ibid., pp. 155–157.

89. Alice Freeman Palmer, *Why Go To College?* (Boston, 1897), p. 9.

90. Ibid., p. 9.

91. Ibid., p. 10.

92. Ibid., p. 11.

93. M. Carey Thomas, "Present Tendencies in Women's Education," *Educational Review* 35 (January 1908), p. 69.

94. John H. Raymond, "The Demand of the Age for a Liberal Education of Women and How It Should be Met," in James Orton, *The Liberal Education of Women* (New York, 1873), p. 44.

95. Ibid., pp. 50, 51 (italics added).

96. Vassar Female College, *Report on Organization*, p. 29. Wellesley also accommodated the students in one large dormitory. Smith and later Bryn Mawr used a string of smaller dormitories, but the sense of a community that bound the administration, faculty, and students remained quite strong.

97. Alice Freeman Palmer, "A Review of Higher Education," in Anna C. Brackett, *Woman and the Higher Education* (New York, 1893), p. 108.

98. Ibid., p. 119. Lawrence Veysey, *American University* (Chicago, 1965), pp. 188–189, 208–209, shows that administrators of male colleges were far more ambivalent about this point. They were more ready to encourage scholarship.

99. Arthur Gilman, "Thoughts on the Collegiate Instruction of Women," *Journal of Social Science* (April, 1888), p. 83.

100. Bryn Mawr College, *Annual Report* 1888–1889, p. 9.

101. Bryn Mawr College, *Annual Report* 1894–1895, p. 18; M. Carey Thomas, "Address," *Smith College Quarter Centennial Anniversary 1875–1900*, p. 189.

102. Dean Briggs, "Address," p. 151.

103. Palmer, *Why Go to College?* p. 16.

104. Frances E. Willard, *Occupations for Women* (New York, 1897), p. 23, 142; Harland, *Eve's Daughters*, p. 258.

105. Arnold B. Wolfe, *The Lodging House Problem* (Boston, 1906), pp. 81–82. See also John Modell and Tamara K. Hareven, "An Examination of Boarding and Lodging in American Families," *Journal of Marriage and the Family* 35 (August 1973), p. 471.

106. Anna S. Richardson, *The Girl Who Earns Her Own Living* (New York, 1909), p. 282.

107. Mary A. Livermore, *What Shall We Do with Our Daughters?* (Boston, 1883), pp. 13, 14; Laura Clay, "Responsibility of Women to Society," Association for the Advancement of Women, Fifteenth Congress, *Proceedings*, 1887, p. 12.

108. Harland, *Eve's Daughters*, pp. 278–279.

109. Livermore, *Our Daughters*, pp. 3, 132, 149; Mary A. Livermore, "Superfluous Women," an undated article found in the WCTU papers of the Sophia Smith Collection, p. 216–17.

110. Edward H. Clarke, *Sex in Education* (Boston, 1874), pp. 131, 133.

111. Raymond, "The Demand of the Age," p. 43; Gilman, *Thoughts*, p. 84; Millicent Washburn Shinn, "The Marriage Rate for College Women," *Century Magazine*, 50 (October 1895), p. 948.

112. Howe, *Health Statistics*, p. 29; Elizabeth C. Boyd, "Vassar College," *Godey's Magazine* (February 1895), p. 197.

113. Willard, *Occupations*, p. 172 (italics added); Boyd, "Vassar College," p. 197; Joseph A. Hill, *Women in Gainful Occupations, 1870 to 1920* (Washington, D.C., 1929), p. 45.

114. May Allison, *The Public Schools and Women in Office Service* (Boston, 1914), p. 6.

115. For the early history of the typewriter see Richard N. Current, *The Typewriter and the Men Who Made It* (Urbana, Ill., 1954); Bruce Bliven, *That Wonderful Writing Machine* (New York, 1954). For the role of the Remington Company as an employment agency, see *The Typewriter and Phonographic World*, 20 (1902), p. 125.

116. Arthur T. Foulke, *Mr. Typewriter* (Boston, 1961), p. 79; G. Shankland Walworth, "How to Get a Situation," in *The Typewriter and Phonographic World*,

18 (Oct. 1901), p. 191; Anna Wade Westabrook, "Young Ladies as Stenographers and Typewriters," *The Typewriter and Phonographic World*, 6 (Feb. 1891).

117. In 1891, for example, there were 239,556 high school graduates in the United States, 60 percent of whom were women; U.S. Commissioner of Education, *Report*, 1891–92, p. 686; Board of Education, Kansas City, Missouri, *Sixteenth Annual Report*, 1887, p. 24.

118. Packard's Business College *Prospectus* 1897–1898, pp. 17–18.

119. Packard Commercial School *Graduation Exercises* (1895), p. 15. See also Jessica Kemm, *Women as Stenographer/Typist: 1880–1900*, unpublished paper (1976), pp. 6, 12.

120. Jean Cunningham, "Character of Office Service," in Allison, *The Public Schools*, pp. 29, 74–75; Hazel Manning, "Home Life Responsibilities" in Allison, *The Public Schools*, p. 166; John F. Soby, "Male Stenographers Required," *The Typewriter and Phonographic World*, 20 (July 1902), pp. 38–39.

121. Grace C. Coyle, *Present Trends in Clerical Occupations* (New York, 1928), p. 13.

122. Ibid., pp. 14, 37. There was also an assumption that the stenographer could and should be better educated than her employer; clearly educational attainments were unrelated to advancement. Potential workers were told: "Your employer may not use correct grammar, but he will want his stenographer to be able to correct his mistakes. He may not understand the proper use of capitals, or be a good speller, but he pays his stenographer for this, and she must not be found deficient" (Westabrook, "Young Ladies," p. 191).

123. Soby, "Male Stenographers," p. 40; *Illustrated Phonographic World*, 14 (January 1899), p. 223.

124. John S. Steck, "Storekeeping in New York City," *Arena*, 22 (August 1899), p. 179.

125. Samuel Hopkins Adams, "The Department Store," *Scribner's Magazine*, 21 (June 1897); Anonymous, "A Salesgirl's Story," *Independent*, 54 (July 31, 1902), pp. 1815–1821; Hower, *Macy's*, pp. 194–199; Helen Campbell, *Darkness and Daylight* (Hartford, Conn., 1892), pp. 256–259.

126. Adams, "Department Store," p. 19; Helen Campbell, *Prisoner of Poverty* (Boston, 1887), p. 173.

127. Campbell, *Prisoner*, p. 174; Siegel and Cooper Company of New York, *Rules and Regulations for the Government of the Employees* (New York, c. 1900), pp. 4–7.

128. Adams, "Department Store," pp. 14–15. Adams also notes that the position of floorwalker invariably went to a man. Generally the floorwalker had been a clerk himself, but in a wholesale house or other business. "Managers of departments are not generally promoted from the ranks or educated to these positions, but are drawn by offers of larger salaries or better opportunities from other establishments where they have attracted attention through their success" (p. 9). See also Siegel and Cooper Company, *Rules and Regulations*, pp. 36–37.

129. Anonymous, "A Salesgirl's Story," p. 1818; Anonymous, "Some Manners," *Nation*, 63 (1896), p. 470.

130. Hower, *Macy's*, pp. 199, 383; Elizabeth Beardsley Butler, *Saleswomen in the Mercantile Stores of Baltimore* (New York, 1913), pp. 143–144.

131. Campbell, *Prisoners*, p. 174.

132. "Memorial of the American Institute of Instruction to the Legislature of Massachusetts in Normal School," January 1837, in Henry Barnard, *Normal Schools and Other Institutions* (Hartford, Conn., 1851), pp. 85–87.

133. Catharine E. Beecher, *An Essay on the Education of Female Teachers* (New York, 1835), p. 18.

134. Thomas Woody, *History of Women's Education in the United States*, I (New York, 1929), p. 491.

135. Willard S. Elsbree, *The American Teacher* (New York, 1939), p. 554.

136. Raymond, "Demands of the Age," pp. 47–48.

137. M. Carey Thomas "The College Woman of the Present and Future," *McClure's Syndicate* (1901), p. 3; Harland, *Eve's Daughters*, p. 271.

138. Massachusetts Board of Education, *57th Annual Report*, 1893, p. 70.

139. Ibid., p. 70; May Sewall, "Women as Educators," in Association for the Advancement of Women, *Proceedings* (1888), pp. 126–127; U.S. Commissioner of Education, *Report,* 1900–1901, II, pp. 2406–2407.

140. See, for example, Massachusetts Board of Education, *Fortieth Annual Report* 1875–1876, p. 160; Chicago, Ill. Board of Education *Report for 1873,* pp. 26–27; Sewall, "Women as Educators," pp. 124–125; Columbus Ohio Board of Education, *Annual Reports* 1875, 1886–1887, and 1891.

Chapter 2

1. Charlotte Perkins Gilman, *Women and Economics* (Boston 1898), p. 164; Sorosis, *Twenty-First Anniversary Report* (New York 1889), p. 45. (Papers of Sorosis in Sophia Smith Collection, Smith College).

2. Jennie Croly, *History of the Women's Club Movement in America* (New York, 1898), p. 169; Jennie Croly, "Sorosis: A History, 1868–1893," from the papers of Sorosis, Sophia Smith Collection, Smith College, p. 222; Gilman, *Women and Economics,* p. 166.

3. Croly, *Sorosis,* pp. 112–113; Mary I. Wood, *The History of the Federation of Women's Clubs* (New York, 1912), pp. 28, 29; Ella D. Clymer, "The National Value of Women's Clubs," in Rachel Foster Avery, National Council of Women *Transactions* (Philadelphia, 1891), p. 297.

4. Croly, *Sorosis,* pp. 33, 111.

5. The First Woman's Congress, *Papers and Letters* (New York, 1873), p. 5; Croly, *History,* p. 24; Croly, *Sorosis,* pp. 30, 111.

6. Rev. Celia Burleigh, "Opening Address," Sorosis Fourth Anniversary *Proceedings,* 1872, pp. 9–10, 13.

7. Frances E. Willard, "The Work of the WCTU," in Annie Nathan Meyer, *Woman's Work in America* (New York, 1891), p. 410.

8. Willard, "Work of the WCTU," p. 401; E.A.D. Barrington, *Industrial Training as a Factor in Temperance Work* (n.d. or place), Papers of the WCTU, Sophia Smith Collection, Smith College.

9. Willard, "Work of the WCTU," p. 402; Frances E. Willard, "Annual Address," Woman's Christian Temperance Union, *Annual Report* 1880, p. 11. Although Willard attached this phrase to "spinsters," it is quite clear that they were to work together with married women, and it is no exaggeration to see all WCTU members as "our Protestant Nuns." See also Joseph R. Gusfield, *Symbolic Crusade* (Urbana, Ill., 1963), pp. 78–85, 129–130, for the social class and marital status of the leaders as well as the breadth of their activities.

10. Alice M. Guernsey, *The Child of the Crusade* [undated pamphlet], WCTU papers, Sophia Smith Collection, Smith College, p. 5. Information about the WCTU kindergartens can be found in Mrs. E. G. Greene, *Pathfinder* (New York, 1884), pp. 104–105; and Frances E. Willard, "Address," Woman's Christian Temperance Union, *Annual Report* 1895, pp. 10, 50.

11. New York Women's Prison Association, *Forty-Sixth Annual Report,* 1890, pp. 14–15. A statement of WCTU policies can be found in Greene, *Pathfinder* pp. 134–135.

12. Greene, *Pathfinder,* pp. 162–163; Willard, "Annual Address," Woman's Christian Temperance Union, *Fifteenth Annual Meeting,* 1888, p. 35. For a more extensive statement of her argument towards female suffrage, see Frances E. Willard, *Home Protection Manual* (Chicago, 1879).

13. "Apartment Hotels in New York City," *Architectural Record* 13 (1903), p. 90; Marion Talbot, *The Education of Women* (Chicago, 1911), p. 31.

14. Josephine Shaw Lowell, *Public Relief and Private Charity* (New York, 1884), p. 98. For an interesting account of women's benevolent activities in the pre-Civil War decades, see Nancy F. Cott, *The Bonds of Womanhood* (New Haven, 1977).

15. George M. Fredrickson, *The Inner Civil War: Northern Intellectuals and the*

Crisis of Union (New York, 1965). Although this is the standard historical account of the U.S. Sanitary Commission, it provides little understanding of the role of women. More can be found in I..P. Brockett and Mary C. Vaughan, *Woman's Work in the Civil War* (Philadelphia, 1867). Brockett and Vaughan reported on the transformation that occurred as women took on this task: "Thousands of women learned in this work, to despise frivolity, gossip, fashion and idleness; learned to think soberly and without prejudice about the capacities of their own sex and thus did more to advance the rights of woman by providing her gifts and her fitness for public duties than a whole library of arguments and protests." (p. 59)

16. A biographical sketch of Schuyler's life can be found in *Notable American Women*, III (Boston, 1971), pp. 245-246. See also Louisa L. Schuyler, "Forty-Three Years Ago: On the Early Days of the State Charity Aid Association," New York State Charities Aid Association *Pamphlet* No. 135, 1915.

17. New York State Charities Aid Association, *Report of the Hospital Committee* (1872), p. 3; New York State Charities Aid Association, *First Annual Report 1873*, p. 25.

18. New York State Charities Aid Association, *Second Annual Report*, 1877, pp. 15-17.

19. Ibid., p. 7.

20. New York State Charities Aid Association, *Handbook for Visitors to the Almshouse* (New York, 1888), pp. 9-10; New York State Charities Aid Association, *Report of a Committee on Hospitals on a Training School for Nurses to be Attached to Bellevue* (New York, 1877).

21. Lowell, *Public Relief*, pp. 91-92, 94.

22. Ibid., pp. 107, 105.

23. Ibid., p. 98; Associated Charities of Boston, *First Annual Report 1879*, p. 3.

24. Lowell, *Public Relief*, p. 111.

25. Elizabeth Wilson, *Fifty Years of Association Work Among Young Women 1866-1916* (New York, 1916), p. 32; Young Women's Christian Association of New York *First Annual Report 1871*, pp. 3-4; *Eleventh Annual Report 1882*, p. 17.

26. Young Women's Christian Association of New York, *First Annual Report*, p. 4; Young Women's Christian Association of New York, *Thirteenth Annual Report 1884*, p. 11; Herbert B. Adams, "Work Among Working Women in Baltimore," *Johns Hopkins Studies in Historical and Political Science* 6 (1889), pp. 8-9. The YWCA in the late 1880s also used the services of a female physician. The Baltimore YWCA employed a female physician to care for the sick, to keep "a careful watch on the sanitary conditions of shops where girls are employed," to call "attention to the simplest rules of hygiene," and to give "lectures on the laws of health" (p. 8).

27. Young Women's Christian Association of New York, *Third Annual Report* 1873, p. 10. The effort to steer the girls toward domestic employment was not idiosyncratic to the New York YWCA; see Wilson, *Fifty Years*, and Adams, "Working Women."

28. Young Women's Christian Association of New York, *Third Annual Report* 1873, p. 16; Young Women's Christian Association of New York, *Eleventh Annual Report 1882*, pp. 11-13. The New York YWCA was the first of the YWCA's to offer these types of courses.

29. Dr. Enoch Stoddard, "Discussion," New York State Conferences of Charities *Proceedings*, 1900, p. 258. The women of the YWCA also visited the factories: see Wilson, *Fifty Years*, pp. 104-105. See also Mary Gay Humphreys, "The New York Working Girl," *Scribner's Monthly* 20 (Oct. 1896) no. 4, p. 5; Mary E. Halley, "Practical Factory Life," Fifth Annual Convention of Factory Inspectors *Proceedings* 1890, pp. 28-29. The female factory inspectors during the 1890s did focus most on the ill effects of a hazardous and unsanitary environment on the workers, but they first entered these establishments to investigate the moral environment.

30. Grace H. Dodge, "Responsibilities of Membership in a Society," *Far and Near* (November 1890), p. 4; L. C. Jarvis, "Country Clubs I. Are they Needful? II. How to Start Them," Convention of the Association of Working Girls Societies, *Sixth Annual Meeting* 1890, p. 106; Mary Haynes, "What is a Working Girl's Society?" Convention, *Sixth Annual Meeting* 1890, p. 11.

31. Robert D. Cross, "Grace Hoadley Dodge," *Notable American Women* I, pp. 489–492; Dodge, "Responsibilities," p. 3; Helen Iselin, "How to Start a Working Girls' Society," Convention, *Sixth Annual Meeting* 1890, p. 13.

32. Iselin, "Societies," p. 15; Emma Illwitzer, "Junior Clubs," Convention, *Sixth Annual Meeting*, 1890, p. 66.

33. M. Josephine Allen, "The Boston Working Girls' New Vacation House," *Far and Near* (November, 1890), pp. 6–7.

34. Grace H. Dodge, "Closing Words," Convention *Sixth Annual Meeting*, 1890, p. 108. In a speech delivered at Chautauqua, Dodge said of the club girls: "They have no practical home training. They need moral elevation, love, confidence, development, opportunities to do for themselves." Grace Dodge Papers, Teachers College; Grace H. Dodge, "Practical Talks: Their Function," Convention, *Sixth Annual Meeting*, 1890, pp. 29–30.

35. Grace H. Dodge, "Some Don'ts in Acquaintance with Young Men." This list is in an 1891 letter that Dodge wrote to her girls, in her papers at Teachers College.

36. Helen Campbell, *Darkness and Daylight in New York* (Hartford, 1892), p. 227; National Florence Crittenton Missions, *Fourteen Years Among Erring Girls* (Washington, 1897).

37. National Florence Crittenton Missions, *Fourteen Years*, pp. 20, 204–205.

38. Campbell, *Darkness and Daylight*, p. 242; Josephine Shaw Lowell, "Houses of Refuge for Women," New York State Conference of Charities *Proceedings* 1900, p. 258; Kate Waller Barrett, *Some Practical Suggestions in the Conduct of a Rescue Home* (Washington, 1903), pp. 34–35.

39. Barrett, *Some Practical Suggestions*, pp. 26–31.

40. Ibid., pp. 28–29; National Florence Crittenton Missions, *Fourteen Years*, p. 81.

41. Lowell, "Houses of Refuge," p. 253; Barrett, "Some Practical Suggestions," p. 48.

42. Leslie Aldridge Westoff and Charles F. Westoff, *From Now to Zero* (Boston, 1968), p. 47; G. J. Barker-Benfield, *The Horrors of the Half-Known Life* (New York, 1976), p. 265; James Reed, *From Private Vice to Public Virtue* (New York, 1978), pp. 34, 391.

43. Mary Wood-Allen, *Ideal Married Life* (New York, 1901), p. 162. John S. Haller, Jr. and Robin M. Haller, *The Physician and Sexuality in Victorian America* (Urbana, Ill., 1974), pp. 100–101.

44. Willard, "Annual Address, 1888," p. 56; Brevard D. Sinclair, *The Growing Sin of the Age* (Boston, 1892), p. 12; Augustus Kingsley Gardner, *Conjugal Sins* (New York, 1870), p. 109. See also, Horatio R. Storer, *Why Not?* (Boston, 1866), p. 14.

45. Barker-Benfield, *The Horrors*, p. 266; see also, James Mohr, *Abortion in America* (New York, 1978).

46. Henry C. Wright, *The Unwelcome Child* (Boston, 1858), pp. 65, 75.

47. John Ellis, *Marriage and its Violations* (New York, 1860), p. 21; Wood-Allen, *Ideal Married Life*, p. 211.

48. Ellen Rodman Church, *Money Making for Ladies* (New York, 1882), pp. 220, 78.

49. Lucy M. Salmon, "The Woman's Exchange; Charity or Business?" *Forum* 13 (May 1892), p. 401.

50. Joseph A. Hill, *Women in Gainful Occupations, 1870 to 1920* (Washington, 1929), pp. 21, 76–77.

51. New York State Charities Aid Association, *First Annual Report* 1873, pp. 6–7.

52. Nurses Training School, Bellevue Hospital, *Twenty-Fifth Annual Report* 1898, p. 5; *Fourth Annual Report*, 1877, p. 10.

53. These examples come from the New York State *Hearings on the Widows' Pensions* conducted by Robert W. Hebberd (1913–1914), unpublished manuscript. New York State Archives, Albany, N.Y.

54. Hill, *Women in Gainful Occupations*, p. 83.

55. N.Y. State *Hearings, passim*.

56. Bloomingdale Day Nursery, *Third Annual Report* 1897, p. 8.

57. National Federation of Day Nurseries, *Report* 1914; Sheila M. Rothman, "Other

People's Children," *Public Interest* (1973). See also Katherine Anthony, *Mothers Who Must Earn* (New York, 1914), pp. 151–154; Cleveland Day Nursery and Free Kindergarten, *Annual Reports* 1891–1897.

58. Adams, "Working Among Working Women," pp. 75–76; Mary S. Ferguson, "Boarding Homes and Clubs for Working Women," U.S. Dept. of Labor *Bulletin*, No. 15 (March 1898); Carroll Wright, "Working Women in Large Cities," U.S. Bureau of Labor *Fourth Annual Report* 1888.

59. Arnold B. Wolfe, *The Lodging House Problem* (Boston, 1906) pp. 46–47; Anna S. Richardson, *The Girl Who Earns Her Own Living* (New York, 1909) p. 273; Wolfe, *The Lodging House*, p. 47.

60. Wolfe, *The Lodging House*, pp. 44, 47.

61. Grace H. Dodge, "Annual Report," Convention Societies, p. 110, and Lucy A. Warner, "Discussion," *Sixth Annual Meeting*, 1890, pp. 107–108.

62. Humphreys, "The New York Working Girl," p. 511; Minnesota Bureau of Labor Statistics, *First Biennial Report* 1887–1888, p. 150. The report also contains middle-class comments on the priority of domestic employment for the factory workers. The Minnesota Survey was undertaken because of a widespread middle-class curiosity about the working girl's disdain for domestic service. In posing the question, "Why do not girls who are paid so poorly in the factories apply themselves to housework?", they commented, "It is the question upon which the public mind is most centered." (p. 149)

63. Campbell, *Darkness and Daylight*, p. 229. It is interesting to note that the typical inmate of the Mission was a girl who had been raised in an orphan asylum. Totally without resources, she was now—as she had been once before—forced to turn to the middle classes for aid. See Barrett, *Some Suggestions* p. 105.

Chapter 3

1. Mary Stanley Boone, "The Kindergarten from a Mother's Point of View," *Education* 25 (November 1904), p. 143.

2. Dorothy Ross, *G. Stanley Hall: The Psychologist as Prophet* (Chicago, 1972), *passim*.

3. G. Stanley Hall, *Youth: Its Education, Regimen and Hygiene* (New York, 1904), pp. 23–27.

4. Ibid., pp. 307, 323.

5. Cora L. Stockman, "Our Nursery," *Kindergarten* 3 (1891), p. 337.

6. Numerous books and periodicals were devoted to the kindergarten in these decades. See, the issues of *Kindergarten*; Agnes Snyder, *Dauntless Women in Childhood Education* (Washington, D.C., 1931); Mary Dabney Davis, *General Practice in Kindergarten Education in the United States* (Washington, D.C. 1925), p. 12.

7. U.S. Bureau of Education Bulletin No. 6, *Kindergartens in the United States, Statistics and Problems* (Washington, D.C. 1914), p. 10.

8. G. Stanley Hall, "Some Defects in the Kindergarten in America," *Forum* 28 (January 1900), p. 580.

9. *Kindergarten* 16 (February 1904), pp. 370–72.

10. Richard Watson Gilder, "The Kindergarten, An Uplifting Influence on the Home and the District," *Kindergarten* 16 (November 1903), p. 132.

11. Mary J. Garland, "The Kindergarten," *Kindergarten* 16 (January 1904), pp. 60–61.

12. Bessie Locke, "Manufacturers Indorse the Kindergarten," U.S. Bureau of Education, *Kindergarten Circular No. 4*, July, 1919.

13. S. H. Weber, "The Kindergarten as an Americanizer," U.S. Bureau of Education, *Kindergarten Circular No. 5*, December 1919, pp. 3–4.

14. Ibid., p. 2.

15. New York Kindergarten Association *11th Annual Report*, 1904, p. 8.

16. New York Kindergarten Association *3rd Annual Report*, 1892, p. 40.

17. New York Kindergarten Association *4th Annual Report*, 1893, p. 18.

18. New York Kindergarten Association *6th Annual Report,* 1895, p. 12.

19. Elizabeth Harrison, *A Study of Child Nature from the Kindergarten Standpoint* (Chicago, 1895), p. 10.

20. Ibid., p. 2.

21. Ibid., p. 11.

22. Evelyn B. Tillman, "Alice Josephine McLellan Birney," *Notable American Women,* I, pp. 147–8.

23. Julian E. Butterworth, *The Parent-Teacher Association and its Work* (New York, 1928), p. 3.

24. The First National Congress of Mothers, *Proceedings,* 1892, p. 273.

25. Mrs. Theodore F. Birney, "Opening Report," *The National Congress of Mothers Quarterly Report* (September 1900), p. 18.

26. Mrs. Edwin C. G. Rice, "The Effects of Mothers Clubs on the Community," *The National Congress of Mothers Quarterly Report* (September 1901), p. 28.

27. "Study Outlines," *The National Congress of Mothers Magazine,* I (1906), p. 12.

28. Birney, "Opening Report," p. 19.

29. See Resolutions for the gist of this program. The First National Congress of Mothers *Proceedings* (1897), p. 168.

30. Ibid., pp. 7–8.

31. Ibid., p. 294.

32. Mrs. Theodore F. Birney, "The Power of Organized Motherhood to Benefit Humanity," *The National Congress of Mothers Quarterly Report* (September 1900), p. 29.

33. Mabel Newcomer, *A Century of Higher Education for Women* (New York, 1959), p. 46; Rudolph C. Blitz, "Women in the Professions, 1870–1970," *Monthly Labor Review,* 97 (May 1974), p. 38.

34. "The College Woman and Motherhood," *National Congress of Mothers Magazine* 3 (March 1909), p. 211.

35. Blitz, "Women in the Professions," pp. 36, 38; United State Bureau of Education, "Statistics of Universities and Colleges," *Bulletin No. 29* (1932), p. 290.

36. Julia Lathrop, "The Highest Education for Women," *Fiftieth Anniversary Addresses at Vassar,* Poughkeepsie, N.Y. (1915), p. 82.

37. M. Carey Thomas, "Present Tendencies in Women's Education," *Educational Review,* 35 (January 1908), pp. 79–80. See also Barbara M. Cross, *The Educated Woman in America* (New York, 1965) for a view of M. Carey Thomas that stresses her determination to use a college training to create professional opportunities for women. Nevertheless, as an administrator Carey did declare that college training would make women better mothers.

38. Alice Freeman Palmer, *Why Go to College* (Boston, 1897), p. 23.

39. Charles Franklin Thwing, *The College Woman* (New York, 1894), p. 140.

40. Thomas, "Present Tendencies," p. 80.

41. Thomas Woody, *A History of Women's Education in the United States,* II p. 218; Mabel Newcomer, *Higher Education,* p. 99; Chicago Association of Collegiate Alumnae, *Public and Social Service as Vocations for College Women* (Chicago 1904), pp. 6–8.

42. Hunter, *Poverty* (New York, 1965 ed.), p. 25.

43. Ibid., p. 47.

44. Ibid., pp. 56–57.

45. Ibid., pp. 64–65.

46. "The Intercollegiate Student Conference," *Fiftieth Anniversary Addresses,* pp. 196–197.

47. Ibid., p. 195.

48. Florence Kelley [Wischnewetzky], "The Need of Theoretical Preparation for Philanthropic Work," New York Association of Collegiate Alumnae *Papers* (1887), pp. 17–18.

49. Ibid. However radical Kelley was on other issues, her views here were typical of Progressive women.

50. Allen F. Davis, *Spearheads of Reform: The Social Settlements and the Progressive Movement* (New York, 1967) and Robert Bremner, *From the Depths: The Discovery of Poverty in the United States* (New York, 1956) describe settlement house activities.

51. Vita Dutton Scudder, *On Journey* (New York, 1937), pp. 139-140.

52. Davis, *Spearheads*, p. 31.

53. Scudder, *On Journey*, p. 136.

54. Davis, *Spearheads*, p. 31.

55. Quoted in Barry D. Karl, *Charles E. Merriam and the Study of Politics* (Chicago, 1974), p. 31.

56. Scudder, *On Journey*, p. 137.

57. Vita Dutton Scudder, "The Relation of College Women to Social Need," Association of Collegiate Alumnae, *Papers* (1887), p. 14.

58. Unpublished diary of the founders of Dennison House, a social settlement in Boston organized by college women. The diary is to be found in the Schlesinger Library, Radcliffe College.

59. Scudder, "The Relation," p. 15.

60. University Settlement of New York, *Annual Report*, 1894, pp. 12-17.

61. Lillian Wald's Papers at Columbia University have lengthy descriptions of the activities of the Mothers' Club of the Henry Street Settlement.

62. Greenwich House, *Second Annual Report*, 1903, p. 12.

63. Henry Street Mothers' Club, *Reports*, Lillian Wald Papers.

64. College Settlement Association, *Fifth Annual Report*, 1894, p. 35. See also Greenwich House, *Second Annual Report*, 1903, p. 8 and Greenwich House, *Third Annual Report*, 1904, pp. 8-9.

65. The diary of Dennison House reports on these activities by workers; also, College Settlement Association, *Tenth Annual Report*, 1899, p. 48.

66. Ibid. *Thirteenth Annual Report*, 1901-1902, pp. 29, 49.

67. The College Settlement Association *Fifth Annual Report*, 1893-1894, p. 46.

68. Henry Street Mothers' Club, *Reports*, Lillian Wald Papers.

69. Jane Addams, "Why the Ward Boss Rules," *Outlook*, 57 (April 18, 1892), p. 870.

70. The College Settlement Association *Eleventh Annual Report*, 1899, p. 12.

71. Davis, *Spearheads*, p. 157.

72. Ibid., p. 104.

73. Ibid., p. 105.

74. Jane Addams, "The Settlement as a Factor in the Labor Movement," *Hull House Maps and Papers* (Boston, 1895), p. 203; James Bronson Reynolds, "Eight Years at the University Settlement," *University Settlement Studies* 2 (July 1906); Phillip Davis, "The Social Settlement and the Trade Union," *The Commons* 9 (April 1904), pp. 146-148.

75. The College Settlement Association, *Fourth Annual Report*, 1892, p. 28.

76. Mrs. Vladimir Simkovitch, "The Enlarged Function of the Public School," Thirty-first National Conference of Charities and Corrections, *Proceedings*, 1904, p. 481.

77. For a detailed account of the activities of the school nurse, see Lina R. Struthers, *The School Nurse* (New York, 1917).

78. This view of the school is explained in John Dewey and Evelyn Dewey, *The Schools of Tomorrow* (New York, 1915).

79. Ibid., pp. 167-168.

80. Ibid., p. 168.

81. Charles R. Richards, *The Gary Public Schools* (New York, 1918), p. 108.

82. Ibid., p. 107.

83. John Dewey, *The School and Society* (Chicago, 1899, 1963 ed.), p. 11.

84. Samuel McCune Lindsay, "Child Labor a National Problem," *The Annals of the American Academy of Political and Social Science*, 27 (1906), p. 73.

85. George M. Kober, "The Physical and Physiological Effects of Child Labor," *Annals of the American Academy of Political and Social Science*, 27 (1906), p. 285.

86. Florence Kelley, "Factory Inspection in Pittsburgh," typewritten manuscript from the Papers of the Consumer League of Massachusetts, Schlesinger Library, Radcliffe College (1908), pp. 13–14.

87. Mary E. Halley, "Observations Gleaned from the Inspection of Manufacturing, Mechanical and Mercantile Establishments in Relation to Women Operatives," Sixth Annual Convention of Factory Inspectors *Proceedings* (1892), p. 24.

88. Florence Kelley and Alzina P. Stevens, "Wage-Earning Children," *Hull House Maps and Papers* (Boston, 1895), p. 75.

89. Florence Kelley, "Child Labor," Eleventh Annual Convention of Factory Inspectors *Proceedings* (1897), p. 37; Kelley and Stevens, "Wage-Earning Children," p. 75.

90. John H. Chase, "Should a Playground Always be Fenced?" *The Playground*, I (Nov. 1908), p. 11.

91. See Clarence E. Rainwater, *The Play Movement in the United States* (Chicago, 1922), p. 47.

92. Ibid., p. 59.

93. New York City Department of Health, *Annual Report* 1920, p. 176.

94. Ibid., p. 150.

95. Ibid., p. 147.

96. Ibid., p. 149. In 1920, there were 3,157 mothers who received this type of care from public health nurses.

97. Ibid., pp. 159–60. The Department reported that in 1913 only 54 percent of the babies visiting the Health Stations were breast-fed; by 1920 the number had risen to 67 percent. In 1925, for reasons that will become apparent later, the number began to drop.

98. See the testimony of Julia Lathrop, Chief of the Children's Bureau, when she testified before a House Committee contemplating the passage of the Sheppard-Towner Bill. *Public Protection of Maternity and Infancy*, Hearings before the House Committee on Interstate and Foreign Commerce 66:3 (Washington, D.C., 1921). See also Grace Abbott, "The Federal Government in Relation to Maternity and Infancy," *Annals of the American Academy of Political and Social Science*, 151 (September 1930), p. 90.

99. New York City Department of Health, *Annual Report* 1920, p. 146.

100. Susan B. Anthony and Ida H. Harper, *History of Woman Suffrage* IV (New York, 1902). For the excellent detailed history of the suffrage movement see Aileen S. Kraditor, *The Ideas of the Woman Suffrage Movement 1890–1920* (New York, 1971).

101. The document is reprinted in Anne F. and Andrew M. Scott, *One Half the People: the Fight for Woman Suffrage* (New York, 1975), p. 57.

102. Anthony, *History*, testimony of Mrs. Mary Seymour Howell, p. 39; Julia Ward Howe, "The Relation of the Woman Suffrage Movement to Other Reforms" in Rachel Avery, *Transactions*, p. 239.

103. Anthony, *History of Suffrage* testimony of Mrs. Lillie Devereux Blake, p. 39.

104. Kraditor, *The Ideas*, p. 107.

105. Ida Husted Harper, *History of Woman Suffrage* (New York, 1922), V, p. 165. Both Harper and Kraditor in *The Ideas*, (pp. 120–121) note that the working girl was outside the movement at this time.

106. Harper, *History*, p. 143; Eleanor Flexner, *Century of Struggle* (New York, 1968) emphasizes the importance of the settlement house strategy to the eventual success of the movement (see especially p. 219).

107. Harper, *History*, p. 178.

108. Ibid., pp. 343–344.

109. Ibid., p. 165.

110. Kraditor, *The Ideas*, p. 124.

111. Harper, *History*, p. 345. Harper does note that while the American Federation of Labor had supported woman suffrage for many years, around 1909 other unions began to adopt favorable resolutions.

112. Harper, *History*, pp. 364–365.

113. Ibid., p. 172.
114. Flexner, *Century of Struggle*, p. 259.

Chapter 4

1. Albert J. Kennedy, *Social Settlements in New York City* (New York, 1935), provides an extended analysis of the small numbers and high turnover of immigrants who actually participated in the clubs.

2. James Stanley Lemons, *The Woman Citizen* (Urbana, 1973), provides a detailed account of the political history of the Act. The Congressional hearings held before the passage of the Act reveal reformers' assumptions. *Public Protection of Maternity and Infancy*, Hearings before the House Committee on Interstate and Foreign Commerce, 66:3 (Washington, D.C., 1921); *Protection of Maternity*, Hearings before the Senate Committee on Education and Labor, 67:1, (Washington, D.C., 1921).

3. F. Kelley quoted in Lemons *Woman Citizen*, p. 155; S. Josephine Baker, "Problems in Connection with the Administration of Well-Baby Clinics," *The Public Health Nurse*, 18 (June, 1926), p. 330.

4. Fred L. Adair, *Obstetric Education* (New York, 1931); American Child Hygiene Association, *Transactions* 1919, p. 79.

5. United States Children's Bureau *Bulletin* No. 203, p. 11.

6. Lemons, *Woman Citizen*, pp. 163–167, describes the American Medical Association efforts in detail.

7. The Illinois State Medical Association and its journal led the fight to support the AMA efforts, but few other state associations repeated their passionate rhetoric.

8. Anne E. Rude, Director, Division of Hygiene, Children's Bureau, to Hon. Morris Sheppard, July 7, 1922. Files of the United States Children's Bureau, National Archives, Washington, D.C.

9. Baker, "Well-Baby Clinics," p. 331.

10. There are numerous complaints about the focus on disease among average private doctors. For a few examples, see E. J. Huenekens, "The Well-Baby Clinic at the Office of the Family Physician and Pediatrician," *American Journal of Public Health*, 20 (July, 1930); American Child Hygiene Association *Transactions*, 1921, pp. 63–64; American Medical Association *Bulletin*, 19 (June 1924), p. 162.

11. Rosalie Slaughter Morton, "Woman's Place in the Public Health Movement," *Woman's Medical Journal*, 22 (April 1912), p. 84; Editorial, "Women Physicians and Public Hygiene," *Woman's Medical Journal*, 19 (November 1909), p. 23.

12. In 1927, of the forty-three states having Sheppard-Towner programs, sixteen had women physicians as directors. Of the eighty-nine full-time physicians employed by the program, forty were women.

13. Florence Brown Sherbon, "The Woman Physician and Her Obligation and Opportunity," *Woman's Medical Journal*, 29 (April 1915), p. 77.

14. The Federal government allocated $1.24 million for Sheppard-Towner for five years (1922–1927). It was a modest stipend for a program that intended to purchase expensive professional services, but not for one that was primarily educative. As a result, its supporters did not find the budget too meager for their programs. See, for example, Grace Abbott, "The Federal Government in Relation to Maternity and Infancy," *Annals of the American Academy of Political and Social Science*, 151 (September 1930), p. 100. Between 1924 and 1929, there were 2,978 prenatal and child health centers established in the country, using, in part, Sheppard-Towner funds.

15. Before the passage of the Act in 1919, the Children's Bureau conducted a "Children's Year," in which it tried to adapt the programs of large cities to fit the needs of rural areas and small towns. For an example of the novel types of programs they devised, see Janet Geister, "The Child Welfare Special," American Child Hygiene Association, *Transactions* 1919, pp. 214–222.

16. Abbott, "The Federal Government," pp. 92–94. Abbott notes that previous to 1920, twenty-eight states had established Bureaus of Child Hygiene or Divisions of Child Welfare. Of this number, sixteen were organized in 1919. She believed this was a result of the intensive efforts of the Bureau and the educated citizens of the various states during the Children's Year. It was the ability of this type of pressure to restructure the Department of Health that led the supporters of the Act to set out these funding stipulations. Under the terms of the Act, each state received $5,000 outright, and an additional $5,000 was available if the state matched the federal funds. The balance of the appropriation was to be distributed among the matching states on the basis of population. In 1927, only five states did not take matched funds. Only two states (Massachusetts and Connecticut) did not participate in the program. United States Children's Bureau "The Promotion of the Welfare and Hygiene of Maternity and Infancy," *Bulletin No. 186*, pp. 22–23.

17. The organizers of the Children's Year relied on the clubs of women to publicize their efforts. See Giester, "Child Welfare," and also yearly reports on the administration of the Act. These reports continually credit women's clubs for aiding their efforts. See especially, United States Children's Bureau *Bulletins*, No. 137, pp. 24–25; No. 146, p. 19; No. 178, pp. 21–24; No. 194, pp. 24–25. In the files of the Children's Bureau are references to the extensive support given by the various chapters of the WCTU, the YWCAs, and the Women's Auxiliary of the Protestant Episcopal Church.

18. In 1926, there were 812 nurses employed by the program.

19. Anne E. Rude to Gertrude Lane, June 25, 1921, United States Children's Bureau Files.

20. *Memorandum* of the Child Welfare Committee of the National League of Women Voters (n.d.), United States Children's Bureau Files.

21. John M. Dodson, "The Growing Importance of Preventive Medicine to the General Practitioner," *Journal of the American Medical Association*, 81 (Oct. 23, 1923), p. 1428.

22. U.S. Children's Bureau, *Bulletin*, No. 156, p. 6.

23. U.S. Children's Bureau, *Bulletin*, No, 137, p. 25.

24. "A report of the Sheppard-Towner Program in Minnesota During 1923," United States Children's Bureau Files. Reports for Michigan and New York indicate a variation of this type of procedure.

25. Alec N. Thomson, "Periodic Health Examinations: What a County Medical Society Can do in the Campaign," *American Journal of Public Health*, 16 (1926), p. 592; B. L. Bryant, "Organization of County Medical Societies for Promoting Periodic Medical Examinations," American Medical Association *Bulletin*, 19 (March 1924), p. 10; Elliott B. Edie, "Health Examinations Past and Present and Their Promotion in Pennsylvania," *American Journal of Public Health*, 15 (June 1925), pp. 604–605; American Child Health Association, *Transactions*, 1927, gives examples of how medical schools conducted this work; see especially in this volume, Bordon S. Veeder, "Washington University Medical School and Child Health," pp. 281–282; Carl Henry Davis, "Report of the Section of Obstetrics, Gynecology, and Abdominal Surgery of the American Medical Association," American Child Health Association, *Transactions*, 1928, p. 36; Editorial, "About Several Things," American Medical Association *Bulletin*, 19 (June, 1924), p. 167.

26. Haven Emerson, "Periodic Medical Examinations of Apparently Healthy Persons," *Journal of the American Medical Association*, 80 (May 12, 1923), p. 1376.

27. Ibid.

28. Ibid., pp. 1376–1377.

29. Ibid., p. 1377.

30. Ibid., p. 1378.

31. Ibid., p. 1381.

32. Ibid.

33. Ibid.

34. Remarks of Dr. Frank Billings, *Journal of the American Medical Association*, 82 (March 23, 1924), p. 967.

35. Harry H. Moore, *American Medicine and the People's Health* (New York, 1927), p. 140. This volume also provides an excellent understanding of the crisis facing the medical profession during the 1920s. John M. Dodson in "The Growing Importance" confirms it.

36. For the mounting tensions between the general practitioners and the specialists, see Rosemary Stevens, *American Medicine and the Public Interest* (New York, 1971), p. 148 and *passim*. Stevens also makes clear that the Sheppard-Towner program provided substantial assistance to the pediatricians and the obstetricians in their campaign to publicize their work (p. 200). For other discussions of these issues, see Bernhard J. Stern, *Social Factors in Medical Progress* (New York, 1927) and throughout the various *Reports* of the Committee on the Costs of Medical Care, Chicago, 1931–1932.

37. L. Emmett Holt, "American Pediatrics, a Retrospect and a Forecast," American Pediatric Association, *Transactions*, 1923, p. 15. Earlier Holt was an ardent supporter of training women for this important task. He frequently spoke to women's clubs on this subject. See, for example, L. Emmett Holt, "Physical Care of Children," Third National Congress of Mothers, *Proceedings*, 1899, p. 233. After the enactment of Sheppard-Towner, he wanted physicians to assume these tasks. To this end he urged medical schools to begin teaching personal health and the hygiene and care of healthy children.

38. Holt, "American Pediatrics," p. 15.

39. Report on Sheppard-Towner, Minnesota 1923, Children's Bureau files.

40. Marshall Carlton Pease, *American Academy of Pediatrics, 1930–1951* (New York, 1952), p. 17.

41. Holt, "American Pediatrics," p. 16.

42. Robert L. De Normandie, "Standards of Prenatal Care," U.S. Children's Bureau *Bulletin*, No. 157, p. 18.

43. Ibid., p. 19.

44. Ibid., p. 17.

45. United States Children's Bureau, "Standards of Prenatal Care: An Outline for the Use of Physicians," *Bulletin*, No. 153, p. 5.

46. U.S. Children's Bureau, "Standards for Physicians Conducting Conferences in Child Health Centers," *Bulletin*, No. 154, 1926, p. 5. There is evidence to suggest that the number of bottle-fed infants rose at this time. See New York City Department of Health, *Annual Report*, 1925, pp. 76–77.

47. *Child Welfare Extension Service*, Hearings before the House Committee on Interstate and Foreign Commerce, 70:2, Washington, D.C., 1929, p. 126. For its part, the Children's Bureau's defense did point to a reduction in infant mortality over the decade. Nevertheless, Bureau arguments for continuation no longer carried political weight.

48. Ibid., p. 125.

49. Ibid.

50. For a complete coverage of this campaign, see Lemons, *Woman Citizen*, pp. 172–176. It is interesting to note that both the maternal and infant death rate declined under Sheppard-Towner. In 1921, the infant death rate was 75 per 1,000 live births; by 1927 it had fallen to 64 per 1,000. Similarly, the maternal mortality rate was 67.3 per 1,000 in 1921 and 62.3 in 1927 (Lemons, *Woman Citizen*, p. 175).

51. Conference on the Care of Dependent Children, *Proceedings*, Washington, D.C., 1909; United States Children's Bureau, "Conference on Child Welfare Standards," *Bulletin* No. 60.

52. White House Conference on Child Health and Protection, 1930, *Proceedings* (New York, 1931), p. 7 (italics added).

53. American Child Hygiene Association, *Transactions*, 1920. Hoover's statements fit well with a change he observed in the 1920's. In 1920 Hoover was an active member of the American Child Hygiene Association, whose president was Dr. S. Josephine Baker, and whose membership endorsed the goals of child welfare reformers. By 1923 the Association incorporated the American Child Health Association and took its name. Its board became increasingly composed of physicians; its

policy towards Sheppard-Towner, in particular, and child welfare reform, in general, became more circumspect. The alteration in title is therefore significant. As a child hygiene association, the group assumed that problems of child care would be solved by the improvement of personal and communal hygiene—by child welfare reform. As a child health organization, it looked to the skills of physicians, to the individual relationship between doctor and patient. See Phillip Van Ingen, *The Story of the American Child Health Association* (New York, 1935).

54. Emilie J. Hutchison, *Women and the Ph.D.* (Greensboro, N.C., 1929), pp. 174-175, 178.

55. Harriet M. Bartlett, *Medical Social Work* (Chicago, 1934), p. 48; H. Douglas Singer, M.D., "The Function of the Social Worker in Relation to the State Hospital Physician," Forty-Sixth Conference of Social Work, *Proceedings* (1919), p. 632.

56. U.S. Bureau of Education, *Bulletin No. 29* (1923), p. 566.

57. Isabel A. Hampton, *Nursing the Sick* (New York, 1893), p. 2.

58. Lina R. Struthers, *The School Nurse* (New York, 1917) pp. 73-74.

59. Willard S. Elsbree, *The American Teacher* (New York, 1939), p. 550.

60. Florence P. Smith, "Labor Laws for Women in the States and Territories," U.S. Women's Bureau *Bulletin No. 98*, 1932.

61. The journal of the National Woman's Party, *Equal Rights,* provides a clear statement of their views.

62. Passing this amendment was one of the major goals of the Party.

63. Doris Stevens, "Suffrage Does Not Give Equality," *The Forum,* 72 (August, 1924), p. 146.

64. Editorial, *Equal Rights,* 11 (March 15, 1924), p. 65.

65. Mary A. Murray, "The Hearings on the Kirkland-Jenks Bill," *Equal Rights,* 16 (February 15, 1930), p. 44.

66. Stevens, "Suffrage," p. 149.

67. Ibid.

68. Harriot Stanton Blatch, "Do Women Want Protection?" *The Nation,* 116 (January 31, 1923), p. 115.

69. Stevens, "Suffrage," p. 151.

70. Blatch, "Protection," p. 115.

71. Murray, "Hearings," p. 44.

72. Florence Kelley, "Shall Women be Equal Before the Law?" *The Nation,* 114 (April 12, 1922), p. 421.

73. Gladys Harrison, "Against Equal Rights by Constitutional Amendment," Hearings of a Subcommittee on the Judiciary U.S. Senate on *Equal Rights Amendments* (January 6, 1931), p. 64.

74. Ethel M. Smith, *Towards Equal Rights for Men and Women* (Washington, D.C., 1929), p. 55. This book was published by the Committee on the Legal Status of Women of the National League of Women Voters.

75. Felix Frankfurter to Ethel Smith, September 8, 1921. Papers of The Consumer League of Massachusetts, Schlesinger Library, Radcliffe College.

76. Alice Hamilton, "Protection for Women Workers," *The Forum* 72 (August 1928), p. 162.

77. Clara Mortenson Beyer, "What is Equality?" *The Nation* 116, (January 31, 1923), p. 116.

78. Hamilton, "Protection," pp. 155, 157.

79. Beyer, "What is Equality?" p. 116.

80. Hamilton, "Protection," p. 160.

81. Florence Kelley, "Equal Opportunity for Wage-Earning Women, Fact Versus Fiction." Pamphlet in the Papers of the Consumer's League of Massachusetts, Schlesinger Library, Radcliffe College, p. 5.

82. U.S. Department of Labor, *Monthly Labor Review* 24 (November 1927), pp. 903-907.

83. U.S. Department of Labor, "Summary of the Effects of Labor Regulation on Employment Opportunities for Women" Women's Bureau *Bulletin No. 68,* 1928, pp. 13-21.

84. Elizabeth Baker, *Protective Legislation* (New York, 1925), p. 427.

85. U.S. Department of Labor, *"Summary,"* p. 22.

86. Ibid., p. 18.

87. G. Stanley Hall, "Some Defects in the Kindergarten in America," *Forum,* 28 (January, 1900), p. 586.

88. Grace Abbott, *The Child and the State* (Chicago, 1938), Vol. I, pp. 265-267.

89. United States Children's Bureau, "Child Labor: Facts and Figures," *Publication* No. 197, p. 48. U.S. Department of Commerce, Bureau of Census, *Historical Statistics of the United States* I (Washington, D.C., 1975), pp. 139-140.

90. Randolph S. Bourne, *The Gary Schools* (Boston, 1916), p. iii.

91. Ibid., pp. 5, 2.

92. See David J. Rothman and Sheila M. Rothman, *The Sources of the American Social Tradition* (New York, 1972) for the relationship of the Lowell boarding-houses to a disciplined work force.

93. Charles R. Richards, *Industrial Work* (New York, 1918), p. 106.

94. Ibid.

95. Bourne, *The Gary Schools* p. 40.

96. Dewey, *Schools of Tomorrow* p. 181.

97. Gary, Indiana Public Schools, *First Annual Report* (1908), p. 2.

98. Dewey, *Schools of Tomorrow,* p. 202.

99. Bourne, *The Gary Schools,* p. 45.

100. Dewey, *Schools of Tomorrow,* p. 202.

101. Bourne, *The Gary Schools,* p. 156.

102. Syracuse, New York Board of Education, *The Gary System* (Syracuse, N.Y., 1915), p. 8.

103. Stuart A. Courtis, *The Gary Public Schools* (New York, 1919), p. 384.

104. New York *Times,* July 4, 1917. See also Martin E. Henner, *In the Court of the Mayoral Election Campaign of 1917,* unpublished manuscript.

105. *New York Globe,* May 17, 1917.

106. For a detailed account of the tensions between vocational education and manual training, see Marvin Lazerson and W. Norton Grubb, *American Education and Vocationalism* (New York, 1974); Massachusetts Commission on Industrial Education, *Report* (Boston, Mass., 1906), p. 16.

107. National Education Association, "Report of the Committee on the Place of Industries in Public Education," *Proceedings* 1910, p. 655.

108. Massachusetts Commission on Industrial Education *Report,* p. 16; National Association of Manufacturers, "Report of the Committee on Industrial Education," Tenth Annual Convention *Proceedings* 1905, quoted in Lazerson & Grubb, *American Education,* p. 90.

109. Sophinisba Breckinridge and Grace Abbott, "The School and the Working Child," Chicago School of Civics and Philanthropy, *Finding Employment for Children Who Leave Schools to Go to Work* (1911), p. 16.

110. John Dewey, "Splitting up the School System," *The New Republic,* 2 (1915), p. 283.

111. Lazerson and Grubb, *American Education,* p. 32.

112. John Dale Russell, *Vocational Education* (Washington, D.C., 1938), p. 5.

113. Ibid., pp. 126-127.

114. Ibid., p. 155.

115. Ibid., p. 154.

116. Ibid., pp. 154-155.

117. Ibid., p. 158.

118. Ibid., pp. 172-173.

Chapter 5

1. Ludwig Lewisohn, "Love and Marriage," Freda Kirchwey, ed., *Our Changing Morality* (New York, 1930), p. 200.

2. Lydia Kingsmill Commander, *The American Idea* (New York, 1907), p. 171. Although stated earlier, this notion prevailed in the 1920s.

3. Phyllis Blanchard and Carlyn Manasses, *New Girls for Old* (New York, 1930), p. 61. For the most comprehensive account of the changing mores in the 1920s, see Paula S. Fass, *The Beautiful and the Damned* (New York, 1977).

4. Charlotte Perkins Gilman, "The New Generation of Women," *Current History* 19 (November 1923), pp. 733-735.

5. Dewey made a similar type of analysis in order to restructure the schools. The sociologists, too, desired to retain older values in a rapidly changing society. Their solution was to restructure marriage.

6. Ernest Rutherford Groves and William Fielding Ogburn, *American Marriage and Family Relationships* (New York, 1928), p. 29. For a contemporary comment on this ideology, see Christopher Lasch, *Haven in a Heartless World* (New York, 1977), especially Chapters 2 and 3.

7. Groves and Ogburn, *American Marriage*, p. 16.

8. Groves and Ogburn, *American Marriage*, Chapter I. See also Lasch, *Haven in a Heartless World*, Chapter II.

9. Robert S. Lynd, "Family Members as Consumers," *The Annals of the American Academy of Political and Social Science*, 160 (March 1932), p. 91; Clifford Kirkpatrick, "Techniques of Marital Adjustment," *The Annals of the American Academy of Political and Social Science*, 160 (March 1932), p. 179.

10. Ernestine Cookson Milner, "Training for Marriage While in College," National Association of Deans of Women, *Nineteenth Yearbook* (1932), pp. 119-120.

11. Ten American College Girls, *The American College Girl, Her College and Her Ideals* (Boston, 1929), pp. 17, 12. See also, Fass, *The Damned*, pp. 82-83.

12. Detailed information on the phenomenal growth of sororities can be found in Fass, *The Damned*, pp. 142-144. Statistical data can also be found in Agnes Wells, "Sorority Standards," National Association of Deans of Women, *Fifteenth Yearbook* (1928), p. 174.

13. Ernest W. Burgess, "Sociological Aspects of the Sex Life of the Unmarried Adult," in Ira S. Wile, ed., *The Sex Life of the Unmarried Adult* (New York, 1934), p. 124. Although the fraternities, which also became popular in the 1920's, were concerned with peer relations as well, their principles differed in many ways from the sororities. For this story see Fass, *The Damned*.

14. Wells, "Sorority Standards," pp. 175, 176.

15. Ethel Chase, "Some Concrete Problems Facing the Dean, National Association of Deans of Women, *Sixteenth Yearbook* (1929), p. 109.

16. Mrs. Frank A. Kemp, "The Chaperon," National Association of Deans of Women, *Fifteenth Yearbook* (1928), pp. 181, 180.

17. Wells, "Sorority Standards," pp. 177, 176; see also Helen P. Rush, "Fraternities in the Building of University Spirit," National Association of Deans of Women, *Fifteenth Yearbook* (1928).

18. Sadie Campbell, "What Should a Social Program in a Teacher's College Do?" National Association of Deans of Women, *Eighteenth Yearbook* (1931), p. 141; Rush, "Building of University Spirit," p. 190; Blanche Davidson, "How Does the Place of Residence Affect a Student's Social Training?" National Association of Deans of Women, *Eighteenth Yearbook* (1931).

19. Lydia Pinkham Co., "Gallivanting Husbands," unpaged (1931) in Lydia Pinkham Papers, Schlesinger Library, Radcliffe College.

20. Robert S. Lynd and Helen Merrell Lynd, *Middletown* (New York, 1929), p. 116.

21. Lydia Pinkham Co., "Gallivanting Husbands."

22. "She Washes Half the Morning," *Ladies Home Journal* (April 1928); "Let Them Dance on Your Floors," *Ladies Home Journal* (February 1928); "The Kitchen Arises to New Heights," *Ladies Home Journal* (April 1928).

23. Burgess, "Sociological Aspects," p. 124.

24. "Spring! . . . For Everyone But Her," *Ladies Home Journal* (June 1929); "Sweet as a Rose," *Ladies Home Journal* (May 1929); "Everyone Knows Instantly,"

Ladies Home Journal (April 1928); "Live Your Romances!" *Ladies Home Journal* (April 1928); "Embarrassed by Dishpan Hands," *Ladies Home Journal* (March 1928); "Step on it, Mother—This Isn't the Polka," *Ladies Home Journal* (March 1928). It is interesting to note that the *Ladies Home Journal* was one of the two most popular magazines in Middletown during the 1920s (Lynd, *Middletown*, p. 158).

25. Robert S. Lynd, "Family Members as Consumers," p. 91; Burgess, "Sociological Aspects," p. 124.

26. Barbara Burke, "New Year Will See Greater Progress," *Beauty Culture Magazine* 2 (December 1920), p. 18; "The Beauty Market," *Saturday Evening Post* 199 (1927), p. 259; Lynd, *Middletown*, p. 117.

27. Paul White, "Our Booming Beauty Business," *Outlook* 154 (1933), p. 133; "Young, Slim and Nice-Looking—How?" *Life and Labor Bulletin* 5 (October 1927), p. 1.

28. Anna S. Richardson, "Is the Woman's Club Dying?" *Harpers* 159 (October 1929), p. 607. The Lynds confirm this trend in *Middletown* (see pp. 293–299).

29. Dorothy Dunbar Bromley, "Feminist—New Style 1927," *Harper's Monthly Magazine* 155 (1927), p. 556.

30. Lynd, *Middletown*, p. 111; Gusfield, *Symbolic Crusade*, p. 129.

31. Margaret Sanger, *Woman and the New Race* (New York, 1920), p. 57. James Reed, *From Private Vice to Public Virtue*, provides a detailed and highly readable account of Sanger and her program. David M. Kennedy, *The Birth Control Movement in America* (New Haven, 1970), focuses on Sanger's dedication to birth control as a panacea for a multitude of evils.

32. Havelock Ellis, *The Task of Social Hygiene* (Boston, 1914), p. 12; Paul Robinson. *The Modernization of Sex* (New York, 1976), presents an interesting analysis of Ellis's ideas.

33. Ellis, *The Task*, pp. 26, 27; ix, 101. Some of Ellis's notions on ideal love were derived from Ellen Key, a prominent Swedish feminist. See Ellen Key, *The Century of the Child* (New York, 1909).

34. H. H. Laughlin, "Eugenicists on the Place of Birth Control," *Birth Control Review* 10 (January 1926), p. 10. For an analysis of the relationship between the birth controllers and the eugenicists, see Mark H. Haller, *Eugenics, Hereditarian Attitudes in American Thought* (New Brunswick, 1963), pp. 88–92. Sanger explained her views on sterilization in, "The Function of Sterilization," *Birth Control Review* 10 (October 1926), p. 299; Margaret Sanger, "Birth Control League," *Birth Control Review* 6 (July 1922), p. 138.

35. Sanger, *The New Race*, pp. 6–8.

36. Ibid., p. 58.

37. Margaret Sanger, *The Pivot of Civilization* (New York, 1922), p. 116. The attitudes towards organized charity and Progressive reform can be found on pp. 107–109.

38. Sanger, *The New Race*, pp. 59–60.

39. Margaret Sanger, "Women's Error and Her Debt," *Birth Control Review* 5 (August 1921), p. 7; Sanger, *The New Race*, pp. 187, 195–96, 9.

40. Sanger, *The Pivot*, p. 140; Kennedy, *The Birth Control Movement*, p. 127.

41. Paul Popenoe, *Modern Marriage Handbook* (New York, 1925); Abraham Stone and Hannah Stone, *A Marriage Manual* (New York, 1935); Margaret Sanger, *Happiness in Marriage* (New York, 1926), pp. 6, 19, 21, 65, 38, 41.

42. Sanger, *Happiness*, pp. 58–9, 60, 61–2, 184–85.

43. G. V. Hamilton, "What is Wrong With Marriage?" Quoted in Groves and Ogburn, *American Marriage*, pp. 54–55.

44. Popenoe, *Modern Marriage*, pp. 179, 156.

45. Sanger, *The New Race*, pp. 101, 107, 231; Sanger, "The Tragedy of the Accidental Child," *Birth Control Review* 3 (April 1919), p. 5.

46. Sanger, *New Race*, p. 74.

47. Margaret Sanger, *My Fight for Birth Control* (New York, 1931), p. 110.

48. Margaret Sanger, *Family Limitation* (New York, 1920), p. 13.

49. Ibid., p. 21.

50. Margaret Sanger, *Dutch Methods of Birth Control* (n.d., n.p.), Sophia Smith Collection, Smith College.

51. Owen R. Lovejoy, "Birth Control and Child Labor," *Birth Control Review* 3 (April 1919), pp. 3-4. After the defeat of the National Child Labor Law, Owen did, if somewhat reluctantly, become a supporter of birth control. See Owen R. Lovejoy, "Birth Control in Relation to Child Employment," *Birth Control Review* 9, (December 1925).

52. Carrie Chapman Catt and Margaret Sanger, November 24, 1920, Sanger Papers, Library of Congress.

53. Gilman, "New Generation," p. 737; Charlotte Perkins Gilman, "Back of Birth Control," *Birth Control Review* 6 (March 1922), p. 32.

54. Sanger, *My Fight*, p. 45.

55. Jane Addams, *A New Conscience and an Ancient Evil* (New York, 1914), pp. 211–212. Some settlement house workers did become ardent supporters of the birth control movement. Dr. Alice Hamilton, a long-time resident of Hull House, believed that the distribution of birth control could close the gap between the social classes. "It is a question," she believed, "of offering the poor who need it most, the knowledge and the power which has long been in the possession of those who need it least." Alice Hamilton, "Poverty and Birth Control," *Birth Control Review* 9 (September 1925), pp. 226–228.

56. Grace Abbott to William F. Wild, February 10, 1922, Children's Bureau Files.

57. Reed, *From Private Vice*, pp. 124–126.

58. Katharine Bement Davis, *Factors in the Sex Life of 2200 Women* (New York, 1929); Blanchard and Manasses, *New Girls*.

59. Lynd, *Middletown*, p. 123.

60. Reed, *From Private Vice*, p. 106.

61. Kennedy, *Birth Control Movement*, p. 172.

62. Margaret Sanger to S. Adolphus Knopf, March 21, 1929, Sanger Papers, Library of Congress.

63. Mary Ware Dennett, *Birth Control Laws—Shall We Keep Them or Abolish Them?* (New York, 1926), p. 201.

64. Margaret Sanger to S. Adolphus Knopf, March 21, 1929, Sanger Papers, Library of Congress.

65. Sanger's efforts to convince private physicians of the desirability of distributing the device can be found in the reports of Dr. James Cooper to Sanger, which are in her Papers in the Library of Congress. See also Caroline Hadley Robinson, *Seventy Birth Control Clinics* (Baltimore, 1930).

66. Margaret Sanger to Mrs. Clarence W. Mitchell, December 9, 1929, Sanger Papers, Library of Congress.

67. Robinson, *Birth Control Clinics*.

68. Rachelle S. Yarros, *Modern Woman and Sex* (New York, 1933), p. 129.

69. Ibid., p. 78; Rachelle S. Yarros, "Birth Control and its Relation to Health and Welfare," *The Medical Woman's Journal* 32 (October 1925), p. 272.

70. Lydia A. DeVilbliss, *Birth Control: What Is It?* (Boston, 1923), p. 55.

71. Lydia A. DeVilbliss to Margaret Sanger, February 2, 1932, Sanger Papers, Library of Congress.

72. Lydia A. DeVilbliss to Margaret Sanger, June 21, 1933, and August 14, 1933, Sanger Papers, Library of Congress. See also her, "Preliminary Report on Sterilization of Women by Intrauterine Coagulation of Tubal Orifices," *American Journal of Obstetrics and Gynecology* 29, 1935.

73. Robinson, *Birth Control Clinics*, p. 109.

74. Ibid., pp. 111–126.

75. Reed, *From Private Vice*, pp. 41, 65.

76. George W. Kosmak, M.D., "Birth Control, What Shall be the Attitude of the Medical Profession Towards Present Day Propaganda?" *Medical Record* 91 (Feb. 17, 1917), p. 272.

77. Papers of the Subcommittee of Public Health Resolution of April 6, 1921, New York Academy of Medicine Archives. Kosmak and Dickinson were both members of this Subcommittee.

78. "Discussion," *Surgery, Gynecology and Obstetrics* 23 (August 1916), p. 190.

79. Robert L. Dickinson and Henry H. Pierson, "The Average Sex Life of American Women," *Journal of the American Medical Association* 85 (October 10, 1925), p. 113.

80. Robert L. Dickinson and Louise Stevens Bryant, "Planning Clinics for Present and Future Needs," in Robinson, *Birth Control Clinics*, pp. 161–162.

81. "Committee on Maternal Health," *Journal of the American Medical Association* 86 (June 19, 1926), p. 1918.

82. Robert L. Dickinson and Laura Beam, *The Single Woman* (Baltimore, 1934), p. iii; Robert L. Dickinson, "Medical Reflections Upon Life Histories," in Ira S. Wilie, *The Sex Life of the Unmarried Adult* (New York, 1934), p. 197.

83. Dickinson and Beam, *Single Woman*, p. 248.

84. Ibid., p. 257.

85. Ibid., p. 252; Dickinson, "Medical Reflections," pp. 210–211.

86. Dickinson and Beam, *Single Woman*, pp. 429–430.

87. John Watson, *The Psychological Care of Infant and Child* (New York, 1928), pp. 12, 69.

88. Ibid., p. 70.

89. Ibid., pp. 76, 78, 80.

90. Douglas A. Thom, "Child Management," Children's Bureau *Bulletin* No. 143, p. 3.

91. Ibid., p. 35; Martha M. Eliot, "Infant Care," Children's Bureau *Publication No. 8.*

92. "Are You Training Your Child to be Happy?" Children's Bureau *Publication No. 202*, pp. 53–55.

93. Ernest R. Groves and Gladys Hoagland Groves, *Parents and Children* (Philadelphia, 1928), pp. 121, 116, 117.

94. Children's Bureau "Are You Training Your Child?", p. 2.

95. Ibid., p. 3.

96. Arnold Gesell, *Exceptional Children and Public Policy* (New Haven, 1921), p. 12.

97. Groves and Groves, *Parents and Children*, pp. 119–120.

98. "The Nursery School," Memo of April 13, 1928 in the Lillian Wald Papers, Columbia University. In 1930, the age at which a child should enter nursery school was not clearly established. Nursery school children ranged between the ages of 2 and 5; kindergarteners between 4 and 6. White House Conference on Child Health and Protection, *Nursery Education* (New York, 1931), p. 52.

99. John E. Anderson, *Happy Childhood* (New York, 1933), p. 280.

100. Washington Child Research Center, *Report 1928–1931*, Papers of the Laura S. Rockefeller Memorial Fund, p. 11.

101. Ibid., p. 10; Esther S. Schell, "The Independent Nursery School," The Institute for the Coordination of Women's Interests, *The Nursery School as Social Experiment* (New York, 1928), p. 13.

102. Grace F. Marcus, "Organization and Technique in Child Guidance Clinic Work," *National Conference on Social Work* 25 (1925), p. 415. The Commonwealth Fund and the National Committee for Mental Hygiene promoted this shift in focus.

103. Smiley Blanton and Margaret Gray Blanton, *Child Guidance* (New York, 1927), p. 7.

104. William I. Thomas and Dorothy Swaine Thomas, *The Child in America* (New York, 1928), pp. 89, 73.

105. Ibid., pp. 75, 77.

106. Ibid., p. 89.

107. Ibid., p. 87.

108. Patty Hill Smith, "The Nursery School and the Present Social Order," Midwest Conference on Practical Education, *Proceedings* (Chicago 1926), p. 91.

Chapter 6

1. William H. Chafe, *The American Woman* (New York, 1972), pp. 107–109.

2. See Sheila M. Rothman, "Other People's Children," *Public Interest* (1973), p. 19; Harvey Bart Campbell, *Educational Activities of the WPA* Staff Study No. 14 (Washington, D.C., 1939).

3. Chafe, *American Woman*, pp. 166–173.

4. United States Children's Bureau, Conference on Day Care for Working Mothers *Proceedings*, Washington, D.C., 1942; Eleanor S. Boll, "The Child," *The Annals of the American Academy of Political and Social Science* 229 (September 1943), p. 75; Ray E. Barber, "Marriage and the Family After the War," *The Annals of the American Academy of Political and Social Science* 229, p. 170.

5. United States Department of Commerce, Bureau of the Census, *Historical Statistics of the United States* I (Washingon, D.C., 1975) pp. 139–140.

6. New York *Times*, June 21, 1960; Kenneth T. Jackson, "The Crabgrass Frontier," pp. 208–220 in Raymond A. Mohl and James F. Richardson, *The Urban Experience* (Belmont Calif., 1973).

7. Herbert J. Gans, *The Levittowners* (New York, 1967), pp. 39–41. It may well be that the Levittowners are not of the same social class as the women who organized the WCTU or became the first settlement house workers. Nevertheless, the private quality of lives in the suburbs tends to cut across class lines. We lack intimate studies that would do for upper-middle-class communities what Gans did for Levittown. There is some evidence, however [for example, from Paul Douglas, *The Suburban Trend* (New York, 1925)], that such a similarity exists. Webster Groves, which was founded in the 1920s and was more "choice" than Levittown, also contained few public facilities, and the women who lived there were reluctant to supply them. It "had no public library, no park or play ground, no community center or any substitute for one like a Young Men's or Young Women's Christian Association. It had very acute problems of sewerage and sanitation, and the development of its public improvements was distinctly ragged." Moreover, the clubs that were central to the lives of women in Webster Groves were essentially recreational (pp. 182–183).

8. Gans, *Levittowners*, p. 162.

9. Ibid., pp. 116–117, 89–91, 120–122, 86.

10. Ibid., pp. 231–244.

11. Betty Friedan, *The Feminine Mystique* (New York, 1963), p. 13.

12. Ibid., p. 23, 13.

13. Ibid., p. 271.

14. Ibid., pp. 250, 254, 261.

15. Ibid., p. 95, 293.

16. Ibid., p. 332.

17. Elizabeth Waldman and Beverly J. McEaddy, "Where Women Work: An Analysis by Industry and Occupation," *Monthly Labor Review* 97 (May 1974), p. 3. See also Elizabeth Herzog, "Children of Working Mothers," Children's Bureau *Publication No. 382*, p. 6.

18. Lois Waldis Hoffman and Ivan Nye, *Working Mothers* (San Francisco, 1975), pp. 5–8, 16; United States Department of Labor, *Handbook on Woman Workers* (Washington, D.C., 1976), pp. 96–97.

19. Arthur S. Fleming, "Oh, If I Could Only Get a Job," *Good Housekeeping* 165 (January 1962), p. 22.

20. Betty Friedan, *It Changed My Life* (New York, 1976), p. 98.

21. Jo Freeman, *The Politics of Women's Liberation*, (New York, 1975), pp. 53–54, provides an excellent and highly detailed analysis of the events that led to the organization of NOW.

22. Ibid., p. 54; Friedan, *It Changed My Life*, supplies a slightly different variation, pp. 81–82.

23. Friedan, *It Changed My Life*, pp. 82, 77.

24. Freeman, *The Politics*, pp. 54–55.

25. A copy of the "Statement of Purpose" can be found in Friedan, *It Changed My Life* pp. 87–91.

26. David J. Rothman "The State as Parent," in Willard Gaylin et al., *Doing Good* (New York 1978) pp. 88–90; Friedan, *It Changed My Life* pp. 90–91.

27. Ibid., p. 89.

28. David L. Kirp, "Student Classification, Public Policy and the Courts," *Harvard Educational Review* 44 (February 1974), p. 32.

29. Robert Rosenthal and Lenore Jacobson, *Pygmalion in the Classroom* (New York, 1968).

30. Eleanor E. Maccoby, *The Development of Sex Differences* (Palo Alto, California, 1966). Matina Horner, "The Motive to Avoid Success and Changing Aspirations of College Women." (Unpublished preliminary Draft 1970.) My point here is not to raise the validity or lack of validity of Horner's research, but to emphasize the origins of the research and its effect when it appeared.

31. Naomi Weisstein, "Psychology Constructs the Female," in Vivian Gornick and Barbara Moran, *Woman in Sexist Society* (New York, 1971), pp. 207, 208, 209.

32. Helene Deutsch, *The Psychology of Women*, I (London, 1947), p. 180.

33. William H. Masters and Virginia E. Johnson, *Human Sexual Response* (Boston, 1966), p. 8; quoted in Ruth and Edward Brecher, *An Analysis of Human Sexual Response* (New York, 1966), p. 85.

34. Mary Jane Sherfey, *The Nature and Evolution of Female Sexuality* (New York, 1966), pp. 46–47.

35. Alex Comfort, *The Joy of Sex* (New York, 1972). For Comfort's views on the desirability of female equality, see *New York Times*, June 2, 1974.

36. Friedan, *It Changed My Life*, p. 98.

37. Comfort, *Joy of Sex*, p. 9.

38. Friedan makes it clear just how much she was forced to respond. See Friedan, *It Changed My Life*, p. 105. See also Freeman, *The Politics*, pp. 55–56.

39. Friedan, *It Changed My Life*, p. 105.

40. Freeman, *The Politics*, p. 99; *Resolution of the 1971 Conference*, p. 16. Found in some papers of the organization in the Sophia Smith Collection, Smith College. Freeman also notes that by 1974 almost half of NOW's members were under thirty; by 1976, NOW had 60,000 members (*New York Times*, January 24, 1976).

41. Friedan, *It Changed My Life*, pp. 157, 163.

42. Joseph Goldstein, Anna Freud, and Albert J. Solnit, *Beyond the Best Interests of the Child* (New York, 1973), pp. 17, 19.

43. Ibid., p. 110.

44. Ibid., pp. 11–12.

45. Selma Fraiberg, *Every Child's Birthright: In Defense of Mothering* (New York, 1977), pp. 62, 4–5.

46. Ibid., pp. 82, 84, 111.

47. Nena O'Neill and George O'Neill, *Open Marriage* (New York, 1972), pp. 242, 79 (see, in particular, Chapters 4 and 12).

48. Gail Sheehy, *Passages: Predictable Crises of Adult Life* (New York, 1976), pp. 11, 243.

49. Ibid., p. 91.

50. Ibid., pp. 15, 90.

51. Ibid., pp. 139, 145.

Chapter 7

1. Jo Freeman, *The Politics of Women's Liberation* (New York, 1975), pp. 202–203; The Equal Rights Amendment Project, *Impact ERA* (Millbrae, Calif., 1976), pp. 2, 16.

2. *New York Times*, September 18, 1975. An NBC poll conducted in December 1977 revealed that the ERA was supported by 53 percent of the public, while 37 percent opposed the Amendment (Poll #91, NBC News).

3. Carnegie Commission of Higher Education, *Opportunities for Women in Higher Education* (New York, 1973); United States Department of Labor *Handbook on Women Workers*, pp. 92–94.

4. U.S. Department of Labor, *Handbook*, p. 94; *New York Times*, July 15, 1977.

5. Carolyn Shaw Bell, "Economic Realities Anticipated," in *Impact ERA*, p. 82; United States Department of Labor, *Handbook*, pp. 130–132.

6. National Commission on the Observance of International Women's Year, *To Form a More Perfect Union* (Washington, D.C., 1976), pp. 192–197; *Oversight Hearings on Federal Enforcement of Equal Opportunity Laws* before a Subcommittee on Equal Opportunity of the Commission on Education and Labor, House of Representatives 94:2 Part III, p. 10.

7. Delbert L. Spurlock, Jr., "EEOC's Compliance Process: The Problems of Selective Enforcement," *Labor Law Journal* (June 1975), p. 399; *Oversight Hearings*, p. 12. See also Phyllis A. Wallace, "Impact of Equal Employment Opportunity Laws," in Juanita M. Kreps, *Women and the American Economy* (New York, 1976), p. 144.

8. *Oversight Hearings*, p. 13; *A More Perfect Union*, p. 192; *New York Times*, December 10, 1976.

9. Wallace, "Impact of Equal Employment," p. 144; *New York Times*, July 29, 1977.

10. Wallace, "Impact of Equal Employment." See also Nancy Smith Barrett, "The Economy Ahead of Us" in Kreps, *American Economy*, pp. 164–165.

11. Victor R. Fuchs, "Women's Earnings: Recent Trends and Longrun Prospects," *Monthly Labor Review* 97 (May 1974), pp. 25–26.

12. Freeman, "The Political Impact," p. 64.

13. White House Conference on Children, *Report to the President* (Washington, D.C., 1970), pp. 227, 232.

14. Ibid., pp. 12, 227.

15. Ibid., pp. 224, 133, 186.

16. Gilbert Steiner, *The Children's Cause* (Washington, D.C., 1976), pp. 14–35; *Child and Family Services Act*, 1975, Joint Hearings before the Subcommittee on Children and Youth, 94:1, p. 143. Margaret O'Brien Steinfels, *Who's Minding the Children?* (New York, 1973), pp. 86–88, contains an account of the women's movement attitude towards Head Start.

17. *Comprehensive Child Development Act of 1971*, Hearings before the Select Committee on Education 92:1, p. 71 *passim*.

18. White House Conference, 1970, *Report*, p. 277.

19. *Comprehensive Child Development Act of 1971*, p. 65.

20. Rochelle Beck and John Butler, "An Interview with Marian Wright Edelman," *Harvard Educational Review* 44, (February 1974), p. 72.

21. Ibid., p. 71.

22. Mary Dublin Keyserling, *Windows on Day Care* (New York, 1972), pp. 4–5; Sheila M. Rothman, "Other People's Children," p. 25.

23. On WIN and the Aid to Families with Dependent Children (AFDC) population, see Gilbert Steiner, *The State of Welfare* (Washington, D.C., 1971); Stephen F. Gold, "The Failure of the Work Incentive Program," University of Pennsylvania, *Law Review* 119 (January 1971), p. 489.

24. United States Department of Labor, United States Department of Health, Education and Welfare, *WIN Sixth Annual Report* 1974–1975, pp. v, 20.

25. Martha W. Griffiths, "Sex Discrimination in Income Security Programs," *Notre Dame Lawyer* 49 (February 1974), p. 542; United States Commission on Civil Rights, *Women and Poverty* (Washington, D.C., 1974), pp. 20, 30.

26. William L. Pierce, *Child Care Arrangements in the U.S.*, 1974 in *Child and Family Service Act, 1975, Part 2*, p. 235; *Comprehensive Preschool Education and Child Day Care Act of 1969*, Hearings before a Select Subcommittee on Education 91: 1 and 2, p. 110; *Child Care Data and Materials*, Committee on Finance, United States Senate 1974, p. 96.

27. Paul E. Mott, *Meeting Human Needs: The Social and Political History of Title XX* (Columbus, Ohio, 1976), pp. 9–11.

28. *Child Care Data and Materials,* pp. 20–21; Rothman, "Other People's Children," pp. 24–25; Keyserling, *Windows on Day Care,* p. 3.

29. Steiner, *Children's Cause,* pp. 111–112.

30. Beck and Butler, "An Interview," p. 69.

31. Steiner, *Children's Cause,* pp. 113, 116.

32. *Child and Family Services Act, 1975,* Part I, p. 135.

33. Ibid., Part 7, p. 1202.

34. Ibid., Part I, pp. 140, 144.

35. Ibid.

36. Ibid., p. 144.

37. Ibid., pp. 1204, 1199, 1200.

38. Ibid., Part 7, p. 1200.

39. Ibid., pp. 1224, 1211.

40. Boston Women's Health Book Collective, *Our Bodies, Ourselves* (New York, 1971), pp. 1, 239.

41. Ibid., pp. 231, 3.

42. Ellen Frankfort, *Vaginal Politics* (New York, 1972), p. xviii; Boston Women's Health Book Collective, *Our Bodies,* p. 270.

43. T. Elaine Adamson and Paula A. Watts, "Patients' Perception of Maternity Nurse Practitioners," *Journal of Public Health* 66 (June 1976), p. 586.

44. Westoff and Westoff, *From Now to Zero,* p. 63; *Griswold v. Connecticut* 381 U.S. 479 (1965); *Eisenstadt v. Baird* 405 U.S. 439 (1972).

45. *Roe v. Wade* 93 S.Ct. 705, 35 Ed. 2d 147 (1973).

46. Christopher Tietze, *Abortion 1974–1975* (New York, 1976), pp. 7, 111.

47. Jeannie I. Rosoff, "Is Support of Abortion Political Suicide?" *Family Planning Perspectives* 7 (January–February 1975), p. 21. Sheila M. Rothman, "Sterilizing the Poor." *Society* 14 (January–February 1977), p. 38. Jean Pakter, Frieda Nelson, and Martin Svigir, "Legal Abortion: A Half-Decade of Experience," *Family Planning Perspectives* 7 (November–December 1975), p. 253; Judith Blake, "The Supreme Court's Abortion Decisions and Public Opinion in the United States," *Population and Development Review* 3 (March–June 1977). As the Blake article makes clear, too much of the results of a poll hinge on the precise way that the question is framed.

48. Tietze, *Abortion 1974–1975,* pp. 8–11.

49. "A Statement on Abortion by 100 Professors of Obstetrics," *American Journal of Obstetrics and Gynecology* 112 (April 1972), p. 994.

50. Linda Ambrose, "The Milwaukee Story," in Tietze, *Abortions 1974–1975,* p. 117.

51. Rosoff, "Is Support of Abortion. . . ?", p. 17.

52. Jeannie I. Rosoff, "Liberalized Anti-Abortion Amendment Becomes Law After Five-Month Battle," *Planned Parenthood World Population Washington Memo,* December 16, 1977; *New York Times,* Nov. 27, 1977.

Index